ALSO BY PAUL HEMPHILL

The Heart of the Game

Leaving Birmingham

King of the Road

Me and the Boy

The Sixkiller Chronicles

Too Old to Cry

Long Gone

The Good Old Boys

Mayor: Notes on the Sixties
(with Ivan Allen, Jr.)

The Nashville Sound

Simon & Schuster

WHEELS

A SEASON ON NASCAR'S WINSTON CUP CIRCUIT

PAUL HEMPHILL

SIMON & SCHUSTER
Rockefeller Center
1230 Avenue of the Americas
New York, NY 10020

Copyright © 1997 by Paul Hemphill
All rights reserved, including the right of reproduction
in whole or in part in any form.

Simon & Schuster and colophon are registered trademarks
of Simon & Schuster Inc.

Designed by Kate Nichols
Insert design by Leslie Phillips
Manufactured in the United States of America

10 9 8 7 6 5 4 3 2 1

Library of Congress Cataloging-in-Publication Data is available.
ISBN 0-684-83017-5

Photo Credits:
1, 2, 3, 12, 13, 14, 17, 21, 22, 23, 24, 25, 29, 30, 31, 32, 34, 35: R.J. Reynolds/Winston
Title page, 4, 6, 7, 20: Photos by Daytona International Speedway
5, 8, 9, 10, 11, 18: Courtesy of Raymond D. Parks
15, 16, 36, 37: AP/Wide World
19: Courtesy of the Gober Sosebee Estate
26: Dixie Speedway/Ted McMahan, Jr.
27: Dixie Speedway
28: Courtesy of Rodney Dickson
33: Performance PR Plus

For Martha Farran Hemphill,
my sunshine, who makes me happy.

CONTENTS

Contents

Hell, what they ought to do is just give everybody a drank o' likker and drop the green flag.

—Buck Baker, circa 1960

PROLOGUE: CAROLINA WINTER

Ominous pewter clouds, relentless as glaciers, had chugged down out of the high wrinkled folds of the Great Smoky Mountains on the first weekend of the new year, dumping their load and moving on, and when the sun rose over the North Carolina piedmont on Monday morning, the undulating tobacco land lay as still and pure as a Grandma Moses. Glistening strands of rime clung to the plump velvet coats of spruce, like tinsel left on Christmas trees. Curlicues of smoke spiraled from the rock chimneys of isolated farmhouses. Tractors and plows and harrows lay stranded where they last had been used. From weathered barns came the puzzled lowing of cows, prodded indoors ahead of the storm, joined in concert by the agitated *caw-caw-caw* of crows, disoriented, circling, scouting for nourishment beneath the blanket of white. The farms and the crossroads villages and the smallest towns were being left to their own devices while intrepid men in yellow bulldozers and dump trucks began to unsnarl the mess out on the highways: grinding gears, clearing snow, spreading salt and gravel, working around the fallen power lines and the jackknifed eighteen-wheelers and the cars abandoned hub-deep in the drifts. There would be no school today, nor much of anything else.

In another time, back when America was still celebrating the end of the Second World War, one of the few signs of human life on a day such as this would have been the movement of one man along a beeline footpath tromped out between the farmhouse and the barn. *Can't do much else, might as well work on the car.* He could have been a farmer or a shade-tree mechanic or even a hardware store clerk during the day, maybe even ran a little liquor into the murky fringes of Charlotte on weekend nights for the extra cash, but his real life was defined by what lay inside that barn: a collage of wheels, tires, axles, springs, brake pads, engines, spark plugs, carburetors, oil pans, gears; the thousands of pieces required for assembling an automobile fit for racing. All through the long cold nights of winter he could have been found in that barn-cum-garage, grinding valves and cleaning cylinders and mounting engine blocks and adjusting springs and tightening bolts until finally, the moment of truth: he would turn the ignition—*Barooom-blat-blat-barooooom!*—bringing terror to the country-side and music to his ears. *Nope, not yet.* He would hunker beneath the hood once again for more tinkering as the night grew longer. One man, one car, one dream; that dream being of the day, come spring, when he would hang a wry hand-lettered sign on the barn door—*Gone Racin'*—and drive away to the nearest little dirt racetrack to find out, fender-to-fender, man-to-man, just who by-God had the fastest car in those parts. With luck, he might earn enough prize money to pay for the gas and tires.

But that was then, and this was now: January of 1996, little more than a month before the new racing season would begin at Daytona Beach in Florida. Those days of one man toiling over one car were in the archives now, in racing museums stuck in the shadows of the soaring new super-speedways or in dog-eared pasteboard scrapbooks or in the fading memories of men with names like Gober Sosebee and Tim Flock and Soapy Castles—heroes in their time but relics now, cobwebs in the attic, gone the way of most pioneers who made it up as they went along—and this new day had brought us, hell, an *industry.* My God! Look what had become of a sport that sprang from deadly cat-and-mouse games between wild-hare young moonshine runners and grim old sheriffs on the twisting back roads of the southern Appalachians during the Great Depression. The racing of "stock" cars at the major-league level—the thirty-one-race Winston Cup Series orchestrated by the National Association for Stock Car Auto Racing (NASCAR) and sponsored by the beleaguered R.J. Reynolds Tobacco Co., testily guarding its flanks against an anti-tobacco administration in Washington—had become the hottest growth sport of the nineties in America. About a dozen of the forty-odd regular drivers on the circuit were earning at least $1 million in prize money each year, and the points champion for 1995, a twenty-four-year-old Christian matinee idol named Jeff Gordon, had taken in more than $4.3 million. Attendance at the tracks was exploding, having doubled from 2.6 million in 1987 to more than five million in '95, and all of the races were being televised nationally. Gross sales in the merchandising of "collectibles," everything from $200 racing jackets to matched sets of lug nuts swept right off the floor of Rusty Wallace's garage ("only $7.95 plus shipping & handling"), was reaching the half-billion-dollar mark. NASCAR's Winston Cup Series had become Corporate Heaven, a place where a manufacturer of, say, automobile batteries fought for the right to pay $5 million a year so a car would parade its logo around a track at speeds sometimes pushing 200 miles per hour.

And so, the truth be known, these new icons of the American sporting scene couldn't *afford* to lollygag around the house on a snowy winter's morn, lugging in some more logs for the fireplace, sipping cider, playing with the kids, pestering the little woman about what's for dinner. Not with this new deal, this new order of things. The first million-dollar check had already come in from the sponsor and been deposited. He barely had time to put away the tuxedo from the season-ending banquet at the Waldorf-Astoria hotel up in New York City, before everybody wanted another piece of him: his owner, his sponsor, his fans, his crew chief, his engine builder, his accountant, his public relations person, NASCAR, the Winston people, the IRS, the magazine writers, the reporters from *Winston Cup Scene*, TNN and CBS and ESPN television and MRN radio (Motor Racing Network). All he had ever wanted to do was race a car as hard and as fast as he could around a track, just stomp it and go, but now everything had changed. He had heard about what ol' Buck Baker had said back there in the early sixties when the changes began—"Hell, what they ought to do is just give everybody a drank o' likker and drop the green flag" —but it was too late for that now. Over at the shop, which is what they humbly insisted on calling their sleek low-slung cinder-block-and-steel warehouses these days, there were a half-dozen racing machines in various stages of production; and not a damned one of 'em was ready for Daytona, not to mention Rockingham, Richmond, Atlanta, Indianapolis, or any of the other tracks on a circuit that now crisscrossed America from Daytona to northern California and from Phoenix to New Hampshire. Some off-season.

Let the new season begin; but first, a word from the sponsors. Having been relegated for so long to the back pages of newspaper sports sections, even in its spiritual homeland of the Deep South, NASCAR had learned to do public relations like few other major sports endeavors in the country. Everybody had a PR staff, it seemed—NASCAR, RJR Tobacco, Goodyear tires, the automakers, the tracks, the forty drivers, the scores of sponsors, the fan clubs, even the wives' auxiliary and the group that held chapel meetings in the garage area on race day Sunday mornings—and from most of them flowed a river of glossy press kits, standard press releases, faxes, managed interviews; anything that might get Winston Cup into the paper or on the air in a favorable manner. Every Tuesday morning following a race, promptly at eleven o'clock, RJR's Sports Marketing Enterprises assembled a teleconference, so the writers—calling an 800 number —could chat up the drivers or owners or crew chiefs made available that week. During the races themselves, it was possible for a writer to cover the whole show from the comfort of his seat in the press box high above the track, where he got lunch, television, MRN, and detailed updates every fifty or one hundred laps. Then, after the race, the winner and maybe his crew chief and his owner or sponsor would be escorted to the press box for a mass interview. Meanwhile, packages of color action photos of the day's race were being prepared; and an avalanche of post-race statements from nearly every driver, gleaned from the hectic garage area by the various PR people, was being dropped in their laps. They were a pampered lot, the "motorsports press," as long as they stayed in line; but they, too, like the sport they covered, had been regarded, not too long ago, as lepers in their own sports departments, and still had to defend against the barroom philosophy that the racing of automobiles wasn't really a sport.

Now, on this second week of January, they were coming together again for what resembled a family reunion. It was the Pinnacle Brands Racing Media Tour, whose official sponsor was grossing $6 million a year on NASCAR trading cards alone. Nearly 100 writers and broadcasters, most of them card-carrying members of the National Motorsports Press Association, had made it through the snow and ice to the elegant confines of the Adam's Mark Hotel in downtown Charlotte, settling into spacious $109-a-night rooms discounted to $60. They called it the "shop tour," because for four days they would be squired around on two chartered buses to several of the racing shops that surround Charlotte Motor Speedway, ten miles northeast on I-85 near the town of Concord, the very bosom of stock car racing. Foisted upon them at every stop would be all sorts of goodies, should they care to partake—T-shirts, sweatshirts, six-pack containers, briefcases, NASCAR umbrellas, key chains, little die-cast cars, RJR cigarettes by the carton, and, by all means, enough press kits to fill a shopping cart—but the tour had its legitimate purposes. With the Daytona 500, the official opening of the '96 season, still more than a month away, this was their chance to have a look at the new cars and talk to the men who had built them and the men who would race them.

There would be the usual mundane matters, good stuff to put away in the files and resurrect on slow news days once the season got underway, to wit: Was this kid Gordon really that good? Could the irascible Dale Earnhardt, "The Intimidator," break Richard ("The King") Petty's record of seven championships? Would Pontiac's new aerodynamic design finally allow it to run with the Fords and Chevys? Were the days numbered for the modest independent operators, now that the fat multi-team conglomerates had begun to dominate? These issues would be answered during the season, but there was a larger one that might take some time to play out. After nearly fifty years as the watchdog, the sanctioning body of stock car racing, NASCAR was riding the crest of its popularity in all ways measurable: prize money, attendance, media exposure, technology, sheer speed.

Now, with so much more money to be made, the directors appeared to be quite ready to turn their backs on the quirky little tracks in the Southern boondocks where the sport was born in favor of the monstrous super-speedways in the more populous corners of the country, places outside of NASCAR's natural habitat. They had been running Winston Cup in Michigan and Pennsylvania and Arizona and California for some time (had even staged an "exhibition" in *Japan*), and now it had just been announced that the classic little track at North Wilkesboro, North Carolina, had been bought into by a millionaire racetrack baron from Atlanta who intended to move one of its Winston Cup dates to the gaudy 163,000-seat speedway he was building in Texas. This same man, in fact, had been quietly checking out locations for a possible new track in New York, on Long Island, of all places. The letters page of the weekly tabloid *Winston Cup Scene*, stock car racing's bible with a circulation of 127,000, flamed with outrage. *Say it ain't so.* To the purists, this represented a blasphemy no less evil than when the Grand Ole Opry was moved out of hard-pewed old Ryman Auditorium and into a carpeted air-conditioned palace. And every old boy who had ever heard the bland strains of Countrypolitan music piped into an elevator knew that country music sold its soul and embarked on a path leading straight to Billy Ray Cyrus and "Achy Breaky Heart" the day that happened.

They were scheduled to begin the shop tour with a visit to Hendrick Motorsports in the nearby little town of Harrisburg, in the shadow of Charlotte Motor Speedway, but the buses couldn't get out of the hotel parking lot, so young Jeff Gordon and his benefactors came to them. The folks at NASCAR had been soft-pedaling their moonshine whiskey roots for several years now, right up to the edge of downright denial, and when this young prince won it all in 1995 they were beside themselves with joy. Here was the future of Winston Cup racing, they said: a handsome clean-cut kid from California, married to a luscious former Winston Model, a wunderkind who seemed born to be a driver; a sponsor, DuPont Automotive Finishes, willing to shell out around $10 million a year; a wealthy owner, forty-six-year-old Rick Hendrick, who controlled eighty Chevrolet dealerships from coast to coast; a thirty-eight-year-old crew chief, Ray Evernham, one of the best in the business, a gung ho sort given to plastering the shop with slogans like "**TEAM**—Together Everyone Achieves More."

In a scenario that would be repeated over the next few days, the three of them were ushered to director's chairs beneath a big banner proclaiming CHARLOTTE MOTOR SPEEDWAY and HENDRICK MOTORSPORTS in a large meeting room off the hotel lobby. With television cameras whirring, Hendrick, whose portfolio included being a minor-league baseball player, a founding partner of the Charlotte Hornets of the National Basketball Association, and an owner of a racing boat that once held the world's speed record, opened by saying it was too bad about the weather: "We wanted to show off our expansion. We've added a hundred and twenty thousand square feet, plus a new museum." Hendrick Motorsports had also added Quaker State motor oil as a sponsor for its three Winston Cup entries— veterans Ken Schrader and Terry Labonte in addition to Gordon—meaning he now had some $20 million worth of sponsorship money for the three race teams and the 165 shop personnel it took to support them.

After Hendrick had finished, Evernham took the mike to speak of some shuffling of duties during the upcoming season. Although he would still be the race-weekend crew chief of Gordon's "Rainbow Warriors," so named for the fanciful paint job on Gordon's number 24 Monte Carlo, he would now oversee the new crew for Schrader's bright red number 25 Budweiser Chevrolet Monte Carlo. "We're gonna call 'em the 'Bud Brigade,' " he mused, as the writers dutifully scribbled notes and the radio people held their tape recorders in the air, with noses twitching as steam tables bearing lunch were being rolled into the carpeted meeting room.

The last they had seen of Jeff Gordon was on national television in December when he dominated the two-hour live telecast of the Winston Cup awards banquet from the Waldorf-Astoria's chandeliered main ballroom before proceeding to the David Letterman show and *Good Morning America*, like Jesus on a victory lap, and still, they found his All-American goodness suspect. The whole New York experience had been "the thrill of a lifetime," he said when his turn came. He had been testing the car at Daytona, and it was "a real thrill to take the champion's spot in the garage." He really talked like that, ever a smile on a dark whiskerless Grecian face that a sculptor would die for. "I still can't believe what's happening. My career started, then skyrocketed, and then . . . *boom!* God was certainly on our side all last year. The off-season goes by so quickly, I really needed to get back in that race car."

With the secondary roads to the shops still impassable for two lumbering tour buses, the venue shifted that night to the Stock Car Cafe, in a strip shopping center right off an exit from I-77 just north of the city. Nearly every stop on the Winston Cup circuit had a place like this, sort of a Hard Rock Cafe for the racing set, throbbing with loud country music, teeming with lip-gloss racetrack dollies and shaggy chain-smoking good old boys wearing matched sets of stonewashed jeans and scruffy Reeboks and shiny nylon racing jackets, a cauldron reeking of cigarette smoke and beer, the air sticky from country-fried steaks and french fries crackling in the kitchen. The general decor—what else?—Late NASCAR. Parked out front in the slush was the black number 2 Miller Ford Thunderbird of Rusty Wallace, that evening's host, and inside was a dizzying melange of hoods and fenders dangling from the ceiling, bleached-blond pine walls adorned with neon signs for Miller's beers, framed racing collages, posters for Die-Hard batteries and Tide soap and French's mustard. Wallace, a handsome devil with beady close-set eyes and a thick mane of razor-cut auburn hair, had finished fifth in the point standings in '95, running his career earnings to nearly $13 million. As he sat beneath two television monitors replaying Rusty's Greatest Moments, he brushed off questions about whether NASCAR's striving for parity had favored Chevy and left Ford holding the short end of the stick: "I drive a Ford. I've driven a Pontiac. I might drive a Chevy one day. These things run in cycles. I just want to win. Right now, I dream of three Fords running side by side to the finish, with me ahead. That's perfect." He tugged at his gray Miller V-neck cotton sweatshirt, winked, and turned it over to his crew chief, Robin Pemberton, who said the new car was "great, it's ready," and everybody headed for the bar.

As the roads began to clear on Tuesday morning, the buses pulled away at daybreak for a long day's tour that held promise. All but a handful of the

Winston Cup shops were located within a short skip from downtown Charlotte, either hunkered together in industrial parks or rising up starkly from rolling land where tobacco once grew, and to visit them was to get to the very heart of big-time racing. The shops were housed in cavernous steel-beamed warehouses dressed up in cinder block or stone or vinyl siding, with demure logos like ROUSH RACING or TEAM SABCO or RCR out front, and the shops seemed to get bigger every year as the racing teams proliferated. Most of them employed about fifty men, mechanics of one sort or another, whose days began early and ended late. The shops had come a long way since the days of humble garages out under the trees behind, say, Junior Johnson's farmhouse. These things now looked like precision Saab factories holding everything under one immense roof, with specialized work going on behind each marked door: Dyno Room, Cylinder Head Department, Engine Shop, Machine Shop, R&D, Paint Booth, even an Exercise Room with Nautilus equipment so the members of the pit crew could get in shape for the critical and frantic pit stops once the races got underway. Now, in most cases, everything having to do with these fanciful racing machines was accomplished in these very shops: from chassis assemblage to the application of sponsors' decals.

In addition to getting a glimpse of the shops, which few would be able to do once the relentless season got underway, the media would be popping in on an interesting mix of drivers on this second day of the tour: the only rookie enrolled in the class of '96, Johnny Benson, too old at thirty-two to be called a "kid" but edgy and rearing to go just the same; Kyle Petty, the restless underachieving son of Richard Petty, The King, the all-time winningest driver in NASCAR's history; Dale Earnhardt, The Intimidator, the man in black, the baddest dude of them all; and Darrell Waltrip, the writers' favorite, a loquacious veteran who would turn forty-nine in a couple of weeks and had seen just about everything since he started out racing go-karts at the age of twelve.

More than a dozen of the shops were located in an industrial strip called Lakeside Park, near Lake Norman, an upscale lakefront community about twenty miles north of downtown Charlotte. With an off-duty state trooper leading the way in a van, probing for dry spots on the ice-crusted streets, the two buses finally slithered to a stop in front of a steel-and-cinder-block building that housed Bahari' Racing. They had beaten the vans that were to cater breakfast, but no matter. Inside, on buffed gray concrete floors so spotless that you could eat off of them, there sat a glistening new yellow number 30 Pennzoil Pontiac Grand Prix, the chariot to be driven that year by Johnny Benson, who had been carefully selected after winning the points championship the previous year in the Busch Grand National circuit, which is to Winston Cup what Class AAA baseball is to the major leagues. Benson, in the Pennzoil team colors—black slacks, black turtleneck, yellow crew neck—looked more like an amiable small-town Pep Boys store manager than a driver entrusted with a race car being backed with something like $4 million from Pennzoil and other sponsors. He had been picked not only for his driving ability but for his dark good manner as well, and for ten minutes he stood beside the sleek racing machine in lockstep with the team owner, a wealthy fifty-five-year-old auto-parts mogul named Chuck Rider, the two of them flashing their teeth and posing as the photographers fired away. Benson had just returned from testing the car at Talladega Superspeedway—the frightening track in east Alabama where drivers used to black out momentarily from vertigo until they got accustomed to speeds of more than 200 miles per hour—and his times had been the fastest of the five Pontiacs there. "We're proud of the car," said his crew chief, about the only notable quote of the morning. Then, breakfast was served.

No one was surprised when things got livelier at the next stop, right up the street at Team Sabco, for this was the bailiwick of the odd couple: Felix Sabates, a Cuban refugee and the most flamboyant and outspoken of all Winston Cup owners, who, in the storybook version of his life, had parlayed a box of Cuban cigars and hard work into a personal fortune gathered through the sales of electronic gadgets ranging from hairdryers to video games; and Kyle Petty, son of The King, NASCAR's different drummer, the least predictable of a stable of drivers who, for the most part, had learned to mind their manners and speak the corporate line. Sabco's shop looked like all of the others, except for the toys. Lining one wall just inside the front doors were eight gleaming chrome Harley-Davidson motorcycles belonging to Kyle, who would be wheeling one of them from California all the way back home to Charlotte during the summer on his annual cross-country charity bike ride. In a garage attached to the main building were some of Sabates's playthings: a silver Rolls-Royce, a white stretch limo, a vintage 1955 Pontiac Chieftain. His latest yacht was on Lake Norman.

There would be no messing around here at Team Sabco, not on this morning. Sabates was being sued by the driver and owner of the Tide car, Ricky Rudd, for allegedly stealing his three principal crew members—crew chief, engine builder, and "engineering data specialist"—and he was livid. While Kyle and two of those crew members sat obediently in the ubiquitous director's chairs on a makeshift dais, Sabates leapt to his feet, tugged at the lapels of his sharp black blazer, and let fly. "I went over to Ricky's shop to see if we could settle the thing between ourselves," he said, his dark eyes flashing. "Ricky told me he'd consider it if I paid him four hundred thousand dollars, plus a hundred thousand for legal fees and sixty grand for something else. I told him to forget it." That was probably the sanitized version, for Sabates once was quoted as saying that the main reason he didn't cotton to Communism was because he had roomed with Fidel Castro, Jr., at Havana Military Academy and "I didn't like the little shithead."

Kyle Petty seemed to be enjoying his owner's performance, and there was little he could do to top it. The most unlikely-looking driver in Winston Cup—with his earrings, receding hair drawn back in a ponytail, a Vandyke beard—he resembled the pop musician known as Yanni. At thirty-five, though, he was no longer considered a promising young man. "Because he's a Petty," one writer had opined on the bus ride over, "he'd own NASCAR if he'd just win a race now and then." He had won exactly eight in seventeen years, against his father's untouchable record of 200, and the charge against him was that he had never really given racing his full attention. (In '95, for instance, he had signed on as a passenger on the supersonic Concorde in a promotional stunt to set a speed record for an around-the-world flight; it was a success, but he missed the preparations for a race while he was gone.) "This is not my first rodeo," he said, drawing smirks from the writers. "We're on a gradual pace here. There's been a lot of turnover, with the new paint and the new design, and these new guys are winners." The new crew chief, a hulking bearded fellow named Billy

Woodruff, who had been working in racing shops for twenty-three of his forty years, said the new Pontiac was "twice as good as last year. . . . We're gonna make *Ford* third, not Pontiac," and then, *voilà!* Somebody on the other side of the main showroom grandly whipped off the nylon wraps to reveal Petty's new number 42 Pontiac Grand Prix, in shiny red-and-blue stripes with the Coors Light logo in a shocking chartreuse on the hood. On their way out the door, at a long laundry table, the writers paused to pick up Sabco press kits and little insulated six-pack containers, perfect for carrying their Coors. "Think I'll hold a yard sale when I get home," one of them said, boarding the bus for the long haul to Dale Earnhardt's place.

The Earnhardt operation, Richard Childress Racing (RCR), was housed in a cluster of low brick buildings beside the railroad tracks in a tiny whistle-stop town named Welcome, south of Winston-Salem and more than an hour's drive from where most of the other Winston Cup shops were concentrated. It seemed fitting that a loner such as Earnhardt would do his business far away from the rest of the crowd; but on the other hand it was ironic that the town would be called Welcome, for Earnhardt was anything but a warm, cuddly, and inviting personality. He was an imposing man at six-two, 180 pounds, downright bulky in comparison to a group of drivers who looked more like racehorse jockeys, and his countenance was that of a gunslinger who had strolled into town, looking for some action: angular, scowling through mirrored sunglasses, a mischievous crinkly half-grin flashing through a bushy mustache that slashed across a face wrinkled and burned by sun and wind and hard knocks. The Intimidator, the Man in Black, Ironhead; his monickers fit him well and he wore them gladly, for he seemed to enjoy his reputation as one tough hombre. He particularly enjoyed baiting Gordon, the clean-cut Christian, twenty-one years his junior (Earnhardt would turn forty-five in the spring). When he said on Letterman's late-night television show that he had been the first man to win a NASCAR race at Indianapolis Motor Speedway, and Letterman said he thought it had been Gordon, Earnhardt brought the house down by saying, "No, I said I was the first *man*." And when Gordon, familiarly known as "The Kid," won the points championship for that year, Ironhead reckoned that for the first time they would probably have milk instead of champagne at the head table during the banquet at the Waldorf-Astoria.

Parked outside in the snow, beneath four flags snapping in the January breeze (American, North Carolina, Chevy, black RCR/3), was the monstrous black double-decked eighteen-wheel car-hauler used to transport Earnhardt's cars from track to track; and inside, crouched side by side in a neat row on the spacious floor of the main room, there sat seven black number 3 Goodwrench Monte Carlo Chevrolets more or less ready for the season. Continuity had been one of the main reasons for the success of the RCR/Earnhardt team. He and Childress, who had never won a pole or a race in a decade of Winston Cup driving, had been together for twelve years. Now, as the media came clattering into the room, they posed beside an enlargement, mounted on an easel, of a contract with Goodwrench, General Motors's service-parts division, that would extend their sponsorship deal to the year 2000; ensuring that Earnhardt, at an estimated $10 million a year in personal income, would continue to be one of the world's wealthiest sports performers. While the members of Earnhardt's pit crew, the "Flying Aces" (formerly the "Junkyard Dogs"), lolled on the fringes, watching in bemusement, strobe lights recorded the handshakes and pronouncements before, finally, Earnhardt, wearing black jeans and a starched white long-sleeved dress shirt, took a seat in a director's chair and was handed a microphone.

There seemed to be an adversarial relationship between Earnhardt and the press, bordering on hostility, and the air crackled with the first question: Would winning the record-setting eighth points championship be the final missing piece to "the Dale Earnhardt puzzle"? There was coughing, and some shuffling in the semicircle of metal folding chairs. Earnhardt's eyes flashed as he bit off his answer: "There *aren't* any missing pieces. If I dropped dead tonight, I would've had a great career." Well, then, can you finally win the Daytona 500? To this, the most sensitive question of all, Earnhardt grinned and snapped, "That's why they run the race, isn't it?" Okay. Well, how about the kid, Gordon? "He pushed the level of competition up a notch. It makes you want to step up to the plate, makes everybody try harder." So, are you ready? "We just ran thirteen hundred miles testing two cars at Daytona last week, and we'll be back again next week.

We've already got an Atlanta car, a Bristol car, and so forth. . . ." It was a classic confrontation between Earnhardt and the media: he could check off another item on his list of errands, and the press could walk away unsatisfied.

It was with some relief that they got the hell out of Welcome and rode on to friendlier surroundings. If the writers and broadcasters seemed a mite intimidated by Earnhardt, they genuinely looked forward to the next stop: a more modest operation, in the lengthening late-afternoon shadows of Charlotte Motor Speedway, the shops of Darrell Waltrip. They were calling him "Ol' D.W." these days, now that he was pushing fifty, and he sort of liked that. "Anytime I need something to write," said Tom McCollister of the *Atlanta Journal-Constitution*, one of only two of the daily newspapermen who would cover all of the Winston Cup races, "I just go up to D.W. and say, 'Darrell, help me out here, I still don't understand such-and-such,' and you can't shut him up." Waltrip had been racing for thirty years now, and had piled up some impressive numbers: tied for third place with Bobby Allison in all-time wins (their 84 wins lagging far behind Richard Petty's 200 and David Pearson's 105), third in earnings with $14 million, three times a Winston Cup points champion, and a winner at Daytona. He had finished nineteenth in points during the '95 season, with eleven DNFs (Did Not Finish), and hadn't won a race in exactly 100 starts, signs that perhaps his time had passed, but he was acting like a young ballplayer on the eve of spring training.

Looking lean and fit in a crew neck sweater and creased wool slacks, not a fleck of gray in his thick crop of black hair, Waltrip was standing at the head of a *receiving line*, for God's sake, glad-handing and carrying on with the media as they came through. When they had all settled into chairs, he bounded onto a makeshift stage and thunked a microphone to be sure it was working and said, "Welcome to the house that Western Auto built." He called for the obligatory unveiling of his new machine, a red-white-and-blue Chevy Monte Carlo with the number 17 in his trademark mirror-silver, and spoke of his new sponsor, Western Auto's Parts America, then said, "Look, I know everybody's tired from running all over the place.

We've got some snacks over there. Maybe you don't have any questions left in you. . . ." Wrong. Soon, D.W. was off and running. He would handle this job all by himself.

"Are you thinking about retiring?" somebody asked.

Waltrip winced. "Bad choice of words."

"Well, let's call it the R word, then."

"Hey"—Waltrip motioned to one of the mechanics hanging around the walls of the shop—"would somebody get that gizmo for me? You know, the plate. It's over there on my briefcase, in the office." He had spun out in practice at Daytona in the summer of '90, shattering his leg and requiring a twelve-inch metal rod to be inserted to hold things together. He finally had it taken out after the last race of '95. Somebody brought it to him and he held it up for everyone to see: a fearsome piece of hardware with eighteen long screws dangling from it, like wind chimes. "I called it my restrictor plate," a wry reference to the metal plates used to artificially limit speeds at the dangerous Daytona and Talladega tracks. "I was waiting in the doctor's office one day, complaining, and this guy said, 'That ain't nothing,' and he rolled up his pants and took his whole danged leg off. Artificial leg, you know. I feel great now. Hey, I can even do the Ickey Shuffle again. Even Earnhardt congratulated me." A theatrical pause, laughs all around. "Well, I *think* he did. He didn't say, 'I *love* you, man,' but it sounded like congratulations to me."

"The R word, D.W."

"I want to win a hundred races. I don't know whether I'll make it, but I don't intend to retire. I'll drive two more years, at least, but the year 2000 has a nice sound to it. I want to be around to get to those new tracks in Texas and Florida and Vegas, too. There's three R words, actually. When I get in the car and start thinking about risks and rewards—do I want this bad enough to take a chance on getting hurt?—then I'll retire."

Waltrip was primed, like a monologuist on a roll. Jeff Gordon? "He's the prototype of the future driver, groomed for it since he was a little kid. He doesn't throw his helmet and cuss NASCAR when something goes wrong, he just goes back to work. The guy's a great driver." The move toward bigger tracks? "Bigger is better. By today's standards, North Wilkesboro isn't the future. Understand, there's nothing I love better than coming off the fourth turn at North Wilkes, sideways, taking the checkered flag, but you've gotta move on." Daytona? "Our sport *is* Daytona. It's got to be on your résumé. It's like the Super Bowl, the World Series, the U.S. Open. I've won eighty-four races, but that wouldn't mean anything if I hadn't won Daytona." The future? "The key is technology. Five or six superteams will be the ones who'll control the sport. We've got some additional property here and we're expanding. I want to see a bunch of men in white aprons running around a big shop, getting ready for Daytona. . . ."

It was a surreal scene that night from high above Charlotte Motor Speedway, on the sixth floor of the posh Speedway Club. All things considered, CMS was the best track on the Winston Cup circuit—115,000 permanent seats, fifty-two condominiums, seventy-six VIP suites, a seven-story office tower, a lighted mile-and-a-half oval, all of it on 2,000 acres in the rolling countryside beyond Charlotte—and for this occasion the lights ringing the track had been turned on to reveal a dazzling portrait of the entire layout buried in snow. After dinner and drinks (and a pitch from the makers of tobaccoless Smokey Mountain Chew, right there in Winston country, akin to cussing in church), there was a half-hour of reflections by three retired drivers who had found second careers as television commentators. Ned Jarrett: "In 1961, my dream was to pay taxes on ten thousand dollars." Benny Parsons: "Somebody up in Ann Arbor or somewhere is tracking the broadcasts, telling Goodyear, General Motors, and all of the other sponsors, 'You've had so many seconds on national television, and that comes to two hundred thousand dollars of national advertising.' " Buddy Baker, Buck's son: "I got into a wreck with Richard Petty at Daytona one year. As it turned out, Petty was the name of one of the track doctors. When I woke up, somebody said, 'You're gonna be fine, Dr. Petty worked on your head,' and I said, 'He sure as hell did, and I didn't even see him comin'.' "

That name, Petty, was always coming up, and the next day they went to visit The King himself. The Petty compound, as it were, was nearly 100 miles from Charlotte, at the little crossroads town of Level Cross. Every year, with their *Rand McNally Road Atlas* denoting the spot, following the bronze markers along a tree-lined country road running south out of Greensboro, some 30,000 racing fans trekked to the Richard Petty Museum, paying $3 a pop, to gawk at the amazing collection resting under the roof of a huge shed: trophies locked under glass, won by Richard and his father, Lee, and his son, Kyle; the 1970 pale blue number 43 Plymouth Superbird, "when cars were *cars*," with its fanciful winged rear spoiler; racing suits and shoes and helmets from the days when Richard, this bony Tarheel with a disarming twang, ruled the tracks; and more crap, in the form of T-shirts, caps, belt buckles, cigarette lighters, and the like, than you would find at a county fair. Once a year, on the front porch of the nearby two-story white framed ancestral home, with traffic backed up for five miles, Petty would sit in a Naugahyde recliner beside a box of felt-tip pens and autograph anything thrust in front of him on Richard Petty Fan Appreciation Day. He was proud to say that he had never refused to give an autograph or an interview in his life.

"If you see something you want to buy, let me know." It was The King himself, sneaking up behind a gaggle of writers clucking among themselves over all of the stuff. He wore his trademark black Stetson, its hatband gauded with a silver buckle and bright feathers, and he was spiffed up like a cowboy come to town on a Saturday night: black jeans, silver-buckled belt, black silver-tipped cowboy boots, crisp blue button-down dress shirt, red-and-blue leather jacket adorned with the number 43 and the oval logo of STP, bushy mustache, blue wraparound sunglasses . . . and a hearing aid crammed in one ear, the legacy of having run in 1,185 Winston Cup races that lasted up to four hours each. For thirty-four years he had driven stock cars, his last win coming at Daytona on the Fourth of July, 1984, with his hero Ronald Reagan in attendance. When he reluctantly gave up the wheel in '92 he became an owner, and in that role, he was yet to win a race.

So that's what this was about: the prospects for the STP/Petty Enterprises Pontiac, the familiar red-and-blue number 43, to be driven again by Bobby Hamilton. Like a father and son (Hamilton, at thirty-eight, is twenty years younger than Petty), the two of them mounted director's chairs to hold what amounted to a chat with the media, arrayed before them in a semicircle of metal folding chairs, as the tangy odors of beans and barbecued pork wafted through the low-ceilinged museum. In this, the twenty-fifth anniversary of the STP-Petty sponsorship, the longest-standing deal in NASCAR history, there would be four different paint schemes on old number 43 to commemorate their years together.

They had tested the car at Daytona, Atlanta, and Talladega during the winter, Petty said, and things looked good. "Bobby's the cog, and now this car, and we've got plenty of sponsorship money."

An executive from STP, hovering on the edge, cut in. "Wait a minute, this is the press, right? I'll pay good money for a tape where Richard says he's got plenty of sponsorship money."

Touché. Petty's down-home grin. "I didn't say it was STP money, did I?"

Upon that amiable note, the press conference rambled along. Hamilton, an easygoing country boy with some streaks of gray beginning to show in his unruly mop of dirty-blond hair, wore a polo shirt and rumpled jeans and sneakers; as though he had been summoned from the shop, told to scrub up and get out there, which very well might have been the case. Petty said the corner speeds and down force appeared to be improved on the new Pontiac. Hamilton said he was "gonna keep my helmet on if I make it to Victory Lane this year, because there's no telling what the fans will do if somebody besides Richard Petty wins in the 43 car." Petty had filed to run for North Carolina's secretary of state position in the coming fall elections, and when somebody asked him about it he had to ask Hamilton to repeat the question, his hearing having become so poor. "I'm doing it to occupy my mind so I won't miss driving so much," he said with an aw-shucks grin. Hamilton again had to repeat a question, this one about what Petty had to say about the move away from the small tracks. "Look how much it's changed since Richard Petty quit driving," Petty said. "I used to drive a lot of tracks, then they'd close 'em, and I'd miss 'em for about two days. The sponsors love these big new tracks. That's progress."

Meanwhile, all across America, the machinery was cranking up for another thunderous round of racing. Goodyear was working out the logistics of delivering 6,500 special racing tires to Daytona International Speedway for the extravaganza known as Speedweeks that would kick off the season. The cars were about ready, the television and radio commercials had been put in the can, the tracks had been preened, the tickets had been sold, the motel rooms were long gone. And the fans were getting cabin fever, if you could judge by *Winston Cup Scene*. There, on the back pages given over to snapshots mailed in by the fans, was a photograph of one Holly Reardon, bundled against the cold in her backyard in Akron, Ohio, posing beside a snowman wearing a T-shirt and cap for her hero Mark Martin, the driver of the number 6 Valvoline Thunderbird, with one of those cartoon balloons that said "How Long Until Daytona?" Enough of this messing around. It was time to go racing.

1

A GATHERING OF EAGLES

The very idea of a place like Florida is anathema to some, especially the good burghers of the rock-solid heartland who sniffily beg to question what kind of values are inherent in a civilization built on sand and sump-pumped swampland and easy credit, but they tend to suspend their judgments when the power lines go down and the pipes burst and they find themselves ass-deep in snow. So now, on the first week of February, after yet another blizzard had hit North Carolina and most of the eastern half of the country—this one even more severe than the one that had brought in the new year—the racing crowd couldn't get out of there fast enough. Poor Brett Bodine, the Winston Cup driver who was trying to unload some of the stuff he didn't need from his $5 million purchase of the retired Junior Johnson's shops, couldn't hold an auction due to the storms; the first two had forced postponements, and now, "the way my luck is going," he was advising people in the North Carolina piedmont to "rent their generators and buy their milk and bread before Tuesday, March 5," the latest date set for the auction. Over in Welcome, the last chances to fine-tune Dale Earnhardt's fleet of black Monte Carlos before leaving for Daytona were saved when Richard Childress activated the emergency generators that would keep the dynamometers and other diagnostic devices going until it was time to load the car-hauler and head south.

So Florida, in spite of all its tackiness, was looking like heaven now to the scores of race teams and the many thousands of their fans who were fleeing south like snowbirds to escape the last blasts of winter and find out if God had just been fooling around. From all corners of the country, California to Maine and every state in between, they had fallen in line on the interstates, a calamitous caravan of pickup trucks and station wagons and Winnebagos and even Harleys and converted old school buses, all of them streaked with the dirty remnants of ice and snow, flying the colors and pennants of their favorite drivers, all roads leading to the relatively balmy shores of Daytona Beach on Florida's upper east coast. With clucks and grins they observed the billboards whizzing past, advising them of some kind of bizarre Land of Oz straight ahead—citrus groves, alligator ranches, snake farms, Disney World and Marineland and Weeki-Wachee Springs, time-share deals on oceanside condominiums, golf-and-tennis spas, "planned retirement communities" slapped out there in the sawgrass —but they kept on going, eighty miles an hour if they could get away with it, because they were headed there not for business or cheap thrills but for a spiritual reawakening, not unlike baseball fans bound for spring training camps.

The good-natured among them called themselves "Motorheads," in the manner of the Grateful Dead's "Deadheads" and the Green Bay Packers' "Cheeseheads." They were stock car fans, racing freaks, everybody hauling ass for Daytona Beach, their journey not ending until they peeled off I-95 and turned onto Speedway Boulevard and got their first glimpse of their Wailing Wall, their Yankee Stadium, their Grand Ole Opry House, their Louvre. And there it was: rising up out of the sand like some giant spaceship, about to become the core of their universe for the next couple of weeks, Daytona International Speedway, the "World Center of Racing."

If Daytona Beach was the spiritual home of stock car racing, then the speedway was its Mother Church. With 110,000 permanent seats and room for at least 50,000 fans encamped around a forty-four-acre lake in the infield, it was the site of eight separate weekends of racing throughout the year, from go-kart rallies to the Daytona 500, and, no matter the time of year or the weather, which can be surprisingly chilly in the winter and hot as hell in the summer, there was always some race team out there running computerized tests on the high-banked 2.5-mile track. The bulk of the racing, though, occurred during the first three weeks of February—Speedweeks—when a daylight hour seldom passed without action of some sort on the track, either practice or qualifying or flat-out racing, by cars of nearly every breed. Speedweeks presented a nonstop orgy of racing, drawing an estimated 475,000 people to a town with a standing population of 60,000 and a county of 370,000. Those sojourners dumped an estimated $215 million each year into the coffers of Volusia County—three quarters of a billion dollars when the Chamber of Commerce's rollover "multiplier effect" was figured in—certainly a potload of cash for a placid little spot on the map that otherwise might have little to do but bask in the sun and create excitement for itself, so the full-time residents had learned to brace themselves and endure. No matter how hard they tried, though, Speedweeks always came with a jolt that rattled the natives from their reverie.

Lord, lord. Out there on U.S. Highway A1A, Ocean Boulevard, the good old boys had arrived. At the beachfront motels, The Reef and Sea Dip and Sunsations and Old Salty's Inn, the signs reading SORRY and NO VACANCY were already going up on the marquees out front by the hour, more than a week before the running of the Daytona 500, their parking lots filled with vans and cars bearing bumper-sticker witness to the owners' allegiances ("Have You Beaten a Ford Lately?" and "Anyone but Earnhardt"), their wrought-iron railings draped with soggy Confederate flag beach towels and bathing suits. There went a tattooed fellow on a Harley-Davidson, long hair trailing from his black Nazi helmet hand-painted with a silver number 3, going into a skid on the sand-blown pavement to avoid a startled blue-haired retiree trying to make it safely across the street from her condo to the Publix market with her aluminum walker. Up and down the boulevard, beneath palm trees swaying in the nippy ocean breeze like grass-skirted hula dancers, a rusty old junker with an Alabama license tag and an orange Tide detergent number 10 Ricky Rudd pennant clipped to its radio aerial, stuffed to the roof with country boys swigging from cans of beer, was cruising back and forth, looking for whatever. For sale, in the temporary shops along the sidewalks: T-shirts, sandals, straw hats, fits-all baseball caps, sunglasses, sunblock, beach towels. Down on the beach, families in sedans and station wagons inched along at a turtle's pace, little boys in the back seat gawked at young things in thong bikinis, walking in pairs or flirting with lifeguards or pretending to ignore Rebel yells drifting down from the balconies of a row of high-rise condos that walled out the morning sun ("Yowww! . . . South gon' *rise* again!"). Filling the skies overhead: seagulls and kites and cirrus clouds, contrails from passenger jets, single-engine planes droning like bees as they towed blurbs for bars and nightclubs and restaurants; and, finally, a sure sign that something must be about to happen in these parts, there was the omnipresent Goodyear blimp, purring along on a course that would put it directly over the speedway. Ten more days, and everyone was counting.

It is possible that none of this would have been happening if a twenty-five-year-old garage mechanic and erstwhile race car driver by the name of Bill France, weary of the winters around Washington, D.C., hadn't packed up his wife and young son and fled southward in the fall of 1934. Tall and handsome, the son of a bank clerk who had named him William Henry *Getty* France in hopes that some of J. Paul Getty's Midas touch would rub off, France had gotten hooked on automobile racing as a teenager, when he would skip school and sneak off to watch open-wheel Duesenbergs fly around the high-banked board tracks in places like Laurel, Maryland, halfway between Washington and Baltimore. More than once, he borrowed his father's Model T Ford for the trek to Laurel and wound up racing it on the thirty-one-degree banks of the Laurel track, having to feign befuddlement, upon returning the car, over why the tires weren't wearing better. He quit high school after two years, to take a job in a garage, and there he began his education in working on cars and racing them. By the time he had become a husband and a father, in the early thirties, he had built a couple of cars from scratch and was running them at board and dirt tracks on a circuit up and down the eastern seaboard. "I started thinking if I was going to have to work all the time fixing automobiles, I might as well fix them where it wasn't snowing," he told Sylvia Wilkinson in her marvelous *Dirt Tracks to Glory*, an oral history of stock car racing's early days. He hooked up a trailer full of tools to his Hupmobile and, with $25 in cash, pointed it toward Florida. One look at the wide hard-packed beach at Daytona, where they stopped for a swim on a perfect fall day, was all it took. They found a house to rent, at $15 a month, and he began working at a garage.

Bill and Annie France had arrived in Daytona Beach just in time to see the end of an era of a particular brand of racing along a strand that ran for eighteen miles, from Ormond Beach to what was known around Daytona as "the inlet" south of town. Show some boy a flat, hard stretch like that, he was going to race something on it, and ever since the coming of the automobile at the turn of the century there had been drag racing on the beaches: rev it up and see how fast it would go in a straight line. France was there on the day in the spring of '35 when Sir Malcolm Campbell, a Brit knighted and known worldwide for his blazing high-speed runs, fired up what was less a race car than a rocket on wheels—his "Bluebird" was powered by the same Rolls-Royce engine that would go in the Royal Air Force's Spitfires and Hurricanes during the Second World War, and his crew was made up of aircraft mechanics rather than automobile grease monkeys—and set a world land-speed record of 276 miles per hour. As though there were nothing else to prove at Daytona, where strong winds and the tides made conditions unpredictable, that whole scene suddenly shifted to the Salt Flats in Utah. For all of those years, the dateline "Daytona Beach, Florida," had flashed around the world as people heard and read of unbelievable speeds being broken there nearly every time one of those dashing adventurers like Campbell crawled into a cockpit, but soon it was over. The departure left a gaping hole in Daytona's psyche, if not its economy, and the Babbitts began to scratch around for some sort of racing activity to replace the speed runs.

The racing of stock cars was catching on, especially in Georgia and the Carolinas, where dirt tracks were being carved out of the red hills to accommodate local daredevils, many of them haulers of moonshine whiskey during the week and race car drivers on weekends, so that seemed to be the way to go. The Daytona city fathers consulted with a well-known driver by the name of Sig Haugdahl, who had been the first man to turn three miles in one minute in a speed run, and he devised a beach-and-road course totaling 3.2 miles: two straightaways of a mile and a half each, one on the beach and the other on A1A, connected by sharp turns at each end through loose sand. The first beach-road race would be a 250-miler, some eighty laps, come spring of '36. It would be open to stock cars only (cars anyone off the street could walk into a showroom and buy), sanctioned by the Automobile Association of America, and the total purse of $5,000 was quite a lure in those darkest days of the Depression, when the minimum wage was $14.50 a week.

When the big day arrived, a couple of thousand curious fans parked their cars on the water side of the beach, then clambered for vantage points on the dunes between the straightaways or atop precarious wooden bleachers thrown up at the turns on either end or along the scrubby shoulders of the highway. They saw a gathering of twenty-seven frisky drivers out squirreling around to get the feel of the wide sandy beach in a smorgasbord of cars: bulky Auburns and Lincoln Zephyrs, a couple of pokey Willys coupes, some nifty little roadsters, and a passel of '34 Ford coupes (darling of the "trippers," the moonshine haulers). The drivers included some dirt-track and open-wheel midget champions from the Midwest and the eastern seaboard, and some trippers from Georgia. The cars were time-trialed—the fastest, at seventy miles per hour, was a super-charged Auburn being driven by an Indy winner named Wild Bill Cummings—and the race began with a staggered start, slowest cars out first. The two Willyses lumbered off to begin the race, and had been circling the track for a full thirty minutes before Wild Bill Cummings, the fastest qualifier and thus the last starter, was let loose. The first to finish the scheduled eighty laps would win the race.

It was a disaster from the beginning, due almost entirely to the sand in the turns. France, driving a '35 Ford he had borrowed from a mechanic friend, had qualified tenth and started eight minutes after the Willyses; and by the time he reached the first turn he came upon heavier cars that had bogged down axle-deep in the sand. He was proceeding better than most, having learned a thing or two about driving in sand during his time living in Daytona. "If you went too slow you got stuck and if you went too fast you turned over," he told Wilkinson years later. The wind came up, bringing the water in ahead of schedule, sending spectators in a mad dash for their passenger cars before the ocean swallowed them up. The race was called after about seventy laps, some 200 miles, when the first turn became completely clogged with race cars either wrecked or hopelessly mired in the sand. France finished fifth, to win $300, but Wild Bill Cummings, like the others in the heavier cars, never finished at all. Appalled, the AAA withdrew its sanction on the grounds that such shenanigans would besmirch its name. The city of Daytona Beach pulled out as well, claiming a loss of $22,000 on the venture, and began to think about less risky ways to bring in the tourists.

The Elks Club stepped in as a sponsor the next year, but what really saved racing at Daytona from an early demise was the discovery that a local clay, known as marl, hardened when it dried and, when mixed with the sand, would at least alleviate the problems in the turns. So there would be another race in '37 after all, shortened to a more sensible fifty laps, and it was won by a local bar owner, Smokey Purser, in a Ford. But one year was quite enough for the Elks Club, and it looked like it was all over until there came a turn of events that would change the face of stock car racing forever.

Bill France owned his own garage and service station by then, on Main Street, and it had become a hangout for the growing number of race car drivers in the area. France was getting deeper into racing now, touring with a '37 Ford at dirt tracks all over Georgia and North Carolina, making connections in what remained a sort of underworld of sports. One day, the Daytona Beach Chamber of Commerce approached him about keeping the beach-road-course race alive. He didn't have the money himself, he said, but he knew who might: Charlie Reese, of Charlie's Grill and Cocktail Bar in Daytona Beach, the sponsor of France's car. Charlie put up the money, France and his wife, Annie, became promoters, and thus began the career of Bill France, the man who would go on to become, arguably, the most powerful czar in the history of American sports. (His only competition, in that regard, was Judge Kenesaw Mountain Landis, who had rescued baseball from the Black Sox scandal, and Pete Rozelle, who would turn pro football into a billion-dollar empire.)

Ragged as racing was on the beach-road course, the benevolent weather and the earnest implorings of France served as magnets to attract the best of the early stock car drivers to Daytona Beach as often as four times each year. Auto racing in America virtually ceased during the Second World War, due to shortages in petroleum, rubber, and metals, but entered its heyday immediately afterward. Genuine dirt ovals sprang up all over the South, *real* tracks with orderly grandstands and ample parking and infield garage areas, but even then there was a cachet about a driver's being able to say he had won at Daytona. Much of this was due to the sheer force of "Big Bill" France's personality as he traveled through the disorganized slew of tracks dotting postwar America, preaching the need for safety and better tracks and a fairer distribution of purses, planting the notion in the minds of the disparate promoters and track owners and drivers that they should all band together in a confederation, convincing them that their passion was not some white-trash folly but a legitimate sport with a boundless future. Thus, the foundation was laid for the two singular events, a decade apart, that would make Daytona Beach, Florida, the center of the universe as far as stock car racing was concerned. First came the formation in 1948 of NASCAR, its headquarters in Daytona, its president Bill France. Second came France's dream: his building of Daytona International Speedway, on converted swampland a couple of miles southwest of the beach-road course. It was a racetrack like no other, a 2.5-mile paved tri-oval super-speedway with swooping straightaways and thirty-one-degree banking on the turns, and when the first Daytona 500 was held there in 1959 it nailed Daytona Beach's claim as the Valhalla of stock car racing.

There had been some action at the track during the early days of Speedweeks '96, sparsely attended, not exactly the NASCAR crowd's cup of tea: practice and qualifying and then the running of endurance races for sports cars and small sedans under the aegis of IMSA, the International Motor Sports Association. Truth be known, Winston Cup fans were famously ornery and downright close-minded about their racing preferences. If a car didn't at least *look* like something they could drive away from a dealership, wasn't big and loud and fast, hadn't been built in an American plant and retooled by some salt-of-the-earth mechanic named Pete or Mike or Harry, wasn't owned and sponsored by Americans, wasn't driven by someone who had come up the hard way (better a Southerner named Bubba), and went around the track any way other than in a counter-clockwise circle . . . well, it hardly counted. Indy cars? Don't ask. *Damned things look like spiders on training wheels, don't use regular gas, and what the hell kind of name is Fittipaldi?* Sure, they would go out to the local track back home to watch the compacts and the homemade jalopies and those little winged mosquitoes from the World of Outlaws slide around in the dirt, if there wasn't some Winston Cup stuff on television, but their hearts belonged to these big mothers now being delivered to the Daytona infield by a veritable convoy of monstrous semi rigs almost as tall as two-story buildings, known variously as car-haulers and transporters, each pulling a gleaming split-level trailer holding two 3,400-pound American race cars and equipment on top and living quarters below, all but a couple of them showing North Carolina license tags.

Virtually overnight, with the speed and efficiency of circus roustabouts off-loading boxcars and hoisting their tents under the light of the moon, a small village had appeared and sprung to life in the garage area by the middle of Week Two of Speedweeks, ten days before the running of the thirty-eighth annual Daytona 500. It had been exactly three months since the end of the previous season, at Atlanta in November, and, even though the mechanics and their volunteer goters belonged to a closed fraternity cloistered around Charlotte, they were treating this like a reunion, a home-coming, a mini-convention. Once the transporters had been parked in close orderly rows and the shiny new race cars had been gently lowered with hydraulic lifts, then rolled to their assigned spaces in a covered garage area with room for 164 cars, the men roistered about, however briefly, playing grabass and comparing vacations and swapping blizzard stories and—they couldn't help it—moseying around, circling closer, leaning, squinting, hoping for a peek under the newly painted hood of each other's machines, anything for an edge. Now and then some fan wandering the garages on a sponsor's pass would ask them for an autograph, prompting one of the more hardened beat writers, Al Thomy of the weekly tabloid *Fastrack*, to opine: "Where else can a guy who changes tires have a uni-form, sign autographs, and be a celebrity? Tell that to the guy who changes tires on *my* car. My guy's just a grease monkey."

That disclaimer aside, these men who made the cars go were the worker bees of Winston Cup racing, the ones who stirred the drink; your friendly neighborhood garage mechanic in demeanor, but several notches higher in expertise. Except for a dozen superstar crew chiefs like Ray Evernham of the Hendrick/Gordon operation, said to be earning as much as $200,000 a year in salary plus various bonuses and five percent of the winnings, the bulk of them were poorly paid and known only inside the brotherhood of Motorheads. They were introspective, patient types who spoke a language of their own—"down force" and "compression ratio," "loose" and "tight," "dyno" and "tunnel test" and "cornering"—as they moved about the garage stalls in team uniforms, their first names stitched over their heart, adjusting belts and tightening bolts and checking tire pressure. *You're only as good as the men in your shop*, the drivers were the first to acknowledge, and it had always been so. The mechanics would have their brief moments in the sun on race days, as members of the seven-man "over-the-wall gang" during pit stops, charged with crawling all over the cars, like emergency medical technicians—changing four tires, wiping the windshields, filling them with gas, adjusting the coils and "track bars" with the cranks of special ratchets, all within twenty seconds or less when things went right— but for the most part their work took place in the shadowy anonymity of the garage. They were paid as little as $35,000 in salary, plus a sliver of the winnings; and, thus, were always prepared to listen to a better offer. "One of the best things about having your shop away from Charlotte," said Larry McClure, owner of the Sterling Marlin entry, based in Abingdon, Virginia, "is being able to keep your team together. I hear that when they go to lunch in Charlotte, they might not come back. And if they do, they've probably leaked some secrets." No matter where they might next tote their toolboxes, they were fervent about their work; NASCAR had decreed that the garages could be open only between seven A.M. and five P.M. because, an official explained with a shake of the head, "They'd stay up all night, working on their cars, if you let 'em. The rule's meant to protect them from themselves."

About the time the crews had set up their garage stalls—roping off the area, arranging their toolboxes, rolling one of the cars into place—in came the drivers, the stars of the show, like leading men entering from the wings. Many of them had flown in with their wives and children, mooring their planes at the city airport adjacent to the track, and it was a rare driver who didn't spend the nights with his family in a posh hotel or a rented villa somewhere on the beaches and the days in a well-appointed motor home in a fenced area of the infield at the speedway where a convivial racing village had been established virtually overnight. They would know few moments of peace during their stints at Speedweeks, if their owners and sponsors and NASCAR had anything to say about it—and they most certainly did—so they felt no compunctions about accepting any little luxury presented to them. Now, with their wives tidying up the kitchen and bedrooms, the kids playing outside the motor homes with other drivers' kids, the drivers made their grand entrances into the garage area. Most of them, like Richard Petty, had long ago learned to walk purposefully through the throngs of fans, signing autographs on the run (Petty, to avoid carpal tunnel syndrome, had perfected a rolling style in which the shoulder was the only moving part involved). And here they came, stage right, into the cocoon of the garage. They weren't treated as heroes by the mechanics, of course, since each side knew full well that it took a driver *and* a car to win, and they had, after all, last seen each other less than forty-eight hours earlier. But their arrival seemed to crank things up a notch, bring springs to steps and smiles to faces, transform a mere reunion into, well, a gathering of eagles.

They were a dashing lot, these forty-odd full-time drivers on the Winston Cup circuit, and as a group they shared many traits. For the most part they had grown up in the small towns of the Southern countryside, sons and brothers and nephews and in-laws of racing families (for the '96 season there would be three Wallaces and Bodines, two Burtons and Labontes and Waltrips). They were religious, often in Victory Lane thanking God and their sponsor in the same breath (one, Morgan Shepherd, had insisted that he be quoted, in his own press kit, as saying that his "greatest achievement" had come on the day he "accepted Jesus Christ as my Savior"). If they followed politics at all, their heroes were conservative Republicans (the longest day in the life of Mark Martin, the only Arkansan in the ranks, had come when he was ordered to squire around the reviled President Bill Clinton as he visited a race, in Winston country, to resounding boos). A couple of them had tried college, but at least half had failed to complete high school. They were 100 percent white; there had been only one full-time black driver in NASCAR history, a former moonshine tripper from Danville, Virginia, by the name of Wendell Scott, who won one pole and one race in nearly 500 tries from 1961 through '73. They were small in stature, averaging around five-ten, 160 pounds. Because their jobs were so intense and demanding, they had to work at keeping their marriages together, many being on their second or third and one on his fifth. Their passions away from the track were hunting and fishing (one, before turning to racing, had spent a year alone in the Virginia woods as a trapper), and flying the planes they now could afford. Although one of them was still being tutored at reading and writing, in his mid-fifties, most had learned by the seat of their pants to be fairly expansive on the dais or during mass media interviews. They were not athletes, in the purest Olympian sense, but they carried the special sort of stamina and courage and temperament required to wheel a car through mayhem at terrifying speeds for three solid hours, in temperatures reaching 130 degrees in the cockpit, with only an occasional "rest" of twenty seconds during pit stops.

In spite of these shared qualities, they also were part of a fascinating stew of personalities that would seem, at first glance, to have been ordered up from Central Casting: Earnhardt for the old school of roughriders from the dirt-track days, the princely Gordon for the yuppies-for-Jesus crowd, the ponytailed book collector Kyle Petty for the free spirits (and any liberal who might be lying low out there on the circuit), the blustery overweight Jimmy ("Mr. Excitement") Spencer of the Smokin' Joe's Camel Ford for the smokers and red-meat-eaters, and so forth and so on, through an eclectic roster that offered a fan a broad assortment of types from which he or she could pick someone to root for. But, no, "root" wouldn't cover it. Fans of Winston Cup racing were notoriously faithful to their favorite drivers and thus to their driver's sponsors, which was the driving force behind those outlays of millions of dollars a year to back one car and one driver. "We always talk about 'the match,' " said a marketing executive for one of the major NASCAR sponsors. "The other day a bunch of us were sitting around, talking about matches, and we found the perfect one. Somebody's making a bad mistake if they don't take this kid on the Grand National circuit, Buckshot Jones, in the double-aught car, and marry him to the Remington rifle people." And, should that happen one day, Buck-shot would have to be taken aside and instructed on what might be the most important of the social graces required of any driver who hopes to hang on to his fans: humility, feigned or otherwise. He must be able to imply, with a tug of the ear and an endearing grin, *I might be rich, but it ain't changed me none.*

Humility was never a problem for Dave Marcis, who, on this day they all came together at Daytona, wore the biggest smile in the garage area. Marcis would turn fifty-five on the first day of March, and he had started more Winston Cup races than any other driver still active on the circuit. True, he had enjoyed only one season in the sun, in 1976, when he won three races, and he had won just two more during his twenty-eight years, the last one coming in 1982. But what made him a hero to the workhorses in the garage, a legend in his time, in this new age of big-bucks multiple racing teams backed by huge corporate sponsorship, was that he stood as the last of a dying breed: the independent owner-drivers. Year by year countless others with names like Jody Ridley and G. C. Spencer had been forced to drop out, unable to compete as the tracks got faster and the cars became more sophisticated and expensive to maintain, but Marcis had survived by doing his own work, taking care of his equipment, running as a "stroker" (playing it safe, staying away from wrecks, hoping for lap money), and earning money on the side as a trusted test driver for, most recently, Dale Earnhardt.

It had always been thus, a love triangle involving him and his wife and his car. After a start on the dirt tracks back home in Wisconsin, Dave and Helen Marcis had towed their mobile home to North Carolina in 1968 to begin a new life, on what was then called the Grand National circuit, out of a modest shop in the little town of Arden, just south of Asheville, far from the cluster of racing teams around Charlotte. Working on a shoestring budget, which included living in that same trailer for twenty-one years before finally building a house for themselves and the two children who came along, they managed. Dave had never been a factor in the points standings, never won anything close to half a million dollars in a season, never been courted by the big sponsors. "It was always a guessing game before a race about what would be on the hood of Dave's car this time," one of the mechanics was saying. "Olive Garden? Big Apple? Who would it be this week?"

But now, for the first time in an intrepid career, right there on the eve of the Daytona 500, a big break had come his way. The word had spread throughout the garages that what had been a race-to-race deal with Prodigy, the computer people, had suddenly turned into a full-season sponsorship worth $3 million. (There was a small irony in that. Marcis Auto Racing was the only team in Winston Cup without a dedicated fax line—"Call in advance" was the advisory in the NASCAR press guide—and now, as part of the deal, he was about to be showered with e-mail and America Online and every other known contrivance of this new era in communications.) *Three million dollars!* He and Helen and the crew had been staying in a motel nearly sixty miles up the road in St. Augustine, out of a lifetime habit of cutting the overhead wherever possible, and now there was this bonanza.

He stood beside his gaudy new purple-and-green number 71 Chevy Monte Carlo, somewhat stunned, accepting congratulations from the mechanics and drivers as they drifted over to shake his hand. The new Prodigy uniforms for him and his crew were on order, but for now he made do with a frayed racing suit trimmed with patches representing dozens of the part-time sponsors who had helped him over the years, in the manner of a world traveler proudly displaying stickers on his worn suitcase denoting every country he had visited. A Prodigy cap was pulled tight over his silvery hair and he still wore the soft pair of wrinkled black wingtip shoes that had become his trademark since his discovery that they were not only cheaper but more nearly heat-resistant than the fancy suede Simpson racing shoes. The wonder of it all! It was obvious that he was trusted and respected, if not revered, by the older mechanics, who understood better than most what it had taken for him to survive for all of those years.

"Hey, Dave," one of them said, "what you gonna do with all of that computer stuff?"

Marcis's Wisconsin accent belied the fact that he had been living in North Carolina for nearly three decades. "Oh, I'll just have to let Helen and Dwayne here take care of that," he said, nodding toward Dwayne Leik, a younger man who doubled as his PR man and an extra hand in the pit and garage. "I've just figured out telephones, myself."

"No more 'Poor Dave,' huh?"

"Hey," he said. "You ever think you'd see the day when Dave Marcis would have a show car?"

With more than sixty drivers trying to make the field, there was a drawn-out system of qualifying for the treasured starting positions in the Daytona 500. The first two spots would go to the cars with the fastest times in the first round of qualifying, on the Saturday a week before the big race itself. More solo time trials would be held on the following Monday and Tuesday, for those who chose not to stand on the time (SOT) they had posted during that first day out. Then, on the Thursday before the 500, there would be a pair of 125-mile races, with the top fourteen finishers in each of those fifty-lappers filling out positions three through thirty in the starting field for the 500. The next eight starting positions would be determined in descending order of speeds during qualifying heats. Positions thirty-nine through forty-two would be filled by the top four teams remaining from the list of leading car owners from the '95 season who had not otherwise made the cut, positions known as "owners' provisionals." There would be a forty-third entry, a "champion's provisional," only if a former Winston Cup champion had not made it in any other way. Simply being in the Daytona 500 was close to being a make-or-break situation for many—a driver who started last and went out after only a couple of laps still could cash a check for more than $30,000, a considerable amount for any of the smaller operations—and, as a consequence, the qualifying rounds and the Twin 125s traditionally were hairy affairs fraught with carnage. The drivers hadn't raced in earnest for three months, for one thing, and so much was at stake that even veterans who should know better were prone to take unnecessary chances, whether on a solo qualifying run or racing in the Twin 125s.

On the Saturday of the first qualifying heats, the tension was thick around the garage area. The Winston Cup drivers had been practicing for two full days—breaking in their new cars, regaining their feel of the track, fine-tuning the engines, refining the "setup" (the perfect balance of spring tension, tire pressure, gear ratio, the works)—communicating by radio with their mechanics in the garage and their spotters perched atop car-haulers, rushing in for adjustments, roaring back onto the track for a few more spins. Now, after lunch, they were walking through a critical routine they would have to follow before every race of the season: passing NASCAR's technical inspection. There was one portal in a certain cinder-block garage through which they all had to pass, the inspection station itself, swarming with NASCAR technical inspectors in uniforms of Winston red and white, with an array of templates and scales and other measuring devices to ensure that the three car makes met NASCAR specifications. The line of cars snaked through the garage area, each pushed along by mechanics and trailed by a little humming portable generator wired to the innards to keep the oil warm. *Next!*

Here came the shiny black Ford Thunderbird of Rusty Wallace, the number 2 on its side, the Miller beer logo on its hood, Rusty himself following in his black racing uniform, helmet under one arm, taking a seat in a metal folding chair to watch every move as the inspectors began by taking a slate-gray aluminum Ford template to see if the car's profile was right. Then they waved it into the garage and onto the scales, and as it was being checked for the minimum of 3,400 pounds, one inspector lifted the hood for a close look underneath and others measured the car's height and width and ground clearance. Rusty had struck up an idle conversation with Bill France the younger, successor to his father as head of NASCAR, wearing khakis and a blue blazer and a brightly striped sportshirt, as the two men lazed in the shade; but he eased to his feet and grinned broadly when he saw one of the inspectors take a blue felt-tip marker and daub a spot on a bright orange decal stuck high on the windshield. A passed inspection. (You never know. The year before, in an inauspicious beginning to his farewell season, the legendary Junior Johnson had been caught and fined $40,000 for trying to slip an illegal intake manifold past the tech inspectors as they checked the Brett Bodine–driven Ford, an indiscretion that the lads in the shops wryly referred to, with some defiance, as "creative engineering.") When two thin vertical metal strips were bolted to the trunk lid, so nobody would mess with the aerodynamics before qualifying, Rusty and his crew were out of there with high-fives, grinning like jack-o'-lanterns. *Next!*

Crunch time had arrived, and there was a festive air in the garages and the pits as the cars were rolled toward their places along pit road for the opening round of qualifying. There had been some cool and windy days earlier in the week, but this one had turned sunny and hot, bringing out the lovelies: there was a curvaceous young Winston Model, dressed in red toreador pants, strolling about with a cardboard box of RJR-brand cigarettes free for the taking; and there was Linda Vaughn, still revered by the old-timers as the buxom Miss Firebird of the sixties, a race queen for the ages, now prancing around the garage area, bursting from a skintight outfit of her own design, turning heads, in her fifties but still bountiful to behold. And all about, lugging camcorders and Nikons, sometimes indistinguishable from the working press, Motorheads with sponsors' garage-and-pits passes strung around their necks trailed behind the cars, rabidly recording the scene, as the last of the cars were moved into place. No semi-celebrity was safe; some of the fans even stopped to have photos or footage made of themselves posing with the television announcers, Ned Jarrett and Benny Parsons and Eli Gold, perceived as stars in their own right.

Mildly amused by all of this, Walter Franklin sat at a picnic table beneath a huge striped tent in the garage area, between a concessions stand and a red transporter serving as NASCAR's information and hospitality center, as good a place as any to follow the qualifying. From there he could hear MRN's broadcast of the proceedings as it boomed over loudspeakers throughout the speedway grounds, and just outside the tent there was an easel set up so a sinewy NASCAR employee in her sixties, wearing a red cowgirl hat, could record the times with a grease pencil. Franklin, balding, about fifty years old, owned a fencing company in Richmond, Virginia, and had been coming down for Speedweeks for "longer than I can remember," as a vacationing volunteer. He simply loved racing, he said, and over the years he had helped in any way he could—basically as a gofer, carting gas cans from the pits to the Unocal pumps and back again, stacking tires, washing cars, whatever—and his thing, these days, was to lament over the proliferation of rich multi-car race teams.

"I've worked off and on for Dave Marcis over the years," he was saying. "Dave's a great guy. He's what racing's all about. Or what it *ought* to be, anyway."

"Guess you heard about his new deal," said a wrinkled old fellow seated at the same table, sporting a nylon gimme cap from a gas station in Gaffney, South Carolina.

"I'm happy for him, but three million dollars still won't compete with the big teams." As if on cue, a qualifying time for one of the multi-team cars was announced, three tenths of a second faster than that of Dave Marcis. "Three million more would've bought Dave that three tenths of a second."

The older fellow said, "Unnerstand Dave's even gon' have a show car now. I figure that's progress."

"Hunh," Franklin said. "Hendrick has so many show cars they can't keep up with 'em. Literally. One time they ran an inventory and came up one short, had no idea where it was. Turned out it had been sitting in Indianapolis for three months. They'd never even missed it."

One by one the cars roared out of the pits on their qualifying runs, one lap to gather speed, two to be timed. This was important enough for ESPN to be covering it live, and intriguing enough to attract a crowd of about 10,000 into the stands. There would be a somber announcement—"Next out, Sterling Marlin, in his number 4 Morgan-McClure Kodak Monte Carlo"—greeted with a roar of football-stadium proportions from Marlin's fans in the crowd, he having won two straight Daytona 500s, and then the scream of the engine as Marlin gunned the race car and burst onto the track for his solo run. Squinting into the sun, peering through binoculars, trying to pick up some driver-to-crew chatter on expensive radio scanners they had keyed to each of the Winston Cup teams' frequencies, the fans in the steep main grandstand and the ones perched atop their RVs in the infield watched as the Kodak-yellow Chevy whizzed around the track, startling coveys of seagulls from their loiterings around the lake in the infield, sailing perilously close to the high-banked walls before dipping precipitously into the corners, zooming past them in a blur, hitting 200 miles per hour on the straightaways, all systems go. When the flagman began madly waving the checkered flag from his perch in a crow's nest

above the start-finish line, Marlin and everybody else seemed to know it
was a keeper, an SOT: 188.814 miles per hour; enough, as it would turn
out, to put him on the second row of one of the Twin 125s. But the biggest
cheers and the biggest boos would come later, toward the end of that day's
qualifying round, when the times were posted. This was to be a major test
for a likable driver named Ernie Irvan, trying to complete his comeback
after damned near being killed during a practice session at Michigan during the '94 season. When the crowd heard that his was the second-best
time of the day they roared and stamped on their aluminum bleacher seats
in approval. The announcement of the best time, though, was another
matter. It was Dale Earnhardt, the man in the black Chevy, ol' Ironhead,
The Intimidator, and even as he approached the start-finish line on what
looked like a fine run, indeed, many fans had clambered down to hook
their fingers in the retaining fence and let him have it. "It's the Daytona
Four-Ninety-Nine, *asshole*," one of them screamed, the veins on his neck
bursting, hitting Earnhardt where he hurt. As Darrell Waltrip had reminded everyone during the shop tour back in January, "you ain't nothing"
until you had won at Daytona.

Sometimes, with all of this going on, one could wonder how the drivers
found time to take care of the one truly important matter that had brought
them to Daytona: running the 500 and winning it. Speedweeks represented
the ultimate business opportunity for the sponsors, the best chance they
would have all year to get the most for their millions, and they weren't
about to squander a minute of it. The drivers were busy enough consulting
with their teams in the garage area and putting in some "seat time" on the
track, whether in practice or qualifying or actually racing in the preliminar-
ies. But they were always being snatched away by public relations types of
one sort or another, escorted through the throngs of fans and media,
shoved into a car or even a waiting helicopter, to be whisked away to fulfill
some kind of obligation. All over the county, at malls and automobile
dealerships and restaurants and motels, show cars were on display in advance of the appearance of the driver himself. The Motorheads knew this,
of course, from reading the daily newspapers and listening to WNDB, the

Performance Racing Network outlet, and since they weren't likely to bump into, say, Jeff and Brooke Gordon while dining out at night—although, Lord knows, they never gave up hope—they tramped around town day and night, whenever they weren't at the track, tailing the stars.

Since the first day of February, the McDonald's restaurants had been bleating the appearance of Bill Elliott at their location near Volusia Mall, directly across from the speedway entrance, even offering a private dinner with Bill himself to five winners of a drawing. Elliott's fans were legendary in their loyalty to "Awesome Bill from Dawsonville," the drawling redhead from Georgia's hill country who had practically owned Winston Cup racing during the mid-eighties when he won the Winston Million bonus (for taking three of four designated races) and everything else, even setting the standing world's record for speed in a stock car with his qualifying run of 212.809 miles per hour at Talladega. For ten of the past eleven years, he had been voted by the fans as Most Popular Driver. (Somewhere in there, suspecting ballot-stuffing, the rules were changed to force fans to pay a 900 phone charge per vote; he won again, anyway.) So he would be there in person, at the Speedway McDonald's, from six to eight P.M. on the designated day, to meet the fans and sign anything they thrust in front of him.

Most of them had simply strolled across Speedway Boulevard after a full day at the track, garbed in everything Elliott that they owned, and as dusk fell they had more or less taken over the asphalt parking lot of Kmart Plaza, an adjunct of the larger mall, now a sea of RVs and cars and pickups, most with Georgia tags, sporting red number 94 Elliott pennants, decals, and bumper stickers. At least fifty of the RVs appeared to have staked out space for the duration of Speedweeks in the mall parking lot or next door at the Shell station, whose bays now served as a souvenir emporium holding racks bending under the load of T-shirts and tables piled high with caps and pins and every other collectible under the sun. Parked at the entrance to McDonald's were Elliott's show car and its transporter, in gaudy red and gold with the Golden Arch logo. There were at least four hundred fans milling about in a line that began at the car and snaked off into the gathering darkness. An employee of the restaurant, wearing a bow tie to dignify the occasion, would hold up three fingers, like a maître d' announcing "table for three," and the anointed fans would grin and squeal and be shown inside the door.

Bill Elliott, in jeans and a striped blue-and-gold polo shirt, had been sneaked in through a back door after a dash to the mall for a radio interview, and now he sat at a table, beneath a small bas-relief rendering of his Thunderbird jutting from the wall, in a corner called the McDonald's McGift Shop that brimmed with souvenirs. It had been a busy day for him, but this was his bread and he knew to butter it.

"Now, *Bee*-yul, I want you to beat that ol' Earnhardt Sunday, you heah?" Elliott's drawl was catching. Close your eyes, you would swear you were hearing Gomer Pyle of the Andy Griffith television show.

"Yes, *may*-yum, I'll try my *bay*-ust."

"You get to the [Dawsonville] Pool Room much, Bill?"

"Ever' chance I get. They prob'ly got the best hamburgers in the world." *Oops.* A grin for the manager. "If you cain't find a McDonald's open, is what I *mee*-yunt."

And so it went, beyond the allotted two hours, Elliott carrying on with the fans and signing everything from worn autograph books to T-shirts. The "private dinner" with Bill for the five lucky couples meant a hamburger feast in a sequestered room, ending past ten o'clock, and it was near midnight before he finally got to sleep in his hotel room up on the beach. With another practice round set for nine o'clock the next morning, his alarm was set for daybreak.

The first door-to-door racing of the new season took place on a Sunday, the day after the opening round of qualifying, exactly one week before the Daytona 500. It was the Busch Clash, sort of an all-star race pitting the sixteen drivers who had won pole positions during the '95 season plus a seventeenth whose name had been pulled out of a hat (Dave Marcis, as it happened, truly on a roll now). The Clash was a pair of ten-lap sprints, actually, with starting positions for the first one being determined by a lottery. There were more than 50,000 fans in the stands on a sunny seventy-degree day when the green flag dropped on the first segment of the Clash at high noon. The winner of that one was Sterling Marlin, having his hopes raised for a third straight Daytona 500 victory, but when the field was reversed (in order of finish in the first segment), he finished second to Dale Jarrett, son of the broadcaster Ned. The first money of the new season had passed hands (Jarrett and Marlin taking in totals of $62,500 and $50,000, respectively, for about thirty minutes of racing; John Andretti collecting $10,000 even though he had pitted with a smoking engine during the pace lap of the first race), but the day had meant more than that. It was best expressed by Darrell Waltrip, ol' D.W., the fading legend who had started third but finished twelfth in the first race and slid from fifth to fourteenth in the second: "We'd like to have done better," he said afterward to a swarm of reporters as he stood in front of his car-hauler, wiping his brow with a bandanna. "But, hey, isn't the Clash something? It's a great way to start the season. It's like getting in the first licks on the opening kickoff of the first football game of the season. Now that we've got that out of the way, let's get on with it."

Win or lose, it was back to the drawing board for all of the Winston Cup teams. No matter how much time and money they had spent in preparation during the short off-season, on the computerized machines in their high-tech shops back home and on the track at Daytona or Talladega, they were never fully satisfied once those first licks were passed. Their race cars might seem to be powerful rocket ships, ready to go with a flip of a switch, capable of running at high speeds all day, but the reality was that they were like the finest thoroughbred racehorses: high-strung, fine-tuned, skittish, always just a step away from some life-threatening catastrophe. Horses are routinely "destroyed" when they break down, God having no replacement fibulas in stock, but for the racing teams it's back to the garage. "We probably spend more time testing here than ten other tracks put together," said Earnhardt, who would seem to have little to complain about after finishing third in the second Clash segment and winning a total of $24,000, but there he was in the garage watching his men tear down his car and then put it back together after the races. What worked in tests, whether at a track or on the dynamometer or in the wind tunnels (NASCAR used two, at the Lockheed Martin aircraft plant near Atlanta and at General Motors in Detroit), wouldn't necessarily work when the real thing began. The number of variable factors in producing a first-place car at a given track on a given day seemed to run into infinity, taking into consideration everything from horsepower to tire pressure.

And there were two other interconnected factors endemic to Daytona and Talladega, the fastest and most dangerous tracks on the circuit. Ever since Bill Elliott's frightening ride at Talladega in 1987, NASCAR had ordained the use of the restrictor plate, a thin piece of metal fitted on top of the carburetor, that drastically reduced the flow of air and fuel and, thus, horsepower, from 700 to around 400. That slowed the cars considerably, from Elliott's record-breaking 213 miles per hour to top qualifying speeds of slightly less than 190 these days, but it also equalized the cars and left a driver hanging out to dry if he suddenly needed a burst of extra power to avoid trouble. So there was that plus a phenomenon known as the "draft," discovered by Junior Johnson in 1960. Junior had felt he had a car that was at least ten miles per hour slower than the best when he showed up that year for the second Daytona 500, but while out tooling around in practice on the eve of the race he found that when he got directly on the tail of a faster car he got swept up in a vacuum and was actually pulled along by the faster car. ("Roll your windows down and get right on the tail of an eighteen-wheeler," is how Kyle Petty explained it. "When the air stops rushing into your car, you're drafting. I wouldn't recommend tailgating a semi, but that's how it works. If you stay with him, you'll not only save gas but he'll pull you all the way to Chicago.") Junior Johnson won the 500 that year, in a car that was woefully slow, and drivers had known ever since that drafting was the only way to go at Daytona and at Talladega. And so it was that in the days between the Busch Clash and the running of the Twin 125s, on the Thursday before the 500, the drivers and their teams had more than enough to occupy themselves: the drivers to check out the aerodynamics of their new machines as they drafted each other in practice, and the mechanics to keep looking for the perfect setup for the race.

While the principals were thus engaged, two quite disparate civilizations had begun to take shape in the infield of the speedway: one for the well-heeled, another for the commoners. The wealthier fans, like, say, the used-car kings from places like Terre Haute and Lubbock, had paid big bucks for prime spots near the garages, some of them separated only by chain-link fences from the drivers' slightly more elegant motor homes, and there they were "roughing it," as they would say with the self-deprecatory chuckles of the nouveau riche, in luxurious $200,000 "recreational vehicles" holding bedrooms and kitchens and lounges and showers and television sets and fully stocked wet bars. But out there on the naked fringes of the lake it was, like, well . . . barbarians at the gate! From the moment the tunnels had opened, the good old boys had been pouring in by the hour, like so many Joad families, having motored down from all corners of the country in an ungodly collection of blocky Volkswagen buses and old pickup trucks and even converted school buses, many painted in the colors of their heroes, and almost overnight they had set up this colony out there in the weeds and the sand. All day and throughout the chilly nights, in a gathering that had the feel of a fraternity party or a hobo camp, the hoi polloi entertained themselves in any number of ways—diligently sawing and hammering away to complete their jerry-built viewing platforms on time, drinking beer, barbecuing great greasy slabs of pork ribs, turning up the sounds of Hank Williams, Jr., on their boom boxes, pitching horseshoes, howling at the thin crescent of a moon, tossing sticks of hardwood on their roaring bonfires, waggling cardboard signs reading SMUT ("Show Me Ur Tits") at comely young women sashaying their way in halter tops and Daisy Mae Yokum cutoffs, announcing a standing offer of a stick of firewood for a "flash" from said lovelies—having about the best damned time they could remember since, oh, hell, last Labor Day at the Southern 500 in Darlington, South Carolina, where this whole idea of camping out at the races had begun nearly half a century earlier. The only times the two classes of citizens ever came across each other was at the souvenir stands in the infield, long strands of tents and trailers reminiscent of the midway at a county fair, to buy T-shirts or radio scanners or pizza, or to pose for a free Polaroid shot of themselves grinning from the cockpit of the Dale Earnhardt show car parked under a billowing blue-and-white-striped tent, courtesy of General Motors and the United Auto Workers.

Meanwhile, from the cinder-block infield media center located near the garage area, the mighty NASCAR publicity machine rolled on. About 1,250 press credentials of varying urgency had been tendered for Speedweeks (1,000 of those for photographers), to journalists ranging from small-town daily papers to low-watt local radio stations to contingents from Europe and Asia, and a reporter didn't have to wait long for another nugget to be dropped in his or her lap. From NASCAR and the sponsors and the teams and the drivers' own personal press agents and the speedway itself, from anybody who had something to sell, there spewed reams of photocopied handouts. "MADD [Mothers Against Drunk Driving] will be joining Cracker Barrel Old Country Stores, Inc., and 2nd Chance Finance [in] sponsoring teams racing on February 16 in the Goody's Dash and on February 17 in the Goody's Headache Powders 300," read one. From Ford Motorsports came the news that team owner Jack Roush had personally flown his vintage Second World War P-51 Mustang to Daytona. Came word from Dallas–Fort Worth that 26,383 fans had shown up for an open house at the 1.5-mile 163,000-seat Texas Motor Speedway, still little more than a hole scooped out of the prairie, a full year away from completion, but already penciled in on the 1997 Winston Cup schedule. Transcribed quotes from owner Bud Moore, at a press conference announcing that Hayes Modem would sponsor the number 15 Ford, driven by Wally Dallenbach: "I'm real happy to be here to make an announcement like we're fixin' to make." A factoid from Goodyear: the cost of one racing tire this year would be $329. From CBS, televising the 500: they would be using nine in-car cameras, thirty-five cameras in all, thirty-eight tape machines, 150 "audio sources," four mobile units, six miles of cable; and they were saddened to announce that Richard Petty wouldn't be in the booth since he was running for political office and there were "equal time" considerations. This just in from Hollywood: a couple of ringers would be in a preliminary ARCA race (Automobile Racing Club of America, Winston Cup's rookie league) as part of the filming of a pilot show for a proposed television series to be called *Daytona Beach*, involving actors Lee Majors and Mac Davis. Whatcha got, Kodak? "On the way to the drawing for starting positions in the Busch Clash, Sterling Marlin, who drives the No. 4 Kodak Monte Carlo, picked up a rental car with four miles on it. He then stopped at a convenience store and bought a Dr. Pepper, some cookies, a car magazine, a banana, and an orange. It came to $4.44. In the draw, he drew No. 4 in his fourth Busch Clash. 'I'll probably finish fourth,' he said." Noted and recorded.

And so the countdown had begun for the biggest race of any Winston Cup season and one of the most famous sporting events in the world, ranking right up there with the Super Bowl and the Kentucky Derby. All of the players were in place now, from the network television wizards high on the windy roof of the grandstand to the scabbiest Motorhead living out of a sleeping bag in the infield grass. There were no more rooms at the inns, not even at the cheapest mom-and-pop motels as far away as Orlando, an hour or so west in the interior, and all along the five-mile stretch of Speedway Boulevard leading from the beaches to the track there were grown men holding cardboard signs scrawled with pleas for tickets that might just as well have read "Will Work For Food." The local newspapers and the airwaves were filled with traffic and weather reports, and overhead the sky was beginning to fill with blimps and small planes carrying such advisories as CIGARETTES KILL RACE FANS. Over there on Ocean Boulevard in Daytona Beach, near the site of the old beach-road course, a handful of old men who had been legends in their time leaned against their lovingly restored thirties-era Ford coupes in the weedy lot of the Christian Drive-In Church, ready to pose in case someone wanted to take their pictures, but hardly anyone cared anymore about the likes of—*who?*—Raymond Parks and Gober Sosebee and Tim Flock. That was then, when the racing of automobiles was regarded as the sport of knaves, and this was now.

Like the first game of spring training in major-league baseball, Thursday's running of the Twin 125s would serve as a full dress rehearsal for the Daytona 500 and, thus, for the season about to unfold. On the poles in the first and second races, respectively, were Earnhardt and Irvan, based on their qualifying speeds of the previous weekend. The pressure was off for those two, but the heat was on for the forty-nine other drivers. Of that number, only twenty-eight would nail down starting positions in the 500, the rest having to sweat it out while NASCAR exhausted the myriad other ways of filling out the field. Now, for the first time since they had convened little more than a week earlier, there would be all the trappings of a full-bore automobile race: sellout crowd of 160,000, live television, decorous prerace ceremonies, the startling roar of twenty-five cars as they flew out of the fourth turn and got the green flag, the high-speed jockeying for positions in the draft, the frantic pit stops. Batting practice and the work on fundamentals were over. Let the games begin.

Except for a mess toward the end of the first race, when five cars got entangled on the backstretch, damaging egos more than anything else, it was a fine afternoon of racing in seventy-five-degree weather. Over the earphones of their $350 scanners, fans could hear the urgent crackling between the drivers and their crew chiefs and spotters: "This thing's loose, all over the place . . . Clear, clear, go, go . . . Stay high . . . Hammer down, now, go, go, go . . . Green's out, go race 'em, buddy . . ." Earnhardt took the first of the two fifty-lap races, marred only by that one wreck and two brief cautions brought on by light rain on the distant backstretch. (This place was so big that the men in the pits didn't know why the yellow flag had gone out until they heard from Earnhardt, calmly giving traffic and weather reports from out on the third turn, "Man, do you believe it, it's *raining* out here!") There was not a single caution during the second race, led by Irvan from start to finish, over with in forty minutes. When the day was done, the field had been set for the big one. As testimony to NASCAR's genius, only one regular Winston Cup driver had failed to somehow make the field for the 500: Bobby Hillin, a thirty-one-year-old Texan whose biggest moment had come ten years earlier when he became the youngest winner in Winston Cup history by taking a race at Talladega (it was he who had set off the wreck in the first 125). Some of the big names made it only by cashing in their owners' provisional chips—most notably, Darrell Waltrip and Brett Bodine—but the fans were assured that, come Sunday, the gang would all be there.

Still, down there in the garage area in the late afternoon, there was the ugly reminder that racing automobiles at those speeds and in such traffic could be a frightening proposition. Side by side in adjoining bays were the brothers Bodine, who had finally patched up a squabble stemming from an on-track accident that had seen them go a year and a half without speaking, and now they were surveying the damage resulting from the wreck of the first 125-mile race. Geoff, the oldest, was going to be all right, although it was going to take a lot of work to repair his car. But for Brett, well, if it wasn't one thing it was another. He had already lost one car due to a fire during practice, and here went another from the batch he had bought in Junior Johnson's closeout sale. Now, over the roar of the Grand National cars spinning around the track in practice for their season opener on Saturday, he stood by morosely while his mechanics salvaged what they could from this one. With blowtorches and pliers and crowbars, they were tearing away mangled pieces of metal skin and tossing them into blue trash barrels. The engine had been pulled and was dangling from a hoist. When they had salvaged what they could, they rolled what was left of this number 11 car to the hauler, Brett following behind with an armful of usable parts, and soon they were engaging the hydraulic lift of the car-hauler to fetch yet another identical number 11 car. They would be allowed to stay late, overnight if necessary, to install the engine in it. But Brett Bodine had made the show, using Junior's owner's provisional left over from the '95 season, and as his mechanics wrestled the engine into the new car he sidled over to chat with a group of fans who had been gawking and whispering throughout the salvage operation.

Finally, late on Saturday afternoon, the countdown for the Daytona 500 began. The last of the preliminary races had been run, the Goody's Headache Powders 300, which had kicked off the Busch Grand National season, and now it was time for the Winston Cuppers to take the track for one final run around the course. They called it Happy Hour, this last chance for corrections before the garages were ordered closed for the night, and, as a measure of its importance, this final practice for the Daytona 500 was being broadcast live by ESPN. Most of the fans were still rooted to their seats as the cars were fired, eased out of their spaces in the garage, and wheeled back onto the track. It was hurry, hurry, hurry: a lap or two, back to the garage for a half-crank on the springs or some more air in the tires, out on the track again—"Sonofabitch still ain't right," on the radio, a driver to his crew chief—then back to the stall. Out for some drafting, looking for a partner, a spotter relays his message from the roof of the hauler to his driver: "Try hookin' up with Kyle and Ernie, up ahead of you on the backstretch." Some, most notably Dale Earnhardt, hadn't even bothered, simply draping the car with its nylon wrap and calling it a day. The garage would officially close at five o'clock, and by four-thirty a deathly quiet had fallen over the garage area.

Kenny Wallace, at thirty-two the youngest of the three Wallace boys in Winston Cup, was hanging around the garage, with nothing left to do, more or less savoring the moment. He had been through this once before, in 1993, when he finished twenty-third to win $27,820, and now he figured he and his number 81 Thunderbird were about as ready as they could be. He had qualified far back in the pack, at thirty-third, not as well as middle brother Mike's seventeenth but a long sight better than older brother Rusty's embarrassing dead last, which forced Rusty to take an ex-champion's provisional and start at the back of the field, and even though Kenny had failed to do so much as qualify his BGN car for the Goody's 300 (he was one of many who drove BGN *and* Winston Cup), all seemed right in his world.

Standing beside the car in his shiny royal blue racing suit, watching his crew give the car a final buffing before covering it and locking the bay doors for the night, he suddenly chirped, "Hey! You know what tomorrow is?"

A mechanic, slyly: "Aw, hell, Sunday, ain't it? Comes after Saturday."

"No, man, it's the *Daytona Five Hundred!*"

"Oh, yeah, I almost forgot. Knew I had to be somewhere."

"Man." Wallace swept his hand through thinning hair. "We've been working three months for this. It gets old, the testing, the practice, the qualifying, and then some more practice. But like they say, it's the Super Bowl, the big one, the big money. I know we've [NASCAR] probably got it all turned around, starting with the biggest race of the year and then playing out the season, but if we did it the other way we'd be worn out by the time we got here."

To simplify the logistics on race day, when more than 100,000 fans would start crowding into the place at daybreak to join the 50,000 already camped out in the infield, he intended to spend the night in his RV right there at the track rather than hassle with the traffic. Somebody would fetch him at nine o'clock Sunday morning and escort him to a tent, where he would spend an hour carrying on with about fifty representatives of Square D Company, a manufacturer of electrical equipment out of Illinois whose ultimate corporate headquarters was in Paris (not Texas, not Tennessee, but France). Then he would attend the drivers' meeting before going back to his trailer to suit up and put on his game face. Would he manage a good night's sleep? "All I can do's try," he said. "Anybody who says they won't have butterflies is lying."

Then, with the five o'clock shutdown fast approaching, there came a grim advisory over the loudspeaker in the garage area, like the voice of God: "You have twenty-five minutes, gentlemen." Nylon wraps bearing the teams' racing colors and the sponsors' logos began to cover the cars. Toolboxes were snapped shut and locked, bay doors were slammed, and the men began drifting away to wash off the grime and find something to eat and think about inducing sleep with a couple of brews. The sun was sinking below the stands now. Where only an hour earlier there had been some 10,000 race fans in the stands, watching the final go-around, there were now hundreds of nattering seagulls, squeaking and flapping and swooping through the empty seats as they foraged for scraps of food left behind.

Happy Hour might have ended on the track, but in the distant lawless reaches of the infield it had just begun. There were the pops and fizzes of beer cans being opened, the sizzling of raw meat on open fires, the sound of Garth Brooks singing "I've Got Friends in Low Places," and the gleeful yips of restless good old boys at play. "Hey, Red, gon' get cold tonight. A stick for a flash, before I change my mind." As dusk began to fall, the first wood fires began to flicker. A piercing Rebel yell shattered the air above a sea of Confederate flags, setting off tribal challenges: *Earnhardt sucks! . . . What the fuck is a Musgrave? Musk rat? Musk ox? Mus-KEE-toe? . . . Heeerrre Comessss RUSS-teeee!* Their bellows and imprecations rent the cool air, like rival Indian war parties speaking in tongues, echoing off the stark empty high-banked turns and the soaring grandstands now silhouetted against the darkening magenta sky. It was going to be a long night.

2

GENTLEMEN, START YOUR ENGINES

None of the eighteen tracks on the Winston Cup circuit had figured out a way to shoehorn these boisterous crowds inside the gates without monstrous delays, and that held to be as true for Daytona as for the smaller places like Martinsville, Virginia, and North Wilkesboro, North Carolina. Two race weekends a year meant huge economic benefits to a city or town, but not nearly enough to justify the grading of spur roadways that would be unused for all but six days of the year. The fans who had been there before knew that the only answer was to leave early; and so, by nine o'clock on the morning of the big day, traffic was snarled for at least two miles in every direction of the main gates of Daytona International Speedway. GENTLEMEN START YOUR ENGINES, read the marquees of some of the fast-food drive-ins strung out on Speedway Boulevard, along with a digital thermometer giving the morning temperature as thirty-nine degrees, but few of the fans cramming the cars and pickups and campers dared lose their place in line for a doughnut and thin coffee. They were inching along, past brokers still lining the roadside with their TICKETS signs, now backing down from their pair-for-$250 prices and waving them with some desperation; past those who had camped outside the track for the weekend and had only to gather up their blankets and coolers for a stroll toward their seats; past homeowners with the audacity to ask $30 for a parking spot next to the swing set in the backyard. The mood of this mass of speed freaks was less festive than it was grim; evidence that fans, too, have game faces.

Fearless Daytona Beach cops had swooped in on five hapless nude dancing clubs during the night, arresting a total of fifty-seven naked women, proof to the randy lads in the infield that their stick-for-a-flash gambit had been the more prudent course. Now, while great hordes of people holding grandstand tickets were stuck in traffic or trudging along toward their gates, the infield crowd was stirring in a more civilized manner. Bacon sizzled, beer cans fizzed, night fires smoldered, impulsive war cries arose—AW-some BILL from DAW-son-VILLE!!—as hungover revelers shuffled off in sandals to the gray cinder-block buildings for a shower and a shave. The earliest risers were already moving about, visiting enemy camps, placing bets, gnawing on pizzas and hot dogs for breakfast, double-checking the frequencies of the forty-three drivers on their scanners. Along the promenades, as it were, the souvenir stands were doing a hearty last-minute business; the most popular being a T-shirtery known as Big Johnson, obviously some regional euphemism for "large penis," that being the running gag in a series of drawings featuring a scrawny little peckerwood with enormous equipment (a shotgun for a penis, surrounded by bosomy guides: "You Need a Big Gun if You're Hunting in the Bush"). Busiest of all was the GM-UAW tent, with a line of customers holding at a hundred feet long, where permed grandmothers and scruffy ten-year-old boys were jauntily posing for Polaroids as they grinned from the cockpit of the daunting black Earnhardt show car.

If there was a major difference between this morning and most of the others over the past three weeks at the speedway, it was the eerie silence. Sure, there was the patter of the MRN announcers with their breathless chatter and taped interviews going out over the loudspeakers positioned throughout the infield and on top of the grandstands; the incessant hawking of collectibles from the trailers on the midway; the random Rebel yells and whoops for one driver or another; the poundings of country and rock music emanating from boom boxes; the occasional scream of a jet engine as another plane took off or landed at the Daytona Beach airport beyond the stands on the backstretch; the tootling from the kids in the Seabreeze High School band as they warmed up for a prerace serenade on the infield grass between the frontstretch and pit road. But something was strangely out of joint this morning, and it took a minute or so before anybody could put a finger on it. Finally, it dawned: for the first time since the beginning of Speedweeks, which had been a virtual nonstop orgy of high-speed racing from sunup to sundown, there was not a single race car on the track. The fierce roar of engines and the pounding *thunkety-thunkety-thunkety* of wide racing tires, even the horrifying screech before the sickening thud of a car slamming into concrete at 190 miles per hour, had been the background music, the speedway's theme song, for so long that one felt oddly discombobulated without it.

The cars were in the garages, of course, about to undergo the sort of last-minute preening accorded thoroughbreds in the paddocks at Churchill Downs on the morning of the Kentucky Derby. The tradition was to open the garages an hour earlier on the day of the Daytona 500, and the security guards had to step back to keep from being trampled when they unlocked the gates at that first gray glimmer of dawn. In strode an army of mechanics and their gofers, nearly 500 in all, like well-rested steelworkers showing up for the morning shift, with steaming cups of coffee in their hands and checklists in their pockets and worry in their eyes. The moment of truth had arrived, the time to find out what all of those hours of toil over the winter had come to, and if there was a man among them who felt his work was done, he wasn't letting on about it. The nylon tarps came off, and the men went to work: taping the checklists to the cars, raising hoods, measuring tire pressure, tightening belts, buffing paint jobs, making sure that the dozens of sponsors' decals were affixed in their prescribed places, repeating what they had done little more than twelve hours earlier. The richer teams like Hendrick Motorsports, with three entries in the field that day, completely disassembled each car and put it back together again under the stern gaze of NASCAR inspectors. The smaller operations, like that of Dave Marcis, simply huddled together and went down the checklist one more time. They were joined, shortly thereafter, by hundreds of "Weekend Warriors," a workforce of shop employees and volunteers who were flown in from North Carolina airports on every race day morning (a dozen on one plane, out of Winston-Salem, in support of Jimmy Spencer alone) to do the grunt work around the garages and pits, from keeping gas cans full to serving as the rear-tire-changer. The schedule called for all cars to be lined up and ready to go on pit road by eleven o'clock, little more than an hour before the start of the race, and much was left to be done.

Finding a driver to talk to or take a picture of or simply gawk at was out of the question at this point in the proceedings. "When it comes down to choosing between a 'commercial opportunity' and an interview," said a writer with three decades' experience on the NASCAR beat, "the writer loses every time." Among the goodies a sponsor bought with his backing, whether $3 million for a Dave Marcis or $12 million for a Dale Earnhardt, was access to the drivers for its executives and key clients. Just outside the speedway, behind the grandstand on the first turn, there was a forest of colorful tents known as Hospitality Village. Each of the major sponsors had invited dozens of their managers and retailers from all over the country, from the guy who sold DuPont automotive paints in Kalamazoo to the biggest Mr. Goodwrench in California, to come on down to Daytona, enjoy themselves, and even see the new line of merchandise; hell, shake hands with ol' Mark Martin himself before the race. Like Bill Elliott on that night without end at the Speedway McDonald's, the drivers recognized a command performance when they saw one. So *there* they were, in the hours leading up to the 500-mile drive that might make or break their seasons: yesterday's good old boys now wearing their casual off-track garb of razor-creased gabardine slacks and Tommy Hilfiger crew neck sweaters and shiny classic Gucci loafers, hobnobbing and dancing the Boardroom Shuffle for the bosses, laying a little Motorhead talk on 'em: "That fourteen-to-one engine, on top of the restrictor plate, just might turn out to be a problem if you need to get on the throttle and get out of there in a hurry." The barons of commerce loved it when the drivers talked dirty like that. *Lemme ask you this, then, Sterling, what's that Earnhardt fella really like? Just between you and I, now* . . . Their duty done after more than an hour of this, the drivers left as quickly as they had come, whisked away by their press agents for the obligatory prerace drivers' meeting and maybe a sweep by the garage area for the Sunday morning chapel service (". . . about two thousand years ago," the preacher began, to a crowd including Brooke and Jeff Gordon in the front row of folding chairs, and a pair of cherubic eight-year-old twins waiting in the wings to sing of Jesus), and finally a dash to the motor home to change into their racing uniforms. They barely had time to worry whether Runt and the boys had remembered to camber the tires like they said they would.

Meanwhile, with or without drivers to photograph at this hour, the paparazzi were having a field day. Loosely translated from the Italian, the word means "bugs," more specifically in this case shutterbugs, and neither Rome nor Hollywood had the corner on them. Winston Cup racing had its own paparazzi, a corps of freelance photographers who found they could make a living by feeding the pages of the score of stock car publications or selling their stuff directly to the sponsors and automakers (one, in fact, was a New York City cop who loved racing and had a deal with Pontiac). In their case, the word was not pejorative—they were pros, or at least semi-pros, with a job to do—but for each photographer with a legitimate press pass there seemed to be ten who were more or less fans let loose in a candy store. They were the . . . *Bubbarazzi!* "Hey, it's The King," somebody would shout, and three dozen of them would run down poor Richard Petty, the man who had never turned down an autograph request, caught like a fox in an open field as he simply tried to make it from the garage to the rest room in the drivers' lounge. "Who was that?" someone asked a fiftyish woman who had just posed with the only black person in the garage area, a handsome young man with a thin mustache, wearing narrow European shades and a crisp beige poplin suit. "I don't know, he just *looks* like somebody," she said, learning only later that he was Brad Daugherty, a retired NBA star and guest of Richard Petty. Daugherty, in fact, had worn Petty's number, 43, as a player. Armed with equipment that even the pros could envy, from camcorders with sound to Nikons with zoom lenses and high-speed shutters, the Bubbarazzi jostled through the garages and the pits and the infield and the grandstands like a network crew working on a documentary. There was the ageless race queen Linda Vaughn again, in her breathless race day getup; and Bill France and the television announcers and the high-profile crew chiefs like Gordon's Ray Evernham and Earnhardt's David Smith; and half a dozen winners of previous Daytona 500s, like Richard Petty and Cale Yarborough and Bobby Allison, those three still plugging away as car owners, men who later would be in the pits overseeing their investments. Nobody was safe, even the grease monkey in Lake Speed's stall, now saying a few words for the folks back in Moline, Illinois, as he tightened lug nuts on the number 9 Spam Ford. The Bubbarazzi had become such a force that the Richmond track had found it necessary to enclose a plea in the envelope holding credentials: "Don't embarrass yourself, the media source that requested your credential, or Richmond International Raceway by asking drivers, owners, or crew members for autographs while you are on assignment in the pits, prerace, Victory Lane, Winston Cup and Busch Series garage, media center, or other work areas. . . ." *Well*, the Bubbarazzi felt, sensing this chance of a lifetime to mingle with the greats, *to hell with that*.

Out on the track, to keep the early arrivals occupied, more than two hours' worth of prerace activity was underway. The Seabreeze High band had cranked up its concert before ten o'clock, in formation on the grassy triangle between the pits and the grandstand on the frontstretch. For an hour there was a parade of vehicles of all sorts—the automakers' new models of sedans and pickups and vans, pace cars from most of the other tracks on the Winston Cup circuit, wreckers and ambulances and fire trucks—while, up there high in the Fireball Roberts Grandstand, a couple from Melbourne, Florida, wearing their go-to-racing jeans and windbreakers, was getting married by a preacher.

Except for the sideshow of the wedding, this stuff was getting old in a hurry. Once the parade of official cars and trucks had ended, hundreds of fans who knew the tradition tumbled through the gate at the start-finish line and either squatted or stood precariously on the steep asphalt track, banked eighteen degrees at that point, for a close-up view of the ceremonies taking place on a temporary stage set up on the grass. There came The King himself, in his jeans and cowboy hat, to present the Richard Petty

STP Achievement Award to his old compadre, Cale Yarborough ("This sport's been good to me, and I hope I've been good for it," said Yarborough, a four-time winner of the 500 between 1968 and '84, drawing respectful applause from those old enough to remember his glory days). A couple of truck drivers were presented checks of $20,000 apiece for the Goodyear Highway Heroes Award, they having pulled three children from a burning car after an accident somewhere out there on the open roads of America. There was yet another welcome to Daytona Beach by the mayor, Bud Asher, but he was drowned out before he got halfway through his spiel. For here they came, the drivers, the stars of the show, each in his racing uniform and balancing on the back seat of a convertible. "Driving the number 5 Kellogg's Chevrolet, from Corpus Christi, Texas [even though he had lived near Charlotte for many years], *TER-eee La-BON-tee!*" This was more like it, the moment the fans had been fancying throughout the long winter, and they were on their feet now, cheering the good guys like Jeff Gordon and letting the bad guys like Earnhardt have it. Racing, they knew, couldn't be far behind.

Nobody in the house knew that better than the boys in the pits. All forty-three of the race cars had just been rolled into place on pit road, in the order of their qualifying positions, and now they crouched there in all their glory: new paint jobs gleaming in the bright sun, hooked up to the ubiquitous generators to keep their engines warm, being wiped and curried by the proud members of the over-the-wall gangs. On the other side of the whitewashed three-foot-high retaining wall, in what amounted to portable mini-garages, the crew chiefs were overseeing the work of the extra hands who would keep things humming during the race. Each car was allowed a maximum of forty tires to start with (although they could borrow more from teams whose cars went out early), and in most of the pits there were ten stacks of tire sets duly marked in chalk with the car's number and the tires' designations—42, RF, RR, LF, LR—their lug nuts glued into place for the anxious moments when they would be thrown onto the cars during pit stops. The Weekend Warriors were hauling red gasoline cans on carts to be filled at the Unocal pumps between the pits and the garages, and dashing elsewhere to fill the familiar orange Gatorade barrels with juice and ice. Each pit, behind the wall, was lined off with ropes or plastic pennants to keep out the fans and media who had pit passes; and inside that area was an array of generators and toolboxes and spare parts like windows and hoods, and television monitors, and computers for figuring gas mileage and receiving lap-by-lap printouts from upstairs in the official scorer's stand in the press box. The temperature was expected to get into the sixties, under a bright Florida sun, so big striped umbrellas had been clamped to the tall director's chairs where each crew chief would call the shots during the race. More than one Winston Cup race was won or lost in the pits every season—by a bad decision on tires, by a simple bungle like not fully tightening one lug nut, by a pit stop lasting more than the desired twenty seconds—and the men down there knew it better than anyone. Now, after an off-season of diligently working out on Nautilus equipment and practicing pit stops back home at the shop, they were making certain that everybody's headset was in working order (no one would be able to communicate without them once the race began) and psyching up for the real thing.

Getting closer now; less than an hour to go. Overhead was the lumbering Goodyear blimp and a hardy little squadron of single-engine planes towing banners promoting everything from Goody's Headache Powders to the Dawsonville Pool Room in Bill Elliott's hometown. Buzzing back and forth along the frontstretch, testing its wings, was a three-foot-long remote-controlled aircraft, of a sort, carrying a CBS camera. Soon, there began a final parade of pooh-bahs and drivers: Busch Pole Award Presentation and Presentation of Rolex Watches to Gatorade 125 Winners (two more opportunities to boo Earnhardt, one to cheer Irvan); Pepsi Fan Appreciation Award; Recognition of Dignitaries; Presentation of 1995 Winston Cup Championship Rings (to the Gordon-Evernham-Hendrick Motorsports consortium); introductions of an honorary starter and a grand marshal; and all of it capped by about twenty minutes of foolishness emceed by the announcer Eli Gold, a pit stop competition among teams of fans. When the laughter over that last had died down and a preacher was clearing his throat at the podium, the estimated 160,000 fans spread throughout this vast playground were already on their feet; for they had hardly missed the stirrings on pit road. The drivers had slipped into the cockpits of their racing machines and locked their steering wheels into place and snapped the chin straps of their helmets and hunkered down into their snug bucket seats. CBS's roving reporters stuck their microphones into the cars for some last thoughts from the drivers, just before the preacher said a few words about God and safe returns. The American flag was raised while the singer Engelbert Humperdinck was losing himself somewhere in the tangle of lyrics to the National Anthem, and suddenly, while 20,000 little American flags that had been passed out at the gate were being waved "in honor of our troops in Bosnia," a pair of Florida Air National Guard fighter jets thundered out of the infinite cobalt sky in a flyover that made the race cars shimmy in their tracks. And then, finally, there came those four magical words: "Gentlemen, start your engines."

A baseball game begins when the umpire, satisfied that the leadoff man has properly taken his place in the batter's box, motions to the pitcher with a flick of the fingers and mutters, if he feels so inclined, "Play ball." In basketball, ten guys wander onto the floor, shake hands, jostle for position in a circle, and then scramble for an opening tipoff that has little consequence in the overall scheme of events. In boxing, the two combatants step to the center of the ring, touch hands, and then try not to do anything chancy for a while. In tennis, golf, soccer, hockey, swimming, sculling, skiing, table tennis, volleyball, and just about all of the other sports known to Americans, the opening thrust is mere formality; you've got to start somewhere. Only in a big football game such as the Super Bowl or a nasty college rivalry is there a truly dramatic overture—the opening kickoff, with two phalanxes of eleven behemoths charging each other on a headlong collision course like enraged armies, adrenaline pumping through their veins and a year's worth of pent-up malevolence beating in their hearts— but even that pales when compared with the beginning of a stock car race. What follows those famous words to fire the engines is a raw explosion of such intensity that seldom does anything that might follow throughout the course of the day, whether spectacular crashes or a photo finish, ever manage to match that single instant in thrilling the senses.

It was not the prissy high bumblebee whine of little open-wheeled Indy cars that the fans heard on the command for the gentlemen to start their engines; nor was it the rude blatting of unruly motorbikes pawing at the dirt. This was an explosion in the most literal sense, an orgasm, a primordial burst of sound and fury, as forty-three drivers simultaneously flipped the toggle switch of their ignition boxes to fire eight-cylinder engines capable of producing 700 horsepower and speeds of 240 miles per hour if anyone dared leave them untethered. Even the throaty roar of enough fans to populate a medium-sized city was drowned out by the thunder of the race cars as they eased away from pit road in low gear, rumbling and bucking, the drivers tapping their brakes and feathering their throttles and swerving from side to side to check out the steering and warm the tires. Straining to be unleashed, they obediently followed a gleaming new Pontiac pace car being wheeled by an old retired race car driver named Elmo Langley, who would have to get up to forty miles per hour just to keep from sliding down off the high-banked corners. Once around the track they went, still bucking and swerving, twenty-one rows of them trailed by the hapless Rusty Wallace in his black number 2 Miller Ford, around the first and second turns, picking up speed ever so slightly on the backstretch, rumbling through the third and fourth turns, and again and again and again. There would be extra pace laps on this coolish day, not yet fifty degrees, to give the drivers more time to heat their tires. On their fourth sweep past the start-finish line, the NASCAR flagman in his crow's nest above the start-finish line suddenly flashed the white flag indicating "one more lap," and when they had passed he furled the white flag and reached for the green one that would start the race. As they came out of the fourth turn, in line and under control, approaching ninety miles per hour now, he began madly waving the green flag and the pace car ducked for safety on pit road and the crew chiefs radioed "Green-green-green!" to their drivers. All together, now, they stomped it and . . . *They're off!* The ground shook. The air shimmered. The startled seagulls on Lake Lloyd went airborne.

Like a stampede of wild horses rushing to see which could make it first to the narrow mouth of a box canyon, they stormed the first corner. Ernie Irvan, on his first big test under pressure since his life-threatening wreck of a year and a half earlier, got off the mark faster than Earnhardt and had the lead when they came flying out of the first two turns. By the time they hit the backstretch, almost out of sight on the farthest reaches of the track, the drivers were getting up to full speed and beginning to look around for drafting partners. Even the lone rookie, Johnny Benson, knew that the only way to survive on this track was to use the draft, likened by all to coupling up with a highballing freight train for a 500-mile ride. During the all-out racing in the Twin 125s, the fans had seen what the drivers already knew; that a driver could lose up to eight places in the blink of an eye if he tried to go high or low—leaving the draft—and didn't make it. Cars in a draft could hit 194 miles per hour, five miles faster than those who had left it, and with one little slip it could take a driver twenty laps to just regain his position. Earnhardt understood the workings of the draft as well as anyone on the track, and that is why he had positioned himself for a slingshot move that threw him into the lead on the fifth lap.

The first words that usually came from the mouth of a driver who felt he had been wronged by another, while waiting for the wrecker to come and tow his wrecked $100,000 car behind the wall to the garage, were "that idiot." But while he sat there fuming, his car and his day ruined, he knew that no fool had slipped through the net to make it as a regular in Winston Cup. To be sure, there were some very good drivers who were a bit more aggressive than others (only yesterday, it seemed, even before the wreck that had jarred his eyesight out of whack for a while, Ernie Irvan was known as "Swervin' Irvan," and the ebullient Jimmy Spencer of RJR's Smokin' Joe's Camel cigarette car might never shuck the sobriquet Mr. Excitement). And there was some sentiment in the pits that a few of the older drivers, like Darrell Waltrip, a year away from his fiftieth birthday and a decade beyond his prime, had lost either their nerve (the "risk and reward" factor Waltrip had openly broached during the media shop tour in January) or their youthful reflexes. But there were no rookies out there on the track on this day or any other that would come up during the '96 season, even if Johnny Benson was officially designated as such, for the aggregate amount of experience in those cars now spinning around at better than 190 miles per hour was staggering. Most of them had been racing in competition since the go-kart days of their childhood, moving up one step at a time through dirt tracks to paved "bullrings" to banked superspeedways, from ARCA to Busch Grand National and finally to Winston Cup, and by the time they had reached the top there wasn't much they hadn't seen.

Forty-three drivers multiplied by twenty years of experience (a low figure) equalled upward of one thousand years of experience; not one thousand hours, nor races, but nearly one thousand *years*. No, there were no idiots out there; only good drivers who would have bad things happen to them when they were least expecting it.

Young Jeff Gordon, of all people, was the first one to get it. The field was still bunched behind the leaders, with everybody back there jockeying for position and scouting for a draft, when The Kid got tapped from behind by Jeremy Mayfield and suddenly was into the wall on turn four of the ninth lap. He tried to straighten his car and save it, but it was too late, his chore compounded by the fact that it was all happening over the "tunnel bump," a slight hump in the track where it passed over the two-way tunnel leading in and out of the infield. A chain reaction set in behind Gordon, putting his car and five others out of commission (for how long, they would have to see) and bringing out the first caution of the day. Gordon and the drivers he took with him obediently unsnapped the canvas mesh nets designed to keep them from flying out of their cars, the universal signal that the driver was at least conscious and mobile, bringing cheers from the hushed crowd and relief in the pits. The race wasn't ten minutes old, and now the defending Winston Cup champion and five others were either waddling along on flat tires or being towed to the garage while Earnhardt and the other survivors of the long season's first scrape either crept along at sixty miles per hour behind Elmo Langley's pace car or ducked into the pits for tires or fuel or minor chassis adjustments. (God forbid that a driver would wish harm upon his competitors—oh, Lord, no, of course not—but it was always wisest to put off pitting until there was a caution, when one was allowed to regain his position, rather than pitting "on green." In fact, two drivers, Darrell Waltrip and Bobby Labonte, had peeled off for a splash of gas during the five pace laps preceding the start of the race.) The radios crackled with instructions, crew chiefs to pit crewmen ("Gimme right side tires . . . windshield . . . splash of gas . . . half a crank on the outside"), as seven cars not involved in the crash pitted.

The tactics that a team chose to follow when the caution went out could be critical over the course of a race. To pit or not to pit was always the question. Most teams chose to pit, if for nothing more than a splash of gas; always a critical matter in itself, since these high-performance engines got between four and five miles per gallon of 110 octane gas and, thus, could barely make forty laps around the 2.5-mile Daytona track on a full load of twenty-two gallons. (Even in the calculation of gas mileage, there could be wild fluctuations, depending on whether a driver was cruising in a draft or burning gas at a faster rate by driving hard: racing to the corners, backing off, then stomping it again.) But NASCAR awarded a bonus of five points for leading a race, whether for only one lap or all of them, and a lot of the weaker cars would choose to stay on the track while the others pitted just to pick up those points. Either way, there was a dark side to these caution periods. When the time came for the restart, the field would be bunched as it had been at the very beginning, and thus the opportunities for wrecks were greatly enhanced. In short, one caution would beget another; and another, and another.

That first caution lasted for six laps, and when they thundered away again on lap fifteen it seemed a matter of time before there would be more carnage. Earnhardt had kept the lead through the caution, choosing to hold his position rather than go into the pits at all, and when they went green a fierce battle developed up front between him and Terry Labonte of the Hendrick team. And while those two were swapping the lead over the next dozen laps, driving hard, on and off the throttle, feinting high and feinting low, several other cars in a draft behind them were steadily closing the gap. It was hot and heavy down there, much door-to-door scrambling for position, a little too early for clearly defined drafting lines to have formed. "Watch your mirror, watch your mirror," the fans were hearing on their scanners as the spotters on the roof of the high main grandstand talked their drivers around the track. "I'm trying to find you a hole . . . Nothing there . . . Go, go, go . . . Aw, *shit* . . . Fall in line there, let's ride . . . We'll get him next time, man . . . That fuckin' *idiot* . . . Dig, dig, dig . . . Clear, clear, clear . . . Good job, good job . . ." And then, after only ten minutes of what the fans had come for, there was more trouble as they headed into the first turn to begin lap twenty-eight. Ernie Irvan had closed in on Earnhardt and was riding right on his tail, in a tight draft, when suddenly Earnhardt slowed. Irvan hit his brakes, was smacked from behind by Wally Dallenbach, and slammed into the wall. So there came another caution, while the trucks came to tow a disgusted Irvan's mangled car to the garage. "When a guy has a problem, you'd rather the guy who had the problem be the one who suffers," said Irvan; end of interview. Over the scanners, the fans heard an Earnhardt who actually seemed repentant: "Guys [to his crew], I want you to tell [Irvan's car owner Robert] Yates and them that I didn't do that on purpose. My ignition went out, and I couldn't help it."

Earnhardt had gone to his backup ignition box, located beside the other on the dash of his car, and got the engine restarted; but then came the yellow flag. This caution would last for four laps, with hardly a car on the track as most of the drivers wheeled onto pit road for gas and tires. The fans who had managed to locate Earnhardt's correct frequency on their scanners—like some of the others, not especially thrilled that other teams could spy on him, he jumped around among three different frequencies— might have gotten a clue about his operation. To wit, the man called the shots himself and ran a tight ship. "Okay, guys, I want two right side tires, gas, and a clean windshield," he was saying, even as he reached pit road and slowed to the sixty-five-miles-per-hour speed limit. He was in and out in less than twenty seconds, a very good stop, indeed, but he had lost the lead to Labonte and Dale Jarrett during his misfortune with the ignition box; a lead he would not regain until fifty-five laps remained. But for now he was pissed. He was roaring out of the second turn, still building speed, when he let the crew have it: "Somebody *painted* the damn windshield." Seconds later, pushing 190 now, he wouldn't let it go: "Next time I'll get out and clean the damn thing myself." Meekly, from his crew chief: "Well, he's new and doesn't like that extension-arm thing we use." They worked it out, apparently, for when he departed after the next stop—on the third caution of the race, when a driver named Derrike Cope missed the turn on four and was hauled to the garage for the day—Earnhardt grumbled, "Good job on the windshield." He looked up to see that the race was being led, however briefly, by an underfinanced independent named Hut Stricklin; the ninth leader after only fifty-six laps.

Down in the defending champion's garage stall, the scene looked like something from *ER*, the television series about a team of emergency-room personnel at a Chicago hospital. The gaudy number 24 Monte Carlo of Jeff Gordon was the patient, the Rainbow Warriors the medical technicians, and they were all over the car in a frenetic attempt to put it back together again. The damages were severe, the major problem being a bent frame, and about all they could hope for was to get it back on the track to save face and earn some lap money. "I got to the outside of [Jeremy] Mayfield going into turn three," said Gordon, standing aside in the shade of the garage, his dark hair tangled and his driving uniform sopped with sweat. "I was up against the wall as far as I could get to make sure we didn't touch. I had a feeling something was going to happen, and it did." He first had slammed the wall with his right front and then, while trying to recover, the right rear swung around and hit the wall a second lick. "I'm sort of on call the rest of the day," he said, grinning and reaching for the hand of his young bride as she walked through the mob of Bubbarazzi milling about. They locked fingers and strolled across the oil-slick pavement to their car-hauler nearby, where they would watch the race on television while the crew took care of the dirty work.

There were a dozen of them under the direction of Ray Evernham, some having been summoned from the other Hendrick teams of Terry Labonte and Ken Schrader, both of whom were out on the track and holding in there quite well. The car had been towed into the garage, having been knocked cockeyed from the violent confrontation with the wall, and it looked a mess; like a fellow who had been jumped by thugs in a dark alley. The frame was bent and the entire right side was streaked and gouged where it had slid along the concrete barrier. Now the car was jacked up on all fours, its front tires and fenders removed and its hood raised so the mechanics could get at the problem. They were glum and intense, wearing headsets so they could hear each other over the roar of the race out there on the track, only vaguely aware that a NASCAR inspector in red trousers and a white uniform shirt was watching their every move. "Gimme a seven-sixteenth!" said a mechanic standing in the tire well, sending one of the men to a toolchest to forage for the right wrench, the aide forthwith returning to slap it in his hands as an intern would pass a scalpel to a surgeon. One man in goggles worked a blowtorch, sparks flying as he cut away loose metal, while two others kept stretching a string to measure distances between points on the axles as adjustments were made to the chassis. At one point, the NASCAR inspector had to shoo away the eager Bubbarazzi, who simply took one step back and resumed firing away with their cameras.

Finally, just before two o'clock, nearly two hours since the race's beginning, Evernham reached through the driver's-side window opening and fired the car. Blue smoke engulfed the car upon ignition, but then the engine began to purr. "Somebody get Jeff," Evernham said over the radio. Gordon was there within a minute, still in uniform, hands jammed in his pockets. The engine was cut and, while the other men put the tires back on and pulled away the jacks, Evernham conferred with Gordon by shouting in his ear, gesticulating and pointing at the car's frame. Gordon nodded grimly, slipped into the car, pulled on his helmet, locked the steering wheel into place, snapped his window net closed, and fired the engine. They would give it a shot, see what they could do.

When Gordon muscled the car out of the garage and rejoined the traffic, he was embarrassed to find himself down by 105 laps, a place he had never been. The leaders were on lap 116 of 200 now, with Bill Elliott forging out front, being drafted by Dale Jarrett, Darrell Waltrip's younger brother Michael, and Earnhardt. ("Hold that line right there, Bill, you're lookin' good," Elliott's crew chief was saying on the radio. "That's a *tee-yun fo-wer*," said Elliott. "You feelin' all right?" "Hey, *ma-yun*," said Elliott, in a joyous yelp, "I feel *great*. I'm leadin' th' *Day-tona Five Hunnert!*") Not so happy was Gordon, out on the track now, chugging along, barely able to steer. The crew had stayed in the garage, not bothering to return to the pits, and from there Evernham radioed, "How's it going, Jeff?" "It's slow, it's pulling," said Gordon, after only four laps. Evernham didn't hesitate: "Better bring it on in, then. We don't want to do any more damage." Thus, the day ended for the wunderkind, the defending champion. He rolled into the garage, made a beeline to his RV without taking off his helmet, and within five minutes was standing in front of his car-hauler in a black leather jacket and checked gabardine pants, hair combed, wearing shades. "We've got a strong team," he said to a dozen reporters who had crowded around. "We'll be ready for Rockingham." And then he was gone, escorted back to his RV by a state trooper. The RV pulled away with ten laps remaining in the race, bumping through the tunnel to beat the traffic, headed back home to Charlotte. They were northbound on I-95 when he heard on the radio that he had completed thirteen laps, finished forty-second, and won $59,052 for a whole winter's work.

Gordon wasn't the only one to be humbled by the track that day, not by a long shot. There were three more cautions after he had chucked it in, on laps 130 and 136 and 160, all of them brought about by spectacular multi-car accidents. The garage area began to look like a field hospital in the midst of a battle, something out of M*A*S*H, the wounded being dragged to safety while the fighting raged on around them. No drivers were injured, thanks to the remarkable roll cages in these modern machines, and most seemed to be handling the sight of their disabled cars with a shrug. Here was Morgan Shepherd, the last of the unlettered boys from Wilkes County, North Carolina, the heart of Junior Johnson's moonshine country, looking like a workingman's Red Buttons with his squinty eyes and curly red hair, calmly explaining to the Bubbarazzi how it was that he and five others had been taken out in a horrible crash on turn four ("That's racin' "). There was Sterling Marlin in front of his car-hauler, in his civvies now, blond mop spilling from a yellow Kodak cap, bemoaning his fate: going for a record third straight Daytona 500 victory, having just taken the lead on lap seventy-nine, his engine had blown up ("It was the same one we won with last year, but the only place you can run on seven cylinders is to the grocery store"). And there was Brett Bodine, one more time, trundling back onto the track with a car that had neither fenders nor hood, and was taped up and using a jury-rigged screen to fit the mangled front end; just trying for some lap money now and wondering how in the world he was going to pay off his whopping debt to Junior Johnson at this rate ("That's three cars we've lost down here, and there's thirty races to go"). When the day was done, there would be a total of fourteen cars failing to finish; and only seventeen of the original forty-three were on the lead lap at the end. One of them, happy to report, was Dave Marcis, who would come through unscathed for a fifteenth-place finish worth more than $52,000.

(That Marcis would take home some $7,000 less than Gordon, even though he completed all 200 laps while The Kid was going out after only thirteen, was due to a complicated payoff system that has been in place for more than three decades. Essentially, NASCAR rewards its stars with "appearance" money, a rule that dated back to the late forties when struggling new tracks would pay a "name" driver cash just to show up for a race. The current system is based on the previous year's final points standings; in effect, ensuring that the rich get richer. The field of forty-odd drivers is roughly divided into three divisions according to the most recent year's final standings—the top ten, the middle of the pack, and the also-rans—and at the beginning of a new season a higher multiplier number is assigned to the more successful drivers. Thus, a lap led by Gordon, the defending champion, would be worth considerably more than one led by Marcis, who had finished thirty-fifth in the '95 points standings. It is contingency money, a reward for the previous year's successes, and the plan has been in place for so long that the drivers never questioned the disparities. "Hey, I didn't argue with it when I was winning," said Darrell Waltrip, "so I don't argue with it now. NASCAR rules.")

After a final caution on lap 160, following a wreck that effectively took six cars out of any chance to win, the ones still in the hunt made their final pit stops. With Marlin and Gordon out of the running early, there was only one major storyline remaining: could Dale Earnhardt finally win a Daytona 500 on this, his eighteenth attempt? He had always done well at Daytona International Speedway over the years—in qualifying, in the Busch Clash, in the Twin 125s, in the July Fourth race—but he seemed snakebit when it came to the biggest one of them all, where three times he had come in second. His inability to win the 500 was clearly beginning to bug him, to bring the catcalls about the "Daytona 499," and perhaps the most galling failure of all had been in '95 when he finished second to Marlin by only sixteen hundredths of a second, about three car lengths. "We spend so much time here that it feels like home," he had said after winning the pole this year, an indication of what the race had come to mean to him and his owner, Richard Childress, not to mention GM's Goodwrench people. He was still regarded by many as the greatest driver in NASCAR's history, and even though he was coming up on his forty-fifth birthday there were no whispers that he might be losing his nerve or his hunger to win. There was just something about the Daytona 500 that kept eluding him, is all anyone could say by way of explanation. "Choke"? Earnhardt, The Intimidator? Forget about it.

So now, as everybody peeled into the pits for what would turn out to be the last stops before the run to the end, all eyes were on the black number 3 car. Some eyebrows were raised when Earnhardt ducked in first, in the lead and under yellow, taking on gas but only two right-side tires to take him the rest of the way. All of the others involved in that critical final pit stop had taken gas and *four* tires. So now Earnhardt would dash the last forty laps with left-side tires that had been on his car since lap 131. It could make all the difference in the world if the race went to the wire and Earnhardt needed to duck low on the rough apron, using one of his patented moves from the fender-smacking dirt-track days, on left-side tires that surely would be ragged by then.

They roared out of the pits and got the green flag to resume racing on lap 165, only thirty-five to go, and very soon Earnhardt discovered the identity of his main antagonist. For the second straight year it would be Dale Jarrett, in a powerful number 88 Robert Yates Thunderbird, a car that everyone would agree, afterward, was the strongest piece of machinery on the track. Also in the mix were a hungry Ken Schrader, the forgotten man of the Hendrick Chevy team, who hadn't won a Winston Cup race since '92 (and had suffered eleven DNFs in '95); and Mark Martin, the wiry little chalk-white Arkansan, in a slower number 6 Thunderbird that wouldn't have been there except for his judicious use of the draft and his crew's work during pit stops. Those were the main players on the stage, then, as the crowd rose as one to watch the final shootout.

Earnhardt and Jarrett had begun swapping the lead as far back as lap 141, with only brief intrusions by Ricky Craven and Schrader. Now they were at it again, *mano a mano*, first Jarrett and then Earnhardt, briefly Schrader, then Earnhardt once more, Martin always there in someone's rearview mirror. The draft; it was always the draft that might skewer things at Daytona by allowing a slower car to overtake a faster one, and that was the focus of the drivers and the more knowledgeable fans as the race wore on. But that would come later, for on the second turn at the start of lap 177 Jarrett's stronger car simply blew past Earnhardt. Up in the CBS booth, a producer looked hopefully at Ned Jarrett and received an assenting nod; yes, if it came to that, he would be delighted to "take your boy home, Ned," just as in '93 when he was given the microphone to describe his son's overtaking Earnhardt on lap 199 to win the 500.

That was a sweet thought, but now Dale Jarrett was sweating through every driver's nightmare: the sight of an outraged Dale Earnhardt filling his mirror with that big ol' mean-looking black car of his. Jarrett knew he had the best race car still on the track, he would say later, but "I also knew I had the toughest guy in the world behind me." Unable to break away from Earnhardt, he proceeded to drive with one eye on the track ahead of him and one on his rearview mirror. He knew Earnhardt's moves by now, in fact had incorporated them into his own style for use on more than one occasion, and so as the number of laps dwindled he anticipated The Intimidator's feints with parries of his own. In short, he blocked Earnhardt when he tried low and blocked him when he tried high. Jarrett's car was stronger and he was in the lead, a comforting reality, but those last laps began to seem like an eternity. His one great fear was that first Schrader and then Martin, both of them hot on Earnhardt's tail, would close up into a tight draft that would give Earnhardt enough of a push to slingshot around him. Such a thing was possible, and it even could leave Jarrett to settle for fourth place or worse.

It never happened. There was much frantic talk on the radio during those last few laps, Chevy-to-Chevy, with Earnhardt's people imploring Schrader's people to help out in a draft against these Ford devils, but in the end Ken Schrader decided he would be damned if he'd take a chance on helping Earnhardt; he was a snap to finish third if he held what he had, benefiting from being pushed along in a draft by the Fords of Martin and Jeff Burton, but if he left the line and nobody followed he could quickly fall back to sixth (at a loss of some $70,000 in purse money). "It ain't my responsibility to worry about where Earnhardt finishes," Schrader would say later. "If I had tucked up tight with him, Michael Waltrip and Mark Martin and those guys were going around on the top of me. I wasn't going to throw third away." So much for the brotherhood of Chevy drivers; Schrader, too long denied any glory to speak of, opted for the bird in hand. Jarrett had to keep on blocking Earnhardt to the very end, with his doting father up in the broadcast booth trying to be cool about all of this, and he poured on the afterburner on the homestretch to make it to the finish line twelve hundredths of a second, two and a half car lengths, ahead of The Intimidator. Ned Jarrett had brought his boy home again.

To the victor went the considerable spoils. The winning of this one race meant $360,775 for Jarrett (Earnhardt got $215,065, Schrader $169,547, fourth-place Mark Martin $118,840), and Jarrett's overall take from the first week of the season, in four races including the Busch Grand National on Saturday, came to nearly half a million dollars. It had been prearranged that the winning car would be confiscated without remuneration and displayed for one year in the glittery new interactive Daytona USA museum on the track grounds, and on Monday he would be flying off to Los Angeles to be on the *Tonight Show* with Jay Leno. But for the nonce, after he had edged the car into Victory Lane for the staged "celebration" to satisfy CBS and his owner and his sponsors and the Bubbarazzi—a bottle of Gatorade on top of the car, a succession of caps going on and off of his sweaty mop, paeans to the Quality Care Ford folks and God and his crew —he opted to be a nice guy, to try softening the blow to Earnhardt. "The last lap was close to five hundred miles in itself," he said. "I tell you, I think I'd rather look in the mirror and see anybody but that number 3 car back there, knowing his history not only here, but Talladega and everywhere else." Yes, he said, he had learned all of those blocking moves from the man himself. "I was thinking if I couldn't win I'd like to see [Earnhardt] go ahead and break his streak here. . . . It's cruel. He's always there, but something always happens to the guy."

Thanks, but no thanks, as far as Earnhardt was concerned. There it was again: failure at Daytona. Now he had lost two 500s in a row, by a grand total of twenty-eight hundredths of a second, giving him four second-place finishes in eighteen cracks. On the radio to his crew, in the moments after Jarrett had taken the checkered flag and everybody was backing off the throttle for the cool-down lap, he said, as much for the media and the fans he knew were listening in, "It's a good start on a new year, that's all you can say. Thirty more [races] to go. It ain't over." There was the customary visit by the runner-up to the Unocal pumps next to the garage area, where the

CBS people were waiting for a live sound bite. Earnhardt took off his helmet, unscrewed his steering wheel, slapped a Goodwrench cap on his head, and squirmed out of the car. He would make this short, sweet, and as diplomatic as he could bear. "The Ford was too strong," he said with a lame grin and a twitch of the mustache. "It's the Daytona 500, and we finished second again." Then he bolted for the nearest gate, sending a Bubbarazzo sprawling on his ass, trailed by a gaggle of two dozen reporters, finally snapping: "They [NASCAR] give 'em [Ford] the damned candy store with all them rules changes. We couldn't do nothin'. You couldn't see that? Just give 'em the damned candy store." With that, he slipped sideways through the opening in a gate and a friendly security guard slammed it behind him and he was out of there, briskly hoofing it to his trailer without a backward glance. Could Dale Earnhardt go low, or what?

Meanwhile, in the infield, the party was over. For two solid hours the thousands of cars and trucks sat in gridlock, their motors running, hardly moving at all toward the tunnel and the extra gates that had been opened to allow the race teams' car-haulers to escape across the track. In the gloaming, the ball of sun was quickly descending over the thick cloud of carbon monoxide and the smoke from the last smoldering fires and the tons of detritus left by the 50,000 campers. Tempers were short enough already when a lone figure began weaving among the overheating vehicles, a fortyish woman with a beer can in one hand and a homemade poster in the other. Scrawled on a torn piece of cardboard was the number 3 in a circle, with a line slashing through the number, and the words NEVER HAS, NEVER WILL. Kicking a man while he was down was the last straw. A chorus of beeping horns arose from the cars and trucks that flew black number 3 pennants, and the woman was loving the sounds of it as she stumbled onward, smirking and cackling with much glee. It seemed to set the tone for the long season ahead.

3

HAULIN' WHISKEY, HAULIN' ASS

It can be said that basketball is a sport indigenous to the United States, but its innocent beginnings don't exactly stir the soul: a schoolteacher nails up a peach basket in a gymnasium, produces a ball, proposes that the lads throw the ball into the basket as a means of whiling away the bleak days of a Massachusetts winter. Not much there to startle the folklorists or set the poets on fire. But the roots of stock car racing, now, that's another matter. A natural outgrowth from several economic and social factors that defined the world of the poor Southern white, which is to say he was poor and stubborn, stock car racing sprouted during the Depression in the thirties and spread as uncontrollably as kudzu. At the center of it was whiskey. The influence of the unforgiving Protestant churches was so profound that, even after the repeal of Prohibition, the vast majority of counties in the Deep South remained dry, meaning that no alcohol of any kind could be sold or consumed. That situation, of course, opened up a market for the home-brewed moonshine whiskey that a Southern mountaineer had always felt it was his birthright to make and drink and even sell if he by-God wanted to, thereby setting up a classic battle of wits between the moonshiners and the law that didn't abate until as late as the seventies when liquor became more nearly acceptable in the Bible Belt.

Once the whiskey had been distilled and bottled, usually on streams far back in the dank forbidding hollows of the southern Appalachians, especially in north Georgia and east Tennessee and western North Carolina, the moonshiners needed a way to deliver it to cities like Atlanta and Charlotte and Knoxville and Winston-Salem where great hordes of their brethren had moved in search of jobs in the factories, making everything from steel to cigarettes. They needed to look no further than the nearest wild hare of a boy whose souped-up car, the first one he had ever owned, was his love, his life, his passion, his passport out of there. He was afraid of nothing—a daredevil who would rather die violently in his car than of boredom in a production line somewhere, punching a time clock to begin each day—and he was perfect for the job. He knew cars, he knew the back roads, and, by outsmarting the authorities, with their "unreasonable" laws, he would be honoring the same tradition that had brought the untameable Scots-Irish settlers to the isolated Appalachian outback in the first place. The surest way to get a "hillbilly" to do something was to tell him it was against the law; such as, in this case, selling whiskey without paying taxes on it.

What a scene it was. The driver would strip the interior of his car so that only a bucket seat remained, leaving room for a hundred or more half-gallon Mason jars of whiskey. He'd install heavy springs in the rear to support the load, refit the engine with up to three carburetors to give it near-supernatural power, and gear the transmission for a high-speed chase. Loaded for the first of at least two round-trips that day, he would ease onto the highway like a rabbit entering a killing field. He had more at stake than the lawmen, and every new trap contrived by the enemy was quickly countered: when the law began shooting out radiators with shotguns from ambush, he installed steel shields; when the law rigged makeshift tongs on the front of their slower government-issue cars (so they could tailgate the bootlegger, grab his rear bumper, and then apply the brakes), he affixed the rear bumper to his car with coat hangers so it would easily fall away; for foiling roadblocks at night, he put police sirens and flashing lights in his grille; for chases he perfected the hairy Bootlegger Turn, a screaming 180-degree spin at high speed; for occasions when it appeared all was lost, with the Feds right on his tail, he would dump a load of tacks and broken glass and then activate a smoke-bomb tank, laying down a screen of acrid smoke caused by the burning of oily cloth saturated in moonshine, creosote, and hot peppers.

A grudging camaraderie developed between the two camps; witness the time a dashing young blond bootlegger named Lloyd Seay of Dawsonville, Georgia, was pulled over for speeding through the town square of Roswell as he returned empty from Atlanta, going back home for another load.

"Well, Lloyd, here we are again," the sheriff told him.

"Reckon so," said Seay, handing him a pair of $10 bills.

"Dammit, son, you ought to know by now the fine ain't but ten dollars."

"Hell, I know that," Seay said, "but I'm gon' be in a hurry comin' back, so I'm payin' in advance."

Lloyd Seay was among the restless young liquor-runners, "trippers," who would find themselves at loose ends in Atlanta on Sundays, having made a half-dozen round-trips to deliver the weekend's whiskey to the big city, with cash in their pockets and time on their hands. Those cars they had built were the family jewels, the proof of their manhood, the pride of their life, and it seemed inevitable that soon they would race them. There would be much drinking and boasting and comparing of cars until finally one would challenge another to put his money where his mouth was. They would all rumble off to the nearest vacant lot or pasture with their cars, jacked up in the back like cats in heat now that there was no load of moonshine to be supported, and after bets were placed and a circular course was staked out the races would begin. Word spread and spectators started to come around, drawing the attention of entrepreneurs, who slapped up board fences and crude grandstands, and soon crowds of more than a thousand were paying to see the races every Sunday at what came to be called Lakewood Speedway, a one-mile dirt track about five miles south of downtown Atlanta. This, of course, created purse money for the winners and made the bootleggers' cars halfway legitimate, and in due time their fame spread beyond the perilous backwoods roads. When Lloyd Seay died in 1941 at the age of twenty-one, the day after winning the big Labor Day race at Lakewood and the $450 pot that went with it—shot through the heart by a cousin in a dispute over sugar, essential to making moonshine— there was an impish obituary that day in the early edition of the *Atlanta Journal*: "When not racing, Mr. Seay divided his time between Dawsonville and Atlanta."

Given some lead time to think about it, the *Atlanta Constitution* decided to stop talking in circles and, in the next morning's editions, came out with the rest of the story, a florid version of Lloyd Seay and the others of those fearless young trippers-cum-racers: "Lloyd Seay was well known in Atlanta and all along the highways in the mountains. Federal, state and county law officers knew him as the most daring of all the daredevil crew that hauled liquor from mountain stills to Atlanta. They had many a wild chase when they hit his trail, but had caught him only rarely, for he hurled his car down the twisting blacktop hill-country roads at a pace few of them cared to follow." The story quoted one revenue officer as saying, "I caught him eight times, and each time I had to shoot out his tires." *Glory!* Now it was out in the open. Good old boys, fast as white lightning, outsmarting the Feds, just trying to make a living. The story caught the fancy of Atlantans, grimly teetering with much trepidation on the eve of another world war, and more than a little attention was paid to the burial of Lloyd Seay that would take place a few days later in the cemetery three blocks off the square in Dawsonville, seat of Dawson County, already well known at the Alcohol and Tobacco Tax division of the Internal Revenue Service in Washington as the Moonshine Capital of the World.

They came from all over to attend the ceremony. Throughout the morning, a virtual caravan of cars steamed up the twisting road from Atlanta to Dawsonville, carrying liquor-haulers and race fans and thrill-seekers and reporters and, for all anybody knew, revenuers with orders to jot down license tag numbers. Among the mourners was a tall, reserved, handsome man in his late twenties, the picture of success, his snappy fedora and pressed brown suit setting him apart from a crowd dressed either in workaday bib overalls or their ill-fitting Sunday Best. A few days later, the townsfolk were startled to see a tombstone marking Seay's grave, a hastily carved granite monument to one of the first great stock car drivers. It was about four feet high, bearing Lloyd Seay's name and the legend "Winner National Stock Car Championship, Sept. 1, 1941, Lakewood Speedway." But there was more: carved in bas-relief was his favorite car, a '39 Ford coupe, and, as though leaning out of the driver's-side window, helmeted and grinning, there was a porcelainized photograph of Lloyd himself. Unknown to the others, it was the quiet man in the fedora who had ordered the tombstone and paid for it in cash. His name was Raymond Parks.

Like most folks in that place and at that time, Raymond Parks had seen enough of formal schooling by the time he reached his teens. Born in 1914 to a Dawson County farm family, he quit school in the middle of the seventh grade and soon, at the age of fifteen, left home. He spent the next two and a half years toiling away in the deep woods of nearby Hall County, "making moonshine with a couple of older men there," your basic gofer, chopping wood and lighting fires and stirring mash and standing lookout. The stock market had collapsed and the Great Depression was on; although, as many would report with not a little irony, there had *always* been a depression in that part of the country. About the only people who could make ends meet, within the law, were those with good bottomland and a lot of sons to help work it, and even those folks dealt not in cash but in bartering food for services. It was that, or make moonshine whiskey. Young Raymond wanted more than a supporting role, and the only place to find a more promising life was in Atlanta. He moved to the big city after his apprenticeship out there in the boondocks of Hall County, to work at an uncle's service station on Hemphill Avenue, a street named for a turn-of-the-century mayor and newspaper publisher, abutting the Georgia Tech campus near the downtown area.

He did a lot more than pump gas. Some people are born to be chiefs, others Indians, and Raymond Parks had the vision and the temperament to be in charge, to be an entrepreneur. With the Depression and Prohibition running concurrently, in a time of great despair, he knew a market when he saw it: cheap whiskey, readily available. He knew who made it and who could deliver it and who wanted it, so he became the middleman in a sprawling operation leading from the low hills of Dawson County to the warehouses and shantytowns of Atlanta. A Moonshine Baron! One thing led to another, and very soon he was dealing in other corners of the "entertainment" industry: renting out jukeboxes and slot machines and pool tables. By the mid-thirties, barely of voting age, he had bought the service station from his uncle and become a wealthy man, too quick for the law: "They called me one time to say they had fifteen of my slots and I could get 'em if I wanted 'em, but I'm no fool. I guess they melted 'em down or something." Money and his gentlemanly bearing brought him respect. He became known as "Mr. Parks" in certain circles, his signature being a wide-brimmed hat; straw in the summer, felt in the winter.

Parks had gotten to know a hotshot automobile mechanic in the neighborhood, Red Vogt, whose fame had spread to the underworld of moonshine runners. Raymond paid Red, in fact, to keep the cars of some of his runners in shape for their hell-bent dashes back and forth between Atlanta and Dawsonville ("Couldn't nobody beat Red as far as working on motors"). When some of those drivers began having Vogt retool those same cars for racing at Lakewood Speedway, using essentially the same skills, it naturally piqued Parks's interest. Maybe it was another way to make some money, he thought. He was already a familiar figure at Lakewood, as a spectator and sometimes as the silent sponsor of a car, when, in 1939, he was approached by a couple of those young bootleggers from up home who happened to be cousins of his: Roy Hall and Lloyd Seay. "Roy and Lloyd got me started in racing," he said, "when they came around and talked to me about building 'em a car to race with. They didn't work for me, and they already had separate cars for running whiskey, but they knew I had some money and I worked with Red." So the deals were struck.

Parks would buy the cars brand-new—usually the same hot little number, the new '39 Ford coupe, that worked just as well on the back roads, fleeing the Feds, as on the dirt surface at Lakewood—then have them delivered to Vogt at his garage on Spring Street. Race cars were still in their rudimentary stage then ("You couldn't put in roll bars, couldn't take the seats out, and the drivers wore what amounted to football helmets"), but Red refitted them a slight bit for racing, mainly changing the gears and springs for the turns and quicker bursts needed on a racetrack. He painted numbers and the drivers' names and "Hemphill Service Station" on them, and kept them under wraps in his own garage. Sundays would bring Hall and Seay to town, pumped up and full of stories about their week of outrunning the law, and off they would go to Lakewood. They won, more often than not, splitting their purses with Parks, then heading back home to Dawsonville that night to take care of business for another week while Vogt got the cars ready for the next weekend of racing. The partnership was on a roll. On the eve of the Second World War, both Hall and Seay won races on the beach-and-road course at Daytona. But then came Lloyd's death, and the war, which caused racing to shut down due to shortages of tires and gas.

When Parks returned from the war, having served as a sergeant in the infantry during the Battle of the Bulge, it was to an America that was vastly changed: winner of the war, leader of the free world, and prosperous like never before. Now there was a proliferation of dirt tracks all over the South and even in the gritty industrial areas of the Midwest, in Pennsylvania and Michigan, and the racing of stock cars took off. Lakewood Speedway was still a showcase for much of it, and Raymond Parks, the sport's first multiple-car owner, became a principal player. Lloyd Seay might have been gone, but there was still Dawsonville's Roy Hall and a fellow by the name of Gober Sosebee. Those two Dawsonville boys were soon joined by a former open-wheel driver from Alabama named Red Byron, and Atlanta's own moonshine-hauling Flock brothers, Fonty and Bob. (Talk about being born to derring-do. Papa Carl Flock, the patriarch, was a tightrope walker. Carl Jr. was a boat racer. Daughter Reo, named for the automobile, was a parachutist and daredevil who walked wings during air shows. Daughter Ethel, named for the fuel, became one of the first female race car drivers. Baby brother Tim would come along in the fifties to become an early NASCAR champion.) The Flocks became so successful on the fledgling racing circuit, blowing the opposition away from Daytona to Langhorne, Pennsylvania, in their Vogt-built Parks-backed machines, that they barely had time anymore for hauling moonshine out of the hills.

But the smudge of their illicit beginnings lingered, particularly in the eyes of the more pious preachers in town—*Common criminals! Racing on*

Sunday!—and it led to a relentless game of cat-and-mouse between the two sides. Everybody's favorite story about the Lakewood of those days involves Bob Flock. The preachers had managed to coax an ordinance that made it against the law for anyone with a police record to race on Sundays at Lakewood, which was on city property; said ordinance, if enforced, would have been tantamount to the death of racing at Lakewood, of course, since few of the drivers had lived the lives of saints. Bob Flock, although not nearly as theatrical as his big brother Fonty, whose pencil-thin mustache and flowing scarf brought to mind Errol Flynn or Clark Gable, showed up for the regular show on a Sunday at Lakewood. So did the cops, who wandered among the cars, peering into the cockpits in search of known miscreants. Bob, the story goes, had tied a bandanna around his head, covering his face like a bandit in a cowboy movie, fooling no one. When he was told to get out of the car, that he was under arrest, he gunned it and removed himself to the backstretch, where he crouched, his engine popping and growling, awaiting the next move. The officer in charge ordered two motorcycle cops to go after him, box him in, get the varmint. Keystone Kops! Flock promptly floorboarded the car, spun into a Bootlegger Turn, and, with roostertail flying, burst through the rickety board fence on the second turn and disappeared onto Pryor Street at 100 miles per hour, haulin' ass, movin' on, headed for the maze of streets in downtown Atlanta.

"Yeah, we had a lot of fun at that track," Raymond Parks was saying one morning in '96, nearly half a century later. Soon he would be marking his eighty-second birthday, but that wasn't slowing him down. Tall and lanky, with thinning gray hair, dressed in a starched white shirt, a tie, and gabardine slacks, he had been in his office since seven o'clock in the morning, overseeing an empire that was still anchored to the liquor business. He owned two package stores, one of them at one of the choicest locations in Atlanta, on the corner of Peachtree and Collier Roads in the upscale neighborhood of Buckhead. He continued dealing in real estate in the same area where he had alighted from Dawson County in the thirties, and still rented out "music boxes" (jukeboxes), pool tables, and pinball machines. It was all legal now, he pointed out. The Olympic Games would be coming to town in the summer, and he planned on having an estimated "nine hundred thousand dollars' worth of stock on the floor" at the Collier-Peachtree store, to satisfy the influx of visitors from all over the world who might get thirsty.

His office was an adjunct of his other package store, on a seedy stretch of Northside Drive, scant blocks from where Hemphill Avenue peeled off and headed toward the sprawling Georgia Tech campus. He owned much of the land between there and a nearby exit ramp of I-75 North, including the bottoms across the boulevard where once stood a steamy little asphalt racetrack known as Peach Bowl Speedway. "You could see it, over where those trees are, if it was still there," he said. He was seated at a cracked leather sofa in an office that looked more like a poor man's racing hall of fame, its thin plywood walls holding shelves laden with tarnished racing trophies, faux-leather albums containing photographs and newspaper clippings from his days in racing (a young Bill France, Sr., in a leather racing helmet, race action at Daytona and Lakewood and Darlington, one of a youthful Raymond Parks leaning against a bar with two lovelies). Under wraps, in the basement garage of the building, sat a perfectly restored black '39 Ford coupe that he drove to Dawsonville every fall to show off during the town's annual Moonshine Festival.

"I got out of racing in nineteen and fifty," he said. "Told my drivers it was time for me to start making some money. I lost money on racing, no matter how well my drivers did. I might should've stayed in it, the way things have happened these days with Winston Cup, and I gave a little thought to getting back in but I decided I didn't really want to. I go to Daytona every February, and once in a while I run over to Darlington or North Wilkesboro. Been to Atlanta [Motor Speedway] a few times. But that's about it. I've got my businesses to look after, and my time was so long ago that not many people know who I am. Who I *used to be* is more like it, I guess."

That was problematical for a long time with the directors at NASCAR. Not unlike the new suits in charge of the country music business these days, who had chosen to sweep country's "tacky" roots under the rug in order to enter the mainstream (abandoning old Ryman Auditorium, metaphorically kicking Ernest Tubb and Hank Williams out the door, replacing the heartfelt nasal twangs with a bland sound they called Countrypolitan), NASCAR went into denial during its orchestrated move on Middle America. Specifically, they didn't much want to talk about *their* pioneers, either, those people like Lloyd Seay and Roy Hall and the Flocks and Raymond Parks. But it was difficult to deny the championships they had won, especially in the early days of the beach course at Daytona. So slowly, over recent years, one by one, the original drivers' names began to appear in the various halls of fame attached to the tracks, at Darlington and Daytona and Talladega, although Parks's name seldom came up in the nominations. Oh, he had been friends for life with Bill France, Sr., who had even raced Parks's cars a few times; and he had been touted by Junior Johnson, the best known of the bootleggers-turned-drivers, as having been "like Ford and General Motors are today." But the elder France was dead and Johnson himself had been a bootlegger, and the new crowd didn't want to get into all of that business about hauling whiskey and such.

The change of mind probably traced back to the day when Ronald Reagan granted a presidential pardon to Junior Johnson, who had served time for hauling moonshine. (That old scalawag Richard Nixon had done the same for country music's Merle Haggard, riding on the crest of "Okie from Muskogee," who hadn't been able to vote since doing time at San Quentin for general boyhood rowdiness.) At any rate, Raymond Parks got the call one day in 1995, nearly six decades after becoming what Bill France the younger now was lauding as "the Rick Hendrick of his time." He had been elected not by the image-makers but by the writers, the National Motorsports Press Association, to their own hall of fame at Darlington Raceway. "What I did was nothing to be ashamed of," he said. And he put on a suit and picked out a suitable straw hat and then drove over to Darlington, on the Labor Day weekend of the Southern 500, to be let out of the closet at long last.

Not all of the Dawson County Boys were in the whiskey business, of course, and one of the innocents was Gober Sosebee. Gober, in fact, was still playing a coy game about all that many years later, even as he approached his eighty-second birthday; as though steadfastly guarding some dark family secret he had solemnly promised to take to his grave. "That's hearsay to me [about Lloyd Seay and moonshine]," was his line, delivered without so much as a wink. "That's told on lots of people, I guess. I never *saw* Lloyd with a drop of liquor, understand. To my way of thinking, he might have hauled whiskey, don't you see, but we talked lots of times and he never actually *told* me he did. He was just a nice-looking clean-cut boy, easy to talk to, and I thought the world of him." *Yeah, well, okay.* The only thing that counted to Gober, in his twilight days of comfortable retirement back home in Dawson County, was that Lloyd Seay and Roy Hall were great race car drivers, pioneers of the sport, and he had been right there with them at the beginning.

Like most farm boys of his era, with all of that machinery lying about, Gober had become fascinated with things mechanical early on. He was born in 1915, less than a mile from where he now lived, one of nine children of a farmer and a midwife. The Sosebees worked about three hundred acres, and it was a busy operation. "We grew wheat, corn, and vegetables. Had about two hundred chickens running loose that gave us three or four dozen eggs a day. My father had a sawmill, and a shop to build wagons and whatnot. We didn't have no money, much, but we were fortunate. We were able to take care of about ten poor families around the place, feeding 'em and the like. Swapped stuff with the barter man for things we couldn't buy. Even rented out some farmland." Everybody in the family pitched in, on the farm and at the mill, and when Gober was ten years old he became one of the designated drivers. "We had this Ford truck for hauling lumber. I couldn't even reach the pedals on it, had to slide down off the seat to work 'em, but I managed. Pretty soon I had to work on the truck to keep it going, so that's how I learned about motors and such." He went to school through the ninth grade, often working on the farm until eleven o'clock at night, and when that became too much he dropped out and began working full-time at his father's sawmill. The closest he had come to racing, at that point in his life, was to take the family car into Dawsonville at night and roar up and down the roads with some of the frisky younger boys in town, among them Lloyd Seay and Roy Hall.

Gober followed the fresh tracks of thousands of other farm boys in poor rural Georgia during the Depression by moving to Atlanta. "Fact is, the first race I ever saw was at Lakewood in nineteen and thirty-nine, and Lloyd was driving in it," he was saying late one morning in a basement den decorated with about a hundred racing trophies, including three he won on the beach course at Daytona around 1950. "I'd left home and was working at Atlantic Steel by then, I guess, living on Hemphill Avenue, and a bunch of us went out to watch the races one Sunday at Lakewood. There was about ten or fifteen of us, mostly Dawson County folks, and after it was over I said, 'Well, that was fun but I'll never see another race 'less I'm in it.' Two or three of 'em just about died laughing, said, 'Well, looks like you won't be seeing no more races, then,' and I said, 'Why not? Watch me. The next one you see, I'll be out there.' So I went and ordered me a nineteen and forty Ford before they were due to come out, even went over to the assembly plant on Ponce de Leon Avenue to see how it was coming along, watched 'em put it together, and I got it delivered in October of '39. Took that brand-new Ford out to Lakewood one Sunday, qualified eighteenth and finished third, racing against Lloyd and Roy [Hall] and Fonty [Flock]. That did it for me. I became a race car driver."

He continued to work the graveyard shift at the Atlantic Steel mill at night, following an all-day stint at a dry cleaner's, but in due time—after he had seen that first race and then begun racing—he gravitated toward the cluster of service stations and automobile shops in the Hemphill–Northside Drive area, getting to know men like Raymond Parks and Red Vogt and the rest of the racing crowd, becoming a regular among them during the week and at Lakewood Speedway on Sundays. "Those were the days," he said. "One time I had me this black Buick with 'Mountain Breeze' painted on the side, for a restaurant in Dawsonville that give me free meals whenever I was up there. One day at Lakewood this old boy from Macon was talking about how he was gonna put my Buick in the lake and then run Lloyd Seay off the track. The track was dusty and Lloyd and myself was going up the back straightaway side by side, Lloyd inside and me outside, when we come up on this old boy on the number three turn. Well, Lloyd hit him on his left rear wheel and I hit him on the right rear, and we folded that car up and it went as high as a ceiling. Lloyd went into the lake, all right, and I kept going until I could run up the bank and get myself stopped. I jumped out to run get Lloyd, because I'd heard him say one time he couldn't swim, but he didn't go down deep enough in the water, the front end just hanging there over the lake. The feller from Macon, he jumped out of his car and ran down the back straightaway as hard as he could and we never did see him no more."

Soon Lloyd was dead, and then came the cessation of racing during the war, which Gober avoided due to his defense-related job in the steel mill, but when peace came he plunged into racing on a circuit that spread far beyond Lakewood Speedway, from Daytona and Birmingham in the South to Reading and Langhorne in Pennsylvania. "We had tow bars to pull our race cars, and sometimes we'd be gone all weekend just to run one race like up at Langhorne. Most of the time I'd stick around home and run three on a weekend, Friday and Saturday nights at the Peach Bowl and Sunday at Lakewood. It was pretty basic stuff. Didn't have no special racing tires, wore these kinda-like Soap Box Derby helmets, and one fellow that had bad kidneys fixed up this funnel so he could relieve himself with the race going on. Didn't have shoulder harnesses, but we did have these nylon lap safety belts we found at Army Surplus, the kind they'd used in tanks. Far as I know, I invented the roll bar after the war when I put this heavy truck spring inside the roof of that '39 Ford and soldered it to a couple of posts coming off the frame. They made fun of me for that, said if I was a good driver I wouldn't need a roll bar, but pretty soon everybody got 'em." The only time he got hurt, amazingly, from running all of those races under such primitive conditions, was when he hit an inside retaining wall and a two-by-eight board flew into the car and broke his pelvic bone.

Gober Sosebee left his mark, no question. From that first race at Lakewood in 1939 until 1964, when he was politely disinvited for winning too often at a track in Rome, Georgia, at the age of fifty—"I won my third in a row up there, even with my engine skipping, and they admitted they'd like to have me back one more time 'just to see how that thing runs with eight cylinders' "—he won about two hundred times in those hellish days of stock car racing's infancy. Three times he won modified races on the beach course at Daytona, one of five Dawson County boys—Seay, Hall, Bernard Long, and Bill Elliott were the others—to have Daytona victories on their résumé, and he even drove a convertible during one of the first races ever held on the high banks of Daytona International Speedway. "I was pretty plain. People didn't much like me till they got to know me. I didn't have no money, backed myself, worked day and night trying to make a good race car driver. But I had some pretty good cars, some *fast* cars."

His all-time favorite was a black '39 Ford coupe, nested in a locked Featherlite trailer under a grove of scraggly trees in the backyard of his airy one-story brick ranch house about five miles from the square in Dawson-ville. He and his wife, Vaudell, a Dawson County girl he first met one day at the Lakewood races, had moved back home in 1968 "when the coloreds starting taking over" the Hemphill Avenue area, building on a hundred-acre spread that backed up to Lake Lanier. Gober, despite his wearing a pacemaker now to counter low blood pressure, still carried a business card for Sosebee Auto Service, specializing not in automobile repair but in grading for driveways in the subdivisions and random vacation getaways sprouting around the lake. Scattered here and there in the backyard were a bulldozer and a dump truck and a couple of modern-era stock cars, rusting in the weeds, that had been driven by his son, David, during a brief Winston Cup career in the eighties. David retired, after a turn at a stock car circuit in Australia, and now was "in the sand business" in Dawson County.

Gober unlocked the trailer, which was hand-painted with his name and a litany of the car's successes, as though it held a thoroughbred horse ("Modified Winner, Daytona Beach, 1949-50-51"), and then swung open the doors to reveal a thing of beauty. If not for his health problems, he would have towed the coupe to Daytona in February, when he and Ray-mond Parks and some of the other old-timers were appearing at the grassy lot of the Christian Drive-In Church during Speedweeks. He had restored it, at considerable expense, to the way it was when he won his NASCAR championships at Daytona those three years running. It was a glistening black, bearing the number 50 and the legend "Cherokee Garage, Atlanta, Ga." on its doors (a garage he owned briefly, and where he did much of his own work), with a fanciful painting of an Indian wearing a warbonnet to cap it off. Everything was the same: V-8 motor, three carburetors, crank-out windshield, special-made replicas of the narrow Firestone tires of that era, the truck-spring roll bar of his invention. This car, he said, would hit 140 miles per hour on the road portion of the old Daytona course, Highway A1A. For years, he and Vaudell had been towing it around to various venues, racetracks and automobile dealerships, to places like Talladega and Daytona and Savannah, "so folks can get the feel of how it used to be."

He dropped a ramp at the rear of the trailer, then climbed into the car. Settling in, goosing the throttle, he laughed at a memory. "You wouldn't believe how many cars used to run on the beach at Daytona. One time they had to call it when the tide started coming in. Any rate, one time I started in ninety-fifth place. You'd draw for positions, see, and there was this guy complaining about being at the end. I told him, 'Here, I tell you what, I drew for the middle and I'll swap.' I'd already learned that the worst place to be was in the middle of that mess, all those wrecks right at the start. So I laid way back in the pack, about two hundred yards behind everybody. They used three pistol shots to start the races then—ready, set, go—and when I heard the first one I fired 'er up. On the second shot, I began moving in low gear. Third shot, I was running full blast. I had the wind blowing in on me from the ocean side, to keep me straight, and when we hit the first turn I was running seventh. Must've lost half the cars before we even made the road." When he cranked the car on this day, four decades later, there was not so much as a puff of smoke. It ran like a sewing machine.

Later, having backed the car out of the trailer and admired it for a while in the blistering noon sun, allowing his mind to wander back half a century to the Cherokee Garage and Lakewood, no doubt seeing visions of Red Vogt and Lloyd Seay and the dashing young Raymond Parks, he put her away and locked the door of the trailer.

"Some car," he was told.

"Yeah. Does people a lot of good to see where racing came from. I don't see how anybody gets hurt in these cars they've got today."

"Folks say it took a lot of guts to drive a race car in those days."

"I can truthfully say I never got scared on a racetrack. I knew what I was doing, had a good car, had my roll bar. Soon as I accelerated on the pace lap, any fear left me just like that."

He watched Winston Cup now and then on television, he said, and liked the way Dale Earnhardt drove. "The way I remember it, the point of racing's to get around everybody and finish first." The money? Unfathomable. "I did pretty good for myself there after a while. After I won at Daytona, I could get a thousand dollars appearance money to run at the Iron Bowl in Birmingham, and that was in nineteen and fifty. Lot of us didn't want to run NASCAR when it started up because we could do better winning races close to home. But, naw, I never thought the money would come to this, that's for sure. I mean, I fed Bill France, Sr., more than once when he was coming up here to race before and after the war. If Raymond Parks had the money he lent France, he'd be rich all over again. And now this. 'Million Dollar Bill' Elliott." That gave him a notion. "Why don't we run over to the poolroom and see what's going on?"

There was a Pit Stop Cafe in town, a homage to "Awesome Bill from Dawsonville" dating to Elliott's 1985 season when he won RJR's special million-dollar bonus and thoroughly dominated Winston Cup racing, but the living and breathing center of town was the Dawsonville Pool Room. Housed in a high-ceilinged red-brick building just off the square, its broad plate-glass window covered with a hand-lettered chronological listing of Elliott's forty Winston Cup victories, it contained a couple of obligatory pool tables smack in the middle of the big front room; but more than anything it was a virtual shrine to Bill Elliott, and, to a lesser extent, the other Dawson County Boys who had made their mark in racing. Chained to the counter were two worn racing tires: one that was on Elliott's car when he took the checkered flag at Darlington to clinch the Winston Million, the other from Gober Sosebee's car when he led the first six laps of the very first Southern 500 at Darlington in 1950. One entire wall was covered with framed photographs of Elliott, from over the years, and the unisex bathroom was wallpapered with newspaper accounts of the highlights of his career. Hanging precariously in odd corners were scarred scraps of Elliott's cars, a hood here and a quarter-panel there, exactly as they had been salvaged. The decor was faux red leather for the booths, black-and-white squares of linoleum remindful of a checkered flag for the floor, and in one corner there was an array of Elliott collectibles for sale: T-shirts, caps, photos, Al Thomy's biography, *Bill Elliott: Fastest Man Alive.* Spotted here and there, wherever room could be found for them, were racing video games.

Gober parked his big white Cadillac on the street outside, near one of those portable balloon-tired marquees with an update on the status of Elliott and the driver of one of his cars in that weekend's races at Michigan International Speedway. (This was at midsummer. Elliott was at home, twenty miles away in his mountain retreat at Blairsville, resting from severe injuries suffered in a crash at Talladega; his relief driver, Todd Bodine, had qualified poorly and had to take a provisional and start at the end of the pack. Ron Barfield, a twenty-five-year-old protégé who was living in a house trailer behind the Elliott racing shops, five miles from town, would be driving an Elliott-backed car in that afternoon's ARCA race at Michigan.) When the screen door of the poolroom slapped behind Gober, he glanced to make sure they still had his Darlington tire on display, and then, noticing there was a boisterous crowd of people chomping down on hamburgers and watching the ARCA race on television sets suspended from the ceiling, decided to take the quieter side room. He picked out a Formica table in the corner, beneath a row of framed oil paintings of himself and the four other Daytona winners from Dawson County.

Soon he was joined by Gordon Pirkle, the owner, a stocky man with steel-gray hair and a bushy mustache. Pirkle was born and raised in Dawson County and now, at fifty-nine, was the walking authority on its history in whiskey and racing. While the sounds of the ARCA race in Michigan droned on and the locals in the booths up front cheered Ron Barfield as he made a run for the lead, the two men swapped small talk. Elliott should be ready to race again at the Brickyard 400, on August 3, Pirkle reported. When Gober told him he had seen the banner for the poolroom being towed above Atlanta Motor Speedway during the March race, Pirkle brightened. "We had it at Daytona, too," he said. "But I tell you, maybe the greatest moment of my life was during the World Series in Atlanta last fall. Furman Bisher [of the *Atlanta Journal*] had it in his column about how Jimmy Carter and Ted Turner were sitting there in the box seats and looked up and saw this banner for 'Gordon Pirkle's Dawsonville Pool Room.' To be mentioned in the same paragraph with those two, I can die now."

"You don't mean that, do you?" Gober said.

"Aw, you know."

"Dawsonville's on the map, that's for sure."

"Has been for a long time, Gober. We've just got to keep spreading the word."

Pirkle looked through the window and pointed out a Fina service station across the street, a stone building that had been there since there were cars in Dawson County. "It used to be a Pure Oil," he said, "and that's where all the trippers hung out. Way out in the country, but it stayed open twenty-four hours, if that tells you anything. There were two pay phones in the whole town then, one at the jail and the other at the station, and that phone stayed busy all night. All the boys would be sitting around, waiting for the phone call to say the stuff was ready to be loaded. And there's this long hill out on the highway, Gober Hill, for the Gober family that owned the land, and they'd be hanging out, waiting for the phone to ring, when they'd hear a car coming, popping and changing gears, four miles away, and they'd start betting on who it was. Lloyd? Roy Hall?"

When thousands of fans and media came from all over the country to attend Bill Elliott Day in November of '85, to celebrate Elliott's Winston Million, it inspired a group of boosters to start thinking about capitalizing on Dawsonville's past. The county's economy had turned around some-what in the sixties, with the introduction of the poultry business on a large scale—long rows of tin-roofed chicken houses now dotted the hills where little besides corn had ever grown—and now they had put together $20,000 as seed money for some sort of tourist attraction centered on racing. "It wasn't easy to talk folks into it," said Pirkle, more or less the point man on the project, "because a lot of 'em still don't want to talk about the moonshine days. But, shoot, we already have the Moonshine Festival every fall, during the leaf season when the tourists come driving through. I used the old line, 'Just call it history and put it in a museum.' This is the birthplace of stock car racing, and I think we ought to make something out of it. Gober, here, he's got stuff for a museum. Lord knows, we've got Elliott cars and things. Maybe a museum with all of that, an authentic moonshine still, a documentary film, sort of a library for re-search. That Robert Mitchum movie, *Thunder Road*, I love that thing, keep seeing it all the time. Dawsonville was headquarters for all that stuff."

Hoots, squeals, and clapping resounded from the front room. Young Ron Barfield had won his first ARCA race, at Michigan, maybe the first step in the building of another champion from Dawson County. Gordon Pirkle got up and went to the front to watch the ceremony in Victory Lane, then got on a stepladder to rewind the tape he had made of the race. When he heard the click he started playing the entire race all over again. Then he stepped outside to get some fresh air. "You know how kids all over the country play cowboys and Indians?" he said. "Well, when I was growing up, we'd go out in the woods and play trippers and revenuers. We'd have to fight over who got to play Lloyd Seay and Roy Hall. The losers had to play the law."

4

TROUBLE IN TURN FOUR

The return of bullish old-fashioned driving was all anybody could talk about following the indelicacies that occurred in only the second Winston Cup race of the season, the Goodwrench 400 at North Carolina Motor Speedway, putting the bad boy Dale Earnhardt smack in the middle of what turned into a storm of outrage. The show had moved back home from Daytona to "The Rock"—the venerable track at Rockingham, tucked into the Sandhills area near the South Carolina line about seventy-five miles east of Charlotte—and when Terry Labonte and Jeff Gordon finished one-two in qualifying, it looked like Hendrick Motorsports might be able to start repaying the good folks at DuPont and Kellogg's for their largesse. Earnhardt had qualified a poor eighteenth, two miles per hour slower than Labonte's pole-winning speed of 156.870, and on that basis he didn't appear to be much of a factor in a race that happened to be backed by his sponsor.

But situations arise during the course of a long hot day, especially at a treacherous 1.02-mile oval such as Rockingham, where, as Earnhardt had mused beforehand, "the patient man usually wins." Labonte had broken away early in the race, leading all but one of the first 137 laps, pumping along on all cylinders, threatening to make a runaway of this thing. When Gordon went out early again, this time with a blown engine only one third of the way into the 393-lap race, it left Labonte squarely in the spotlight. The friends and the enemies of Earnhardt should have known better, though, for The Intimidator had all but told them so when he saw steam rising from Labonte's Chevy up ahead. "He's not gonna make it," Earnhardt had radioed to his pit, more than once, as he relentlessly weaved his way toward the front, finding himself up to third place by the time the first full pit stops on the eighty-eighth lap came around. Labonte had begun to overheat—from a random piece of paper clinging to the air dam of his car, just another of those odd happenstances that can befall even the best of them—and suddenly his engine blew, taking him out of the race. "That's racin'," was how they always put it.

So now, like Darth Vader, here came Earnhardt in his ominous black Monte Carlo, picking his holes, thundering onward; into the lead for the first long stretch at lap 236 after Labonte's departure, briefly giving it up to such pretenders as Ricky Rudd and Jimmy Spencer and Dale Jarrett and, finally, Bobby Hamilton, but just as quickly taking it back. When Earnhardt and Hamilton began swapping the lead, lap by lap, with about fifty to go, the crowd clearly rallied on the side of Hamilton and his car owner, Richard Petty. Should they pull it off, it would be the first Winston Cup victory ever for the mop-haired country boy and for Petty as an owner. The very sight of that familiar old blue-and-red STP car bearing Petty's number 43 had the fans on their feet, hearts and fists pumping, visions dancing in their heads of the good old days when The King ruled. Back and forth it went, Earnhardt taking Hamilton low and then Hamilton returning the favor on the next lap. It was thrilling stuff, the best piece of racing in the early season.

Then Earnhardt did it. Never is a car more vulnerable and potentially unstable than when it is coming out of a turn, about to power up for a run into the straightaway. The laws of centrifugal force are momentarily suspended when, in racing lingo, "the air is off the spoiler," leaving the car hanging in a sort of limbo, with its flank exposed for only an instant. Hamilton was thus caught midway up the track on the fourth turn, a sitting duck, and he presented a target that Earnhardt couldn't resist. He had Hamilton in his crosshairs now, a submarine stalking a destroyer. Reaching all the way back to the raucous dirt-track days of his hard-driving father, about the only man he was known to accord homage to, Earnhardt went full power a split second before Hamilton could react and vigorously popped the 43 car on the left side of the rear bumper (had there been bumpers on these machines), rudely kicking Hamilton out of the way, up against the wall, and roared into the lead. *Bye-bye, see you later, that's all she wrote.* At first the fans didn't believe what they had seen, were startled by the audacity of it all, and then they began raining a thunderstorm of displeasure down onto the track. Hamilton soon went out with handling problems caused by that initial lick, and Earnhardt took the checkered flag, under a late-race caution, for his first win of the season, tying him for the points lead with Dale Jarrett. He collected nearly $84,000 for first place, while Hamilton got $27,000 for finishing way back in twenty-fourth. When Earnhardt, holding his seven-year-old daughter and grinning through his mustache during the obligatory interview from Victory Lane, kissed it off as "a little bumping," his words going out over the speedway's public address system, the crowd was not amused.

The firestorm that followed wouldn't go away. Over the next ten days, *Winston Cup Scene* would receive a total of 158 letters about the incident, only five of them defending Earnhardt. A woman from Tennessee: "The [*Nashville*] *Tennessean* quoted Earnhardt as saying, 'Look at the tape, you'll see what happened.' I have looked at it, and it was intentional." A fellow from Virginia: "Just like the days of old, Dale Earnhardt couldn't find a way to beat another driver cleanly, so he knocked him out of contention. And then, just like old times, NASCAR didn't raise a finger and Earnhardt went on to win." An unabashed fan of Richard Petty recommended that The King employ another trick from the good old days: "a tire iron wrapped in newspaper to greet the 'Ironhead.'" The only voice of reason came from a fellow, taking neither side, who once had been a student at Petty's driving school: "Ever since I took a ride around Charlotte Motor Speedway at a speed in excess of 160 mph, experiencing the buffeting, the bumps, the dips and the sensation of holding a 3,400-pound car on the track, much less in a perfectly straight line, I'm not so quick to judge the courage of a Ken Schrader, the integrity of a Dale Earnhardt or the will of a Darrell Waltrip. . . ." The fans seemed to be as hard on NASCAR as they were on Earnhardt, complaining once more about a double standard; that Earnhardt was too big a gate attraction to be forced to sit out a race under a penalty for dirty driving. NASCAR chose to lie low, behind a terse statement: "The penalty box has been used when we have no doubt the incident was intentional. We did not get that in this situation. We saw a lot of hard racing, but in that situation, we didn't see anything intentional."

On the weekly Tuesday morning teleconference, the media was waiting. Earnhardt came on the line first, offering a final word or two about his failing to win at Daytona ("Peanut butter's fine until you've eaten steak"), then bracing for the questions about Rockingham. "Jarrett got into me twice, but nobody talks about *that*," he said, showing no remorse. "There were other accidents, and several wrecks. I didn't do it intentionally. If they [Petty and Hamilton] want to ride around all day [this] Sunday at Richmond, looking to knock out the 3 car, it's their prerogative, but you can't cry over spilt milk." *Prerogative?* From Dale Earnhardt, the high school dropout? Hamilton, the reporters were advised, was "busy getting ready for Richmond" and thus "unavailable." Speaking for him and for Richard Petty was Dale Inman, general manager of Petty Enterprises and the team's spotter from high in the press box at Rockingham that day: "There's no question that who's the best driver in the history of Winston Cup racing is between Dale Earnhardt and Richard Petty. I've seen 'em all, going way back to the Flock boys. The thing that's so disturbing is, Earnhardt's better than that. I'm not saying he hit us on purpose, but he could've missed us. It cost us a lot of money, if we had won, and I think we would've won if it hadn't happened. I know how much it cost us, but I'm not saying."

The whole experience had been instructive on several levels. First of all, the lick itself: it was, indeed, a masterful move, as old as racing, one known to every driver on the track that day at Rockingham and utilized every weekend in the relative obscurity of dirt tracks all across America. Secondly, in defense of Earnhardt, similar moves took place in nearly every Winston Cup race; but far back in the pack, out of camera range, and not involving someone with the bad-boy image that Earnhardt had built and allowed to fester. Finally, what was NASCAR to do? Just when stock car racing was on a roll, trying to shed its old image of brawling yahoos and join mainstream America, it had gotten caught putting on not a sporting event but a mere "show," a word that NASCAR itself often used. All of the other major sports in the country had been dealing harshly with miscreants over the years on the grounds that rules were rules—baseball with pitchers doctoring the ball and hitters corking bats, football with overzealous college recruiters, basketball with point-shavers—but there was plenty of evidence, for those fans and media who taped the races, that there really was a double standard for Earnhardt. It would become evident as the season bore on that he was, in a real sense, the franchise. There had been a downside to all of NASCAR's careful selection and grooming of its drivers: it had produced a generation of men who seemed driven more by a desire to share the considerable wealth than by the old-fashioned raw greed to win at any cost. Thus, the promoters at NASCAR were stuck in a situation of their own creation. They knew better than anyone that the fans loved to hate Dale Earnhardt.

When everybody showed up at Richmond later in the week for the third race of the season, the Pontiac Excitement 400, the debate was still roiling. The first piece of paper to show up in the infield media center was a handout from the Pontiac Racing office that spoke of Earnhardt's "needless tag" and his "roughhousing tactics," and then proceeded to present the Earnhardt people with what was more or less a bill for damages. Apparently, Dale Inman of the Petty team had decided to go ahead and lay it out there. The tab, as it were, came to a total of $460,000, only $30,000 of it listed under "cost to fix car." The bulk of it was money that Hamilton would have won that day or might have earned in the future on contingency bonuses, had he gone on to win the race. As for Hamilton himself, who said he had turned and walked away when Earnhardt tried to talk to him upon their arrival at Richmond on Friday morning, he had seen enough of the accident on tape: "That man can come up on a fifty-two-car pileup, and always get through it. So how can he get into just one car? He's the best there is. He don't make mistakes. When something like that happens and it's Earnhardt, you don't think 'mistake.'" "Nope," wrote columnist Bob Lipper of the *Richmond Times-Dispatch*, "you think multiple offender," then quoting Benny Parsons, the driver-turned-broadcaster: "Earnhardt's going about [racing] all wrong. NASCAR doesn't *need* to do something about this, they've *got* to do something." The quote had been resurrected from 1987, when Earnhardt was in the midst of his stampede to glory.

Earnhardt was playing it cool, minding his own business, while several of the other teams wrestled with damage to their cars and their drivers and their egos. After only two races, the toll was high. A back-of-the-pack driver named Loy Allen had broken his shoulder when he slammed into a wall at Rockingham, causing a ten-minute red flag while they cleaned up the mess and whisked him away in a helicopter to a hospital, and it looked like he would be replaced for quite a while by David Letterman's favorite driver, the wonderfully named old trouper Dick Trickle ("I didn't get off the first banana boat; the second, maybe, but not the first"). The forty-seven-year-old Geoff Bodine had broken two ribs in his entanglement at Daytona, being replaced by his youngest brother, Todd, at Rockingham, and he would gamely try to slip behind the wheel again this weekend. The lone rookie, Johnny Benson, had pneumonia but would see what he could do. There had been more than a dozen crashes already, after only two races, and Geoff Bodine's middle brother, Brett, wasn't the only one who was cannibalizing mangled cars back at the shop to keep others going. Except for Hamilton's stirring run before his "incident" with Earnhardt at The Rock, the six Pontiacs had been awful so far; journeyman independent Rick Mast's tenth-place finish at Rockingham and Kyle Petty's eighteenth at Daytona being the best they could do. The most noteworthy disasters of them all, however, had befallen Jeff Gordon, NASCAR's bright young hope for the future, who had completed only 147 of the total 593 laps in the first two races. "We've been humbled," said the defending champion, his twenty-fifth birthday still five months away. The only heartwarming note to be found amidst all of this pain and squabbling was that the new duds for Dave Marcis and his crew had finally arrived from Prodigy.

But the show had to go on, wrecked cars and psyches notwithstanding, even with forecasts for a dreary weekend that might bring snow. There was a debate of another sort raging in the old Confederate capital, about whether to place a statue of the black native son Arthur Ashe, the tennis great now dead from AIDS, alongside those of beloved Confederate heroes on a downtown boulevard. Neither tennis nor Arthur Ashe was of any concern to the Winston Cup crowd on this day, or any other, their interests focusing on Richmond International Raceway, one of the choice stops on the Winston Cup circuit. The track dated back to 1953 when Lee Petty won the first race there, and steadily over the years it had been upgraded into a neat place to watch an automobile race. (Thoughts of tennis and Lee Petty reminded the old-timers of the day in the fifties when a reporter was talking to the curmudgeonly old father of the King-to-be when Lee abruptly asked him, "What's your favorite sport?" When the writer said tennis, Lee said, "Well, we don't have anything else to talk about, then, do we?" and spun on his heels and found something better to do.) RIR sat in the middle of the state fairgrounds, close to downtown and its ribbony maze of interstate highways, and was a classic short track: three quarters of a mile, D-shaped, relatively flat (fourteen-degree banks in the corners), completely encircled by about 80,000 grandstand seats that rose high and close over the track, giving the intimacy of Wrigley Field or a cozy little minor-league baseball park. The camping set had to entrench on the hillsides outside of the track, there being no room for them in the small infield, but they had learned to pitch a tent and start a bonfire anywhere.

Bonfires they needed. It was bitterly cold, on this first weekend of March, and that would become more of a problem for the drivers and their crews than for the fans. The temperature of the track surface was yet another variable involved in setting up a car for a race, and it affected mostly the tires. Back in the earliest days of NASCAR, when the first paved tracks were being built, drivers rode on what they could find, at tire stores or even junkyards; wider truck tires or thin-ply "maypops," as they were known, for you never knew when they might. The wide treadless doubletubed racing slicks—a tire within a tire—came along in due time, and even those required further experimentation. Most Winston Cup track surfaces were asphalt, a couple of them concrete; some were smooth, others rough; some tracks were high-banked, some were relatively flat. If there was one area of technology that continued to evolve, nearly half a century since the first paved track showed up on the circuit, at Darlington in 1950, it was in tires. The engineers at Goodyear, the sole supplier of Winston Cup tires since a failed hostile incursion by Hoosier tires in the early nineties, were constantly testing new rubber compounds not only for the four distinctive groupings of tracks—four short tracks of less than a mile, two serpentine road courses, two breathtaking superspeedways that require restrictor plates, and ten others of a mile or more in length—but for the specific demands of every single track within those groupings, as well. There seemed to be variables within variables; to wit, times would be slower on concrete, on a cold day, simply because concrete doesn't heat up as quickly as asphalt. Was the track high-banked, or flat? Rough surface, or smooth? Drafting, or no drafting? So there were all of these choices to be made as the crews arrived at the track on Friday at daybreak and trudged off to the mammoth Goodyear trailer to place their orders for the weekend: tires for the cold morning, tires for the warmer afternoon; tires for practice, tires for qualifying, tires for the race itself. What would it be, "stickers" (new tires with the factory stickers still on) or "roughs" that had been run a few laps? Soft rubber "gumballs," or hard compounds? It was a never-ending search for the right tire on the right track in the right temperature for the best safety and speed and endurance.

And then there was the matter of qualifying. Everybody, even the poorer operators like Dave Marcis and Rick Mast, brought one car for qualifying and another for the race. Each required an entirely different setup and approach, the basic difference being that qualifying involved one mighty solo burst around the track, a flat-out run with no consideration of drafting or traffic or strategy or pit stops or conserving gas and tires, while the race called for endurance throughout three or more hours of combat in traffic and changing track conditions. Qualifying well wasn't nearly so critical for the strong teams, who could overcome a poor qualifying position with their superior experience and resources, as it was for the lesser ones. Winning the pole position meant a lot more to the independents than just having a head start when the green flag dropped; with it came a check for $5,000 from Busch beer, an automatic spot in the field for the next year's Busch Clash at Daytona, and a day in the spotlight by way of headlines all over the country ("Musgrave Claims Bristol Pole"). And because the lesser teams didn't always have a former champion's or an owner's provisional to fall back on in the event of a disastrous qualifying run, they always had to sweat out the feared DNQ—did not qualify—after all that work in the shop, the expensive testing, the long haul to the track, the chancy preparations in the garage, the practice rounds, and the qualifying run itself. Nothing was quite so depressing for everyone at the track as the sight of a team loading up the car-hauler around noon on a Saturday, having failed to qualify after two cracks at it, trying to clear the infield before the gates were locked for the beginning of the Grand National race; home before dark.

The weather would wreak havoc throughout the weekend. There might be snow, but for sure it was going to be cold, in the thirties and forties. All during the first day there was the steady roar of practice and qualifying for both the Winston Cuppers and the less experienced Busch Grand National drivers, who would be running Saturday afternoon in a 250-lapper called the Hardee's Fried Chicken Challenge (well, why not, if the folks in Shreveport could live with a Poulan Weed Eater Bowl and San Franciscans would allow Candlestick Park to be renamed for a corporate benefactor?), and it became a mess out there from the moment the machines were unloaded from their haulers. The villain, of course, was the cold. "Once the race starts, I don't see it as being a problem," said Richard Petty. "All the exhaust and stuff will get the track warm, and the brakes will be warmed up, so that'll kind of preheat the tires." But for now, on Friday and again on Saturday morning, when patches of snow were found at daybreak, it seemed that there was a screech and a thud somewhere on the track every ten minutes. Ernie Irvan, who had wrecked in each of the first two races of the season, raised more eyebrows when he slammed into the wall only moments after going out for a few practice spins on new tires. Earnhardt, Kyle Petty, and Jimmy Spencer met the same fate. And what was happening in those cold conditions to the major-leaguers, the best stock car drivers in the world, was nothing when compared to their Grand National wannabes.

Busch Grand National was only a step away from the big time, albeit a very long step. Johnny Benson had blown 'em away in BGN for two straight seasons, but so far in his rookie year he was trying just to stay on the track with drivers who had from ten to thirty years' experience in Winston Cup racing. Except for Patty Moise (*maw-EEZ*), the wife of driver Elton Sawyer and the only female competitor in the upper levels of NASCAR, the BGN drivers were good old boys on the way to becoming men on the racetrack; their hair was a little shaggier, their uniforms less tailored, their speech a little less articulate, their sponsors regional (Farmers Choice Fertilizer) rather than national. While the Winston Cup teams were set up under covered garages, a short jog from the pits, the BGN teams were scattered on the outer fringes of the infield in the open air, their modest car-haulers parked in some disarray. In their exuberance, coupled with sparse knowledge of the Richmond track, particularly in such weather, they would squeal out onto the track with a new set of tires and next be seen immobilized against the wall on the third turn, squirming out of the car, signaling for a wrecker. (Indeed, one of them would go out for the day when he wrecked on the pace lap of Saturday's race.) Whenever one of them was hauled into the warmth of the big infield media center for the first press conference of his career, plopped down in a director's chair and handed a microphone to replay his round for several dozen reporters seated in deep chairs beneath soft fluorescent lighting, it was reminiscent of Junior Johnson and the good old days: "Yeah, well, the dang thang run pretty good at first, but then that idiot come up behind me out o' no-*whurs*." They were, in short, not quite ready for prime time.

When qualifying began on Friday afternoon to determine the first twenty-five starting positions in Sunday's race, many in the crowd of 10,000 or so who had bundled up and come out for the cheaper admissions and the action left their seats and strained against the catch fence to let their anger be known. They had seen the Rockingham race on television, if not in person, and they knew how they stood on the "little bumping"

Earnhardt had given Hamilton. Even as Earnhardt and Kyle Petty stood beside their cars on pit road, the crinkle-eyed Intimidator and the pony-tailed wild child just chewing the fat as they bided their time to qualify, the jeers and taunts flew. What Earnhardt was wont to do on such occasions was to grin and tweak his mustache, never *ever* looking their way, and that was enough to *really* piss 'em off. Hamilton went out on his qualifying run before Earnhardt, and when he nailed down what turned out to be third place they were cheering him like a homeboy. When Earnhardt turned in a time that would start him in ninth place, although he was only two tenths of a mile per hour slower than Hamilton, they whooped sarcastically like a baseball crowd cheers a wild pitcher when he finally throws a strike. Terry Labonte and Jeff Gordon again would start side by side on the pole, as at Rockingham. The crowd had doubtlessly fancied Hamilton and Earnhardt on the pole, but at least they had been able to let the Man in Black know where they stood. It had all of the elements of Friday Nite Rasslin'. And somewhere, in the comfort of the corporate suites high above the Winston grandstand, a NASCAR mogul had to be smiling.

After all of the jangle and controversy surrounding the first two races of the season, everything turned out to be downright peaceable at Richmond. A record crowd of 88,000 was assembled in the gleaming new aluminum bleachers at RIR, in spite of the biting cold and patches of snow elsewhere in the city, and the only sniff of controversy was provided during the introduction of drivers, easing down the frontstretch on the rear seats of convertibles, when the fans were given one more chance to let Earnhardt have it. There was the usual round of welcomes and prerace awards and introductions by and for executives representing the race sponsors, GM and Pontiac; the invocation by David Smith, Earnhardt's crew chief, whose conversion from a hell-raiser to a born-again Christian had been getting much ink in the trade press; and, finally, the singing of the National Anthem by a county police officer. If there was any tension in the pits as the drivers cranked their engines and rolled away for an extraordinary five pace laps, two or three more than usual because of the cold, it was in the defending champion's stall. Gordon had finished fortieth and forty-second in the first two races, and the Rainbow Warriors had seen enough.

It took a while, but The Kid finally took the lead for good with fifty laps to go. Around and around the track they had gone, almost without incident, in a 400-lap race that would take less than three hours. In all, there were twenty-five lead changes among eleven drivers, not an uncommon number in the tight confines of a short track. Like an NBA game, where it all comes down to the last two minutes, what drama there was came toward the end. There had been only three cautions over the first two hours of the race, but when Darrell Waltrip hit the wall on lap 350 to bring out the yellow, the real race began. Gordon had led at various points for a total of seventy-four laps, and when he whipped into the pits on the caution following Waltrip's crack-up he was running fifth. But he had three things in his favor—a background in Midwestern sprint racing, the most efficient pit crew in Winston Cup racing, and the choice defending champion's pit area at the end of pit road (allowing a speedier return to the track)—and when he slithered back onto the track he was suddenly in the lead.

There would be a total of five cautions over the last fifty laps, with the usual mayhem resulting when the field bunches up during restarts, and each time Gordon was able to sprint away ahead of the rest. On the last caution, with only five laps to go, his crew chief, Ray Evernham, got on the radio like a stern big brother. "Okay, Jeff," he said, "you're the Winston Cup champion. Now sit up straight in your seat and let's win this thing." The green flag dropped and Gordon floorboarded it, bursting away once more, and even before it was officially over the Rainbow Warriors were celebrating. "I can't tell you how proud I am of you today, Jeff," Evernham radioed to Gordon. "No, no," said The Kid, "you guys did it. You guys did a great job. [This, while tooling around on the next-to-last lap at about 120 miles per hour.] The Rainbow Warriors, working together. That's what it's all about." Well, yes, indeed. When Gordon crossed the start-finish line and took the checkered flag, he shouted into his radio: "Yaa-*hoooo!*" The Kid was on the board, at last.

About the only excitement the Pontiac Excitement 400 had to offer those without a vested interest in Jeff Gordon's future came in the aftermath. Earnhardt never really got it going all day and came down with brake problems toward the end, finishing thirty-first in a field of forty; and, as usual, ducked out of the post-race interview with MRN for parts unknown. Ernie Irvan had been involved in yet another crash and didn't care to discuss it, loading up and escaping early through the tunnel. It was left to Bobby Hamilton, still smarting about the incident with Earnhardt at Rockingham, to bring life to the proceedings. He and John Andretti had begun to mix it up toward the end of the race—Hamilton had rammed Andretti to effectively put himself in sixth place and knock Andretti back to twelfth, and then on the cool-down lap following the checkered flag Andretti had gotten on Hamilton's tail and popped him twice—and Hamilton was not pleased. Having spun out at the entrance to pit road, he got out of his car and was standing there waiting for an ESPN microphone to be shoved in his face. "The first lick, I thought he was congratulating me, but then he hit me again," he said with a lopsided smile. "So I locked the brakes down and was getting out to talk to him about the weather. Hey, it turned out to be a beautiful day, didn't it? But then he took off for the garage. I don't know what his hurry was." Boys, boys, boys.

5

WIN ON SUNDAY, SELL ON MONDAY

It would appear, at first glance, that William Henry Getty France was taking on the impossible when he pondered bringing some order to the chaos that was automobile racing at the end of the Second World War. These people were, after all, about the most independent cusses in all of the United States: Southern mountaineers, for the most part, who would be damned if they would let *anybody* tell them what to do. They were still living the lives of their Scots-Irish forefathers, who had crossed a mighty ocean to get away from the Brits and then had settled into the hollows of the southern Appalachians to avoid yet another form of big government. No, they weren't the organizing types, any more than their forebears had been. Many of their kids had even refused to participate in the Civil War, on the grounds that they owned no slaves and therefore had no dog in that fight. Those who had chosen the side of the Confederacy had done so because they fancied it as another heroic rebellion against some distant ruling class. The backbone of that sprawling southeastern quadrant of the

United States, the Appalachian spine and its foothills, was reviled by most of the rest of the country. The people who lived there were regarded as "hillbillies" and "briarhoppers" and "rednecks" and "lintheads"—incorrigible yahoos who made whiskey, chewed tobacco, lived by the gun, married their cousins, ran rabbits, romanced sheep, prayed over snakes—and the objects of all this bile had responded by burrowing deeper into the mountain folds where they could live on in blissful protest of other men's laws. Such was the lineage of the men Bill France would try to organize.

But these were the sons and the grandsons of all that, a new generation of men who had been flushed out of the hills and forced to see a larger world during the war, and when they got back from Bataan and Bastogne and the steel mills of Birmingham they were a mite less intractable than before. They were still stubborn and independent, mind you, about the last body of Americans to join unions, but they could see how it might help if somebody wrote down some rules for their protection when they went out and risked their necks racing cars. It was a mishmash out there: no insurance if you got hurt or worse, dangerous little outlaw tracks with clapboard fences for retaining walls, promoters who might pay off and might not, nobody to check on the cars to make them halfway equal, nobody keeping records on how the boys were stacking up against each other, no kind of public notice except on the police blotter when a dispute at the track got settled with a tire iron upside the head. The factories across the land were turning out new automobiles now, rather than tanks and planes and ships, and it was as though the rural South had been born again. And many thousands of the younger ones, not just the old moonshine trippers, had looked around and seen that it just might be possible to earn a living from racing them against each other. If they didn't get killed first.

Bill France knew what they were thinking because he had been there himself, both before the war and immediately afterward, from his work at Daytona and his perambulations around the South as a driver and a promoter. He had become well connected by then, in the sprawling underground of mechanics and drivers and promoters and land barons itching to build a little track and become racing moguls, and so in the middle of December in 1947 he called together thirty-five of them at the Streamline Hotel in Daytona Beach; promoters, mostly, but with a smattering of men

like Red Vogt, the mechanic from Atlanta. They met for three days, in the
Ebony Bar overlooking the ocean from the roof of the hotel, at first swapping horror stories of racing widows and nonpayment of purses and
drunken racers and unbeatable moonshine tripper cars, then hunkering
down to decide how to make sure those things never happened again.
Slowly, a charter began to evolve. They laid down rules that would bring
some parity to the cars, set up a points system that would declare a
national champion, arranged insurance programs for drivers and guaran-
tees that they would win the purses they were promised, tossed in a
few rudimentary safety regulations requiring helmets and seat belts and
reinforced wheels; and, even then, they talked about the image of the
sport. "I brought it up at the first meeting," France would say years later.
"I felt if you were racing a junky-looking automobile, even if it had started
out as a new Cadillac and you pulled the fenders off and let it get real dirty,
then it would be a jalopy in most people's minds." It was Red Vogt, of all
people, he with one foot in the world of moonshine whiskey, who came up
with the name for the group: the National Association for Stock Car Auto
Racing. They got a straitlaced racing champion named Cannonball Baker
to be their "racing commissioner," overseeing the technical business. They
formally incorporated two months later, in February of '48, and named Bill
France as president. Their mailing address was France's service station and
garage on Main Street in Daytona Beach.

The founding of NASCAR was the first major milepost on a journey
toward respectability and acceptance by the general public that would still
be a work in progress fifty years later. In fact, that was the primary message
delivered in the wake of the very first event sponsored by this new govern-
ing body: a 200-lap race over a three-quarter-mile dirt track at Charlotte, in
June of 1949. The founders had organized NASCAR racing into three
divisions—Strictly Stock, Modified Stock, and Roadsters—and this race at
Charlotte was for Strictly Stock, months later to be renamed Grand National, which in turn would evolve into Winston Cup. This was to be the
showcase division, for boxy American cars no more than three years off the
showroom floor, very little tinkering allowed beyond the reinforcement of

right front hubs to keep lug nuts from popping off in the turns. Nine different makes were represented among the thirty-three cars entered in the race (led by ten Fords, the old standby of the trippers), and the Georgia gang of bootleggers was well represented when the green flag dropped. The thinking, even then, was that fans should be able to relate to the cars they saw on the track; to want to root for the car make as much as for the driver.

What happened was instructive. First across the start-finish line was a North Carolina bootlegger named Glen Dunnaway, in a '47 Ford, but when Cannonball Baker's inspectors broke down the car afterward they found that a wedge had been placed in the rear springs to keep the car from swaying in the turns. It was an old bootlegger's trick; and it was learned that the car, indeed, had been used for hauling whiskey earlier in the week. NASCAR couldn't have that, of course, so they disqualified Dunnaway and gave the $2,000 first-place purse to a driver from Kansas, of all places, named Jim Roper, who had steered a '49 Lincoln. (Second, third, and fifth places had gone to the Georgians Fonty Flock, Red Byron, and Tim Flock, who, in commiseration with their maligned fellow bootlegger, shared their purses with Dunnaway.) The owner of the Dunnaway car sued, forcing the issue into an open court, which was the moment NASCAR had been waiting for. In his arguments, the lawyer for NASCAR spat out the word "bootlegger" over and over, the epithet ringing through the courtroom, effectively making the point that there would be no place in this new scheme of stock car racing for such riffraff. NASCAR won the case and, it hoped, a lot more. Notice had been served that theirs was a classy operation, and maybe this would be the beginning of the end for the moonshine trippers.

Lots of luck. Even when the automakers got involved in NASCAR racing, not long after that first race at Charlotte, technology developed by moonshine mechanics stayed ahead of the refinements discovered by formally educated white-jacketed engineers in Detroit's racing factories. The trippers had a leg up on the engineers in finding ways to make an automobile go faster: boosting horsepower, distributing weight, adjusting suspensions to withstand torque at high speeds, experimenting with tires that would stand up on long runs. Hell, they had to; it was either that, or go to jail. The most famous of all the trippers who became stock car legends, Junior Johnson, still swore, after a forty-year career as a champion NASCAR driver and an owner, that he "never saw a better race car than what we built for haulin' whiskey." Junior had also said, while he was still driving, "I always think someday I'm gonna look in my mirror on the racetrack and see a flashing blue light." Junior was arrested for hanging around his father's still in 1955, a full six years after NASCAR's courtroom pronouncements about cleaning up things by running off the bootleggers, and as late as 1971 a NASCAR driver was caught for running moonshine between race dates. Even now, in the glitzy world of Winston Cup racing at the end of the twentieth century, a season never passed without one of those uniformed mechanics, born-again Christian or otherwise, being nailed at the on-track NASCAR inspection stall for trying to slip past with a "refinement" that would make a tripper smile: a wedge in the coils that would fall away during the race to drop the nose and the rear of the car, a slightly larger hub for the right front wheel to make it corner easier, a block of heavy cadmium to add weight to the driver's side, a phantom pipe that might hold an extra dollop of gas. It had always been "us" against "them." Only the "them" had changed.

The fifties would become known as the glorious age of the automobile in America. There was the grim "police action" in Korea, of course, but the country was basically at peace and the mills were able to begin producing steel for automobiles and for buttressing the bridges and roadways for President Dwight Eisenhower's new interstate highway system that would carry them. The automakers in Detroit couldn't build passenger cars fast enough for an American public that suddenly had disposable income on its hands. "I Like Ike"? They loved him, this grandfatherly retired war general, for it was on his watch that they were slipping behind the wheel of big plush touring machines so they could get out there and See America First. It was a sellers' market. The waiting lists were long at car dealerships all over the nation, at least six weeks in many towns and cities, and it was considered grand entertainment for whole families to traipse downtown on an appointed autumn evening for the dramatic unveiling of the "brand-new 1951 Dodge Coronet," rotating on a pedestal beneath gleaming lights at the showroom of, say, Liberty Motors in Birmingham, Alabama. Those old prewar Fords and Plymouths and Chevrolets had been nursed along for nearly a decade, hard times made harder by shortages of rubber and fuel, but now they were being traded in for a new generation of winged machines with real chrome and white-walled tires and wraparound windshields and snout noses and rear fins that bordered on the sensual. What'll it be: sedan, hardtop, or convertible? two-door or four? whitewalls, or those old tacky black ones? radio? automatic transmission? felt seats, or vinyl? want that beauty painted two-tone, or plain? We'll let you know when they call and say it's going through the line up at *Dee*-troit. Lord, Lord; every man a king!

And nobody was more swept up in all of this than the Southerner, who was, as ever, the last American to share in the nation's bounty. For reasons that were more practical than aesthetic, he had appreciated the gas-propelled vehicle more than anyone else in the country. People in the cities of the North and the East could get by without wheels, being concentrated in urban settings where there was most likely to be public transportation; but, except for a handful of cities like Atlanta and New Orleans with their trolleys (streetcars), the South even after the war was still a land of farms and small towns scattered out there in the boonies miles apart. Entire generations of Southerners had spent their lives in the same crossroads farm village or county—the big day of the week being Saturday when they would hitch the mule to a wagon and go into town to buy supplies and maybe see a "picture show"—but now they were being liberated first by the coming of the tractor and the harrow and other farm machinery and then by the truck and the automobile. And, given their relative poverty and an innate pride in taking care of their hard-earned possessions, they learned how to do the repairs themselves.

So NASCAR and Detroit found themselves running on parallel tracks; the one in the business of racing cars, the other in making and selling them. They had begun dating, as it were, as early as 1949, the year of that first NASCAR-sanctioned race in Charlotte, when Oldsmobile stuffed its biggest engine into its smallest chassis to create a car especially made for racing. Ford responded by jumping in the next year to win the inaugural race at Darlington International Raceway in South Carolina, NASCAR's first paved superspeedway; Chrysler came aboard the next year with a powerful V-8 engine; and in '53, Hudson introduced something called a 7X dual-carburetor engine at the express request of NASCAR drivers. The car wars were on, then, creating a marriage between NASCAR and the automakers. (There would be tire wars, as well, involving Goodyear and Firestone and, for a short while, Hoosiers.) Bill France hardly needed to pick up the phone to get the carmakers' attention; being in fierce competition with each other, they didn't need anyone to point out the commercial value of having their products win on France's racetracks. It would be a fitful relationship at the beginning—they all backed off for a period in the late fifties and early sixties in a self-imposed ban designed to save themselves from an enormously expensive endeavor—but they always came back, to one extent or another, and they were still a presence in this Winston Cup season of 1996. They had always liked to bleat about how they were giving the average American car buyer a better and safer product through their experiments with race cars, and there was ample truth in that. Over the years, Detroit's engineers would blaze the trail in all areas of automobile refinements they had developed while trying to build better race cars: horsepower, durability, stability, handling, braking, safety, reinforced bodies. These refinements would be passed on, whenever it was deemed economically feasible, to the cars they put on sale to the general public. But the bottom-line reason they devoted all of that time and money to building a better race car was expressed in a simple pragmatic motto that still propelled Winston Cup racing at the end of the century: "Win on Sunday, Sell on Monday."

The only driver to be killed during a Winston Cup race in the nineties was a struggling independent named J. D. McDuffie, who was driving with hand-me-down parts and tires when he blew a tire and lost his brakes at the road course in Watkins Glen, New York, in 1991. The old-timers found it amazing that this latest generation of cars could turn 240 miles per hour if anyone dared try it; for it seemed to them like it was only yesterday that hot-to-trot kids were rolling in off the street and announcing they were ready to race. That's about the way it was in the beginning, according to one of the originals, a storied mechanic from Daytona Beach named Smokey Yunick, in an interview some years ago with Dr. John Craft for his *The Anatomy and Development of the Stock Car*, the one book every Motorhead ought to own: "A lot of guys drove their race cars to the race and then took the back-up plates and the headlights off, took the windshield wiper arm off, wound both windows down on the left side, took a strap and wrapped it around the roll bar, which was supposed to be one of the few add-on parts in it. In some cases, the roll bar was two-by-fours nailed together right at the racetrack. You couldn't run without some kind of a roll bar, so some guys would get the two-by-fours and cut them off and nail them together inside the car. We would get some wire or cable or something, and wrap it around them. Lots of cars ran with the license plate on them. We weren't allowed to take any upholstery out. In the beginning, if you had a full front seat, you weren't even allowed to take that other front seatback out."

They were unsafe at any speed, even on the short dirt tracks that dominated the scene during the fifties, and no one knows precisely how many men were killed during races in those perilous early days. (Some estimates put the death toll as high as 1,000 in stock car racing of all types, during races and practice and testing, in the half-century since '47.) Stock cars right off the production line simply weren't built to go tearing around racetracks without severe modifications, especially in regards to tires, and yet that is what was called for in Bill France's original plans for the Strictly Stock division. NASCAR's Official 1950 Grand National Rule Book, in fact, was a terse one-page affair listing thirty-one items. It called for "1946 through 1950 models of American made passenger cars only," which had to have "complete bodies, hood, fenders, bumpers and grilles." The word "stock" meant "any part which is listed in the manufacturer's catalog for the year, model and type car entered." The last item read, "It is recommended that wheels, hubs, steering parts, radius rods and sway bars be reinforced and strengthened in any manner." There was no mention of safety belts or roll bars; the only safety requirements being that doors had to be strapped shut, mufflers removed, headlights and chrome and other potential flying parts "protected by masking tape." For the most part, the rules were wide open to interpretation—made to be broken—which is what the mechanics like Smokey Yunick, who had learned about engines while working on bombers with the Army Air Corps, proceeded to do forthwith. The cars would never be truly stock again.

Handed such a vague set of rules, the mechanics began pushing the outer limits of creative engineering and became stars in their own rights. The drivers were always the main feature, then as well as now, but all knowledgeable fans began to know and applaud the work of a group of independent mechanics: Ray Fox of Junior Johnson's team in Ronda, North Carolina; the Wood Brothers of Virginia; the renegades like Banjo Matthews and Cotton Owens and Smokey Yunick; John Holman and Ralph Moody of Holman-Moody in Charlotte. The mechanics' thinking was that if a certain refinement wasn't specifically against the rules, that must mean it was all right or at least worth a try. Yunick, working out of his garage in Daytona Beach ("The Best Damn Garage in Town" read the hand-painted legend on cars he had worked on), was the most creative of them all, and every time one of his cars rolled into the NASCAR inspection station at a track, the inspectors went on alert and pored over it like customs agents searching for drugs. Once, they had gone so far as to drain the gas tank to see if he had somehow managed to expand the capacity beyond the legal limit. Finding nothing wrong there, they nevertheless advised him that he had violated a dozen rules. Smokey then calmly cranked the engine and said, "Make it thirteen," as he drove away.

When the first big paved superspeedway was introduced at Darlington, in 1950, quickly followed by four more in that decade and another four in the sixties, it presented a new horizon and an entirely different set of problems for everyone involved. These tracks were bigger and faster and, most problematical, paved with asphalt. There was never any doubt that the mechanics could make a car go fast—some of those with moonshine backgrounds had built tripper cars capable of running 140 miles per hour back in the thirties and forties, to hear them tell it—but now the cars had to do it in malevolent traffic, on tire-eating pavement, through chassis-wrenching banked turns, for as long as five hours without rest. "When they first brought the cars to the first race [at Darlington], there was six hundred and eighty tires blowed that day," Yunick told Craft. "Everywhere you looked, there were tires all over the race track. It got to the point where they couldn't stop the race often enough to move the caps." Those big old bullet-shaped 3,600-pound '51 Hudson Hornets looked like a million dollars in a showroom, slowly revolving on a turntable under benevolent lights, but they were nowhere near ready for racing; as any father with a gum-snapping son begging to take the new family car out for "just a little spin" could attest. They were built for driving to work or cruising down a highway, not for running flat out through violent turns on a high-banked asphalt racetrack. There was nothing about them that could withstand the punishment, neither tires nor chassis nor cooling system nor brakes, and to go racing in them without severe modification was tantamount to suicide.

The evolution of the race car from those hot little '39 Ford tripper coupes to the sleek racing machines of the nineties was a painful step-by-step process; expensive, fraught with death, learned by the seat of the pants. Formal extensive tire tests weren't held until Goodyear latched on to the idea in 1958. The drivers themselves rankled that shoulder harnesses were too confining and pointed out with horror the death of a driver at the Atlanta speedway, around 1960, caused when he couldn't duck and was virtually decapitated. It took the death of the dashing star Fireball Roberts (an eerily appropriate nickname from his baseball-pitching days), burned to a crisp when his gas tank exploded in a wreck at Charlotte in '64, to bring about the virtually leak-proof fuel cell; and that took three years of development before it became standard equipment. Tubular steel roll cages and mesh window nets and formfitting cockpit seats, all designed to encase the driver in a near fail-safe cocoon even if he became airborne, didn't become standard until 1970. Bill France had backed off from his fanciful dream of ordinary production-line cars spinning around a track early on, given the dire results, and year by year the NASCAR rule book grew longer and more complicated. What he had really meant, he grudgingly conceded, was that there should be at least an *illusion* of a real American automobile out there on the track in order to fulfill his original intention: a car that a red-blooded American could sink his teeth into. By the end of the sixties, when stock car racing was on the verge of entering its modern era and reaching out for fans beyond the South, NASCAR was beginning to emphasize the word "parity" in its pronouncements. "We just want it to be a safe, even race, so nobody gets hurt and the fan knows that his favorite driver can win any race on any given day," France said. It was a noble proposition, even though he knew as well as anyone that some drivers and some mechanics would always find a way to excel; rules, or no rules.

Those "good old days" referred to by the fans in their letters to *Winston Cup Scene* in the aftermath of Earnhardt's run-in with Hamilton at Rockingham meant the late fifties and early sixties; and the implications extended beyond mere events on the racetrack. For better and for worse, for reasons not entirely admirable, that would turn out to be the most vivid era in the history of stock car racing; one that NASCAR, in its later strivings for respectability, would simply have to live with. Until then, the blue-collar white South had been able to function almost as a sovereign nation, virtually unaffected by the social upheavals occurring in the rest of the country. Its boilerplate, its underpinning, its infrastructure, was the segregation of the races; the South being protected, up until that point, by the clever shenanigans of such powerful tenured legislators as Senator Strom Thurmond of South Carolina. But now, with the passage of President Lyndon Johnson's Civil Rights Act, the legislation that would empower his Great Society (a *Texan?* a so-called *Southerner?* a damned *turncoat!*), the heat was on for the white Southerner to change his ways or else. Bubba was being told to clean up his act, put away his Confederate flag, stop insulting his black brothers with the singing of "Dixie," come on and join the nation before the troops got sent in. To help him along, to show him the way to truth and light, he was already seeing his turf invaded by phalanxes of lawyers and clergymen and social workers and college students from up East (Catholics, Jews, hippies, a bunch of damned *liberals!*). It was the Civil War all over again, a full century later.

And so Bubba closed ranks and went racing. Those stock car tracks scattered throughout his domain, in little pockets of the Appalachian piedmont like Darlington and Rockingham and North Wilkesboro and Martinsville, became his camp meeting grounds. For it was there, amid trappings he could understand, that he could loudly celebrate his way of life without any meddling from outsiders; from "them." He could tolerate the only black driver who dared show up, ol' Wendell Scott (hey, he'd been a bootlegger, hadn't he?), as long as he stayed humble and didn't win; just as Nashville could abide its token black, "Country Charley" Pride, who could sing "Kaw-Liga" better than Hank Williams himself. There, at the track, he had the numbers on his side. So after work on Fridays he loaded the pickup or, better yet, a car much like the one his hero drove, with everything he would need—beer, pork ribs, cigarettes, blankets, the little woman—and headed off to the track for a weekend of howling. In a later time he would be called "politically incorrect," but he didn't much give a damn about what anybody said. He thrived on calling himself a redneck, in fact, before somebody else did; and as the beer flowed and the ribs sizzled and the Confederate flags ripped in the breeze of the infield campground, the sons of the South fired up their Fords and Chevys and Plymouths for an afternoon of banging around the track in a maddening, ear-piercing, thunderous affirmation of life as Bubba understood it.

The glory of it all! There was nothing abstract or foreign about any of it: not Linda Vaughn's blossomy breasts as Miss Firebird proudly flounced around the pits in her halter and short-shorts and stiletto heels; not Banjo Matthews's laconic explanations of how he had found a way to "get a few more horses" out of his 427-cubic-inch Impala; not George Wallace's snarling prerace descriptions of "pointy-headed Harvard intellectuals that cain't park their bicycles straight"; not the words to "Dixie" as it was played over the loudspeakers; certainly not that first mighty blast as three dozen unmuffled engines started up at once without anybody needing to say anything. He and most every other old boy there knew all there was to know about machinery of various ilk, they holding down jobs as mechanics or heating-and-air-conditioning repairmen or truck drivers, and they would just as avidly haul ass down to Cape Kennedy in the late sixties to camp out in the Florida swamps for a close personal look at the first attempts to put men on the moon; on the grounds that they knew a thing or two and even had a vested interest in the stuff it took to get those mothers off the ground.

It was an incestuous closed society, white and rural and Southern to the core, and the heroes were mirror images of the fans. In those days long before the arrival of public relations gurus and elocution tutors and various other spin doctors, each driver seemed to be a tour de force on wheels; a visitor from another planet, an original untouched by modern civilization, some exotic creature out of a Southern gothic novel. Here and there you might find a law-abiding clean-living Christian who could talk in cogent paragraphs, but they were greatly outnumbered by an arrant semi-literate crowd of hell-raising drinkers and womanizers and eye-gougers and alimony-jumpers and bootleggers or sons of bootleggers. They went by names like Junior, Buck, Fireball, Little Joe, Pops, Tiny, and Lee Roy. They came from the obscure little villages and black-dot towns hidden in the forests and hollows of the Carolinas and Virginia: Timmonsville, Easley, Ronda, Wilson, Level Cross, Mount Airy, Ninety Six, Christiansburg. Except at the Daytona 500 on the big new superspeedway, the crowds seldom exceeded 10,000, and even the Southern newspapers paid them scant attention, but the drivers and mechanics didn't much concern themselves with that. It beat working for a living, they would joke, these country boys who had dropped out of high school because it was boring or they needed to help out on the farm. They were perturbed, naturally, when they were sniffily refused accommodations at the Holiday Inn in Atlanta, that tight-assed image-conscious capital of the New South where a modern super-speedway had gone up in the forests far south of the city, in 1960, but they learned to swallow their pride long enough to park their race cars and trailers around the corner and put on a clean shirt and slick their hair down and stroll into the lobby like any other regular American, just passing through, in town on business.

None was as outrageous as Curtis Turner. He had come out of the ragged hills of southwestern Virginia, son of a moonshine whiskey baron in an area rich only in coal and timber, and learned to drive by hauling whiskey as a teenager. A large, garrulous man nicknamed "Pops" because of the way he popped cars out of his way en route to the checkered flag, Turner was bigger than life: a winning driver from the early dirt-track days and on into the superspeedway era, a hell-raising womanizer with a penchant for Stetson hats and silk suits and what he called "doll babies" and bourbon-and-Coke and airplanes and Lincoln Continentals. With money he had made from moonshine as a kid, he made and lost millions of dollars more than once by dealing in timberland in the South and South

America; and it was his money that launched the construction of Charlotte Motor Speedway. A body of stories grew up around him that one might take or leave, but never forget: of his all-night parties before races, of his derring-do on the track, especially of his exploits in the air. Once, on a dare, he had set his plane down on the backstretch at Darlington, but that was nothing. The story told the most often was about the day when he and a pal were flying from Atlanta to Charlotte when they realized it was Sunday and they didn't have any whiskey. The fellow said he had a couple of bottles at his house, in Easley, South Carolina, so Pops landed the plane on the road while his buddy went to fetch the whiskey. Airborne again, Pops saw a traffic light and a maze of power lines looming ahead, so he pulled up his wheels and flew *under* everything; or so he thought, clipping some lines and knocking out phone service in Easley for the rest of what should have been a calm Sabbath. When he died from crashing his plane into a Pennsylvania mountain in 1970, at the age of forty-six, they threw away the mold.

During the mid-fifties, when stock car racing was going through the awkward throes of its adolescence, there occurred an odd interlude that would be a harbinger of the well-financed multi-car team operations of the nineties. A stumpy cigar-smoking millionaire from Wisconsin by the name of Carl Kiekhaefer, owner of the outboard motor manufacturer Mercury Marine, had discerned from market research that the fans who followed NASCAR also had the wherewithal and the inclination to sport about in motorboats. His idea was to field a competitive team of race cars, emblazoned with the Mercury Outboards logo, and sell his motors through these rolling billboards. So he rented a Pure Oil station in Daytona Beach and set it up as the shop for Team Mercury Marine, ordered a half-dozen spanking-new two-door Chrysler New Yorkers, hired a corps of the best mechanics and drivers he could lure, and announced that his Great White Fleet would be entering the Grand National campaign of 1955 on a grand scale.

Kiekhaefer was a methodical, hard-driving Teutonic sort, a Groucho Marx look-alike who was born to command. His mechanics set about to converting the identical white Chryslers into powerful racing machines that NASCAR had never seen before: big mamas with 355-horsepower V-8 engines and heavy-duty three-speed manual transmissions and reinforced undergirdings for speed and handling on the corners of what remained mostly dirt tracks. He was the first to buy enclosed car-haulers to transport his machines to the races; the first to establish a large orderly shop with production-line capabilities; the first to outfit his mechanics and drivers in identical (white) team uniforms; the first to consult meteorologists about the race day weather prospects; the first to analyze track surfaces in order to maximize setups for the race cars; the first to rent out entire hotels for his "superteam" and its entourage on racing weekends; the first, and the only, owner to turn over the entire winning purses to his drivers. The downside of all this was sometimes hard for the drivers to swallow—at dawn on race days he had someone blow a bugle to awaken the troops, and he segregated the sexes, even the husbands and wives—but he was putting together the makings of a dynasty and they could certainly live with that.

It goes without saying that Team Mercury Marine was virtually unbeatable for two straight years. With drivers like Buck Baker and Speedy Thompson and all three of the Flock boys, they won forty-nine of the 101 races during the 1955 and '56 seasons; in one stretch taking sixteen in a row. Tim Flock reported that he pocketed $55,000 in that first year with Kiekhaefer, setting a single-season record of eighteen victories that would stand until Richard Petty broke it a dozen years later. Flock quickly added that he also saw his health break under the strict regimentation of racing and making personal appearances at certain of Kiekhaefer's 2,700 Mercury retail outlets across the country.

But then, to no one's surprise, the scheme backfired. What was happening to the invincible New York Yankees of that era began to visit Team Mercury Marine. Bored fans were beginning to boo the Great White Fleet's cars and stars as they were introduced at the tracks, and attendance began to flag. Greatly disturbed by all of this, Bill France started siccing his own teams of rabid NASCAR mechanics on the Kiekhaefer cars in meticulous post-race inspections, tearing down the engines in hopes of finding something—anything—that was against the rules; but not once did the cars fail to pass. Ironically, Kiekhaefer's meteoric appearance on the scene ended the way it had begun. The sales of Mercury outboard motors had risen dramatically during the Great White Fleet's first year, but fell just as abruptly during the second season. When he realized that he was making more enemies than friends with his success on the racetracks, Carl Kiekhaefer summarily shut down his operation. But his grand experiment had left the stock car racing community with two truths to ponder: first, for future car owners, that a well-organized multi-car operation was the way to go; second, to Bill France and NASCAR, that parity was an absolute imperative.

It took a "Yankee," if that word could be applied to someone from Elmhurst, Illinois, near Chicago, to propel NASCAR into what could be called its modern era. His name was Fred Lorenzen, movie-star handsome and articulate, the square-jawed blond son of a carpenter, a champion of the paved tracks in the Midwest when he decided to try Grand National racing in the South during the early sixties. The automobile factories had gotten back into racing at full tilt by then after a self-imposed hiatus, having determined that the exposure was well worth the time and money spent in developing better race cars, and in Lorenzen they found a gold mine. Few of those Southerners had the sort of persona that the PR people in Detroit wanted as their public face—the drinking, the brawling, the drawling half-educated grunts—but Lorenzen was a dream: a wonderfully smooth driver who took care of his equipment, went to bed early the night before a race, acted the gentleman that he was, and won more often than not. It was the dashing and dependable "Fast Freddy" Lorenzen, driving for Ford Motor Company, who brought to fruition the motto "Win on Sunday, Sell on Monday." Sales of Ford cars skyrocketed during Lorenzen's reign in the late sixties and led directly to the next milepost in the growth of NASCAR: the big-bucks sponsorship of race teams and drivers that, in this season of 1996, kept the whole enterprise going.

Until Lorenzen came along, sponsorship was a sometimes thing. The cars might be decorated on the sides with hand-lettering or stencils proclaiming Ford or Chevrolet, as part of the deal with the factories, but beyond that it was small-time stuff: little decals stuck here and there, on the fenders or the rear side windows, for companies that had supplied the batteries or oil or tires or spark plugs. In many cases, the deals would be local one-time arrangements; a service station in Martinsville, Virginia, say, was interested in paying for space on a car's body only during the race in Martinsville. That changed, though, when the marketing people at STP gasoline treatment approached Richard Petty before the race at the road course in Riverside, California, with a proposition. Petty, not quite thirty-five at the time, had already won three Grand National championships and was clearly the cream of the NASCAR crop. He wasn't as slick as Fred Lorenzen, who by then had abruptly quit and gone back home with ulcers and a pile of money, but this son of Lee Petty, a crusty old dirt-track driver from crossroads North Carolina, oozed with rustic charm and was on his way to becoming The King on the track. Petty and STP shook hands, a big oval red-and-blue STP logo went onto the hood of his car, and it was the beginning of the most enduring sponsorship in the history of NASCAR.

It was around the same time that the biggest step of them all occurred, without a whole lot of fanfare. The American tobacco companies had acquiesced under pressure from the federal government and agreed, under much pressure, to stop advertising their cigarettes on radio and television, effective in January of 1972. One of the giants was R.J. Reynolds Tobacco, headquartered in Winston-Salem, North Carolina, smack in the middle of tobacco and NASCAR country. RJR had dabbled in limited race sponsorships, but all of that changed on a November day in '69 when Junior Johnson drove over to Winston-Salem from his farm an hour or so west, hat in hand, to ask if RJR might sponsor his car in the upcoming season. In those days, a year's sponsorship cost little more than $100,000; Junior, by then a car owner, had lost his sponsor, an auto parts dealer from Detroit, when the man died in a plane crash. RJR said no, they were looking for something bigger to make up for the impending loss of advertising; well, hell, said Junior, why don't you just sponsor the whole show then? It seemed a natural fit for RJR—good old boys and racing and cigarettes were as natural a mix as Brits and cricket and tea—so they got in touch with Bill France to begin the mating dance. Beginning with the Daytona 500 of 1971, NASCAR's Grand National division became the Winston Cup circuit.

■ ■ ■

All through the fifties and the sixties, at the insistence of Bill France, the original dirt tracks were either dropped from the NASCAR circuit or paved; with RJR kicking in a little money for improvements in roads, grandstands, infield amenities, and press facilities. France built himself a second track in 1969, Talladega Speedway in the low hills of eastern Alabama—a course so fast that soon the auto racing fraternity, much like the days when Air Force test pilots were straining to break the sound barrier, was making bets on who would be first to break 200 miles per hour in a stock car—and now the Southernization of America was underway with Winston Cup taking its show outside of the South, to big tracks in places like Michigan, Pennsylvania, California, Delaware, and New Hampshire. Now there were crowds of more than 100,000 at tracks other than Daytona, with winning purses in the mid–five figures, drivers who could say they had won more than $1 million in racing, and sponsors representing products other than those related to the auto industry. Nationally televised Winston Cup races, the final milestone in NASCAR's long climb toward acceptance, seemed to be just around the corner.

Like God surveying the world he had wrought, seeing that it was good and choosing to rest on the seventh day, William Henry Getty France picked this juncture to pass the leadership of NASCAR to his eldest son, William C. France (known by all, for the sake of convenience, as "Bill, Jr."). The old man felt he had taken it far enough, that it was time to pass the baton, and the change became effective in January of 1972, on the eve of RJR's second season of sponsorship. "He and Bill, Jr. were the toughest czars there ever were, but in different ways," said Clyde Bolton of the *Birmingham News*. "When the old man started NASCAR, racing was the lowest of the low, had a terrible reputation, but he had a vision. Unlike baseball, which was more established, racing would have been killed by a strike [the two times one was threatened] and France, Sr. knew that. His son is just as tough, but in a different way: dealing with corporations, sponsors, television, sales, the big new tracks. I have the greatest respect for both of them, each in his own way." The elder France kept his hand in, overseeing his dream tracks at Daytona and Talladega, until his health began to fail around 1990. "He called me one day and said he wanted me to do his biography. 'We'll go out on my boat for a couple of days and you'll have enough for *two* books,' he said. So I drove over to Talladega one day and they had me wait a few minutes, and I went into his office, and pretty soon I saw he didn't know who the hell I was. He must have asked me seven times if I wanted a glass for my beer. It turned out he had Alzheimer's. I went home and cried, literally cried." France died in '92, at the age of eighty-three.

There had been some television over the years—with NASCAR under the aegis of Bill France, Sr.—usually only tape-delayed highlights or severely edited versions (read: spectacular crashes) for weekend sports shows, but under Bill, Jr., Winston Cup racing would enter the television age. In 1976, one of the major networks televised the Daytona 500 live. That was the race with the most astonishing finish in the history of NASCAR. David Pearson led Richard Petty by one car length when they got the white flag signaling one lap to go, but they were side by side when they reached turns three and four: Pearson high, Petty trying to take him low. It looked as though Petty was on his way to victory, when suddenly, he began to shimmy as he came out of the fourth turn, hit the tunnel bump, and touched with Pearson at 180 miles per hour. Both cars caromed off of the outside wall and headed out of control for parts unknown. Petty was sent skidding onto the infield grass, the hood and right side of his blue number 43 STP Dodge a crumpled mess, but Pearson managed to save his battered number 21 Mercury and stay on the track. While Petty sat in the grass, futilely trying to restart his engine and screaming for a push from his men in the pits, Pearson managed to amble across the start-finish line at about twenty miles per hour to take the checkered flag. The drivers forgot it immediately—it was "just racin' "—but the fans did not.

Three years later, with fond memories of that dramatic finish, an audience of nearly 30 million tuned in for the '79 Daytona 500, the first flag-to-flag network television coverage of a NASCAR race; and, hard to believe, this one managed to top the '76 race. Again, it had come down to the last lap. Donnie Allison of Hueytown, Alabama, had a slight lead over Cale Yarborough of Timmonsville, South Carolina, as they went flying into the third turn. When Yarborough attempted to pass Allison on the low side and Allison tried to drop down and close him off, they began to bang away at each other, neither giving an inch, and the inevitable happened. Both spun out and went into the wall between turns three and four, immobilized and out of the race, leaving the door open for a startled Richard Petty to clear the opening and take the checkered flag. But the cameras didn't stay on Petty for long, because Allison and Yarborough had crawled out of their cars and were having words right there on the high-banked track. Finishing his race but now roaring back around the track, Donnie's brother Bobby stopped his car where now helmets were off and fists were flying, and jumped into the fray himself in defense of his brother. Had the circumstances been different, Bill France and his image police might have delivered stern fines and admonishments. But they knew that America had just seen a show. Millions of people out there across the land had just seen a real fight, live, right there on the television set in their dens. *Damn! You see that? Who the hell* are *these people?* For better or for worse, that was the precise moment when stock car racing entered the mainstream of American sports.

6

REDNECKS NEED NOT APPLY

But for its sense of propriety, expressed in 1886 by *Atlanta Consti-tution* publisher Henry Grady when he coined the term "the New South," the city of Atlanta could have become the spiritual and operational home of two uniquely Southern pursuits that evolved into giant industries to-ward the end of the twentieth century: country music and stock car racing. Atlanta had a head start on the two cities that opted to become headquar-ters for those endeavors, Nashville in country music and Charlotte in stock car racing, but flatly chose not to participate. The city that Union General William Tecumseh Sherman had practically burned to the ground in the anticlimax of the Civil War, effectively dispersing the Confederacy to the winds, had been desperately seeking affirmation by the more advanced and sophisticated East ever since its rebirth from the ashes. A long succession of mayors and millionaire businessmen and sundry other tub-thumpers had devoted their lives to competing not with the Birminghams and the Chattanoogas but with the New Yorks and Philadelphias. They were white-shirted blueblood captains of commerce, not men with necks reddened from working in the sun, and they dreamed of the day their city would become known as the New York of the South. The last thing they wanted was to have a bunch of peckerwoods like hillbilly singers and race car drivers hanging out on street corners, giving the place a bad name.

It's an oft-told story about how an announcer by the name of George Hay took the microphone at radio station WSM in Nashville one Saturday night in October of 1925, following the weekly syndicated program of music "largely taken from grand opera," and puckishly announced that now his listeners would be treated with some "grand ol' *op-ree.*" Hay had grown up on the music and felt, as he wrote in his memoirs, that it "expressed the heartbeat of a large percentage of Americans who labor for a living." A mountain fiddler started sawing away that night, live from the studio, and thus was born the Grand Ole Opry and everything that followed to make Nashville "Music City USA," the bosom of a zillion-dollar industry. A few years earlier, though, there had been Atlanta's WSB, another of the handful of powerful 50,000-watt clear-channel radio stations pulsating across the South. WSB also produced a weekly show of live country music, but instead of having a George Hay to nurture it they dumped the assignment on a couple of persnickety college graduates who saw the great Fiddlin' John Carson not as a folk artist but an unlettered hillbilly. One of those announcers, in *his* memoirs, gave WSB credit, "if such it may be called," for introducing such dastardly works to the Atlanta public. Fiddlin' John, he wrote, was an "itinerant musician who enjoyed a reputation of sorts" but was also "a man of somewhat unstable habits" who liked to guzzle "corn squeezings." Atlanta was too busy putting up buildings and attracting investors from the North and East to be bothered with such trash.

The story was basically the same when it came to Atlanta's view of automobile racing. Lakewood Speedway, not far south of downtown, was already a major destination for race car drivers when young Bill France stumbled onto the scene at Daytona Beach in the mid-thirties, when the best and brightest spent their weekdays hauling moonshine and their weekends racing. Atlanta's administrators did more than just look down their blue noses at the proceedings at Lakewood; they determined that such caterwauling represented a blight on their fair city and went after it tooth-and-nail. (For what it's worth, the young police lieutenant who ordered the motorcycle cops to chase Bob Flock around the track that Sunday at Lakewood, Herbert Jenkins, grew up to become the Atlanta police chief who calmly kept the rabble-rousers like Lester Maddox at bay throughout the racial turmoil of the sixties.) But Charlotte, on the other hand, was an overgrown country town in those days, less interested in its skyline than was Atlanta, and a lot more forgiving of the working class and its entertainments. There were thousands more Lloyd Seays in North Carolina than in the Georgia mountains, anyway, and when Atlanta succeeded in closing down Lakewood the action quickly shifted to the Carolinas and, ultimately, the hub city of Charlotte. By the nineties, when six Winston Cup races were being held each season in North Carolina and nearly all of the teams were clustered around Charlotte, the state of Georgia had no more than a half-dozen sanctioned stock car tracks, most of them dirt, and the only native son among the forty-odd drivers was Dawsonville's Bill Elliott. Now the only Georgia stop on the Winston Cup tour was Atlanta Motor Speedway, and it was still a work in progress.

Easily the largest city on the tour, the Atlanta of the nineties still looked with some disfavor toward the racing crowd. The March and November races at AMS, plopped down in the low rolling forests thirty miles south of the city's gleaming new skyscrapers—so distant that the Atlanta newspapers used the dateline "Hampton, Ga.," on their dispatches from the track —were far down on the list of hot tickets for Atlanta sports fans. They had given their hearts to the Braves, who had finally won a World Series, in 1995, and had become major-league baseball's "Team of the Nineties." Even the perennially woeful Falcons of the National Football League and the Hawks of the National Basketball Association were held in higher esteem than the Winston Cup shows; and now, with the Braves in spring training and the Hawks playing out the string and the National Collegiate Athletic Association's East Regional basketball tournament on its way to town, the Purolator 500, Winston Cup's fourth race of the season, was being overshadowed by the countdown for the upcoming Summer Olympics. Maybe "disinterest" would be a better word than "disfavor" to describe mainstream Atlanta's attitude toward racing; no longer did the motels blatantly deny room at the inn for racing teams, as some had done in the sixties, but they were much more interested in hosting expense-account conventioneers than feverish Dale Earnhardt fans wanting to triple up in their rooms and raise hell for a weekend.

There were some good reasons to look with some disdain at the speedway, for it had gone through some shabby times. It was born in 1960 as Atlanta International Raceway, a specious name for a place that was, depending on the weather, a dust bowl or a pig wallow. The builders were real-estate speculators from Alabama, not racing people, and it showed. They had guessed wrong on the sight lines, forcing fans in the front rows to stand or relocate in order to see over the retaining wall; the speedway office was in a house trailer; and the toilet facilities in the garage area consisted of a three-holer with flopping doors. An estimated 28,000 fans occupied the wooden bleachers for the inaugural race in July of that year (six weeks after Charlotte Motor Speedway had attracted about 40,000 for its opener, and more than a year after the first Daytona 500), and it didn't get much better for a long time. Their two dates were in the early spring and the late fall, the most fickle times of the year in north Georgia, in terms of weather, and traffic was a problem no matter the weather or the time of year. Worst of all, management was a mess; for nearly thirty years there was the constant turmoil of power grabs and threats of bankruptcy. Just when stock car racing was in the ascendancy, pulling huge crowds at such little places as Bristol and Darlington and even in the East and Midwest, Atlanta was fumbling the ball.

Ironically, it took racing people from Charlotte to bail them out. Bruton Smith had been just another pushy young race promoter when he went in with the volatile Curtis Turner to build Charlotte Motor Speedway. The track there had its problems in the beginning, just as Atlanta, resulting in the dismissal of both Turner and Smith in the early sixties. Smith went off to make a fortune in selling automobiles and playing the stocks and dealing in real estate, and when he had quietly amassed controlling interest in CMS, in 1975, he was named its chairman of the board. The best move he made was to install an imaginative young promoter named Humpy

Wheeler as general manager, and very quickly they made Charlotte the best all-around operation in all of NASCAR. The mile-and-a-half asphalt oval there had always been a favorite of the drivers, due only in part to its proximity to their shops and homes, and soon it became a dazzling show-case for Smith and Wheeler's visionary dreams: 115,000 permanent seats, VIP suites and condominiums sold or leased to drivers and sponsors, a fancy seven-story office tower holding the Speedway Club and the best souvenir shop and museum in racing. Well ahead of Winston Cup's televi-sion age, they installed sites for cameras all around the track and put in superb lighting for night racing. They made sure that there was always something going on at Charlotte Motor Speedway—Richard Petty's driv-ing school for fans, testing by the teams and such suppliers as Goodyear, racing of everything from Winston Cup cars to school buses, filming of movies like *Days of Thunder*, automobile fairs—and once, to break the tedium, they even hired 6,000 people and a covey of helicopters to stage an "invasion of Grenada."

In 1990, Smith pounced on the opportunity to buy the old Atlanta International Raceway and add it to his Speedway Motorsports, Inc., to go along with Charlotte and Bristol and a piece of Darlington and his pro-jected monster track in Texas. In a blink, it seemed, he had begun to remake AMS in the image of Charlotte, and soon Atlantans were begin-ning to take notice of the superspeedway out there on Tara Boulevard, *Gone With the Wind* country, for the first time. Up went forty-six condos for sale at an average of $500,000 apiece (to many a chuckle from David Letterman), plus ninety-two luxury VIP suites for those who wanted nei-ther the roar of the engines nor the smell of the crowd, all of those crowning grandstands that now held more than 100,000 fans, with more on the way. And Smith, who physically resembled the abrasive comedian Don Rickles with his jutting jaw and balding round head, wasn't stopping there. For the 1997 season, he would have the mile-and-a-half track completely reconfigured so that the start-finish line would be where the backstretch had always been; and, since nobody else seemed to want to help him out, he intended to build some roads in and out of the place all by himself. He may have infuriated many of the racing purists by buying a half-interest in (and effectively burying) beloved old North Wilkesboro, just so he could take one of its two Winston Cup dates for his own Texas speedway, but this was a big thinker at work here. He had already been spied checking out property for a racetrack on Long Island, and now he was talking about putting a dome over weather-cursed Bristol Motor Speedway to take God out of the equation. What less could one expect from a man who once bought an Israeli jet, wing-mounted machine guns included, formerly the property of the Ugandan strut-about Idi Amin?

Smith knew that he had better get something done, and fast, about the traffic problems at AMS, because he had severely tested the patience of what were clearly the most devoted fans in all of American sport. It took a lot of time and money and energy for a Motorhead and the Bubbarazzi to follow the Winston Cup circuit. A single seat high up in the Weaver Grandstand, at the start-finish line, cost $75. The cheapest seat in the house could be had for $30, and that was in the bleachers on the lonely backstretch. There were other ways to go—from $35 for camping out all weekend in the infield's "Winston Cup Corral" to a single $130 race day ticket in the "VIP hospitality area" that fetched breakfast, lunch, closed-circuit television, and protection from the elements—but none of it was worth a dime if you couldn't get to the track on time. Horror stories abounded from the finale of the '95 season, when Jeff Gordon hung on by his fingers to win the points championship from Earnhardt, and the letters page of *Winston Cup Scene* was full of them. "It will have to get a lot colder in hell than it was in Atlanta for me to go there again for a race," wrote a fan who had driven the 350 miles from Jacksonville, Florida, in about the same amount of time it took him to cover the twenty-six miles from his motel to the track. The last fifteen miles to AMS were along Tara Boulevard, two lanes northbound and two southbound on an old U.S. highway, and many fans had abandoned their cars and walked as far as four miles, lugging their coolers and blankets along the grassy shoulder of the road, simply to claim their seats and huddle in the bitter cold for up to five hours. Indeed, one Atlanta sportswriter had waited until nine o'clock in the morning to leave downtown for the one o'clock start, thinking that surely it would be better this time, and missed nearly half of the race.

But the season was engaged now, three down and twenty-eight to go ("That's a pretty depressing thought, isn't it?" said Darrell Waltrip, whose best finish so far had been a sixteenth at Rockingham), and the show had to go on in spite of forecasts for wintry weather throughout the weekend. Slow advance sales had already virtually assured that the unspeakable would happen on Sunday—a blackout in the Atlanta area of ABC's telecast, one of only five noncable television races of the year—but the sponsors and the drivers were committed to going through their paces. All over the sprawling metropolitan Atlanta area, especially in the blue-collar towns outside the city's interstate perimeter, the plastic banners and checkered flags and pennants were fluttering in the winds of early March, welcoming the drivers and their show cars: John Andretti and his number 37 Kmart/ Little Caesars Ford at a Ford dealership in Conyers, Bobby Labonte's Interstate Batteries Chevrolet up at Cartersville, Bobby Hamilton's STP Pontiac down at Riverdale, Ricky Rudd's Tide cars everywhere. On Friday night in the town of Griffin, just south of the speedway, with the winds up and the temperature below freezing, there was a Festival of Lights Parade, the spectators nearly outnumbered by the hundreds of troupers who *had* to be there: some thirty drivers from the Winston Cup, Busch Grand National, Craftsman Truck, and ARCA series; local cheerleaders, clowns, and city officials; fire trucks, emergency medical vans, and even a guy driving a 1960 Edsel convertible. The country music radio stations were filled with paid promos and chummy interviews of the drivers; the Atlanta papers, as would happen at every venue during the season, had put out a special Purolator 500 section; and over at the Airport Hilton Eli Gold was hosting his live weekly prerace show for TNN, featuring call-in questions for his driver guests. Stock car racing had come a long way since the days of promoters running around town, nailing posters to telephone poles, luring drivers with appearance bonuses.

If there was ever a time for the press to stay huddled up in the media center, another of those cinder-block reminders of RJR's quarter-century sponsorship of Winston Cup, this was it. AMS was reputed to serve the best meals on the circuit—barbecue one day, fried chicken the next—and, besides, the morning temperatures outside were barely edging out of the teens. Forthwith, the little mail slots nailed to the walls began to fill up with handouts: data on the cars and drivers who would be entered in the ARCA, Busch Grand National, and Winston Cup races over the weekend; something about how Speedway Children's Charities Foundation was giving $70,000 to shelters and various other good-works programs in the area; a release from AMS about its plans to break the world's record for a "one-day ticketed concert" in July, with the Fruit of the Loom All-Star CountryFest '96; invitations to a brunch of "Spam 'n Eggs" in the infield Saturday morning with the esteemed Lake Speed, driver of the number 9 Spam Ford, known to the writers as the "Spam-mobile." Here came Richard Petty, with a few words about his driving school and an answer to the impish question of whether auto racing should be an Olympic sport ("Why not? They got everything else but marble-shootin'"); and Earnhardt and his third wife, Teresa, a titular board member of Dale Earnhardt, Inc., to introduce the fellow who would drive their Chevy truck on the new NASCAR truck circuit; and a howdy from Lynyrd Skynyrd, the Southern rock band, who had shown up just to meet Earnhardt.

And out there on the front straightaway, trying to wriggle his six-one, 185-pound frame into a comical-looking little orange-and-brown go-kart, was Dawsonville's own Awesome Bill Elliott, preparing to give his all for yet another of his sponsors, Reese's Peanut Butter Cups. (In one of the better television commercials of the season, two "crewmen" on a "pit stop" in Elliott's den jack up his recliner and give him a Reese's Piece. He takes a bite and smiles and says, "Awesome," and there is the sound of a race car roaring away with tires screaming; and that was it, Elliott's kind of "interview.") A bespectacled forty-two-year-old NASCAR fan from Maine, now being playfully billed as "Hot Rod" Roderick, had won a trip to Atlanta and would race against the clock with Elliott. If he won, he got $1 million; if he lost, he got a new Ford Thunderbird and Reese's would donate $10,000 to a children's hospital fund. Either way, Roderick was happy to be there; he owned 5,000 racing cards and avidly watched Winston Cup on television, but he had never seen a race in person and until now had flown in a plane only once. The go-karts could do sixty miles per hour, it was said, although even Elliott wasn't about to risk it. At any rate, Elliott went first and negotiated the short slalom course, a series of turns through some orange traffic cones, without incident. Everything was going all right for Hot Rod Roderick until he tried to cut it too fine on his return, spinning out and taking a cone with him. The boys and girls in the pressroom had been observing from a closed-circuit television set hanging from the ceiling. "Poor guy just never got it dialed in," one of them said. Lunch was served.

The drivers and the teams had no quarrels with Atlanta and its speedway. The track itself was a fast mile-and-a-half asphalt oval with corners banked at twenty-four degrees, sort of in between the steeper turns at Daytona and Talladega and the flatter ones at Michigan and Pennsylvania, and qualifying speeds there (about 185 miles per hour) were as fast as anywhere on the circuit. There was plenty of room in the infield for their car-haulers and their RVs, an airstrip was right next door, some could stay in one of the condominiums there, and it was a relatively painless trip down the interstates from Charlotte. All of those factors made Atlanta Motor Speedway one of the favorite places to go for tests of all sorts, whether for tires or searching for the proper setup for the summer races on the similar-sized tracks in the East and Midwest. And it was, after all, the location of the last race of every Winston Cup season, where first-place money could reach six figures and the points championship could be determined; the place where the long campaign finally came to an end, in the big city and before increasingly large crowds, where a fellow could lie back in style and reflect on the season without worrying about a next race. That had more or less been the situation with the frizzy redhead Morgan Shepherd in 1993 after he had won the season-ending race at AMS and decided to stay over in his glitzy penthouse at one of Atlanta's glossiest motels. This had been only his fourth victory in thirteen full seasons of Winston Cup racing, and it had been a long haul for the aging son of a western North Carolina bootlegger. Over the years he had fathered six children by five wives, and in the shank of the evening one of the daughters from the first one popped in for a surprise visit. They chatted for a while, about grandchildren and his newfound Christianity and his latest young wife (this one only two years older than the daughter now standing before him), and as she was leaving he blurted after her: "Tell your mama I made seven hundred eighty-two thousand five hundred and twenty-three dollars this year!"

Earnhardt practically owned this track, it seemed. He had won there seven times, starting with the spring race of his coming-out season in 1980, and with one more he would surpass the hall-of-famer Cale Yarborough for most wins at AMS. The track was made for him—not too fast like Talladega and not too risky like the calamitous little half-milers where anyone might get lucky and win—and he could power his way through a long afternoon of heavy traffic requiring patience, endurance, and savvy. (As testimony of how much time he spent flying over from Charlotte for tests and for commercial work, he owned one of the condos perched atop the main grandstand.) The last the Atlanta fans had seen of him was during the '95 NAPA 500, the final race of the year, when he had the slimmest mathematical chance to overtake Gordon and win his record eighth Winston Cup championship. The only way Gordon could lose it, though, would be to finish dead last in the race; and the way to ensure against that, using an old ruse that even the Earnhardt people themselves had resorted to three years earlier, was to put in a ringer whose duty was to run a couple of laps and then head for the garage for an official last-place DNF. "They're too far out to get in anybody's head," Earnhardt had said of the Gordon team beforehand, in a rare cozy fireside chat with some writers at his car-hauler, "but if it was a forty-point game I'd go to work on him right now." Starting at eleventh position, he roared into the lead early on and poured on the coals like a runaway locomotive to make a shambles of the race. Gordon ambled along without a care, assured of the points championship and RJR's $1.5 million bonus from the instant his ringer went behind the wall, and finished thirty-second. Earnhardt's final words before trekking off for a winter of pondering The Kid and counting his money: "Don't forget me next year. I'll still be around."

Nobody was forgetting him for a second as the long hours of practicing and qualifying droned on. His black Chevy hovered over every gathering of the clan like a shadow, a storm on the horizon, and there wasn't a man in the garages and the pits who didn't think he would be a factor, if not the winner, every time the green flag was dropped. The man was a competitor, born to race, the most tenacious driver in the long history of NASCAR with the possible exception of The King. "Every misconception there might be about Earnhardt is due to one simple thing," said one of the marketeers at RJR. "The man hates to lose." His thirty-first-place finish at Richmond had been not just an aberration but an egregious insult as well, like poking a stick at a rattlesnake, and few jocularities were being passed back and forth over his radio on Friday morning as he hit the track for the tedious process of spinning around on practice laps in order to dial in the car for that afternoon's first round of qualifying. After the controversial win at Rockingham and the near miss at Daytona, he was already only a heartbeat away from the lead in points for the young season and Gordon was nowhere in sight.

Cale Yarborough, the man whose record of seven wins at Atlanta was on the line and there to be broken on Sunday by Earnhardt, had a few words to say about that in the course of talking about his young driver, a jumpy twenty-six-year-old crew-cut Kentuckian named Jeremy Mayfield. Cale, like Bobby Allison and Richard Petty, had become a legendary driver but in a time when the purses were barely sufficient to keep a man afloat; meaning that all three were still obliged to work for a living as team owners and confidants. (The Motorheads up in the stands loved to tune in on Mayfield's frequency to hear the fatherly Yarborough try to keep his eager young charge in line. "Jesus Christ, did you see that? I'd like to run over that motherfucker right there," Mayfield had yelped from the backstretch, turning about 180 during a practice round. "Well, you didn't hit him, son, that's the important thing," was Cale's laconic response.) "It's harder to find aggressive drivers today because the salaries and the money create a lack of desire," Yarborough was saying, quick to exclude his boy, Mayfield, from that general assessment. "Some just want to stay out of trouble and draw those big paychecks, and the young ones are reluctant to go after it if they don't think they have the perfect car. But I'll tell you what. They're paying close to a hundred thousand dollars to win this thing, right? Earnhardt would go for it if they were paying a nickel."

The rookie, Johnny Benson, won his first Winston Cup pole with a run of 185.434 miles per hour, the best thing about that being that it automatically qualified him for the next February's all-star Busch Clash at Daytona; but then, out on the track for a final whirl during Happy Hour on

Saturday, he smacked a wall head-on and totaled his Pontiac and thus would have to start from the rear, in a backup car taken off the hauler, in Sunday's race. (NASCAR rules were firm on this. Whenever a car was destroyed after qualifying—and it happened at an alarming rate, often during Happy Hour—the backup car had to start at the rear, no matter how the original had qualified. Most teams used one setup and engine for qualifying, another for the race, but this rule related to the car itself.) "I just lost it," he said, blaming no one but himself. Earnhardt and his crew never got the setup right for qualifying and ran exactly two miles per hour slower than Benson, to qualify eighteenth, and Gordon would start even further back at twenty-first. But their troubles were nothing compared to the woes that befell Jeff Burton, Ward's younger brother. Here he was, the '94 Rookie of the Year, currently second in points after three races, a full-fledged member of the brotherhood who was committed to running in all thirty-one Winston Cup shows during '96, and he failed to qualify. He was, of course, "devastated," and the fact that NASCAR couldn't somehow find a way to fit a full-timer such as he into the field with a provisional set off a storm of grumblings in the garage area. "How can you be second in points with a team that's signed up for the whole deal and send those guys home?" said Kenny Wallace. Dale Jarrett thought it was "pretty crummy," strong words from such an unflappable Christian gentleman. Burton's owner, Jack Roush, he of the P-51 Mustang, stomped and yelled at the NASCAR officials on the scene, but to no avail. The Burton entourage loaded up their cars and left during the Busch Grand National race early Saturday afternoon. It was small consolation that at least they were able to beat the horrendous traffic.

In a little prerace entertainment on Sunday, as if to remind the fans of how far Winston Cup racing had come, the old champion, David Pearson, second to Richard Petty in all-time wins, was invited to take a ceremonial lap around the track. The hard-charging Pearson had driven a Purolator-sponsored car in his heyday, from 1960 through '86, and much was made of the fact that his total earnings in those seventeen years amounted to nearly $2.5 million less than Earnhardt's take during the previous season alone. And finally, in the swirling winds and bitter cold of Sunday, the drivers buckled up and fired their engines. The pace car led them around for three extra laps to give the tires time to warm up, and Terry Labonte jumped out from the outside pole (now that Benson had been pushed to the rear) to lead the way for nearly half an hour. But then, niftily picking his way through the traffic, here came Earnhardt; sliding high, dipping low, flat out, belly to the ground, a man on a mission. He had moved up from eighteenth to sixth after only five laps, an astonishing insinuation, and when he first took over the lead on the forty-ninth lap it was as though the Grim Reaper had arrived. It turned out to be about as clean a race as Winston Cup ever sees, with only three caution periods totaling thirteen laps, a situation that takes away such factors as pit strategy and track debris and bunched traffic; the sort of happenstances that can allow a lesser machine to win. Hammer down, roaring onward, Earnhardt won in a breeze to become the all-time champion at Atlanta Motor Speedway. He was $91,050 richer, as well, and, more important in the larger scheme, only fifty points behind Jarrett in his quest for a record eighth Winston Cup championship. (Consistency pays in Winston Cup racing. Although Earnhardt had won two of the four races, his thirty-first-place finish at Richmond, while Jarrett was finishing second, had left him trailing in overall points.) Gordon had finished third, enough to make him forget those disastrous first two races, and it appeared that now, finally, The Intimidator and The Kid might be about ready to get it on again.

7

DALE EARNHARDT™ AND THE KID®

There was a time when NASCAR's biggest stars were famously accessible to the press, even to writers who weren't a part of the family of beat reporters. They had no pressing engagements to speak of, beyond getting the car ready for the next race, and there was always time for sitting around and telling war stories. They had been ignored for so long by the mainstream media that they would just about dance a jig for an author or a writer from some publishing house or national magazine whose influence extended far beyond that of the chummy trade press. Everybody remembered the time in the mid-sixties when the writer Tom Wolfe, a New York dandy given to wearing white suits and spangled vests, checked in with Junior Johnson on his farm in western North Carolina and for a racing weekend at North Wilkesboro to produce what turned out to be a 16,000-word portrait in *Esquire* magazine: "The Last American Hero is Junior Johnson. Yes!" It was a wondrous piece of work that was viewed at first with some anger and puzzlement by the racing crowd—Wolfe, dabbling in a creative style being touted as "the New Journalism," was dead-on in capturing the laid-back flavor of Southern stock car racing as it was in those pre–Winston Cup days—but soon came to be embraced, especially when it was turned into a movie. The writers who would follow Wolfe into the world of NASCAR found it to be a pleasurable assignment even as RJR got involved and the stars became more and more preoccupied with having to satisfy their sponsors. About all a writer had to do was look them up in the phone book (it being well nigh impossible to keep an unlisted phone number in Level Cross or Ronda, North Carolina), get directions to the farm, pick a time, and show up with a tape recorder.

In the mid-seventies, gathering fodder for what would become one of the better books ever written about stock car racing, *Fast as White Lightning*, a writer named Kim Chapin asked Humpy Wheeler of Charlotte Motor Speedway to recommend an up-and-coming star for him to interview. "Ralph's boy," he was told, meaning Dale Earnhardt, the twenty-four-year-old son of a legendary dirt-track driver named Ralph Earnhardt. Chapin found him bivouacked at his mother's house in Kannapolis, North Carolina, sleeping on the sofa there after having been kicked out of the house by his wife. Earnhardt would enter his first Winston Cup race that summer at Charlotte (finishing twenty-second, one place ahead of Richard Childress, now his owner), but at this point he was raw and, Chapin found, "painfully shy." Earnhardt on his father: "I think him and the Pettys were the same-type people." On the salaried job he once had, working on Great Dane trailers: "I done a good day's work for people." On the change from dirt tracks to asphalt: "It weren't hard for me." Chapin tracked him down again five years later, when he had been the Winston Cup Rookie of the Year in '79 and was on his way toward his first points championship, and found only some slight material differences. By then he was divorced and living alone on exclusive Lake Norman, sporting a new mustache, wearing cowboy boots and a belt of rattlesnake skin, and about to be featured in *People* and *Sports Illustrated* and the *New York Times*. Despite the attention, he remained "polite but nervous; uncomfortable at rest. He would rather have been fishing" than being interviewed. It didn't get a whole lot better in the eighties, when Earnhardt became The Intimidator and the championships and the money began to pile up. "He couldn't put two words together, couldn't make a sentence," said one beat writer. "Joe Whitlock [his PR man at the time] would sit with him in an interview and nudge him along. It was embarrassing."

Now, in this Winston Cup season of 1996, everything had changed. Earnhardt was a millionaire, an icon, NASCAR's main man, obsessed by his mission to become racing's greatest champion. "He doesn't speak to anybody these days, except at press conferences," that same writer reported, adding that as far as he knew, the last extensive one-on-one interview Earnhardt had granted was to an Atlanta newspaperman in 1994. Earnhardt had polished his English somewhat (he was, after all, a high school dropout), at least to the extent of eliminating double negatives and inserting words like "prerogative" into his public pronouncements, but he clearly cringed at the thought of appearing in any media situation that wasn't firmly controlled: the obligatory interview up in the press box after winning, the little sound bites for the soft television and radio "reporters" like the former drivers Ned Jarrett and Benny Parsons, the packaged television infomercials, the commercials for GM Goodwrench and NASCAR. And when he had lost, forget about it. "He can be abrasive when he figures he's got a reason, like if he's lost or people think he's caused a wreck," said Neal Sims of the *Birmingham News*. Earnhardt was the bane of MRN, the radio racing network that liked to get quick post-race interviews but played hell finding him if he hadn't won, as in the aftermath of the Daytona 500 when he had ducked through a gate to leave the press cooling its heels. Generally speaking, in spite of the pains he had taken to polish his act, Earnhardt plainly was a driver and not a diplomat. Not soon forgotten by members of the media was another of those January shop tours when Earnhardt, who had promised some one-on-one interviews, was found off in a side room chatting with a gaggle of favored beat reporters. "Just what the goddamn fuckin' hell is *this* shit?" bellowed another writer who had stomped off to find him. Earnhardt, startled, looked at the PR man beside him for help. "I'm not talkin' to your flack, I'm talkin' to *you*, Earnhardt!" the writer shouted. Earnhardt had never heard such a tirade, not from any man, and began stuttering apologies: "Hey, I'm sorry . . . I didn't mean to, you know . . . We're just talkin' . . . Hey, y'all come on in . . ." Without a smooth PR man to guide him, Earnhardt stayed in trouble.

He had lost a friend and a patient handler when Joe Whitlock, one of the beloved earlier reporters on the stock car beat, committed suicide. Now his press relations person was a combative fellow named John (J.R.) Rhodes, of Champion Sports Group, Inc., in Charlotte, who had reached that station in life not through journalism or public relations but as a bartender at a watering hole in Daytona Beach that was popular with the racing crowd. He had latched on as a gofer at the NASCAR offices in Daytona Beach and then, at the death of Whitlock, suddenly become the spokesman for one of the most successful figures in American sport. Often he could be seen at the track, a burly man wearing mirrored wraparound sunglasses just like the boss, leading interference for Earnhardt as he brushed past the Bubbarazzi on his way to his race car. Only the principals would know whether Rhodes's job was to brush off the press, rather than cooperate, but for sure there was a lot of animosity and paranoia at play. The Earnhardt people were still smarting from an unauthorized biography published in '91, Frank Vehorn's *The Intimidator*, a benign pastiche of quotes from clippings and racetrack handouts, and then came their curious response to a piece in late '95 by Ed Hinton of *Sports Illustrated*. "God knows what *that* was all about," said one of the PR minions in NASCAR. "You've gotta follow this closely. When Joe Whitlock died, Hinton married his widow. Hinton showed up to talk with Earnhardt at his office for *SI*. The piece came out and Earnhardt felt, rightly or not, that Hinton had put Whitlock's blood on his hands. Somebody guessed that Hinton got pissed when Earnhardt kept going through his mail and signing autographs, saying, 'Naw' and 'Unh-hunh,' rather than giving him anything substantive. Who the hell knows?" Still, trying to argue in Earnhardt's defense, Chris Powell of RJR's Sports Marketing Enterprises said Earnhardt "can be the nicest guy in the world when he's feeling good. There'll be a gleam in his eye, a genuine likableness, but you don't see it often. The man hates to lose, and if things aren't going right, well, look out . . ."

Early in the '96 season, a writer with a book contract followed the protocol in trying to line up some time with Earnhardt. He sent a one-page fax to Rhodes, explaining the book and requesting the interview, but heard nothing. Three weeks later he faxed the note again, this time adding, "Please respond." Two hours later, his phone rang. It was J.R. Rhodes, testy and growling, with a series of evasions: Earnhardt was "on vacation for ten days," "very busy," and never did interviews at the track because "that's his office." Fair enough; it was a long season. Then Rhodes said, "Who have you talked to so far, *sir?*"

"I've just been hanging out at the—"

"Who have you *talked* to, *sir?*"

"I told you, I—"

"*Sir*"—bartenders do this just before they eighty-six a drunk—"I just don't think so."

"What? *The* driver in all of Winston Cup?"

"*Sir*, you *do* understand that both his name and his image are trademarked."

"Christ, so are mine. I've published books. What the hell does *that* mean?"

"It means"—a sigh—"it means that if we win this eighth championship we'll be doing our own book."

"But wait. It doesn't work like that."

"Yes, it does, *sir*."

Alas, he was right on that score. Following the lead of show business and politics, Winston Cup racing had finally stepped in line with all of the other major sports in America vis-à-vis relations with the media. This same writer who now found himself groveling to get an hour with Dale Earnhardt remembered with some uneasiness the time in the early eighties when he tried to finagle a telephone interview with Arnold Palmer, the great golfer and king of endorsements, for a magazine piece. Palmer's right-hand man, Doc Giffen, the former press relations person for the Professional Golfers' Association, sweetly advised that this would be impossible: "Arnie's so busy with his endorsements and playing golf, you know. But I know what he's got to say about everything, so just pretend I'm Arnie. First question." The quotes that appeared in the piece were by Arnold Palmer, as surmised by Doc Giffen, as told to *Goodlife* magazine. Now the same game was being played in Winston Cup racing. "I've called J.R. [Rhodes] to get quotes from Earnhardt," said Birmingham sportswriter Neal Sims, "and I'm sure Rhodes just made 'em up. Dale's always 'testing' or 'appearing' somewhere or just plain 'out.' What else are you gonna do?"

This had become a golden age for public relations. The myth-makers in Hollywood had always played the game better than anyone else, demanding an approved cover photo of their starlet in exchange for an "in-depth interview" that was anything but. Washington, D.C., came right along behind showbiz—hard to believe now that few Americans knew, until he started going to Warm Springs, Georgia, for polio therapy, that Franklin Roosevelt was bound to a wheelchair—offering access to its presidents only at "pool" press conferences and "photo opportunities" and other managed events. The lesser magazines and tabloids had always been happy enough to make a deal with the "information" people, but now, in the nineties, the virus had spread to the mainstream media. "Mr. Pacino, approached through representatives, did not respond to requests for an interview," reported the *New York Times*, wanting a word with the actor Al Pacino about a Broadway production forthcoming in '96. The glossy magazine *Vanity Fair*, with one of the largest circulations in the country, seemed to have no compunctions about promising the actress Demi Moore a prior-approval cover photo of herself in some stage of undress in exchange for a "revealing" interview in which she said motherhood was cool.

There was such a glut of media outlets that the American public was confused about which was real and which was not. More than ever before, the medium was the message. The quadrennial national political conventions were staged shows now, not news events. The presidential debates were about style, not issues. Even the mini-wars like Desert Storm in Iraq and the "invasions" in Grenada and Somalia were staged spectacles filmed and reported not by intrepid combat photographers and correspondents but by the government's own military "information specialists"; for the government had learned its lessons well in Vietnam, where there had been not an iota of press censorship. Now there were commercials and infomercials and public-access cable television and e-mail and the Internet and trade publications on the one hand, and the legitimate independent journals such as the *New York Times* and *The New Yorker* on the other, but to the average working stiff out there in Akron the lines were blurred. "Well, I saw it on TV," one might say, not delineating between a program produced and paid for by the Republican National Committee and a muckraking spot on *60 Minutes*. Even the *New York Times*, America's one great newspaper, was adding to the confusion by reporting what a sleazerag like the *National Enquirer* had "reported" either in a paid interview or a piece of unabashed slander.

Winston Cup wasn't show business or politics—it was "just racin'," in the vernacular, a commercial venture with an element of competition and danger—but its managers had latched on to the desirability of managing the way the public might perceive it. Unlike that day in the distant past when the champion driver Ned Jarrett aspired to pay taxes on $10,000 a year, very big money was involved now. About a dozen drivers were taking down at least $1 million a year in purse money, and that was just a start. (The sensational young Davey Allison of "The Alabama Gang," who died at the age of thirty-two when he crashed his new helicopter in 1993, had been drawing a salary of $1 million a year, plus half of the purses, plus a cut of collectibles sales, all of it coming to some $3 million a year.) If sponsors were going to pay out between $3 and $12 million a year to finance a driver and a team, they expected not just success on the track but a winsome image for their products, as well. Often that was a lot to ask of drivers who were, for the most part, of rural Southern stock; men who had grown up in the dangerous and gritty world of racing, not in banquet halls and television studios; men who had been high school slackers or dropouts, not valedictorians.

For some, most notably Darrell Waltrip, hamming it up came naturally; he knew a sound bite when he got one off, and at one point between races during the '96 season he pinch-hit as the emcee for TNN's *Prime Time Country*, sort of a country fan's *Tonight Show*, flawlessly handling a monologue and carrying on with guest musicians as though he had created the show. Jeff Gordon, with his good looks and his gee-whiz goodness, was a dream even if he never really said anything beyond platitudes. There was a whole group of handsome and articulate charioteers—Ricky Rudd, Terry

Labonte, Dale Jarrett, Kyle Petty, Rusty Wallace and his brothers Kenny and Mike—who could move as well among clients at a corporate gathering as through traffic on the racetrack. And for many of the others, there was, well, *school!* Not that he needed it any more than the others, for he was a vibrant good-looking blond with the pleasant hint of a twang in his voice, but Sterling Marlin (along with his crew chief and his owner) spent an entire winter's day prior to the '96 season in front of video cameras brought to the shop in Abingdon, Virginia, by his sponsor, Kodak, learning how to use his hands and speak in colorful sound bites. For the least sophisticated, especially the rookies coming up to the big time from Busch Grand National, there was what amounted to a finishing school: how to eat, dress, walk, chat, and lollygag. (Yes. One of the tutors making the rounds emphasized that the proper way for a manly race car driver to put his hands on his hips was with the knuckles out, thumbs behind; none of that sissy stuff with the palms back there on the small of the back like some woman or, God forbid, *worse.*) And then there were those who were left to wing it as best they could, like Morgan Shepherd, the born-again son of a Wilkes County bootlegger. "It's to his credit that he's still learning to read, at fifty-four," said one of the NASCAR press people. "But one day I ran him by a Charlotte radio station to do a promo and they gave him something to read on the air. They were just deejays, they didn't know. I wanted out of there, didn't want to be a witness to it, but then I saw him 'reading' from the piece of paper and faking it. He knew the gist, the routine. 'Hi, this is Morgan Shepherd in the number 75 Remington Ford, and I hope to see y'all at Charlotte Motor Speedway this Sunday . . .' Nobody knew the difference."

Here, again, it was remarkable how the changes in stock car racing since the sixties paralleled those in country music. Before Nashville turned slick and Countrypolitan in the early seventies, it was still possible for some old boy to get off a Greyhound and hoof it a couple of miles, guitar case in one hand and an AWOL bag in the other, and start knocking on the doors of dilapidated houses along Music Row until somebody asked him to hum a few bars of the songs he had written back home. Willie Nelson, broke and hungry, was known to pitch songs by doing just that over the pay phone at Tootsie's Orchid Lounge until he got an invitation to trot on over to the

1

Arguably the best driver of his time, Dale Earnhardt—"The Intimidator"—saddled up and ready to roll.

A familiar sight throughout the NASCAR season: Earnhardt in his black #3 Chevy leading the pack.

Stock car racing really
blossomed at Daytona just
after the Second World War.
More than once, though,
the races were called when
the tide came in or when the
cars got bogged down
in the sand.

Earnhardt's main competition: Jeff Gordon (left), aka
"Wonder Boy" and "The Kid," movie-star handsome and
Madison Avenue–approved—talks to his crew chief,
Ray Evernham, after a race.

With some 150,000 fans on their feet, the green flag
drops for the start of the 1996 Daytona 500.

5

6

The 1996 Daytona 500: The elusive missing piece to Dale Earnhardt's storied career evaded him once again when Dale Jarrett (#88) finished just twelve-hundredths of a second ahead of the #3 car.

Not a bad way to kick off the 1996 season: Dale Jarrett celebrates his victory at Daytona and the $360,775 check that came with it.

7

Dawsonville's Lloyd Seay, left, and his barefoot cousin Roy Hall, at Lakewood Speedway circa 1940. Many of the early stock car drivers were fearless teenaged mountain boys who hauled moonshine during the week and raced on the weekends, usually with the same car.

The legendary Lloyd Seay entertaining the fans at Daytona with one of the moves he had learned from outrunning the law. Seay would die six weeks later, shot by a cousin in a dispute over sugar—an essential ingredient in the making of moonshine.

One of early stock car racing's most popular tracks: Lakewood
Speedway in Atlanta, circa 1947.

Nobody ever said it was easy sliding through the turns at
Lakewood in a stock Ford coupe.

Terry Labonte—the
"Ice Man"—driver of the #5
Kellogg's car and winner of the
1996 season-long Winston
Cup championship.

12

13

A good crew is just as in-
valuable as a good driver. Here,
a seven-man over-the-wall
gang attends to Ricky Craven's
car during a critical pit stop.

The cars and the tires are no longer
the same as in the good old days.
Nowadays, a tire within a tire
can help avert sure disaster.

14

15

Swept up in the 200-miles-per-hour traffic on the frontstretch at Talladega, young
Ricky Craven in the #41 car sails toward the catch fence on the first turn.

Shedding tires, sheet metal, and even its battery as it catapulted off the catch fence,
Craven's car looked like a skeleton when it finally came to rest on the track. "It
goes with the territory," a virtually unscathed Craven said after the race.

16

President Ronald
Reagan made Richard
Petty's day at Daytona
in 1984 when he showed
up to watch The
King take the last of his
record 200 Winston
Cup victories in the
Firecracker 400.
Reagan is flanked by
Petty, in sunglasses, and
NASCAR great Bobby
Allison.

17

Multi-car owners like
Rick Hendrick and Felix
Sabates owe the innovation
to stock car pioneer Ray-
mond Parks (right).
Wealthy from his moon-
shine dealings, Parks
backed his Dawson County
cousins Lloyd Seay (left)
and Roy Hall at Lake-
wood Speedway in the late
1930s.

18

19

A pit stop during the 1996 Daytona 500. The fate of many a race has been decided in the twenty seconds or so it takes to change four tires and take on a full tank of gas.

Opposite page

Another one of the early champion drivers from the Georgia mountain town of Dawsonville: Gober Sosebee, posed here with his restored '39 Ford coupe, the favorite of the early stock car drivers.

NASCAR fan's perennial choice for Most Popular Driver: Bill Elliott, "Awesome Bill from Dawsonville."

21

22

23

The men behind the high-tech machines: Dale Earnhardt's crew of mechanics prepares a new engine for his black #3 Chevy.

Kyle Petty—son of The King and grandson of Lee Petty (another NASCAR legend): the first third-generation driver to win a Winston Cup race.

24

Just some good old boys lighting up and hunkering down
for a weekend of racing at Darlington.

Winston Cup fans sent a strong message to President
Clinton when he and his administration stepped
up their anti-tobacco campaign.

Saturday night at Dixie Speedway, a classic half-mile dirt track thirty miles north of Atlanta.

Unlike Winston Cup racing, where high-tech engineering and aerodynamics play a major part in a driver's success, skill and daring are paramount on dirt tracks.

28

29

Top. Rodney Dickson,
the 1996 Late Model cham-
pionship winner at Dixie
Speedway, holding the
checkered flag.

Center. Jimmy Spencer,
"Mr. Excitement," so
dubbed for his early days
of reckless abandon on
the racetrack.

Left. After several
practice runs, Dale
Earnhardt's crew goes
through what amounts
to a last-minute pre-
flight check.

31

Temporarily sponsorless, one driver did his bit for the Republican party.

Below, top. Rusty Wallace (right), master of the short tracks, talks shop with his crew chief, Robin Pemberton.

Below, bottom. NASCAR's First Couple: Brooke and Jeff Gordon, during the annual Winston Cup awards banquet at New York's Waldorf-Astoria in 1995, when Jeff won the championship and more than $4.3 million at the ripe age of twenty-four.

32

33

The forces of good and evil: The Kid (right) and The Intimidator "chat" a little before a Winston Cup race.

Closely monitored by a white-uniformed NASCAR official, Earnhardt's car pits at Darlington.

The Intimidator does his thing at Rockingham: In his black #3 Chevrolet, Dale Earnhardt ducks low to take the lead after tapping Bobby Hamilton from behind. Hamilton's car was never the same; Earnhardt went on to win the race.

Earnhardt's chance for a record eighth Winston Cup Championship was effectively ruined after a horrific accident during the summer race at Talladega. Although he would heroically soldier on, a fractured sternum and collarbone made it impossible for him to catch the eventual winner, Terry Labonte.

37

Tulane Hotel, where Decca had its recording studio, and make a demo if not a full-blown record. Everybody knew that a new day was coming when a secretary named Jeannie C. Riley cut a twangy classic story song called "Harper Valley P.T.A." that hit the charts; but, before they dared let her sashay out the door and hit the road, the new moguls hired tutors to "show me how to *wawk 'n' tawk 'n' fix mah hay-yer.*" Now all of the old venues in Nashville were either gone or déclassé—Tootsie's, the Tulane, Ryman Auditorium, the old houses on Music Row—replaced by shiny buildings with peephole doors to keep out the riffraff. Bill (Whisperin' Bill) Anderson, a top country songwriter and star of the Grand Ole Opry in those earlier days, might have been echoing the stock car racing purists when he talked about Nashville in the nineties: "I host the half-hour television show that leads into the Opry every Saturday night, and it's a break to be a guest. I can't tell you how many times a new singer has shown up with his press agent—can you believe it?—and the agent has given me a sheet of paper with a list of questions to ask his client. I just roll it up and throw it away. Tell *that* to Grandpa Jones."

Forty cars, forty sponsors, each of them convinced that they could move a lot of "product" if they picked the right driver as a spokesman. "We call it the 'inspired fit,'" said Steve Saunders, field marketing manager for Coors beer, which had been sponsoring Winston Cup cars since the early eighties and now was backing Kyle Petty's number 42 Pontiac. (It was Saunders who had opined that the perfect match would be a marriage of Buckshot Jones in the number 00 car with the Remington gunmakers.) "It's got to make some sense. In the NBA, Windex gives a Clean the Glass Award for rebounding, and Allstate has the Good Hands Award for steals and assists. It's a fit when Goody's Headache Powders gives an award for the Winston Cup team that has the worst luck during a race, gets the biggest headache." But some of the commercial pairings, in the '96 Winston Cup season, didn't make much sense at all. The bland Lake Speed, or anyone else for that matter, selling cans of Spam seemed a specious endeavor (seeing Speed's number 9 Spam car running around the track "doesn't give me a sudden urge to eat pig snout," wrote the columnist

Steve Hummer in the *Atlanta Constitution*). Except, perhaps, for his Italian name, the only connection between John Andretti and Little Caesars pizza seemed to be that Andretti, at five-five and 140 pounds, was the littlest Winston Cupper. The fortyish Rick Mast, with the stern demeanor of a Quaker uncle, was driving for . . . *Hooters?* It seemed as though it wouldn't make much difference who drove for Heilig-Meyers Furniture or Exide Batteries or the QVC shopping channel or Pennzoil; although if the driver became successful enough the connection might stick after enough trips to Victory Lane. But there was a sufficient number of those "inspired fits" like the devil-may-care Jimmy Spencer in the Smokin' Joe's Camel cigarette car and the all-American-boy Bill Elliott in the McDonald's Ford and the goodtime-buddy Rusty Wallace in the Miller beer car, and, best of all, the macho Earnhardt in the GM Goodwrench ("like a rock") Chevy, to keep the sponsors coming, checkbooks open, ever hopeful.

Coors beer, out of Golden, Colorado, had gotten into Winston Cup racing in 1983 by plastering its logo on the hood of Bill Elliott's car. "We wanted exposure, *media* exposure, with a winning driver," said Saunders, who had flown into Charlotte for a meeting of Coors distributors from around the country; they would tour the Team Sabco shop, hang out with Kyle Petty, and then buckle into Richard Petty Driving School cars for a spin around Charlotte Motor Speedway. "So that's the way we measured it," Saunders was saying. "How many times Bill Elliott won, how many minutes and seconds the logo was seen on television, how many times pictures of the Coors car showed up in newspapers and magazines. We had a sort of 'sports calculus' rating system we used, with eighteen elements worth, say, ten dollars a point, and we'd do the numbers and say, 'Well, we can spend X thousand dollars on *that,*' which might be show car appearances, and then move on to the next element, like, say, the driver himself being brought in for a convention." It was a propitious time to be picking Bill Elliott to carry the Coors colors, for in their nine-year relationship he became Awesome Bill from Dawsonville and won the Winston Million and set the speed record for stock cars. When Elliott moved on to McDonald's, Coors sponsored Wally Dallenbach for two years, without favorable results, before finally going with Kyle Petty, son of The King.

"From Coors's perspective," said Saunders, "we had to make sure we were doing the right thing by advertising beer in a sport as dangerous as auto racing. Beer and driving don't mix, of course, so the owner and the driver would have to be comfortable with a beer sponsor. The driver doesn't have to drink, but he and the owner have to be a good match for us, be enthusiastic and comfortable supporting our product, or it won't work. And the driver can't run lousy; he's got to be a proven winner. We advertise to the male between twenty-one and twenty-five years old, and he has to like the driver's persona. We want him to say, 'Kyle's a good driver, I like him,' and go out and buy Coors Light. The fan isn't likely to visit the brewery and meet Mr. Coors himself, so Kyle *is* Coors Light to him, and he's sold a lot of beer for us, no doubt about it. The other area where it works for us is with the retailers. We have six hundred distributors around the country whose job is to sell to retailers, places like Winn-Dixie, and when the buyer at Winn-Dixie begins to associate Coors Light with Kyle Petty it makes the distributor's job easier. The retailer will take all of the Kyle Petty standup displays and commemorative cans we can give him." And if they are lucky they might be slipped garage passes for a Winston Cup race, making them eligible for membership in the Bubba-razzi.

Team Sabco and Petty were getting $5 million a year to carry the Coors colors. Although they were being furnished with only one show car to haul around the country—most teams had two, Ricky Rudd a record dozen—the deal was fairly standard. Kyle was obliged to make twenty special command appearances per season, of two hours' duration, getting paid $10,000 for each of the last five. Those appearances ran the gamut: at malls around the country, on a Coors float at the Mardi Gras in New Orleans and at the St. Patrick's Day parade in Savannah, at such Coors gatherings as the one Steve Saunders was now orchestrating in Charlotte for his distributors. He even spent two hours tending bar at the Harley-Davidson Cafe in Manhattan one summer's night during the '95 season, pouring drinks and signing autographs and swapping Harley stories, before moving on to that weekend's race in New Hampshire. Although there was concern about his faltering performances on the track, he was perfect in many ways: garrulous, trustworthy, voluble, able to converse on many levels. Like the Buck Owens song, all he had to do was act naturally. Coors would drink to that, and so would Felix Sabates. "The contract is actually with the owner, not the driver," said Jon Sands, Team Sabco's PR man. "Say Felix is at a convention and he's introduced to President Clinton as the owner of a Winston Cup car. The president says, 'Oh? Who's your driver?' and if Felix has to say, 'Ricky Craven,' he'll just get, 'Well, nice talking to you.' But if he can say, 'Kyle *Petty*,' the president goes, 'Hey, son of The King!' and they're off and talking. So it's like Saunders said, everybody's got to be happy with the deal, all the way around."

With the exception of Richard Petty's arrangement with STP, there was never a more natural pairing of driver and sponsor than the one involving Earnhardt and GM Goodwrench. He had driven for a while under the aegis of Wrangler blue jeans, not a bad marriage in itself, and by the time GM Goodwrench came along with its tons of money, becoming his primary sponsor in 1987, his image was already in place. "Dale was always smart and it didn't take him long to figure out where the money was," said the Atlanta papers' Tom McCollister. "He fully understood the 'Man in Black' and 'The Intimidator' and all of that. He was the first of the new breed. He didn't take no shit, and it came to him naturally. D.W. [Darrell Waltrip] was a hard racer in his time, too, although he never did some of the things Earnhardt does on the track, but he never capitalized on it." Whereas it might be a stretch to imagine what in the world the connection might be between, say, Ricky Rudd and Tide soap, the Earnhardt-Chevy-Goodwrench alliance was a no-brainer. The crinkle-eyed cowboy, king of the road, came barreling down the track in a macho black Everyman's car, both the car and the man built like a rock, as though to say, *Outta my way, I can take care of this job all by myself.* The parking lots and the infield camping areas at every track on the circuit were filled with black Chevys of every make—muscle cars, Blazers, vans, balloon-tired monster pickups—and their owners tended toward the pugnacious, even belligerent. It was the same audience that followed Hank Williams, Jr., of the strutting go-to-hell Southern country swagger, a prospect that had always left the promoters of outdoor country music concerts somewhat fearful. "They come, a *lot* of 'em come, but those Confederate flags and the guns in the back of their pickups scare the hell out of me," one of them said during Williams's surge on the waves of his defiant song about how things would be different in this country, by God, "if the South had won."

By 1996, Dale Earnhardt was an industry unto himself. The high school dropout who once was a welder and tire mounter in a trailer factory was more than holding his own in an era when sports heroes were wallowing in millions of dollars raked in through endorsements and the sale of T-shirts and other collectibles. The professional basketball stars Michael Jordan and Shaquille O'Neal led the world in income from endorsements alone, with $38 and $23 million, respectively, followed by the ageless Arnold Palmer with $16 million. Earnhardt's advisers weren't disputing the consensus that he was grossing $50 million a year on collectibles, mostly through a T-shirtery that he had bought out (his T-shirts grossed $28 million, putting him ahead of the Rolling Stones and country superstar Garth Brooks), and that he was in the top ten of the world's richest athletes. Dale Earnhardt, Inc. (DEI), was a conglomerate with many holdings: Sports Image Racing Souvenir and Apparel, the factory and warehouse, whence 1,000 boxes of T-shirts and caps and decals and other froufrous were shipped out every day; Dale Earnhardt Chevrolet, a car dealership in Newton, North Carolina; a working farm and a bunch of poultry houses; five racing teams (his, a Busch Grand National, a SuperTruck, and those of his two sons and his daughter); plus various investments. The $3.2 million he had won in purses during the '95 season, running his career Winston Cup earnings to more than $25 million, paled in comparison to the outside money; although, to be sure, without his success on the track there would have been nothing. Sports Image alone employed seventy-six people, and the total number of DEI employees came to 237. Earnhardt found it necessary to have a Learjet to make it to all of his appointments, whether to Phoenix for a race or to Daytona for testing or to New York for the post-season banquet at the Waldorf-Astoria.

The grandfather of sports marketing was Mark McCormack, who had known Arnold Palmer when Arnie was playing collegiate golf at Wake Forest in Winston-Salem (where, only incidentally, Winston Cup's R.J. Reynolds Tobacco Company is headquartered). "Arnie's Army" was at its peak, in the mid-sixties, with Arnie Palmer taking golf out of the country clubs and to the masses, when McCormack convinced his old pal that he ought to get ahead of the curve; take the money he was generating before somebody else did. That made McCormack a hero to a generation of sports consultants and marketeers that followed, and in the case of Earnhardt, his Mark McCormack was Don Hawk. A Pennsylvanian in his late thirties, Hawk came into Earnhardt's life in 1993. He had spent eighteen years as an executive "in the car business" for Ford and General Motors, dealing with the shops and service departments, but in the late eighties he had dabbled on the side in helping with the business affairs of a Winston Cup driver from Wisconsin, Alan Kulwicki. Thus initiated into the NASCAR family, Hawk got to know Richard Childress, Earnhardt's car owner at Childress Motorsports. Kulwicki's death in a plane crash early in the '93 season, at the height of his career, happened just as Earnhardt was charging toward his fifth Winston Cup championship and thus was too preoccupied with racing to avail himself of the flood of business opportunities coming his way. Hawk, who had narrowly missed getting on the plane with Kulwicki, continued to work on race weekends with what was left of the Kulwicki team.

"The way we met was in typical Dale Earnhardt style," Hawk was saying one day during the '96 season as he surveyed the empire he had helped establish. "Childress and I had gotten to know each other when I was working on some research-and-development projects with him, for GM, and I guess he liked me. Everything had gotten too big for Dale, and Childress had recommended me to him. It was at Dover in June of '93, three months after Alan had died, and I was in the pits, right next to Earnhardt, so I walked over to meet him. He was already in his car, helmet on, waiting to qualify, and I said, 'How's it going, Dale? You ready to race?' He stuck his hand through the window to shake hands and said, 'I don't want to talk about racing with you, I want to talk about you going to work for me.' Later in the day we went into his hauler to talk and he asked a lot of questions. I told him some of the things I had done for Kulwicki, but I think he respected me when I said I couldn't tell him how much Kulwicki's estate was worth, that I couldn't talk about a client's business to *anybody*. At any rate, that's how it started."

Earnhardt's affairs were "like a Rubik's Cube," said Hawk, with "a lot of interesting colors in there, but all mixed up." Earnhardt and his wife, Teresa, were trying to handle it as best they could, but "she was busy being a housewife and a mother and he was driving for another championship. So I came in with Dale on a salary, plus some other considerations, which is still the way we work, and what I did was turn the wick up. I can't say that Dale and I always agreed on everything, but I stole a line from Benjamin Franklin: 'If two people agree, you don't need two people.' I convinced him that if the offer is ten percent and two oranges, you ought to shoot for fifteen percent and three oranges; that if you sign a T-shirt deal with four people, they're going to be competing with each other and so you ought to deal with only one of them; and that you don't have to sign every deal that comes along, because sometimes less is more. We bought the apparel company [the T-shirtery] and I sorted out all of the businesses under one holding company. I think I did a really good job of it. The highest compliment is when somebody says, 'You know, that reminds me of Mark McCormack and Arnold Palmer.' But let me say this about Dale Earnhardt. I think he's a phenomenon. He might be a country boy who quit school in the eighth grade, but he's got a master's degree in street smarts."

From the standpoint of marquee value, there was an awful lot of deadwood back there in the field of the forty-plus drivers who showed up for the qualifying rounds every weekend at a Winston Cup race. Three of them were in their mid-fifties—Shepherd, Marcis, Trickle—and they were among about a dozen drivers who were years away from their last victory and seemed to have little hope for another one. Few people in the world outside of racing, the audience that NASCAR was straining to reach, had ever heard of drivers like Steve Grissom, Ted Musgrave, Rick Mast, Elton Sawyer, Robert Pressley, or Joe Nemechek. It was, again, like the Grand Ole Opry, where a performer would be anointed as an Opry regular on the basis of one hit song; and then, thus tenured, could hang around for decades as long as he or she showed up willing and able and sober for a certain number of Saturday nights each year. (Anybody heard from Jeanne Pruitt, of "Satin Sheets," since 1973?) The faded stars of both the Opry and Winston Cup had their devoted fans, of course, but their hanging around and refusing to quit was causing a logjam. "One thing you do have to consider," said a NASCAR official in a mild defense of the system, "is how long it takes to find a sponsor and train a rookie, both on the track and off, and to build a following. It's a gamble, a lot of hassle, and most owners and sponsors would just as soon stick with the Golden Oldies." There were many thousands of young stock car drivers out there across the land who would kill for a chance to join Winston Cup, and yet, in this season of '96, there was only one rookie, Johnny Benson, among the forty drivers. (Most major-league baseball clubs carry two or three rookies on their twenty-five-man rosters.) NASCAR, with its guaranteed provisional starting spots for yesterday's heroes, was stuck with them.

All of this made the arrival of young Jeff Gordon seem like either a promoter's dream or a blessing from above. There had been a long dry stretch between infusions of fresh blood in the Winston Cup family. Some had died just as their stars were in the ascendancy, most notably Kulwicki and Davey Allison, while others like Darrell Waltrip and Derrike Cope weren't finishing in the top ten so much anymore and were in danger of becoming faithful family pets. There was still a strong coterie of about a dozen high-profile drivers with solid sponsorships who appeared capable of beating Earnhardt on any given Sunday, and with some panache—Rusty Wallace, Terry Labonte, Mark Martin, Sterling Marlin, Ricky Rudd, Dale Jarrett among them—but it had been quite a while since a driver in his twenties had come onto the scene possessing "the whole package," as the marketeers would put it (driving ability, enthusiasm, charm), to not only challenge Earnhardt but bring new fans to the sport as well. Winston Cup racing had become a weekly television event now, on the order of the NFL's Monday Night Football, and what NASCAR desperately needed was a teen idol to demonstrate to the nation that stock car racing had come a long way since the incestuous days of bootleggers and "creative engineering" and tire-iron fights in the pits. What they were praying for was someone who could share center stage with the indomitable Earnhardt, who, in many ways, represented the past. Enter, Gordon.

Jeff Gordon would be called the "first test-tube driver" when he showed up for Speedweeks at Daytona in '93, just twenty-one years old, for his first ride in a Winston Cup race. Earnhardt and most of the others in the old guard had been born to race cars, many of them as worshipful sons of doting dirt-track drivers, but Gordon's story had a new spin; he was a California kid who had spent his young lifetime racing nearly everything *but* stock cars. Much of the credit goes to his stepfather, John Bickford, an auto parts maker who was wealthy enough and caring enough to stake him all the way through his serendipitous climb through the racing world. The kid was racing bicycles in motocross competition when he was four; and, by the age of eight, racing every weekend all over the country. He became the national champion in quarter midgets: six-foot-long open-wheel sprints with single-cylinder 2.85-liter engines. He moved up to slightly more powerful go-karts the next year and kept winning, at age nine, until kids nearly twice his age rebelled and sent him packing, back to sprints. A sort of midlife crisis came when he was fourteen and found that he was too young to drive the bigger sprint cars that he and his stepfather were interested in, so they solved that by building a 1,300-pound, 650-horsepower sprint car and moving to Indiana where there was a racing series with no minimum age requirements. He won three races before he was old enough for an Indiana driver's license, and every year he moved up to more powerful cars and won more championships. It seemed that he would be a natural to join the Emerson Fittipaldis and Ray Mearses on the rich IndyCar circuit, but it took more money to join that exclusive European-flavored body than even John Bickford had, so the family picked up and moved to North Carolina to try another tack. By the time Gordon discovered full-bodied stock cars, he had already won some 600 races of all kinds.

His introduction to the big NASCAR machines came when, out of curiosity, he attended Buck Baker's driving school at the Winston Cup track in Rockingham, North Carolina. Slipping behind the wheel of one of those big mamas, just before his nineteenth birthday, was akin to a kid going to Yankee Stadium for the first time and falling in love with baseball. *Hey, man, this is it.* He spent the next year shuttling between NASCAR and the United States Auto Club, winning Busch Grand National's Rookie of the Year in the big stocks and USAC's Silver Crown championship in Indy-type sprints, and in '92 he turned his full attention to Busch Grand National. In March of that year, at the BGN race in Atlanta, he caught the eye of Rick Hendrick by outrunning Earnhardt and the legendary Harry Gant. Hendrick said, "I thought, 'Man, that guy's gonna wreck, you can't drive a car that loose.' " Three months later the richest owner in Winston Cup was signing the brightest star NASCAR had seen in years to a long-term contract. Gordon began driving the number 24 DuPont Chevy in '93 at Daytona—at twenty-one becoming the youngest driver ever to win one of the Twin 125s—and went on to be named Winston Cup's Rookie of the Year. In his second year he won the inaugural Brickyard 400 at Indianapolis (celebrating his NASCAR-record $613,000 payday by ordering a pineapple pizza from room service) and the Coca-Cola 600 at Charlotte, finishing the season eighth in points. And in '95 he blew everybody away: eight poles, seven wins, most miles and laps led, record purse winnings of more than $4.3 million.

The Kid had it all: good looks, a respectful manner toward his elders, taste and grace, a beautiful ex-model for a bride, every instinct of the great race car driver, and, not the least, favored status with the richest team ever assembled in stock car history. Rick Hendrick, his owner, coddled and exalted him as though he were heir to a throne. Ray Evernham, the crew chief for the Rainbow Warriors, calmly worked with him in the manner of a wise and patient older brother. Elfin, five-seven and 150 pounds, Gordon was every sponsor's dream: a twenty-five-year-old who loved movies and *People* magazine and video games, water-skiied and shot baskets in the driveway, thanked the Lord for his good fortune at every opportunity, moved as easily among DuPont executives twice his age as with goggle-eyed young fans who finally had a driver they could relate to, and could bubble like a teenager ("cool, man, awesome") after going door-to-door with the gnarly Earnhardt for three hours at hairy speeds. When Earnhardt began his needling campaign, trying to "work on his head," Gordon acted as though it were a fun little game, just a little joshing from a favored uncle. Remembering that Earnhardt had groused that when "Wonder Boy" accepted his honors they would "probably serve milk instead of champagne" at the Winston Cup banquet in Manhattan, Gordon went along with the gag by having a waiter bring a silver champagne bucket to the dais at the Waldorf-Astoria and pouring himself a flute of milk so he could toast the grinning Earnhardt down there in the front row.

Even his courtship and marriage to the former Brooke Sealey read like a fairy tale, embraced by thousands of dreamy teenaged girls who could have been Dave Marcis's granddaughters. Their first meeting had taken place when she, as a Winston Model, had presented him the trophy for winning a Twin 125 at Daytona in '93. They had been admiring each other from across crowded rooms and garages for some time, but there was a problem: Winston Models couldn't mingle with drivers. Thus began a courtship so furtive that friends of each began to wonder why such a handsome young man and an effervescent beauty never showed up at functions with a date. Earnhardt even walked up to Gordon one day and bluntly asked him if he were gay. They became experts at meeting on the sly, at restaurants and other places where the racing crowd wasn't likely to be found ("I became a master at sneaking in and out of hotels," said Gordon, and Brooke learned to case a restaurant for kitchen-door exits when she first walked in), but they finally came out of the closet one year to the day from their first meeting, when Brooke had finally ended her reign as a Winston Model. In a dark corner of a French restaurant in Daytona, ostensibly there to celebrate their first anniversary, he proposed and she accepted. The young prince married the princess, and soon they moved into an airy, tastefully appointed manse hard by the campus of Davidson College, north of Charlotte.

No doubt about it, Winston Cup racing had a dream pairing on its hands: the grizzled old son of a dirt-track terror versus the preppy Christian child prodigy who had teethed on open-wheel sprints. It was like the uncouth Gas House Gang of the St. Louis Cardinals against the regal New York Yankees; a brawling club fighter against a clever dancing counterpuncher; a souped-up hammer-down pickup truck against a purring Lamborghini. Earnhardt hunted and fished and did grunt work on his farm; Gordon played Nintendo and watched *Seinfeld* on television every Thursday night and shot hoops in the driveway with his young bride. It was, simply put, a promoter's fantasy—a villain in black against a young challenger in white—and NASCAR could only sit back and enjoy the show. It was about to begin.

8

THE EVIL WEED

Every track on the circuit had a distinct personality, making its own demands of the drivers and crews, and one of the meanest of them all was Darlington Raceway up in the piney woods of northeastern South Carolina. This was the original superspeedway, christened on Labor Day of 1950, and that was the problem. It had been built for a different generation of race cars, souped-up hot rods and overbred jalopies that were barely a step away from hauling moonshine; but now, nearly half a century later, these new monsters that had replaced them were qualifying at speeds nearly twice as fast as in the beginning. The track was uneven in many ways —rippled from having been laid on sand, pear-shaped, slick from a new layer of asphalt, and too narrow to accommodate side-by-side racing in the turns—and although the teams respected the track for its place in history, they also cussed it. "It's like running through a mine field at a hundred and sixty miles an hour," said Rusty Wallace. "It has an invisible hand that'll slap you if you're not paying attention," said Earnhardt. Said Dale Inman, the team manager for Bobby Hamilton's Petty Enterprises car: "I'm always saying you need a couple of breaks to win a race, but here you need about four."

When the car-haulers rolled in at daybreak on Friday, past the usual encampment of rowdy fans already queued up in their jangle of pickup trucks, waiting for the gates to the infield to be opened for them the next morning, the crews could only cluck and shake their heads when they saw the track. Jim Hunter, who had been one of the beat writers in the earliest days of NASCAR and had grown up to become president of the speedway, had chosen not to whitewash the retaining walls since the last race, on Labor Day of '95, which had seen eighty-seven of the 293 laps run under caution. Everywhere they looked, the walls were still streaked with the previous year's "Darlington Stripes," scars left by cars that had gotten out of control, ominous warnings of the treacherous hours of racing that lay ahead. The black streaks and gouges on the retaining walls served the same purpose as the clusters of white crosses one sees planted on highway shoulders to mark the site of traffic fatalities. "The problem is," said Ken Schrader, who had been wrestling with the track for all of his adult life, "the grooves are so narrow that there's nowhere to run if there's a crash in front of you."

Oh, the horrors! The Lady in Black would turn out to be as wicked as ever. A combination of temperatures in the seventies and a softer new tire being tried out by Goodyear had led to a record qualifying speed (by Ward Burton, at nearly 174 miles per hour) but much carnage during practice and qualifying, as well. "To get around that fast," Burton had said after his exhilarating ride, "you have to pump yourself up and hold on." Gordon had qualified second, Earnhardt only twenty-seventh (putting him in one of the less desirable pits on the backstretch of the cramped track, whence no driver had ever won), Kyle Petty a distant thirty-ninth. There was mayhem everywhere once the race began, with Dick Trickle spinning out on his own oil slick and crashing on just the second lap. Gordon slipped past Burton on the eighth lap and was in the lead for most of the long afternoon, using his patience and getting good pit stops from his crew, as the yahoos in the infield hooted over the demolition derby going on in his wake. There were a total of eleven cautions for fifty-six laps, with only seven cars finishing on the lead lap, and an even dozen went out in crashes or with engine failures; six others simply running out of gas while desperately gambling at the end, one of those being Earnhardt, who finished fourteenth. Gordon led 189 of the 293 laps and won the race by five car lengths, on a roll now, moving up to ninth place in the point standings at this early juncture in the season.

The coming of spring and the emerging battle between The Intimidator and The Kid should have had them dancing in the labyrinth of carpeted corridors and cubicles at the headquarters of the R.J. Reynolds Tobacco Company in Winston-Salem, but it would take more than that to resuscitate them from the gloom that had been hovering over the big house for many months. For a quarter of a century now, ever since that day Junior Johnson came by to see if they might sponsor his race car on NASCAR's old Grand National circuit, RJR had been sponsoring stock car racing's big show. The makers of Winstons and Salems and Camels and other cigarette brands had created Sports Marketing Enterprises to handle all aspects of Winston Cup, from press relations to rights fees to the considerable purse money, and RJR estimated that it had laid out three quarters of a billion dollars in the endeavor over those years. They wouldn't give out a figure on how much they were spending each year, except to say there was some $6.5 million in "visible" money for various point funds and bonuses ($1.5 million of that going to the winner of the points championship), but experts in the field of sports business estimated an outlay of between $15 and $20 million each year. Even at those prices, it was considered well worth the returns in exposure to RJR's products. But now, due to a crusade against tobacco led by the Clinton administration in Washington, that cozy relationship between cigarettes and stock car racing was being severely threatened. It seemed quite possible that RJR would be forced out of the game if and when Clinton and the Food and Drug Administration declared nicotine an addictive drug.

They were in it for the promotional value, of course, and therein lay the rub. Everywhere one went on the circuit there were constant reminders of RJR. The company sponsored only one car (Jimmy Spencer's Smokin' Joe's

Camel Thunderbird) and one points race (the springtime Winston Select 500 at Talladega), plus a nonpoints all-star spectacular under the lights at Charlotte in May, but those expenditures were hardly necessary. It was, after all, called Winston Cup racing, and all of the eighteen tracks were ablaze with red-and-white banners and billboards carrying the Winston logo. It was just as impossible for television cameramen to follow the cars around the track without showing the Winston colors as it was for sports editors to refer to it as anything but Winston Cup racing. RJR had gotten into it in the first place to circumvent the ban against cigarette commercials on radio and television, effected in January of 1972. Over the years, as the dangers of cigarette smoking were revealed, the tobacco manufacturers had been under the gun from Washington. If it wasn't one restriction, it was another: health warnings on cigarette packages (1965), the surgeon general's report on secondhand smoke ('72), mandated no-smoking areas on airplanes ('73), the first employee lawsuit to prohibit smoking in the office ('76), a call for higher health insurance premiums for smokers ('84), the banning of all smoking on domestic flights and interstate buses ('90), a Supreme Court ruling that cigarette manufacturers could be held liable for secondhand smoke in tobacco-related deaths ('92). Now, in this Winston Cup season of '96, President Bill Clinton was going for the jugular. His approach was straightforward: kids shouldn't smoke, kids watch sports on television or in person, so they shouldn't be exposed to tobacco advertising.

It didn't take any special prodding for the troops to rally behind RJR, even if their pronouncements did sound as though they had been memorized from a playbook. "This is America, isn't it?" was the key phrase, whether uttered by Earnhardt on an infomercial as his wares were being hawked on a split screen or by some other driver during an interview. So what, if only one of the forty or so drivers still smoked, the line went, they didn't need some big-government *liberals* telling 'em what to do. This was conservative country, *tobacco* country, certain of its denizens still yammering about Yankees and the Civil War and states' rights, code words left over from George Wallace in the face of integration in the mid-sixties. Brian Murphy, editor of *Sports Marketing Letter*, noting that "injuries might result from sponsors tripping over themselves to get to the phone to call up NASCAR to be new sponsors" should RJR lose out, made a valid point: "This is the national sport of the South. If the Confederacy had won, NASCAR racing would be the national pastime." And all of the teams and the drivers who were clustered around the old tobacco lands of North Carolina knew where *their* government was. It wasn't in Washington, D.C. It was in that fierce granite fifteen-story monolith on Main Street in the middle of downtown Winston-Salem, a tired old hill town of about 145,000 where there was no such thing as a no-smoking section, the world headquarters for the stupendously wealthy R.J. Reynolds Tobacco Company.

The president of RJR's Sports Marketing Enterprises, a garrulous man in his late forties named T. Wayne Robertson, could look through the window of his office in a modern annex and see the big house next door, the focus of *Barbarians at the Gate*, a scathing book and cable movie about corporate extravagancies at RJR Nabisco. Grave meetings were taking place over there nearly every working day as Washington continued to tighten the screws, and, as a measure of Winston Cup racing's place in the scheme of things, Robertson was one of the regulars around the conference table. If there was an irony in the fact that only one Winston Cup driver still smoked cigarettes, then how about this one: Robertson's father, a retired farmer, lay dying of lung cancer in a Winston-Salem hospital. "I tried to get him to quit, but he enjoys it," he was saying. "Who am I to deprive him of one of his last pleasures?" His mother and his wife were smokers, he said, but neither he nor his twenty-one-year-old son partook. The real issue at stake, and this was the tack chosen by RJR, was one's constitutional right to make the decision for himself. Hanging on one wall of Robertson's office was a framed photograph of his son, Toby, with aspirations of becoming a Winston Cup driver, posing beside the red Pontiac race car that he currently drove at the short paved track at Hickory, in one of NASCAR's lesser divisions. Robertson was the owner and the sponsor of the car. Painted on the hood was the legend, in block capital letters, TOBACCO PAYS MY BILLS, and on the rear quarter panels there was THIS IS AMERICA.

"Look," he said, patting his expansive gut and smiling, "I'm thirty pounds overweight. I can't eat at McDonald's or it might kill me. I know that, so I try to stay away. But the point is, I don't want Bill Clinton or anybody else telling me I've got to get on a scale and weigh in every week, that I can't go to McDonald's ever again until I've lost my thirty pounds. It's big government that we don't like. I've been a registered Democrat all my life, and so has my father, but I wouldn't vote for *this* one." He was smitten by his analogy between fast food and smoking. "These fast-food restaurants are smart. They start hooking kids on cholesterol by putting up those swing sets, having games and sandboxes, doing Ronald McDonald, and then they have the audacity to play the smoking card with the parents by having no-smoking sections. You see? They're throwing rocks, but they live in a glass house."

In many ways, Robertson fit the profile of the men in the boardrooms of NASCAR and Winston Cup. He was born and raised on a farm in the North Carolina countryside, and got a degree in fire safety engineering from little Rowan College in Salisbury, thinking one day he might become a fire investigator for insurance companies. But he had loved automobile racing as a kid, and he and his father had a side business in fuel additives. RJR was into it in a limited way in the late sixties, mainly sponsoring road racing through its Carter Hall pipe tobacco division, and young T. Wayne signed on with the company in 1969 to haul show cars around the country. "I'd tow a Petty Plymouth behind a station wagon to shopping centers all over America. I was just a kid, getting to see the country, and it was a lot of fun." Then came Junior Johnson, in November of 1970, looking for someone to sponsor his race car on the old Grand National circuit.

"You could sponsor a car for about a hundred thousand dollars a year back then," said Robertson, "but we needed to do something bigger than that. We [tobacco makers] had caved in on the advertising ban and needed some way to sell our products. So a man here named Ralph Seagraves got in touch with Bill France in Daytona, and we put together a five-year plan called Winston Cup. Nobody, in 1971, had any idea how it might work out. But it became evident early on that it was a good marriage. We were from tobacco country and we had advertising expertise, and racing fans smoked. The money wasn't the big thing to NASCAR then. Stock car racing had been regional, with that background in moonshine, and we not only had marketing capability but we were nonautomotive. So the most important thing we did was to give racing affirmation, if you will."

Of the current drivers, only the handful in their fifties could remember when RJR wasn't lord of their realm, the sugar daddy of big-time stock car racing. Until RJR got into the game, NASCAR had been a haphazard confederation of regional auto-and-farm-supply sponsors and scores of ragged tracks mixed in with a few modern superspeedways, the purses financed for the most part by race-to-race gate receipts. It wasn't uncommon for the full-time drivers on the circuit, such as it was, to compete in fifty or sixty races every year in a desperate attempt to make a decent living. The first race to be held when NASCAR's Grand National Division became Winston Cup was the 1971 Daytona 500 (although all "Winston Cup records" cover the pre-RJR days, back to the formation of NASCAR). In that first year the points fund from RJR was a total of $100,000; and now in this season of '96, Robertson pointed out, the payout to the points champion would be a cool $1.5 million and the twenty-fifth-place finisher in the point standings would receive a check for $25,000. But it was more than the money. RJR had brought a well-oiled public relations juggernaut into NASCAR and had become such a presence that nobody in the business could imagine life without Winston Cup. The "Coke Cup"? The "Kellogg Stakes"? The "Hooters Chase"? Forget about it. In late '95 there had been a syndicated sports cartoon in the newspapers, showing cars racing side by side in the "Annual Surgeon General 500," with the cars bearing the legends "May Cause Cancer" and "May Be Hazardous to Your Health." No one at RJR or NASCAR or the Winston Cup shops was amused.

"This sentiment's been going on for over thirty years," Robertson was saying, invited to take his best hold. "I don't mean to minimize it, but we've been facing it for a long time. Philip Morris, Chesterfield, Marlboro, and some others have all sponsored sports events and concerts, but the Kool Jazz Festival is no more and all of them seem to be buckling just like we did in '69 with the ban on advertising. At the same time, I've seen the saccharin scare and the red meat scare, but they stood up to 'em [the government]. But now look; we can't even get an appeal, an audience, a chance to be heard. 'No, no, it's a fact, cigarettes are bad, case closed, that's it.' Let me say that the government has done an excellent job of advising people about the risks involved, but let me add that it's totally untrue that four hundred thousand people die every year from smoking cigarettes. How about cholesterol and heart disease? They don't play a part? We try to respond, but they won't even listen. What kind of a democracy is that? This is *America?*"

RJR was hitching its wagon to the rural conservative elements in the country, which happened to be Winston Cup racing's natural constituency, and calling Washington's incursion just more evidence of a big liberal government running amok and stomping on free enterprise. "Tobacco is a legal product that thirty percent of the American people are buying," said Robertson, heating up now. "Cars, racing, fast foods, alcohol, cigarettes, there's a risk involved in all of them. Plenty of people *do* smoke, so we don't have to convince people to smoke. We just want them to smoke our product, not somebody else's. We want the legal right to advertise our own product, that's all. It's not true, by the way, that we're trying to hook kids on smoking. We've got studies showing that not that many underaged kids come to our races, anyway. Jeff Gordon came to us and said he'd like to do a commercial that would warn kids against smoking, and we said, 'Fine.' The commercial starts soon."

Robertson was seen at the Winston Cup races almost every weekend, hanging out in the media centers and the garages and the executive suites; a jolly sort with a full head of hair and eyes that disappeared when he laughed, which was often, wearing a nametag that simply read T. WAYNE. "It's not me, I'll always have a job," he was saying as he arose and stood in front of the wide windows opening up a splendid view of hilly little Winston-Salem on the eve of spring. "We're not barbarians. I still think like I did when I was a kid, milking cows at five in the morning, but you wouldn't think so to hear some of the stuff I get. I was on a call-in radio show not long ago and a woman said, 'How does it feel to have killed four hundred thousand people last year?' What do you say to something like that? Do you ask a guy on the assembly line in Detroit how he feels about killing fifty thousand people last year? How about the cook at McDonald's?" This was not going to go away anytime soon.

But there was a season of racing to be played out, too, and the sixth stop of the year would be at Bristol, a town of fewer than 25,000 souls, high on the Tennessee-Virginia border, where funny-looking little nursery-rhyme hills blip across the horizon as though scrawled with a kindergartener's crayon. This was Daniel Boone country, where the first frontier outpost was established the year the Declaration of Independence was signed, and the area known to the Tri-Cities tub-thumpers as the Mountain Kingdom was still a place of wild beauty. Ominously looming to the east and south were the clouded ridges of the Great Smokies and the Appalachian Mountains, home over the centuries to the mighty Cherokee Nation and then a succession of log-cabin Scots-Irish settlers and hunters and trappers and moonshine runners. Even in this time of development and the intrusion of Interstate 81, not to mention television and automobiles and small factories paying decent wages, the dank forests and deep hollows of east Tennessee were populated by a mean breed of hillbillies from another time. Hikers along the nearby Appalachian Trail had learned to walk softly around brooding Roan Mountain, never to go alone into the small villages in search of supplies, for if the native yahoos weren't simply harassing them they were burning the ATM shelters to the ground just for the hell of it.

Maybe because of this isolation, the racing fans in the smaller places like Bristol and Rockingham and Martinsville seemed to welcome the Winston Cuppers with more fervor than at, say, Atlanta. For one thing, the economic impact of each of Bristol's two racing weekends was an estimated $55 million; and, for another, not a whole lot happened during the year in those parts. And so, as early as the Thursday before Sunday's running of the Food City 500, the towns of Bristol, Johnson City, and Kingsport were swarming with show cars and meet-the-drivers autograph opportunities like the Food City Family Race Night at the Eastman (Kodak) Employee Center. There might have been a few fans who had waited all their lives to visit the building in downtown Bristol where, two days apart in August of 1927, the first commercial recordings in country music history were made by a tubercular cab driver from Asheville named Jimmie Rodgers and the Carter family of the nearby mountains of western Virginia, but mostly the folks were there to hear the engines roar. Raw weather with the threat of rain and snow and freezing temperatures notwithstanding, the dank bottomland outside Bristol International Raceway had become a sprawling campground by midweek. It beat staying at the distant motels, where the cost of a single in a fleabag on the Virginia side jumped from $30 to $60 overnight.

For anyone looking for an introduction to Winston Cup racing, this was the place to be. The track had opened in 1961, and over the years had evolved into the "Fastest Half Mile in the World," as it was proclaimed in huge white block letters on the outside facade. The track was set in a bowl, surrounded by 81,000 seats in steeply rising aluminum bleachers topped by light standards for the late-summer night race and for times when dusk fell in the early spring, and following a race from high in those seats was like watching theater in the round. The turns were banked at a perilous thirty-six degrees, the steepest on the circuit, and drivers were constantly fighting G-forces during their 500 laps around the course. "It looks like one o' them county fair deals for motorbikes," Richard Petty had said when he first laid eyes on the track, referring to the high-banked portable velodromes. It was so tight that a driver going into turn one couldn't see the exit to turn two. And if the vertigo from G-forces didn't get you, the rough concrete would; this and Dover being the only two tracks on the circuit so paved. "We call this our 'concrete' car," said Robbie Loomis, Bobby Hamilton's crew chief, as he pulled the wraps off the number 43 Pontiac and shifted into Motorspeak. "It was built for the high banks. Every time we'd go and run the high-bank tracks all the interior sheet metal would be warped up, you know? We thought the chassis was flexing. So we went home, put the car on a steel platform and twisted it, and built this car that has all these stiff bars and braces on it." The bottom line was that what worked for a car and a driver at Bristol was almost the opposite of what worked at the high-speed tracks such as Daytona and Talladega. The qualifying speeds at Bristol were some sixty miles per hour slower than at the monster tracks, but the torque and the rough concrete and the G-forces created more problems for the drivers and the mechanics than did the speeds and the necessity for drafting at most other tracks.

When they gathered on Friday morning for practice and the first round of qualifying, there was some off-track news that most of the drivers preferred not to discuss. The long, sad saga of the Allison family—the

Alabama Gang—was playing out in the courts and in the family compound at Hueytown, a rough old steel town on the outskirts of Birmingham. The brothers Bobby and Donnie Allison had abruptly uprooted their families from Miami, in 1963, and moved to Alabama with the vague notion that it would be a good location for their racing operations. Donnie did all right as a driver, but Bobby was the spiritual leader of the family and would become one of the most renowned drivers in NASCAR history. A hardworking, hard-driving man of craggy features and a lead foot, he was a three-time winner and a three-time runner-up in the Daytona 500, a Winston Cup champion once, a six-time winner of the Most Popular Driver award, winner of nearly $8 million in purses during a period when they were still relatively small, and still ranked in a tie for third (with Darrell Waltrip) with eighty-four career NASCAR wins. But now, after a series of tragedies unmatched in the history of automobile racing, he and his wife of thirty-six years were divorcing and just about everything they owned was being auctioned off.

The calamities had begun at Charlotte Motor Speedway in 1981, when Bobby won the World 600 race but Donnie suffered serious head injuries in a crash that effectively ended his career. Seven years later, in a four-month period during the '88 season, Bobby would go from the highest high a father could know to the end of his own career as a driver. He won the Daytona 500 in February of that year, and his promising young son Davey finished second. But then, when a tire went flat on the first lap of the Pocono race that June, Bobby lost control of the car and slammed into the wall in a wreck that not only ended his driving career but left him with multiple broken bones and internal injuries and, worst of all, a scrambled brain resulting from a severe cerebral concussion. There would be more tragedy, much more, the death of his adored father by cancer in April of '92 being just a beginning. Four months later, just as Bobby had slowly begun to regain some of his memory and was back in Winston Cup as a car owner, his youngest son, Clifford, was killed during practice at Michigan. ("I walked up close to his car, as close as I am to you, and he wasn't disfigured or anything," he once told an interviewer, "but I could see that he was dead.") Eleven months after that, in July of '93, his thirty-two-year-old son, Davey, who had already won eighteen Winston Cup races and was

NASCAR's hope for the future, died when he crashed his own new helicopter while landing at Talladega to watch a friend test a car. Then, during the first practice session for the 1994 Daytona 500, Bobby lost his best friend when Neil Bonnett, an honorary member of the Alabama Gang, died after a wreck.

Bobby Allison had become a sad apparition as he dutifully showed up at the Winston Cup tracks every week, overseeing the Bobby Allison Motorsports cars driven by Derrike Cope in both the Winston Cup and Busch Grand National circuits. They were sponsored by Badcock furniture outlets and Mane 'n Tail, not exactly heavyweights with millions to throw around, and after the first five races of the '96 season Cope had finished in the top ten only once and was running thirty-sixth in the Winston Cup points standings. Allison had worked hard for years to regain his senses— giving much credit to his Catholic faith, his many therapists, even the working of crossword puzzles—and was proud to say that he was back in the cockpit of his private plane after passing rigorous examinations to become recertified. But still, to the other members of the racing brotherhood, it was painful to watch as he shakily mounted the steps of the tall chair at the number 12 pit stall in order to radio directions to his driver during a race. There, but for the grace of God or at least a good set of tires and clear sailing in the turns, go they. Bobby Allison served them as a living reminder of the precariousness of their profession.

> HUEYTOWN, Ala. (AP)—Model cars made by the late Davey Allison will be among the items up for sale Saturday when racing great Bobby Allison auctions off his Alabama home and its contents. . . .

It was there, in the papers, when everybody arrived at Bristol, and nobody quite knew what to say as the number 12 Thunderbird was being off-loaded from the hauler in the garage area. The marriage between Bobby and Judy Allison had never been the smoothest, there having been many rancorous separations over the years now totaling nearly four decades, but it had finally collapsed under the relentless series of disasters. Said Neal Sims of the *Birmingham News*, closer to the situation than any of the regulars on the beat: "Bobby's way of coping was to throw himself into his work, but that work was what had cost Judy her sons and, in a way, her husband. She had no way to deal with her grief, the way Bobby did. A marriage counselor hadn't been with them for fifteen minutes when he said, 'I've never said this before to any couple, but you folks need to get a divorce.' " Judy had rented an apartment, and Bobby was drifting between his mother's house in Hueytown and his condominium above Charlotte Motor Speedway. All of their money had been gobbled up during Bobby's protracted rehabilitation, and now they were auctioning off not only their 5,000-square-foot lakefront home but a trove of memorabilia that could never be replaced: hats, T-shirts, jackets, shoes, photographs, newspaper clippings, even signed racing tires; artifacts representing the racing careers of Bobby and his two dead sons.

Compared to the travails of the Allisons, the other news of the Winston Cup world over the soggy weekend amounted to little more than amusing tidbits. When Mark Martin, the chalky little Arkansan, hit town, he had to shoot down a wild rumor on the racing grapevine that he was dying of cancer when he wasn't even sick ("If they'd said I had AIDS, now, it would o' made me pretty mad"). Earnhardt and his owner, Richard Childress, held a press conference to announce that they were joining the move to multi-car teams by adding a second car to be driven by Mike Skinner on a limited basis, sponsored by the makers of Realtree camouflaged hunting gear. Showing that football was still the king of sports in Tennessee, the honorary starter for Sunday's race would be University of Tennessee coach Phillip Fulmer, making this his first Winston Cup race. Earnhardt and Rusty Wallace would be flying to Japan immediately after the race to run tire tests for the exhibition road race there in late November. In the media center, there was a stack of Fort Worth newspapers splashed with a front-page photo feature about Bruton Smith's Texas speedway—"Raceway Rises from the Prairie"—and, while Smith was on their minds, they wondered just exactly why he intended to put a dome over this Bristol track when it already held in the noise to the point that crews could barely hear their drivers over their headsets. Terry Labonte was being called NASCAR's "Iron Man," now that he was one race away from tying Richard Petty's record of 513 consecutive Winston Cup starts, and it was announced that in mid-April he would throw out the first ball at Oriole Park at Camden Yards alongside baseball's new "Iron Man," the Baltimore Orioles' Cal Ripken, Jr. (A harried sportswriter for the local paper, with five other bylined stories in one edition, wrote an entire column on Labonte from a Chevrolet press release.) Somewhere in the mix was a professional wrestler known as Sting, a blond hunk in a gaudy nylon purple-and-yellow windbreaker and shades, opining that he was "big-time pumped up" about the Cartoon Channel's sponsorship of driver Steve Grissom's "Yabba-Dabba-Doo" car. "One question, Sting, can you take Hulk Hogan?" said a reporter. "Take him? I'll *kill* him," said Sting, who was still babbling when the cars were cranked for qualifying.

Martin found the simplest way to stanch the rumors of his cancer by winning the pole with a speed two miles per hour slower than his record of the year before, due to the low temperatures. (He would go on to win Saturday's Busch Grand National race as well.) Unlike most of the other drivers, who felt that a good spotter from the roof of the grandstand was essential in the tight confines of Bristol, he said it didn't matter much because "by the time he tells you there's a wreck up ahead you're already a part of it." There was room for only thirty-seven starters, on such a short track, and five big-name regulars on the circuit, including Kyle Petty and Bill Elliott, had to settle for provisional spots at the end of the field. Six other lesser names failed to qualify at all. The cold weather had something to do with it, making tire decisions more critical than ever, but qualifying on a half-mile track was always a gamble. As in greyhound races, when one tiny slip could mean the difference between first place and last, there was not the distance to recover from a mistake that there was on a two-and-a-half-mile superspeedway. The rookie, Johnny Benson, didn't make it; nor did a young Texan named Bobby Hillin, who had hauled his car to Bristol for tests two weeks earlier and had to personally shovel snow off the track in order to get in a few practice laps. Even Dale Jarrett had his troubles, crashing his car after qualifying seventh and being forced to start at the rear with a backup car. Saddest of all the qualifying stories, though, was the sight of the beloved Dave Marcis, arm around the waist of his wife, Helen, scrawling autographs as he hurried to get out of the infield before the start of Saturday's Grand National race.

Horrid weather forecasts or not, the hordes piled out of their motels at daybreak Sunday for the maddening trek to the little racetrack. (Most churches in the Tri-Cities area had learned to hold only a nine o'clock morning service on racing Sundays, and the wise parishioners had found that the one sure way to part the waters as they tried cutting across the thick lanes of traffic was to tape a sign in the windshield that read "Going to Church.") More than the figures showing their "brand loyalty," more than the size of the fan clubs, more than their gobbling up every silly souvenir and tacky T-shirt known to mankind, this day offered absolute evidence of the stock car fans' devotion. All day long, the bitter winds whistled and the dark clouds boiled with trouble, but they nestled into their seats—more than 80,000 of them in all manner of foul-weather gear —and hooted and howled and roared as though it were a sunny day at Daytona. Sensible people would have stayed home, swallowing their tickets and settling in before the television set, but nobody has ever referred to stock car fans as sensible people. There were three red-flag rain delays throughout the long day—the delays consumed two hours and forty minutes, the official driving time was only one hour and fifty-nine minutes— but the fans found the Wave and other diversions to keep themselves engaged. All in all, it was a mess, with only six cars finishing on the lead lap and three not finishing at all due to crashes.

The end was almost anticlimactic. Mark Martin had burst away from the pole to lead the first sixty laps, Skinner and Elliott taking over for a while until Gordon took the lead for 100 laps. There followed a numbing succession of rain delays and caution flags, and a confusing period during an abrupt red-flag stop when the cars pulled into the wrong pits and the rain poured down and nobody seemed to know exactly who was in the lead or just what the hell was going on. They cranked up again and drove for about twenty laps, Gordon clinging to the lead, before the third red flag sent everybody to the pits with only 342 of the 500 laps having been completed. For more than an hour, with the track lights on and fans finally beginning to leave under blackened skies, the drivers and crews hunkered down in their pits and garage stalls and car-haulers, eating sandwiches and giving out television interviews. Gordon, in fact, was talking to ESPN, live, when Earnhardt stepped into the interview and said, in a burst, "You win. Congratulations. I'm outta here." *Well, golly.* The Kid sloshed through the puddles to Victory Lane, saw that the stands were nearly empty, shook hands with somebody, and then headed home. Just that quietly, he had pulled into sixth place in the standings and was knocking on Earnhardt's door.

9

JUNIOR AT EASE

On a chilly Thursday morning in mid-April, when the racing teams were loading their cars onto haulers in preparation for the next-to-last Winston Cup race ever to be run at the raggedy little track in tiny North Wilkesboro, less than an hour's drive up the road from the shops around Lake Norman, Robert Glen Johnson, Jr.—aka Junior Johnson, Tom Wolfe's "Last American Hero"—had more important matters of his own to attend to. After forty-three years in the business, about the last of the living icons in the relatively brief history of stock car racing had abruptly retired on the day after the final race of the '95 season, sold off the remains of his huge stockpile of equipment for a tidy $5 million, took his punishment from the courts for ditching his longtime wife for a woman less than half his age, and settled in on his 200-acre spread to spend the rest of his days—as a husband to his young bride and father to their two small children—in a life of relative ease and prosperity in the swooping dales and hollows of Yadkin County. Instead of staying up half the night, fidgeting about tires and engines and carburetors and chassis setups for Sunday's race at what had been his home track for four decades, he had gone to bed early and gotten up at five o'clock to make some coffee in the silence of his majestic 14,000-square-foot granite Georgian mansion before heading outside to check on the 200 head of black Santa Gertrudis cattle wandering about the rolling meadows. They needed some more grass to chew on, and this was the weekend Junior had chosen to plant it.

At nine o'clock, a visitor to the double-winged white-columned palace on the knoll could look through the thick beveled windows of the oaken double doors and see the new Mrs. Johnson, an attractive thirty-year-old strawberry blonde, wearing a shiny jogging outfit and listening to her Walkman as she trudged in place on a treadmill. The children were on the floor, playing games, and through the plate-glass picture windows at the rear of the house there could be seen a backyard playground holding swing sets and slides and monkey bars and a sandbox. A middle-aged housekeeper answered the door and said, "You the book writer? You drove right past him. He's down there on one of the tractors."

The morning fog had burned off to reveal a brilliant sunny day in this, a reluctant spring, and an artist would have reveled in the vivid colors: sleek black cattle, cobalt sky, rich ocher earth, velvety blue-green grass. Down by the old country road, next to the Oak Grove Cemetery, four tractors pulling discs known to farmers as rotary rock rakes were chugging along in clockwise circles, raising swirls of dust, as they chewed at the rocks and roots and moist clumps of dirt. It wasn't difficult to pick out which one was being driven by Junior; it was the one with a photographer hanging on for his life, like a ball-turret gunner on a Flying Fortress, firing away with his cameras as the faded red tractor bumped along its rounds. His subject, contentedly jouncing on the wide seat, was something right out of a *Progressive Farmer* photo spread: great shock of white hair over a leathery bronze face, sparkling set of teeth, outfit of bib overalls and tan work boots and a blue nylon windbreaker and a gimme cap from a North Wilkesboro auto parts store. He had been in the celebrity business long enough to know how to strike a pose, and for another ten minutes he peered right and squinted left and furrowed his brow and flashed his fine teeth until the photographer, clambering all over the tractor to get the proper angles, seemed satisfied. Then Junior cut the engine and descended from the tractor, peeled off his leather work gloves, fished some Chap Stick from the pocket of his jacket, and began slathering the balm on his cracked lips as he surveyed his handiwork.

"Bet you figured you were done with the press," he was told.

"Aw, well, with the race at North Wilkes this weekend and all, I reckon I'm still sorta news. Magazine fella's comin' by tomorrow, and so's ESPN."

"Seen any of the car-haulers go by yet? You can see your house from the main road."

"It's a mite early. Truth is, I ain't been lookin' for 'em."

"Thought you might show up at the track Sunday."

"Aw, naw. When I quit, I quit. I might pass by the TV to see who's winning. But I've gotta get this fescue down. Sunday looks like the best time to do it."

. . . Junior Johnson was over in the garden by the house some years ago, plowing the garden barefooted, behind a mule, just wearing an old pair of overalls, when a couple of good old boys drove up and told him to come on up to the speedway and get in a stock car race. They wanted some local boys to race, as a preliminary to the main race, "as a kind of side show," as Junior remembers it. . . .

When *Esquire* magazine published Tom Wolfe's article about Junior Johnson in 1965, in a flashy style that affected, for better and for worse, a whole generation of young journalists smitten by its reliance on italics and exclamation points and stream-of-consciousness riffs ("Ohmigawd, it was . . . *yesss* . . . *Junior!!!*"), stock car racing got its first big-time national exposure. Wolfe had spun a lavish tale of a near-mythological creature who had sprung from the deep woods of the southern Appalachians, the shambling semiliterate son of a bootlegger who had gone on to become a legend in what was then a little-known subculture, an amusing footnote, of American folklife. This Junior Johnson was an original, a force of nature, some kind of primordial form of life that had oozed up out of the forest primeval without an instruction manual. His speech was sprinkled with strange backwoods resonances like, "Yee-'uns" and "Hit don't bother me none," and he was given to showing up at racetracks garbed in bib overalls and scruffy old clodhopper work boots. Junior was in his mid-thirties at the time of Wolfe's visit, trailed by an entourage of good old boys and a durable childhood sweetheart named Flossie Clark, and he was at the top of his game as a driver on NASCAR's Grand National circuit before he inadvertently led to its becoming Winston Cup. He had spent much of his youth hauling moonshine out of Ingle Hollow and the Brushy Mountains in Wilkes County, an isolated tangle of impenetrable coves and ridges and hardwood forests, and had even served nearly a year at the federal penitentiary in Chillicothe, Ohio, after getting caught waiting for another load at his daddy's still. He was still hauling whiskey on the side even after he began racing; fell asleep at the wheel of a liquor car and killed a woman in a wreck, in fact, less than a year after his release from prison (pleading guilty to manslaughter and getting off with a $300 fine and a suspended sentence). Incorporating many of the skills he had learned as a liquor tripper, knowing no fear, seeming to have an innate *feel* for preparing a car and then racing it, he won a total of fifty races—taking thirteen of the circuit's thirty-six races in '65—before retiring as a driver and becoming a car owner in 1966.

He was only thirty-five years old when he quit driving, a decision hurried along by the on-track deaths of such old friends as Joe Weatherly and Fireball Roberts when driving stock cars was truly a perilous piece of business, and it was as an owner that he excelled. During those thirty years, when Junior's shops were in his backyard, a total of twenty-three drivers ran under his banner. It was a love-hate relationship in many cases, Junior being a cantankerous perfectionist who did not suffer fools gladly, but the arrangement was profitable for those who stuck it out. His best years were in the seventies and the mid-eighties, when his drivers—most notably Cale Yarborough, Bobby Allison, Bill Elliott, and Darrell Waltrip—won 107 races and six Winston Cup championships, Waltrip alone winning forty races in one span of five years. In all, as an owner, Junior put 139 cars in Victory Lane and won more than $22 million; a take that still ranked him third, in 1996, behind Rick Hendrick and Richard Childress. But only nine of those victories had come during the nineties, five of them by Elliott in '92, and he got off some parting shots when he stepped away from it all.

"Money is the root of all the problems we have in our sport," he said, directing his fire at the emergence of the superteams run by men like Hendrick, whose fortune derived from sources outside of racing. "You can't *buy* everything you want. You've got to be smart enough to figure out how to do it without the finances everybody else has, and I've always been able to do that." The politics had gotten nasty, he said, to the point where "there's no pride in any of 'em." Hell, the man some felt had always enjoyed special dispensations from NASCAR couldn't even cheat anymore. He had been fined and suspended for twelve races (reduced on appeal to three) for running an oversized engine in '90; again caught the wrath of NASCAR inspectors during Elliott's hot streak of '92 when he was found tampering with the camber of the rear wheels, a fine piece of country "creative engineering" that brought about new rules; and it was only fitting that he would get nailed for the illegal intake manifold found during inspection before his very last Daytona 500.

For Junior, times had been changing off the track as well. He and Flossie had gotten married soon after Tom Wolfe's visit, and outwardly they had evolved as NASCAR's First Couple. They were as down-to-earth as Moon Pies and Dr. Pepper, country folk with huge appetites for good food and lots of laughs with friends, and Flossie became legendary in her own right for her artery-clogging breakfasts held for the racing crowd on the weekends of races at the North Wilkesboro track. "Junior was liked," said Darrell Waltrip, "but Flossie was loved." It became a barren marriage, in due time, and Junior began to stray. They had unofficially adopted a boy named Brent Kauthen, whose mother had married the head of General Motors' motor sports division, and he was calling their home his and being staked by them to his education at North Carolina State, in Raleigh, when he was killed in an automobile accident. It was a double blow for Junior; he had lost not only a son but an heir to his racing operation as well. Flossie had been unable to give Junior the children he said he always wanted, and soon, at the age of sixty, he was seen slipping around with Lisa Day, a twenty-six-year-old registered nurse who had grown up right down the road in Wilkes County. Junior and Flossie separated, and the lawyers were working things out as amicably as possible until Flossie heard the whispers about Junior's wanderings. "It tore my heart out," she said, and the divorce proceedings took a turn that cost Junior a big chunk of his considerable holdings; right down to half of his 200,000 chickens. They divorced in October of '92, Junior marrying Lisa two months later in a fancy affair at the Ritz-Carlton in Atlanta, and soon the babies began to arrive: Robert Glen Johnson III in August of '93, and Meredith Suzanne in July of '95.

The countryside had also changed since that day in the early fifties when Junior's brother came to fetch him out of the garden patch and take him racing for the first time, at the North Wilkesboro track, when it was little more than a dirt bullring with plankboard fences and flimsy bleachers. One had to strain now to imagine how it must have been in the forties and fifties when the night air would explode with the thunderous roars of trippers, scores of them, as they bumped up out of the hollows and squealed onto the pavement to begin their nightly runs into Statesville and Winston-Salem and Charlotte. The moonshiners had the money then in those parts, but all of that changed when the mechanized Holly Farms poultry plant came to the valley, bringing salaried jobs and more paved roads, opening up the territory. Now, tenuously clinging to the ridges and looming over the little white church steeples and long rows of tin-roofed chicken sheds and the bleached old barns and double-wide house trailers with satellite television dishes planted out front, there were spanking-new timber-and-stone aeries belonging to wealthy Florida retirees or to executives from Charlotte who could zip up there on I-77 in less than an hour to spend their weekends posing as country squires.

If there was a single word to describe Junior at rest, it would be "contented." He had undergone triple-bypass heart surgery in March of '93, while Lisa was carrying their first child, but he had come back as hale as ever and was holding his weight at 220 pounds under Lisa's regimen of salads and pasta rather than the grease-and-gravy diet of the past. He was early to rise, early to bed, except when he and Lisa might go into Statesville or Winston-Salem or Charlotte for a movie, and his towering physical presence—the hair that had turned white when he was a teenager, the leathery skin, the hooded gaze, the measured resonance of his voice (now devoid of the twangs and the double negatives, for the most part)—

reminded one of Paul (Bear) Bryant at the end, or maybe even Ty Cobb between debaucheries. His holdings came to 378 acres, distributed over five different parcels in the valley, and the cattle numbered 500. He had no cash-flow problems, not since the whopping sale of his racing operations, and the great joys of his life were working the soil on the farmlands beneath a high benevolent sky and gamboling with two little kids who called him Daddy. Except for occasional visits from faithful old friends like Cale Yarborough, whose relationship had been forged in the raging fires of many a chaotic race day, he had just about disassociated himself from automobiles and racing. On this weekend, he expected a couple of visitors —Jimmy Spencer, whose only two Winston Cup victories had come in '94 as a driver for Junior; and Junie Donlavey, a longtime car owner from Richmond—while, in the meantime, down the road at the old homeplace, Flossie would be having Bill Elliott for breakfast and Darrell Waltrip and his wife for dinner.

Only when someone came around, asking him for reflections, did he even talk about the old days. "These guys today don't know where [racing] came from, what it was like. We used to go on the road for two weeks, and had to find a gas station or a level piece of ground to work on the car between races." Great drivers? "It takes three things: physical strength, natural talent, and the willingness to never give up. The drivers were better thirty years ago. It took unbelievable nerve to drive back then because the safety equipment wasn't as good and the cars were flat unsafe. I had eight or ten die around me when I was racin', includin' Fireball and Joe [Weatherly], and one day at Darlington there was four or five boys got killed in the pits. The thing about fear is, any driver who's afraid is no good. You might get afraid *after* the race, when you see the film and realize what might have happened to you, but even then you say, 'It's not going to happen to me.' Anyway, I'd say the best were Cale and Darrell and Curtis [Turner] and Fireball and Bobby Allison. Richard Petty kept drivin' to the point that he couldn't win, and that hurt his image to my mind. Earnhardt was a good one, but he's about forty-five now and a driver's reflexes start to slow when he's forty. Jeff Gordon, now, I'm not takin' away from the boy, but the car's a big part of it with him." He still maintained that the best race cars ever built were "whiskey cars," especially the '40 Ford, and that the move toward multiple teams was ill-advised: "They're spreadin' them-selves too thin. Say if you've got three cars and none of 'em qualifies, then you got three sponsors to explain things to. It's hard enough to make *one* car win." What about Tom Wolfe, the writer who had made him famous? "Some folks got mad at first, thought he was makin' fun of us, but then they got to seein' that he was doin' a different type of writin'. He's got friends over in Asheville, rich folks at the Biltmore estate, and I've run into him over there a time or two. He's a good old boy." He would leave it to others to say that he had played a pivotal part in the development of stock car racing: the driver who discovered drafting, the inventor of the seat belt as we know it today, the mechanical genius fully appreciated only by the boys in the shops, the one who led to RJR's creation of Winston Cup, the star of the first major national exposure in the media, the very embodi-ment of the sport's astonishing growth from liquor hauling to million-dollar sponsorships over a period of less than half a century.

"Some men would kill to be where you are right now," he was told. "Young wife, kids, all of this."

"Well, it took me a while to get here, you know."

"Any sadness about the end of racing at North Wilkesboro?"

"It's a shame it's got to end, but I reckon that's progress for you." That last question seemed to interest him least of all. Junior Johnson smeared his lips with some more Chap Stick, tugged at his cap, wriggled into his work gloves, and climbed back onto the wide bucket seat of the tractor. He squinted into the sun and saw that it was halfway up, ten o'clock. A few more turns around the plowed field and it would be time for Daddy to walk up to the big house and see what the kids were up to.

North Wilkesboro Speedway, some fifteen miles west of Junior's new digs, was one of the two original NASCAR tracks remaining on the Winston Cup circuit, the other being at Martinsville, Virginia. It had been scooped out of the red Carolina earth in 1947 by a local man named Enoch Staley, to accommodate the postwar madness for the new sport of stock car racing, and it became the home track for a gaggle of good old boys and moonshine trippers from Wilkes County, one of the premier moonshine havens in the nation. It was a half-mile dirt track in the beginning, the scene of many tire-iron fights and fender-bangings and roostertail slides into the flat corners, and among the heroes was Ralph Earnhardt of Kannapolis, who often brought along his young son Dale to observe the proceedings and maybe learn a thing or two. The track was paved with asphalt in '57, while Junior was away in prison, and he became the biggest favorite of them all. Once, when Junior got outfoxed and was passed during a race by another driver, a man who turned out to be an uncle of his flung a jar of moonshine at the offending car and was escorted from the premises during the ensuing red-flag pause in hostilities to pick up the shards of glass. Another time, a race had to be postponed when thousands of earthworms wriggled to the safety of the asphalt surface following a heavy rain. In more recent times, Junior was invited to dedicate the new Junior Johnson grandstand by smashing a jar of moonshine against the facade. "I told Enoch, 'Well, I don't know, I've had a lot of trouble with that stuff, you know,' " but he obliged, anyway, and a good time was had by all.

The problem with the track now was that it had simply outlived its usefulness. It was relatively flat and slow, a five-eighths-mile oval with an all-time record qualifying speed of only 119 miles per hour (contrasted with the 200-plus at Daytona and Talladega, and, at the slow end, the 91 at the road course in Sonoma, California), and there were only 40,000 fixed reserved seats with room for another 20,000 on the weedy banks and in the infield. It had a certain rustic charm, to be sure—a hydraulic lift was used to raise the winning car to the checkerboard-painted roof of the infield media center for Victory Lane ceremonies, and a wooden four-by-four timber had been erected to fill a gap in the concrete retaining wall on pit road—and camping on the steep little hills was where you found it. Luxury seating meant metal folding chairs arrayed on the concrete steps at the front straightaway, and the whole place had the jury-rigged feel of an add-on carport in a trailer camp. With room for so few fans, the problem was pure and simple: lack of revenue. The teams and drivers saved a lot of overhead by spending every night back home in their own beds (Kyle Petty even rode the 100 miles from his home to the track, each day, on his Harley), and the countryside was so sparsely populated that they didn't have to mess with show cars and personal appearances there, but the fact was that a win at North Wilkesboro was worth peanuts when compared to the take at most of the other tracks.

Enoch Staley had died during the '95 season, and the track went on the block when neither his survivors nor the area Chamber of Commerce showed the will to continue. In a blink, a pair of racetrack barons swooped in to divvy up the track: Bruton Smith of Speedway Motorsports, Inc. (Charlotte, Atlanta, Bristol, and the new monster track going up in Texas), and Bob Bahre of the track in the wilds of New Hampshire. They each bought fifty percent of North Wilkesboro, not to modernize it but to take its dates and move them to their own tracks; Smith for his 163,000-seat Texas Motor Speedway in the spring, Bahre for a second race each year at New Hampshire. There were some lamentations expressed around poor Wilkes County, which stood to lose about $10 million a year it had been raking in from the two Winston Cup weekends ("I think Enoch Staley's gonna be turnin' over in his grave," said a woman who lived across the road from the main entrance to the track), but nearly every single driver and owner and sponsor and NASCAR executive understood that it was a business decision, cut-and-dried, whether they liked it or not. There were vague promises to offer Busch Grand National and pickup truck and modified races to North Wilkes—no one seemed to want to let racing there go completely belly-up—but that seemed scant compensation. "You don't move a top-of-the-line sport away and bring in something else," said Junior, predicting that the citizens of the county wouldn't support anything less than Winston Cup. Ashes to ashes. The folks at little Martinsville Speedway, a similar track that also traced back to NASCAR's first year, were shaking in their boots.

Although Junior had made it clear that he would be leaving no light on in the window for the racing crowd as they turned off of I-77 and headed west on old U.S. 421 in order to make it to the track at daybreak Friday, surely the older men in the car-haulers pointed out to the younger ones Junior's mansion on the hill, not a half-mile to the north, as they grabbed gears and negotiated the massive eighteen-wheel rigs along the familiar undulating road. It had been a long struggle for the old-timers who were still hanging on in the business, as crew chiefs or fabricators or tire changers or truck drivers, and a Junior Johnson sighting at that time of day —"Gawdam, why, it's, it's . . . *Junior! . . . out there plowin', and it ain't even sunup yet!!!*" Wolfe might have written—would have been worth a mighty blast on the air horns. *Way to go, Junior, stick it to 'em, boy!* Such was the legacy of a man who was like a granddaddy to them all, their own Last American Hero, in a very real way the father of all of this. But duty called and they moved on; to save the air horns for the early-arriving fans who would be lining the main entrance at dawn, waving pennants for their heroes, hoping to get a glimpse of, say, Mark Martin riding shotgun; to ease across the silent racetrack (no tunnel here) and find a place to park in the cramped infield; to unload the cars and the portable garages; to find something to eat at this ungodly time of day. They reckoned that if Junior could have done this for forty years, so could they.

The companion event for Sunday's First Union 400 Winston Cup race would be something called the Lowe's Home Improvement Warehouse 150, a ninety-three-mile race in NASCAR's Modified Division, Lowe's being based right there in Wilkes County. If Winston Cup was the major leagues and Busch Grand National Triple-A, then this was a rookie league. The drivers were kids from small towns in the area, like Kernersville and Wallburg and Mount Airy; the sponsors were small local firms such as Salem Plumbing and King Plaza Flea Market and Clarence's Steak House; the cars low-slung lightweight little open-wheel numbers capable of zipping around the North Wilkesboro track at six miles per hour faster than the hulking Winston Cup machines. While the big boys would be competing on Sunday for $1.2 million, the first million-dollar pot in North Wilkesboro's history, the purse for the Modified race came to a measly $20,250. There were no "bird-dog" scouts in NASCAR, as in baseball, where wizened old part-time talent-hunters working on finder's fees could always be found sitting in lonely high school bleachers in hopes of discovering some raw teenaged phenom, so the only way for a kid to get out of the Modifieds and make it to the next level was to completely blow away the opposition, week by week; better yet, on a weekend such as this when the Winston Cuppers were sharing the track. Although there would be no more than 15,000 people in the stands for the Lowe's 150-lapper on Saturday afternoon, which was carried only on local radio and by ESPN on a same-day tape-delay telecast, there were those fans who preferred the laid-back earnestness of these hairy little affairs to the thundering predictability of Winston Cup spectacles, and the kids did not disappoint. There were wrecks galore as they shimmied into the narrow corners, tires squealing and thin panels of sheet metal flying, the sparse crowd bellowing its encouragement, and there was a feeling that if this was, indeed, the future of North Wilkesboro Speedway then the fans just might be able to live with it in spite of Junior's dire prediction that the fans had seen the best and wouldn't settle for less.

Junior's name kept coming up, in spite of his absence. There was, of course, the Junior Johnson Grandstand over there on the backstretch, so proclaimed in big block letters atop what was actually just a section of ordinary aluminum bleachers. But when the qualifying got underway, it was discovered that he was connected with four of the cars and/or drivers who qualified in the top twenty. The man of the moment was Terry Labonte, the pole winner, whose start on Sunday would tie him with Richard Petty for the most consecutive races in NASCAR history and deliver him to Camden Yards for Baltimore's home opener. Labonte was getting the full ride from the spin doctors on this weekend: the familiar red and yellow Corn Flakes colors of his Chevy had been painted over with battleship gray to symbolize his new stature as the Iron Man of racing; and it was announced that he would finally see his picture on a Corn Flakes box, after eighteen so-so years in Winston Cup, alongside The King himself. The Labonte connection with Junior was that he had driven in eighty-seven races for the Johnson team, from 1987 through '89, winning both the pole and the spring race at North Wilkesboro in '88. "When I drove for Junior," he said, "this was the most important race of the season. I think we put more effort into this one than we did the Daytona 500." Junior's touch was felt by three others, as well, all of them driving Fords he had unloaded in his closeout sale: Elton Sawyer, who had qualified for the outside pole in the number 27 car; Jimmy Spencer, whose number 23 had been a Johnson machine; and, of course, Brett Bodine, whose car number 11 (the number made famous by Junior Johnson, the driver) had been the centerpiece of the sale.

There were the usual shenanigans, rumors, low-comedy routines, breathless press releases, and other entertainments to keep the folks in the garages and the infield media center occupied as the first truly hot days of the season arrived. A fellow who looked and sounded exactly like Don Knotts's character on *The Andy Griffith Show*, all ears and teeth and jumpy high-pitched shriek, had found a second career as Barney Fife (moving to the Concord area, buying the television show's Mayberry Sheriff's Department squad car, and making a living from personal appearances and commercials); and here he was, in full fine fettle, moving about the infield in his tan Mayberry uniform and crushed hat and deputy's badge, answering to catcalls in his falsetto yelp. Kyle Petty's annual charity motorbike ride from California back to Charlotte was coming up soon, and already seventy Harley freaks had anted up $7,500 apiece to ride cross-country with him. A little gay-bashing by one of the *Winston Cup Scene* columnists: "Considering that [fitness guru] Richard Simmons's kind aren't appreciated around race tracks...." A letter in *Scene* from a fan in Pennsylvania, responding to charges of desecration of the American flag if Earnhardt went with a red-white-and-blue paint job on Memorial Day: "I fly the American flag twenty-four hours a day, with a light on it at night.... I still get a tear in my eye when I hear taps, because I am a veteran. I also fly the Earnhardt flag under the American flag every Sunday...." The reckonings that this might be the very last Winston Cup race at North Wilkesboro were shot down when the track announced that tickets for the fall race had been printed and would go on sale Monday morning, besides, the more modest operators had argued, they had budgeted to run up the road to Wilkesboro in September, not to undertake a costly trek to Texas or New Hampshire. On a bleak note, for the second week in a row Dave and Helen Marcis found themselves leaving early Saturday, with another DNQ.

"Gentlemen ... *and Jimmy Spencer* ... start your engines." The honorary grand marshals for the Sunday race were John Boy and Billy, a noted country music disc jockey team out of Charlotte, widely syndicated and wildly popular with the stock car set, and they were about to become the latest to learn about the fierce loyalty Motorheads held toward their favorites. The affable Spencer, still known as Mr. Excitement for his impropitious gambles on the track, was "a little hurt, myself, at first, but I figure they were just a couple of old boys havin' some fun"; but for the fans, it meant another opportunity to get published in *Scene* ("I know it's a God-given right to be stupid, but he [John Boy Isley] abused the privilege," wrote a woman from New Jersey). Start their engines they did, the thirty-six gentlemen *and* Jimmy "Smokin' Joe" Spencer, and off they roared for another Sunday drive in the country. For the first couple of hours, the fans were presented with some plain good racing—few accidents, dramatic green-flag pit stops, a dozen lead changes that gave that many drivers ample hope—but when the shadows grew long it appeared to be shaking down as a duel between Terry Labonte and Rusty Wallace.

More often than not, a Winston Cup race came down to the wire. Wallace, a premier short-track driver over his sixteen-year Winston Cup career (in the eight short-track races in '95, he had two wins, two seconds, two thirds, and a fourth), seemed to have his black number 2 Ford dialed in for this one. He and Labonte had been going back and forth since the halfway point, and he had taken a commanding lead on lap 321 when all of a sudden, like a bolt of lightning streaking out of a cloudless sky, disaster struck with only twenty-seven laps to go. Just when he might have been rehearsing his post-race remarks for Victory Lane, he saw the 37 car driven by little John Andretti, of the famous Indy family and the hideous purple Kmart/Little Caesars paint scheme, spinning like a top in front of him on the frontstretch. "Go *low*, go *low!*" Rusty's spotter radioed as Andretti, who had been smacked from behind by veteran Geoff Bodine, slammed into the outside retaining wall. Wallace obeyed the spotter and took the lowest groove, but now Andretti was caroming off the wall and diving across the track to the apron. "No, go *high*, go *high!*" his spotter yelped, but it was too late. Andretti, helplessly hung out to dry, was sideswiped by Joe Nemechek and slammed into the cluster of protective water barrels at the pit road exit. He then bounced back into the line of fire and sat there like a sitting duck as Wallace hit the brakes—his tires smoking and laying rubber—and T-boned the crippled car with a sickening sound, like somebody crunching a beer can. They could add a new definition to the expression "That's racin'." Two cars, neither on the lead lap, had ruined the leader's day, and

Rusty didn't even collect the feared Goody's Headache Award; that honor going to Andretti. If that wasn't a headache, what was?

It took eleven minutes under a red flag to clean up the mess—Andretti's car had caught on fire, bringing on the boys with the foam to blow-dry the bits of metal and rubber and refill and rearrange the water barrels—and Labonte managed to keep his Hendrick Motorsports teammate Jeff Gordon in his mirror to win by a car length. Wallace collected only $21,615, mainly for leading so many laps. Because he took the $129,200 Unocal Challenge Bonus for winning from the pole, Labonte gathered in a total of nearly $230,000 for this one day's work. It was a good thing Junior hadn't come to the races after all, for in his fourteen years as a driver his total winnings had come to a paltry $275,000 and Labonte's take might have made him a little testy. Maybe now, as the dusty car-haulers lumbered past Junior's mansion on the hill at dusk, somebody would hit the horn in a salute.

10

UNSAFE AT ANY SPEED

In the late sixties, taking stock of the kingdom he had wrought since those frenetic early days of the beach-road course at Daytona, Bill France, Sr., might have sat back and proclaimed a seventh day of rest like any ordinary god. The creation of NASCAR would have been enough of an accomplishment for most mortals, given the degree of difficulty inherent in organizing such a motley crew of cowboys, and certainly his building of the first giant racetrack for stock cars, Daytona International Speedway, had assured a living monument in his memory. He had become the most powerful czar in the history of any sport in America—king of kings, caller of all shots, head of an organization with more than 20,000 members, the one man to talk to whether the subject was tire size or admission prices— and if anybody had ever doubted his power he had famously dispelled such thoughts when, in 1961, Curtis Turner and Tim Flock tried to align the drivers and mechanics with Jimmy Hoffa's Teamsters; France shooting them down before they got off the ground by calmly advising them that if they joined the union they couldn't race. But France was a big thinker, still in his fifties, and he wasn't about to stop there.

Toward the end of the decade, scouting locations for a monster track of his dreams that would be even bigger and faster than Daytona, he zeroed in on the state of Alabama. There were plenty of NASCAR tracks in the Carolinas and on up the eastern seaboard, but none in the very belly of the Deep South, whence came the soul of stock car racing. The search led him to a little jerkwater town known as Talladega, in the low rolling hills of east Alabama, fifty miles east of Birmingham and 100 miles west of Atlanta. A friend of France's, a car dealer in nearby Anniston, told him of the weedy sad remains of an abandoned Second World War military air base sitting amidst some 2,000 acres. The price and the location were right (France had found that 15 million people lived within a 300-mile radius of Talladega), and when Alabama's governor, George Wallace, promised to speed the completion of I-20 on the Alabama side and to open more roads to the track, the bulldozers descended. Not only had France gained a powerful new friend—he would serve as Florida campaign manager during Wallace's two runs for the presidency—he created the damnedest racetrack the world had ever seen.

This thing, Talladega Superspeedway, was terrifying. It was a tri-oval, with a backstretch nearly a mile long, and its 33-degree banked turns were slightly steeper than those at Daytona. The first drivers to let it all hang out in test runs rumbled back to the garage area with white knuckles and the shakes, reporting momentary blackouts from vertigo caused by the G-forces. Soon enough, it would be found that the draft was an even bigger factor there than at Daytona. In fact, the drivers balked and threatened to boycott the track when it came time for the inaugural race in September of 1969. They had formed the Professional Drivers' Association by then, electing Richard Petty as president, and to their list of general demands—bigger purses, better health insurance, a pension fund, improved bathrooms and showers, better seats for spouses and kids in the infield—they added their fears that Talladega might be unsafe at any speed. As he had dealt with the Teamsters threat, so did France deal with the PDA: *you don't want to race, somebody else will.* Only one regular on what was still called the Grand National circuit raced that first day (Bobby Isaac, who was presented an expensive gold Rolex watch from France afterward in appreciation), and when there were no serious accidents the drivers drifted back into the fold in time for the next Talladega race in the spring of 1970. This was Bill France's baby, and they would have to learn to live with it.

As the drivers developed a feel for the track and technology expanded, improving aerodynamics and boosting horsepower and creating the need for special "Talladega" tires, the qualifying speeds began inching upward year by year, from Bobby Isaac's 186.834 miles per hour in 1970 to David Pearson's 197.704 ten years later. Even Isaac could see what was happening, and in the middle of a race at Talladega four years after the inaugural, he got spooked, "heard somebody talking to me," and abruptly wheeled the car to the garage, never to return; an action that effectively destroyed his career, although he would continue driving until he died of heart failure, soon after, during a race at another track. Everybody knew it was only a matter of time before somebody would hit the magical 200, and to some that figure was as symbolic as breaking the sound barrier had been for jet test pilots. "Yeah, when I saw *The Right Stuff*, about Chuck Yeager and those boys out at Edwards Air Force Base in California trying to go supersonic, it reminded me of how breaking two hundred was for us," said Benny Parsons, now a Winston Cup announcer, the first man to qualify a stock car at those speeds (200.176, in '82, at Talladega). It had become a familiar sight at Talladega to see a car lose the draft and suddenly lift skyward, going airborne at more than 200 miles per hour. When Bill Elliott set the all-time record, hitting nearly 213 miles per hour in 1987 ("*Awe*-some," he said, bug-eyed), the time had come to mandate restrictor plates at both Talladega and Daytona. And that brought another problem that most drivers felt was even more dangerous than the raw speed; the plates were installed over the carburetor to restrict the flow of oxygen and fuel, cutting the standard horsepower from roughly 700 to 400, which kept speeds below 200 but also equalized the cars and robbed them of the reserve power necessary to stomp it and get out of there when trouble developed.

Now, as the teams rolled into Alabama on the last weekend of April, they resumed their cursing about the vagaries of the schedule. They had just completed what was referred to as the "short-track schedule," consecutive weekends at the shortest tracks on the circuit (Bristol, North Wilkesboro, Martinsville), and now ahead of them lay two tracks of an entirely different nature: Talladega, the fastest; and the serpentine road course at Sonoma, California. It seemed like a macabre practical joke, some devious obstacle course laid out to addle the troops at Parris Island, and especially aggravating was the fact that the grinding Winston Select 500 at Talladega followed right on the heels of the race at Martinsville, the slowest track in Winston Cup other than the two road courses. The half-mile Martinsville Speedway, just over the North Carolina line in southern Virginia, was shaped like a paper clip; the shortest and second-flattest track on the circuit, where braking and handling were more important than nerve and flat-out speed. The record qualifying speed at Martinsville was only 94.129 miles per hour, and the race usually went to one of the craftier veterans, like Earnhardt and Rusty Wallace, with dirt-track sensibilities; indeed, Wallace had taken the past weekend's race, his fourth straight Goody's Headache Powders 500 at Martinsville, by nursing his brakes and staying out of trouble. Now came mighty Talladega, where qualifying speeds would be 100 miles per hour faster. To the drivers, the change of pace was like having chased a studious little curveballing relief pitcher from the mound, only to look up and see some snarling flamethrower with a blinding fastball striding in from the bullpen with malice on his mind.

Also on the agenda for the weekend were a 500-kilometer ARCA race and the second round of the IROC (International Race of Champions) series, pitting a dozen stars from four different types of racing, but the focus was on Sunday's Winston Cup race and the track itself. Here, again, was further evidence that the large well-heeled superteams with deep reserves were the future. There was no way for, say, Dave Marcis, even with his new sponsorship from Prodigy, to compete with Hendrick Motorsports's 165-odd shop personnel and a stockpile of more than 300 engines and in-house dynamometers and other state-of-the-art accoutrements of the big-time modern racing shop. Nor could he afford to load up and go to Talladega for tests, dropping $30,000 just like that, as owner Robert Yates had just done in behalf of Ernie Irvan and Dale Jarrett. Earnhardt repeated the metaphor scripted for him in a television commercial, that driving at Talladega was "like hooking up with a 500-car freight train," adding that it resembled "flying a plane or steering a boat, where you don't want to make any sudden turns." Lately, the masters at Talladega had been the veteran drivers with deep pockets, like Earnhardt and Irvan and Elliott and Marlin; and that wasn't likely to change anytime soon, according to a middle-of-the-pack driver named Bobby Hillin: "Only the very best teams have the good stuff, and not too many rookies are going to be in those cars." Tell that to Johnny Benson (the only rookie in the field): "It's not just the driver. It's the whole program—engines, body, crew, the whole nine yards —and then there's experience."

In a long chat with reporters before the cars went out to qualify on Friday afternoon, Jarrett went off on a monologue about the perils of running at Talladega: "It's pretty much hell. Anybody that tells you it's not the most nerve-racking place we race, they haven't been up in that lead pack and been a part of what goes on. Two eyes, a mirror, and a spotter aren't nearly enough to keep up with everything that's going on around you out there. It's fun, and it's great to sit there all day and try to outthink everyone else, because that's what it is, a thinking game. Obviously you have to have a good car to get yourself in that position [up front], but it's a thinking game, a chess match, all day long, to get yourself into position for the last twenty-five laps of this race." Then, he said, came the crunch. "You've got to start positioning yourself with about seventy-five laps [of the 200] to go. You need to be well within the top ten, because the leaders will start checking out [pulling away] about that time. By the last twenty laps, you've kinda determined who you're gonna have to race the most for the lead and to get to the front. You size up the competition and decide who you want to hook up with [in the draft] and who you need to stay away from because their car isn't strong enough to help you. As the laps dwindle down, you plot what you might need to do if certain scenarios unfold; who you want to link up with, who you want to avoid, and where and when you want to attack. Everybody talks about helping each other, but I can assure you there's no help to be found out there with ten laps to go in the race. Everybody needs some help at times during the race, and you want to repay the guys that help you at some point in time, but the last ten laps of this race isn't the time to repay any favors. The front's the best place to be. I'd much rather have Dale Earnhardt and a number of others trying to pass me than me trying to pass them. It's a lot easier to block than pass." Somebody asked him about fear, recalling the apocalyptic finish in 1993, when he came in third after Rusty Wallace went airborne and had his car demolished following a series of barrel rolls. "I lost my mind there, along with some other guys. That was probably the wildest two laps I ever remember racing. It scared me. It was pretty frightening to do it, and even more frightening later when I saw a replay on television. Hopefully, nothing like that's going to happen this weekend, but yet that's kinda the way this race could go all day."

And so most of the talk around the garages was about danger and courage, raw power and restrictor-plate racing; and whatever bets might have been placed on the outcome surely were going down not on the patient finesse drivers like Rusty Wallace, men much more at home on the short tracks, but on the daring veterans who would be buckled into rocket ships: the Irvans, Jarretts, Marlins, Earnhardts, Martins, and even Elliott after all those years. Although his was a dissenting voice, Jack Roush, owner of the powerful Ford teams of Mark Martin and Jeff Burton, had some interesting commentary concerning restrictor-plate racing at Daytona and Talladega: "The old saying, 'Be careful of what you wish for, because you might get it,' is true here. That's what happened to NASCAR. They wanted the cars to be even, with restrictor plates, and they got it. It's gotten so tight now that a first-year team can buy what it needs to finish up front. A lot of people don't have the experience or the good sense to stay out of trouble here, and the best drivers simply don't have the speed to get away from 'em. The fortieth-place driver, if he has the courage to stand on the gas, has a chance to win. One of the *truck drivers* could win. The trick at Talladega is to have the good sense to back off. But that's the problem; if you do that, then you don't have enough power to catch back up."

Roush's main man, the bony little Arkansan Mark Martin, leveled as few drivers were wont to do when asked about danger on the racetrack, specifically at Talladega. "If your typewriter shocked you," he said to a gaggle of reporters, "you'd go right back to it because it's what you do. Most of us [drivers] don't have anything else in our lives. That doesn't keep us from complaining about the tracks, the horsepower, the wrecks, the stupid driving, but it's what we do. I've never seen a race car driver who was semi-hurt who wouldn't race. One of his greatest fears is that he'll see his car out there racing and somebody else driving it. My goal this weekend is to get on the plane Sunday night with a smile on my face. The last four times I've raced here, I've had three wrecks, and I decided just recently that I'm not real crazy about coming to Talladega. It's great for the race fans, understand. They love it, with the side-by-side racing and everybody bunched together, that big old track and the competition. But it's scary and it's dangerous." Like his boss, Martin decried the restrictor plates: "I have no solutions, no ideas, not a clue about what to do about restrictor-plate racing. Daytona is slightly safer because the corners are sharper, the pavement is slicker, and handling is more important. It separates the best [drivers] from the mediocre. But anybody can go out and buy an engine and a chassis and run Talladega, and stay in the race if he doesn't wreck. The real problem here is, you're running too slow and you can't get away from anybody. It's a catch-22. I don't see how we can run any faster here, but that's what you need to do to stay out of trouble."

When the qualifying runs got underway later in the afternoon, to determine the first twenty-five starting positions, it looked as though it would be just another day at the track. A goodly crowd had gathered in the grandstands, under benevolent skies and mild weather, while down in the pits and the garages and on top of the car-haulers scores of mechanics, crew chiefs, owners, and even some of the sponsors' minions clutched their stopwatches in anticipation of the moment their man would be released for his warmup lap and the two more that would be timed. "Next out, in his number 12 Mane-'n-Tail Ford Thunderbird, Derrike *Cope!*" a voice would intone over the loudspeakers, eliciting a roar from the crowd, that being the car owned by Alabama's beloved Bobby Allison, grand patriarch of the now-defunct Alabama Gang. The cars would slither out of the pits, their drivers briskly shifting gears to get them up to speed, then gently steering them from side to side to heat up the tires, and by the time they had hit the backstretch of the monstrous track they would be approaching full-throated flight. As they finished their runs, the official elapsed times and the corresponding miles per hour would flash on the pylons in the middle of the infield, bringing cheers to some corners and groans to others. If there were any surprises, it was that seven of the top ten qualifiers were drivers who had never won a Winston Cup race. But nobody, not anywhere in the house, seemed surprised when the top two positions were won by the Fords driven by Ernie Irvan and Dale Jarrett, of the Robert Yates Racing combine. Yates, a veteran of the racing wars, had secured healthy sponsorships for both of his aces (Texaco for Irvan, Quality Care/Ford Credit for Jarrett) and hired two of the best young crew chiefs in the business for them (Larry McReynolds and Todd Parrott), and the term "powerful Yates engine" was the standard identifier whenever a writer typed the names Yates, Irvan, or Jarrett. As with Junior Johnson for many years before him, Yates seemed to know something about squeezing extra horsepower out of an engine that his brethren couldn't quite figure out.

Then, when the last driver had made his run, the shit hit the fan. NASCAR, in its eternal search for absolute parity among the machines, had responded to a request from unnamed car owners to conduct a spot check of the fastest qualifiers. They had gone so far as to buy a new toy for Gary Nelson, their Winston Cup director, a title translated to mean chief inspector of all things technical. It was a portable dynamometer, rigged with rollers and computers that would measure a car's horsepower once it was revved to its maximum revolutions per minute. Hardly anyone had noticed, during the qualifying runs, that a flatbed trailer had been eased into place just inside the wide gate leading from pit road to the garage area. Nor did anyone pay much attention when Nelson's army of uniformed inspectors hailed the fastest Ford (Ernie Irvan) and the fastest Chevy (Sterling Marlin) and ordered them to the trailer. (They wouldn't bother with the Pontiacs, which had been of little consequence so far.) Irvan's car was rolled up a ramp to the deck of the flatbed and wired to the computer like a heart patient. Nelson, who had shucked the red blazer he normally wore to distinguish him from the grunts and slipped into the usual red-and-white NASCAR worker's garb, wriggled into the cockpit of Irvan's number 28 Texaco Thunderbird and put on a headset so he could communicate with the owner, Yates, who stood beside the car in a state of considerable trepidation. Irvan and some of his crew hung back, hands jammed in their pockets, wondering just what the hell was going on. Then Nelson fired the engine and began to noodle the accelerator. He was going through the gears, building the rpm's, when suddenly—*blooey!*—he inadvertently slipped the clutch and a burst of smoke billowed from the exhausts. Yates and Irvan and the others were beside themselves, panic-stricken, but Nelson backed off and then resumed revving the car until— *ka-pow!*—the engine blew. Ruined: one $100,000 race car, double that price when the costs of transporting and testing were figured in. The only person smiling was Sterling Marlin, who now could get his crewmen to help roll his Chevy to the garage stall since the dyno's computer had blown as well.

This was a hell of a note for the normally placid Yates, who had already lost one car to NASCAR that season when he had to turn over Jarrett's winning Daytona 500 car for display in the new museum at Daytona International Speedway back in February. But all he could do now was live with the consequences. "Basically, we're all pretty good liars," he said of the men in the garages, grinning sheepishly through his wispy blond mustache, looking for a gentlemanly way out of this mess. "This was an attempt by NASCAR to get its own answers, and I can't quarrel with that. But this thing [dyno test] is really hard on a motor. I think they now realize that. Hey, I grew up working on chassis dynos, so I'm familiar with them. When you can isolate the gears and wheels and all of those things, it's a good deal, but this went a little far. We know you can hurt engines lugging them. All truck drivers in America know about lugging; when you go up a hill and miss a gear and go to the next one up and you don't have enough rpm's, you have to start over. That kills these engines, especially these restricted ones. The second round [after smoking the clutch], Gary did a good job driving it." Yates was frustrated. NASCAR had always dealt the cards, owned all of the balls and bats and marbles, and he found himself obliged to register an official complaint ("I'm not happy with what happened here") while, at the same time, acknowledging NASCAR's absolute power even in matters such as this obvious travesty. "Look," he said, hoping to close the issue, "there's a dirt track across the street, and I guarantee you I'd rather be racing here. If they told me to put water in my gas tank, I'd probably do what they say."

Most of the reporters had stayed in the infield media center during qualifying, where it was easier to catch the action and the times as they came in over MRN and the television monitors suspended from the ceilings, but they had witnessed the dyno test through the wide plate-glass windows, some of them rushing out to the truck when they saw the billows of smoke, and now they were clamoring for the NASCAR press people to go fetch Gary Nelson and bring him on the carpet to explain himself. Although Nelson was an amiable sort who had worked his way up through the garages, as a gofer and then a mechanic and finally as a crew chief, and he seemed to be respected and highly regarded by all sides, the boys and girls in the media center had every reason to doubt that they would get a crack at him. ("When something goes wrong, like a bad accident or a failed inspection, you'd be amazed how quickly the lines of communications shut down," said one of the feistier reporters.) But they were heartened to see none other than Kevin Triplett, NASCAR's chief of PR, rush out the door to corral Nelson ("Kevin," the same reporter explained, "stays in trouble with his bosses for being 'too helpful' to the press"). While they waited, another press relations type reported that if the Irvan engine was, indeed, blown, NASCAR was offering to fly it to the Yates shop in Charlotte for repairs or to do whatever else they could to ameliorate the situation. "Needless to say, we regret what has happened. Robert Yates has been very understanding."

Then came Nelson, being escorted by a grim Triplett to the lectern where routine interviews were conducted. Normally easygoing, with thinning blond hair and an affable grin, Nelson was a tad grim himself as he leaned into the microphone to summarize the situation. "I didn't dream up the test we did today," he said. "We've been to the wind tunnel several times, trying to figure out the differences in aerodynamic drag. Then the car owners said they wanted to compare motors. They came up with this machine and we said we'd give it a try. The machine is pretty good, but we had a computer problem. Robert Yates, the car owner, had the option to say no to the test. If he had, we would've done the test after the race. Anyway, he was there on the radio and I was the driver. He walked me through the whole procedure. He was nervous because that was their race engine. I smoked the clutch a little bit the first time. Once we got that sorted out it was basically no different than driving the car at full throttle. But then the computer malfunctioned and we lost all the data. Rather than do another run, we decided to scrap it for now, get our problem solved, and do it again at another time." He took a deep breath and got to the crux of the matter. "NASCAR strives to have close competition among various makes of cars. We have aerodynamic data so we're able to discuss intelligently what a Pontiac does, what a Chevrolet does, and what a Ford does with hard facts that we know are accurate. We're looking for the same thing on horsepower." He paused again and then said, laying himself bare, "Okay. I did it. Take your best shot."

There was a rush of shouted questions: "*Which* owners? . . . Is the engine wasted? . . . How's the dyno work?"

Nelson said, "I repeat, this was done at the request of the car owners. Nobody objected when I talked to the top teams I thought might have a chance to be in the top couple of spots, and that was about twenty teams' owners, engine builders, and crew chiefs. Not one guy said no, and most said, 'I hope it'll be me that you pick.' Qualifying was the best example of the peak that your car could do, because most guys detune their cars for the race. In a perfect world, the qualifying number would be the one you'd want."

"You're not a driver, *Irvan* is. Why didn't you let *him* do it?"

Ruffled, Nelson snapped, "I'm not going to answer that. Next question."

"Is this leading to artificial horsepower restrictions? Is this the future?"

Nelson sighed. It was at the heart of the issue. "The idea of NASCAR racing," he said, "is to try to get the cars to run side by side, to let the guys work within the rules to make the cars the best they can and to let the best driver go to the front. The drivers' talent should be displayed on Sunday."

For Ernie Irvan, the driver now being forced to use a backup engine and start from the rear after winning the pole (rules were rules), if it wasn't one thing it was another. He had been under close scrutiny since his near-fatal crash at Michigan in August of '94, and the questions persisted about his eyesight and courage and reflexes. Since the debacle at Daytona, when he started on the outside pole but went down early when he struck Earnhardt from behind and finished thirty-fifth, he had recovered handsomely by taking fourth at Atlanta, sixth at North Wilkesboro, and second at Martinsville, but now there was this. "In a way, my comeback was complete when they said I could go racing," he said. "My body and my mind have been through a lot of things since the accident. I'll go see the eye doctor again in December, but my vision is just about as good as it was, except for the little droop in the left eyelid, and I'm using normal glasses now. My vision is a hundred percent as far as the racetrack is concerned. I mean, hey, I won a 125 at Daytona, finished second at Martinsville, and qualified best today." How about his wife, who had been badly shaken since that day at Michigan when someone tapped on the door to the trailer in the infield to say there had been a little accident? "She sits in the motor home and watches on TV now, but mainly she's nervous because I haven't been running so well." Well, someone asked, how about the wasted car? "I'm not too sure what this dyno thing is all about. Gary Nelson was the driver"—a bit puckish here—"and you know, I wasn't aware until today that Gary was a driver."

There was no doubt that American automakers, down through the years of developing stronger and safer race cars, had been able to apply some of that technology to the improvement of the ordinary passenger car; which was, after all, their main piece of business. General Motors and Ford and Chrysler and all of the others who had waxed and waned in the stock car business might have overstated the case from time to time—straining a mite overzealously to create the illusion that, say, a Ford was a Ford, whether it was driven by Rusty Wallace or John Doe—but nobody would argue that American passenger cars had benefited from the lessons men had learned from tests at wind tunnels and on dynamometers and in the NASCAR shops and garages. John Doe's four-door sedan was sleeker and faster and more stable and efficient now than ever before, thanks to everybody from Junior Johnson in the sixties to Robert Yates here in the nineties, but nobody was kidding himself about safety. These racing machines were exactly that, with their drivers encased in reinforced steel cocoons and high-tech crash helmets and fail-safe seat belts that enabled them to survive just about any calamity that might occur at 190-plus miles per hour in heavy traffic. They even had roof flaps that caught the wind and sprang up vertically to stabilize the car when it went into a spin. In the meantime, while the debate raged even about the safety of the newfangled air bags in late-model passenger cars, about 50,000 Americans were still being killed each year in traffic accidents. The automakers' response was to disclaim the premise of Ralph Nader's *Unsafe at Any Speed,* to say that the costs of outfitting sedans with roll bars and other reinforcements would be prohibitive, and to remind everybody to buckle up.

If Bubba had any delusions that his sleek black Monte Carlo (with a discreet silver-and-red number 3 decal on the rear window) made of him a Dale Earnhardt, the meanest mother on the road, impervious to danger, he was brought back to his senses late that Friday afternoon. After a full day of action both on and off the track, capped by Winston Cup qualifying and the ensuing fiasco with Gary Nelson's dyno, thousands of fans and various officials fired their vehicles and embarked on a mad dash for the exits. It was a wild scene, with no discernible traffic patterns on the dusty traces of the old Army Air Corps airfield, and one of the departees was a fifty-five-year-old grandfather named Bob Loga, who happened to be the president of ARCA. With his brother and another man riding along in his Dodge Intrepid, Loga had just driven through the tunnel from the infield and was easing into the maze of traffic when he was suddenly T-boned, on the driver's side, by what was described as a "large sports utility vehicle" that was going much faster than the posted speed limit of ten miles per hour. The two passengers were banged up a bit, but Loga suffered massive internal injuries and would die in a Birmingham hospital the next afternoon even as the ARCA race was being run. For those who were keeping score and remembered a similar accident that had killed two fans in a van near the main entrance at Daytona in February, right there at the intersection of Bill France and International Speedway boulevards, that made the death toll Fans 3, Drivers 0, thus far in the young Winston Cup season. In light of the carnage yet to come on this weekend at Talladega, it seemed to be a chilling omen.

Although the International Race of Champions series was in its twentieth year, the NASCAR fans' lack of enthusiasm for it was both palpable and instructive. The idea behind IROC was to take a sampling of some top drivers from four distinctive types of racing (Winston Cup, IndyCar, road racing, World of Outlaws), put them in identical cars (Pontiac Firebirds this year), and let them have at it in a series of four races held as preliminary all-star shows during the Winston Cup season. They were relatively short races of about 100 miles each, on the big tracks at Daytona, Talladega, Charlotte, and Michigan, and the overall champion this year would receive a tidy check for $225,000. Not surprisingly, since the races were held on Winston Cup turf and its drivers outnumbered the others, NASCAR had dominated the series by winning forty-two of the total seventy-seven races held over the years. The premise seemed promising enough—a chance for the notoriously provincial NASCAR fans to root for their boys against these interlopers from other types of racing—but it wasn't quite working out like that, to judge by the fans' reaction when the introduction of drivers got underway late Saturday afternoon.

The biggest Saturday crowd in Talladega history, estimated at 90,000, had gathered for a full day of action. In the morning, there had been Winston Cup practice and the second round of qualifying for Sunday's Winston Select 500, followed by the ARCA 500-kilometer race at noon, and then the Cuppers' Happy Hour at mid-afternoon. All along, over the public address system, attention had been directed toward the dozen IROC machines down in the garage area, with breathless promises of a real old-fashioned shoot-out. Much was made of the fact that the three Indy-Car drivers had been involved in qualifying at a track in Nazareth, Pennsylvania, that morning and would be arriving momentarily at the Talladega airstrip adjoining the track; sure enough, their plane landed and they were helicoptered to the infield, in full view of the fans, and soon were taking practice laps in their awaiting IROC cars. But if the fans were thrilled by the possibility of seeing Dale Earnhardt drive an orange Pontiac against someone named Al Unser, Jr., in a white Pontiac, they failed to express it during the introductions, except to roar lustily for the seven Winston Cup entries and good-naturedly boo the "outsiders" before walking off for another hot dog or one more glob of soggy fries before dusk descended.

If these IROC races proved anything, it was that Winston Cup fans wanted more than just pure racing. They wanted the whole package, the extravaganza that had been created by the sponsors and the owners and the drivers and the spin merchants. They wanted the morality play that pitted the bad boy Earnhardt in his menacing black number 3 Chevy against the wunderkind Jeff Gordon in his multicolored number 24 car.

They wanted the frenetic pit stops, the continuing storyline of a Winston Cup points race, the distinctive personalities of forty separate drivers, the legend of those "powerful Robert Yates engines"; they even wanted to be able to root for Spam, for God's sake, as it ran to catch up with Kodak and Budweiser and Skoal. There were none of these elements in an IROC race: no pit stops, no cars splashed with the familiar numbers and garish sponsors' logos, no bitter rivalries to be settled, no spotters from on high, not even driver-to-crew radio communications for the fans' eavesdropping pleasure. What you had was twelve identically prepared Pontiac Firebirds distinguishable only by a color and a number and the name of the driver in block white letters (the powder blue number 10 was PRUETT [*who?*], the lime [*what?*] number 5 was MARLIN), and when the green flag dropped and the cars burst away at speeds approaching 190 miles per hour there were few in the stands who, on such short notice, could tell who was driving what. *Whoaaa, lookit Earnhardt . . . Naw, wait, the black car, that's, that's . . . Gordon? What th'—?*

The format was a recipe for disaster on the track, as well. These were twelve veteran drivers, to be sure, champions all, but what worked for, say, Steve Kinser in a skittery little World of Outlaws "skeeter" (with a top-mounted airfoil) on a dirt track in Indiana had little in common with what happened in a full-bodied stock car on the swooping expanses of Talladega Superspeedway. What made driving on America's interstate highways so dangerous was the volatile mix of drivers with all sorts of disparate backgrounds and capabilities and personalities: experienced interstate truckers riding high in their monstrous rigs, little old ladies in old Buicks joining the traffic from one exit to another en route to the grocery store, good old boys in pickup trucks with a dog in the back, sixteen-year-olds zipping in and out of traffic with the radio turned up; each of them with a different concept about driving. Among the reasons there were relatively few crashes during Winston Cup races was the fact that there was so much shared experience on the track; they had been racing against each other for so long, on the same eighteen tracks, year in and year out, that they had learned to anticipate each other's moves. The veterans such as Earnhardt and Wallace and Martin dreaded having to endure the apprenticeship of a rookie, who usually didn't even know his own moves yet, and this danger was multiplied in an IROC race. To the seven Winston Cup drivers in this race, IROC XX, the five outsiders might as well have been rookies.

The twelve drivers had barely gotten up to speed and begun scouting for drafting partners when half the field got wiped out in a nasty crash on the fifth lap. They had been running four abreast through turn three when Earnhardt, who had started last by virtue of his having won the first race at Daytona, decided to duck in front of Marlin for the lead. As Earnhardt made his move, Marlin hit him from the rear to send him into the wall. "I got turned around so quick, I knew it was going to be a helluva wreck," said Earnhardt, and indeed it was. Marlin made it safely through the spinning cars and flying metal, but Earnhardt and five others weren't so lucky; the other casualties being road racer Tom Kendall and the Winston Cuppers Gordon, Martin, Benson, and Rusty Wallace. With most of their boys already out of the race, the fans turned their attention to the infield, where, as it happened, an RV had gone up in flames at about the same time as the wreck. There was a long red-flag delay to clean up the mess on the track, and when racing resumed the remaining six drivers fell into a draft line until, with ten laps to go, it came down to a duel between the IndyCar drivers Unser, Robby Gordon, and Scott Pruett. "Sterling and Terry [Labonte] worked together really, really well in the draft," said Unser, underscoring the difficulties of driving on a foreign track, "where Robby and myself and Scott tended to lose our patience a little bit. We'd try to make a move on each other and then we'd fall back." But Unser, latest of the famous racing family from Utah, had driven with his mirror and fended off Robby Gordon and Pruett to take the checkered flag. Marlin and Labonte were right behind, in fourth and fifth places; proving nothing, as far as the NASCAR fans were concerned. By sundown, there seemed to be more people entering the track than leaving as the infield campers checked in for another night of howling under a full Alabama moon. Hell, the *real* race hadn't even started.

Sunday broke hot and windy, a perfect day for the races, and a crowd of about 150,000 had assembled when the call came, at half-past noon, for the gentlemen to start their engines. No one on the premises understood the dangers that lay ahead any better than the forty-three drivers, now buckled into their customized seats like astronauts preparing to blast off; but, hey, as Mark Martin had said, "it's what we do." Besides, awaiting them at the end of the day would be a pot of more than $1.5 million. And so they were off, under sunny skies, with the low bluish hills of east Alabama ringing the horizon, a whole afternoon of the sort of racing found only at Talladega ahead of them—three-by-three even in the corners, the fastest speeds in stock car racing, the elusive draft always in play, a place where once (in '84) the lead had changed a dizzying *seventy-five* times— and they had barely begun to get wound up and shop around for drafting partners when the first trouble came. The caution flag went out on lap five when Morgan Shepherd and Jimmy Spencer "got together," as they delicately put it in the pits, slamming into each other and caroming off the wall, effectively ending each man's day before it had really begun. Earn- hardt had already bobbed and weaved up from his starting position at sixteenth and was running fourth, after only five laps, but he and everyone else knew how fleeting that could be. Sure enough, he had drifted all the way back to thirty-third by lap forty-eight. This was, after all, Talladega.

For the next hour or so, it was pure hammer-down Talladega racing, with only one minor caution period to clear the track of pieces of sheet metal resulting from the relentless banging. A total of fourteen drivers took the lead at one point or another in the constant shuffling in and out of the draft, even Dave Marcis for a couple of laps when he stayed out while others pitted on green. So far, so good. But then, out of nowhere, out there on turn two in the backstretch, on lap seventy-nine, Bill Elliott's red-and-yellow number 94 Thunderbird suddenly arose from the pack of bunched cars like a gawky pelican trying to fly. There had been no touch- ing, as far as anyone could discern later from the slow-motion replays; Elliott had simply ducked too low as he came out of the turn, and when his left-side tires hit the rough apron as he tried to regain control the swoosh- ing air got under the chassis and sent the car airborne. With the others still roaring past at full speed, Elliott's car appeared to be in slow motion as it lifted some forty feet into the air like a magic carpet. "The sound of [silence] is not a good deal," he would say later. "When I got up in the air, I told myself, 'This ain't going to be too good.' " The roof flap kept it from flipping over, fortunately, and the car landed on a vacant expanse of the grassy infield with a series of violent *whomps* until it finally came to rest in a billow of dust.

The yellow flag went out immediately while everybody, in the stands and on pit road and at the infield medical center, breathlessly waited for some sign that Elliott was okay. A roar went up from the stands when Elliott's arm finally appeared through the window, waving none too gallantly, and soon there were workers all over the car. It took about ten minutes for them to cut through the roof with torches and saws and pliers in order to extricate him, and the race had resumed when a groggy Elliott, wincing in great pain, was lifted out of the infield by helicopter and flown to the roof of a hospital in Birmingham. He would undergo surgery the next morning for a shattered left femur (the thigh, the largest bone in the human body), and he wouldn't be racing until, at best, the Brickyard 400 at Indianapolis in early August, three months away. It was the worst accident he had experienced in more than thirty years of racing, but he was accepting it with the same stoicism that most drivers use when they have looked death in the eye. "What happened to me could have happened by falling off the back porch," he would tell Tom McCollister of the Atlanta papers, who was, as the ghostwriter for Elliott's weekly column in the *Journal-Constitution*, about the only reporter the driver was talking to these days; a result of his innate shyness and, most writers guessed, a growing self-consciousness about his one-of-a-kind mountain drawl.

Then, about an hour later, there came the damnedest wreck of the year; one that would make Elliott's adventure seem like a fender-bender in a parking lot. There had been only one other brief caution since Elliott's misfortune, but the lead had continued to change hands an inordinate number of times and it seemed only a matter of time before a new horror might unfold. As everyone had been warning all weekend long, the combination of the draft at high speeds and the plates that restricted power when a driver might need it the most could spell big trouble. The field had been bunched perilously since lap 120, following a caution when Dave Marcis had lost it in turn two. Over the next ten laps, another series of breathtaking lead changes took place. This was flat out powerful racing, dicey and frightening to watch, with Jarrett and Marlin and Terry Labonte roaring back and forth in the draft, tit-for-tat, back and forth, like jet fighters in an air show, with a large squadron of cars hot on their tails. That second pack was the one to watch, for they were running three and four abreast as they jockeyed through the tri-oval on the frontstretch at nearly 200 miles per hour, every single driver looking for a drafting line. Then the inevitable happened. Gordon had been pinched against the wall, and when he tried to straighten his car he tapped Martin, left front to right rear, which put Martin into a screeching sideways slide that slung him directly into the path of Ward Burton. Thus, the mayhem began. It was not unlike a massive pileup on the highway caused when a cluster of speeding tailgaters comes up over a rise or a bend in the road and discovers, too late, that there is trouble up ahead.

Brakes smoked, tires blew, cars shimmied, metal flew, as the disaster unfolded. Suddenly one of them was flipped on its roof and then took off like a rocket headed for parts unknown—the green-and-white number 41 Kodiak Chevy of Ricky Craven, the '95 Winston Cup Rookie of the Year—getting more lift from the thirty-three-degree bank on the first turn, shedding its tires and thin skin of sheet metal and even its battery as it sailed into a high catch fence that had been installed just three years earlier after a driver had soared clear over the wall and down a forty-foot embankment. Craven's car, or what was left of it by now, was catapulted off the fence as though from a slingshot and hurled back in front of the incoming traffic, taking several cars with it before finally settling on the edge of the infield grass like a duck that had been blown to smithereens by buckshot. The wreck had heavily damaged a total of fourteen cars, five of them too extensively for them to continue. Among them was the unlucky Irvan, who managed to return but finished thirty-first. There was a couple from Rhode Island who had paid a scalper $164 apiece for two tickets in the grandstand on turn one, right where it had happened, and only now could they figure they had gotten their money's worth.

Amazing. The red flag went out, the engines were cut, and a pall of black smoke and silence fell over the entire valley. There came the arm of Ricky Craven, waggling through the cockpit window, letting the folks know he was alive and reasonably well. The car, stripped of its sheet metal to reveal the intricate weaving of its steel roll cage, looked like a medical school skeleton. A cheer of great relief went up from the ashen fans, who had seen about all of this that they could take in one day, and now they settled back to glumly watch the cleanup. Time stood still while Craven was plucked through the roof of his demolished car and lifted out of the infield on yet another helicopter headed for yet another Birmingham hospital. As dozens of men struggled with the catch fence and the speedway's emergency trucks went about scraping the flotsam off the track, the fans, to relieve their anxieties, tried to get a Wave going. (Earnhardt, ol' Ironhead, took the occasion to bum a ride in the pace car, since the remaining race cars were parked during the red flag, for a visit to the drivers' rest room in the infield.) It took exactly fifty-two minutes and six seconds to clean up the mess and resume racing. When it was all over, Sterling Marlin's Kodak yellow Chevy had taken the race and $110,000 in a thrilling dash to the end with Jarrett and Earnhardt. Mindful of the spectacular smashups they had just witnessed, not to mention the death of Bob Loga in his passenger car while driving away from the track on Friday, the fans departed Talladega in a most courteous manner.

And then, on Tuesday, hard to believe, there was none other than Ricky Craven on the other end of the line for the weekly media teleconference. He had spent Sunday night under observation at the hospital ("I saw the replay on a TV at the hospital and said, 'Boy, I feel sorry for that guy,' and then I saw it was *me*; I'd blacked out, and I still can't put it all together"), but now he was back home in Carolina feeling, well, "just a little sore is all." His left eye was swollen, there was a bruised lung and a fractured vertebra, but he was rearing to go. "We assume the risk," he said, almost jauntily. "If they told me I had to go back and race at Talladega this Sunday, I'd do it. I love what I do." The car, now, that was another matter: "People have been calling to get what's left of it for their museums. I wouldn't mind the public seeing this car, to see how safe they are. The first thing to come off are the tires, and when those other pieces leave it gets dangerous. I landed hard, not having any springs or tires left, and that's what hurt. But I had a lot going for me: the harness, the helmet, the seat tailored to my body, the catch fence." Would he be gun-shy the next time out? "Nah," he said. "It goes with the territory."

11

PÂTÉ, OR PORK RINDS?

All things considered, the Winston Cup folks had every reason to feel downright full of themselves as the summer approached. There were some nettles, to be sure: the White House was still trumpeting its case to ban tobacco advertising at sports events, taking RJR out of the game; those horrific crashes at Talladega had brought on more hand-wringing about the need to do something, *anything,* about the dangers of restrictor-plate racing; and there were whispers that Rick Hendrick, the biggest racing team operator since ol' Carl Kiekhaefer in the fifties, was under federal investigation for shady maneuverings vis-à-vis his automobile dealerships. But these concerns were easily forgotten when the accountants looked at the pluses in this, Winston Cup's twenty-sixth season. All of the numbers were at record highs—attendance, television ratings, purses, even sales of collectibles—causing a delay in what was known as the "silly season," that time of the year when panicky owners begin firing their drivers; changing partners in the middle of the dance, as it were. Four drivers had already won more than $600,000 apiece in purses, and the promoters' dream matchup was taking shape: The Intimidator was leading the points race, but The Kid was closing fast. *Sports Illustrated* and even the *New York Times* were covering the races like never before; *TV Guide* was working up a splashy cover story on the Winston Cup phenomenon; and it seemed like every week either Earnhardt or Gordon was a guest on a popular network television talk show, either *Oprah* or Letterman or Jay Leno's *Tonight Show*. Obeisance was being paid the rabid Motorheads and Bubbarazzi, as ever, but the sport continued to reel in people who never thought they would be caught watching an automobile race.

That, in fact, was the group about to come under some heavy courting as the long Memorial Day weekend approached. For years now, one of the premier races in any NASCAR season had been held on Memorial Day Sunday—the Coca-Cola 600 at Charlotte Motor Speedway, Winston Cup's longest race, at perhaps its finest track—but it had gone relatively unnoticed by the public at large because that was also the day of the famous Indy 500, for open-wheel cars, at Indianapolis Motor Speedway. The eighty-year-old Indy 500 had always drawn upward of 400,000 fans, plus a huge television audience, and was the *only* automobile race as far as the average American was concerned. Indy had reached that highest plateau in sports: the one event of its type that might attract even the most casual observers, that great body of people who could take sports or leave it. In that respect, the Indy 500 was right up there with the World Series in baseball, the Masters Tournament in golf, the Super Bowl in football, the Kentucky Derby in horse racing, the Olympics in track-and-field and gymnastics, the NBA or NCAA championship games in basketball, and any heavyweight championship fight in boxing. The housewife and bank clerk in, say, Joplin, Missouri, would watch those on television and figure they had gotten their dosage of sports for the year. The other stuff, like the 162-game regular season leading to the World Series, seemed mere foolishness to them.

Winston Cup had brazenly tested its broadening popularity in August of '94 by taking its show directly to the mother church of open-wheel racing, the hallowed Indianapolis Motor Speedway, the Brickyard itself, and sponsors perked up when the first annual Brickyard 400 turned out to be a smashing success both at the turnstiles and in the television ratings. Now, on this Memorial Day of '96, Round Two was in the offing; and suddenly, after years of coasting along as the most recognizable automobile racing event in the country, the Indy 500 itself was in trouble. Unlike NASCAR, whose drivers and owners had meekly acquiesced to the despotic Frances, *père et fils,* Indy racing was in the midst of a full-blown mutiny among its drivers. Concerned that the Indy 500 had become elitist, the president of the speedway, Tony George, had formed the Indy Racing League and made the noble announcement that the gates would be open for any driver who could qualify in time trials. The truly big names in open-wheel racing, whose reputations as international playboys with supremely rich sponsors were not unfounded, were so incensed that they formed CART (Championship Auto Racing Teams) and announced that they were boycotting the '96 Indy 500. They booked the big superspeedway at Brooklyn, Michigan, for a new race, the U.S. 500, to be held, thank you very much, on the same day as the Indy 500 and Winston Cup's Coca-Cola 600 in Charlotte.

So the lines had been drawn for a showdown on the last Sunday in May, with all three of the races scheduled on national television: the Indy 500 on ABC at noon, the U.S. 500 on ESPN at two P.M., and NASCAR's Coca-Cola 600 on TBS at five o'clock in the afternoon. There would be full houses totaling more than half a million fans in actual attendance at the races, but in this era of television both sides in the duel—Indy racing aficionados and the stock car faithful—seemed more interested in how their respective shows would be received by the millions out there in TV land. And no one was taking it more seriously than the NASCAR people, who rightly perceived the proceedings not only as a showcase of two distinctive types of racing but as a contrast of lifestyles. The mention of Indy-car racing, whether at the Brickyard or in Michigan, brought certain visions to Bubba's mind: spidery little foreign racing machines with prissy whines, streaked blondes wearing lamé tights and gigantic Audrey Hepburn sunglasses, effete rosy-cheeked drivers with funny-sounding European names, tailgate fare featuring pâté de foie gras and Brie and Chablis. Unlike their fans, the Winston Cup drivers seemed to hold a genuine curiosity and professional respect for the open-wheel drivers—not unlike big-city American cops mingling with English bobbies at a police convention—although never did a Winston Cupper jump over to Indy cars; because of the money and the exposure, it was always the other way around. At any rate, Bubba, for his part, didn't intend to change his routine; he would still show up at Charlotte Motor Speedway in his pickup truck, wearing his jeans and his favorite driver's T-shirt, lugging his coolerful of beer and barbecue and pork rinds, making sure the little woman had dialed in all of the cars on his scanner; ready to whoop as the big American muscle cars rumbled. These weren't just races; it was, once more, *us* against *them*.

For a sustained orgy of racing, nothing on NASCAR's calendar could compare with Speedweeks at Daytona, but the folks at Charlotte Motor Speedway came close to it every year in the week that was climaxed by the Coca-Cola 600. There were bigger and faster and steeper and more historic tracks in NASCAR, but CMS held a special place in nearly everyone's heart. Being located just outside Charlotte, in the vortex of the stock car racing industry, it had been the very first big-time superspeedway ever seen by most of the current drivers, whose accounts of first laying their eyes on it as kids were similar to those of country music fans remembering the first time they had seen Ryman Auditorium. It was at once the track where many of the all-time greats had roared to their most stirring victories, and also the place where Fireball Roberts had burned to death in a horrifying crash. Thanks to the deep pockets and the blessings of Bruton Smith, carte blanche had been granted to Humpy Wheeler, the track's flamboyant president and general manager, an imaginative promoter who believed that racing was only half the package. There was never a dull moment at Charlotte, which held some sort of racing-related event on 280 days each year, from full-blown Winston Cup races to such sideshows as Humpy's "invasion of Grenada." The seating was the best on the circuit, and the same could be said of the many other amenities: the ingenious lighting system utilizing arc-lighted mirrors in the infield to go along with the powerful lights ringing the grandstands, the elegant glass tower housing VIP suites and condominiums and an airy press box and CMS offices and the posh Speedway Club, the roomiest garage area in Winston Cup.

As usual, Humpy had pulled out all the stops for the last days of May at CMS. For eleven days, actually, from early afternoon until near midnight, there would be something for everybody: practice and qualifying and then the running of an ARCA race; Legends Car races, a pet project of Wheeler's, with retired stars like Ned Jarrett driving cartoonish little toy cars (five-eights-scale replicas of thirties models powered by motorcycle engines) around a special oval course in front of the main grandstand; the third round of the IROC XX series; the Red Dog 300 Busch Grand National race; the feverish Winston Select, an all-star shoot-out patterned after Daytona's Busch Clash; and, finally, the eleventh race of the Winston Cup season, the Coca-Cola 600 on the Sunday of Memorial Day weekend. Much of the racing would take place under the lights, a special treat, with sparks flying as the glittering cars braked in the corners. Having run the road race at Sonoma, California, on the first weekend of May (won by Rusty Wallace, a master of road courses and short tracks), the Winston Cup crews and drivers welcomed the chance to spend most of the month at home before embarking on the usual summer schedule of racing up East and North, for the most part. The first three months of the season had taken their toll in equipment and injuries, and they needed the time to rest up and fine-tune their machines. At CMS, as at North Wilkesboro, they could sleep in their own beds and tootle out to the shop or the office or the track in their own sweet time. They were treating it like Old Home Week, an extended home stand in their own ballpark.

Meanwhile, at Indianapolis and Michigan, the rival Indy-car camps were spending more time firing volleys at each other than actually racing; and, when they did race, the results were unsettling. Seventeen of the thirty-three drivers in the field at Indy would be rookies, boys from the open-wheel bullrings dotting the Midwestern landscape, and some of them were so poorly financed that they were choosing not to practice in traffic for fear of losing their one and only car. The veteran CART drivers up in Michigan, the Andrettis and Fittipaldis and Unsers and Zanardis, had been sniffily predicting calamity for the Indy 500, what with all of those rookies (and even a woman, Lyn St. James) tooling around the Brickyard at 240 miles per hour for their first time. Sure enough, hours after he had won the pole for the Indy 500, a young driver named Scott Brayton was killed when he crashed a teammate's car during a mindless routine practice

session. It looked a lot like Replacement Ball, major-league baseball's answer to the players' strike during spring training of '95, which had found
thirty-year-old former college hotshots and minor-league washouts pre-
suming to fill the shoes of superstars like Barry Bonds. A full week before
the showdown, the *New York Times* gave affirmation to what the Winston
Cup managers had known all along: "The rift comes at the worst possible
time for Indy-car racing. NASCAR and its stock cars are doing something
in television ratings that they could never do on a race track: leaving Indy
cars in their dust."

The crowds were so large and the traffic so calamitous during Race
Week at Charlotte Motor Speedway that one would have thought some
sort of week-long community holiday was in progress; which was true, in a
way. As it was in Nashville every year when the Opry stars came home for a
celebration called Fan Fair, a boosterish tribute to the city's best-known
industry, so did Charlotteans turn out to thank God and Bill France and
Bruton Smith for CMS and stock car racing. Banking had become the
major economic force in Charlotte, and the city now had franchises in the
NBA and the NFL, but it was still best known as the spiritual home of
daring young men and their flying machines. The local media and Humpy
Wheeler were fanning the flames, and the fans were responding by mo-
toring out to the speedway, every day, no matter what was on the schedule.
"Super Saturday . . . Dog Day Afternoon!" is how Humpy's ads were billing
the day before the Coca-Cola 600, when a fan could pay as little as $15 to
sit in the stands and glory in Winston Cup practice, a "special match race"
among a batch of middling country music stars driving the funny little
Legends Cars, the Busch Grand National Red Dog 300 race; all of it topped
by the Winston Cuppers' late-afternoon Happy Hour, normally a standard
piece of business that now was being touted as "the final shakedown for
drivers in the Coca-Cola 600! Who has the best race setup? This final
practice is always intense!" It had all of the trappings of a gala family
reunion; and the key word, given the squabbling in that other world, the
one of Indy cars, was "family."

In that spirit, there was no way the voluble Darrell Waltrip was going to pass on the opportunity to hold a little open house of his own so he could hobnob with his pals in the media. He was easily the most articulate, beloved, and accessible of all the Winston Cup drivers, but now the sobriquet he had coined for himself, ol' D.W., was taking on a sad irony. He would turn fifty on his next birthday, during Speedweeks at Daytona in '97, and suddenly he had become an elder statesman, a lion in winter, a ghost of the driver who had been hell on wheels in the late seventies and throughout the eighties. This had been an absolutely awful year so far for the three-time champion who was tied for third in career Winston Cup victories—twice he had been forced to take provisionals to make the race, his best finish had been fourteenth at Sonoma, and he stood a distant twenty-sixth in the points standings—and his musings about the "three R's" during the media tour back in January (risks, rewards, retirement) were coming back to haunt him. The general feeling was that D.W., at his age and as an owner responsible for paying the bills, had lost the will to go charging willy-nilly into the turns without considering the consequences. Thus, it seemed a most propitious time for the third annual "Danish with D.W." gathering at his DarWal racing shop, on the far edge of the Charlotte Motor Speedway property. Several of the beat reporters had checked into motels for the duration of the festivities leading up to Memorial Day and the big showdown with Indy racing, and they had gleefully circled the date of D.W.'s brunch. In this new era of managed media access and pool press conferences, every bit as restricted as when Norman Mailer became just another writer in the crowd for the Apollo 11 moon shot in the late sixties for his book *Of a Fire on the Moon*, they hungered not so much for Waltrip's coffee and Danish but for his puckish candor.

"Maybe I've been brutally honest with you guys through the years," he began, when everybody had settled in, and he was off and running. Ford had just been allowed to lower its roofline by half an inch, as a means of managing parity with the Chevy Monte Carlos, and Waltrip, a Chevy man himself, chose to start there. "Everybody in this sport is the master of deception, and I think that's one thing that makes it hard for NASCAR to get a handle on what everybody's doing. Whether they take a car to a wind tunnel or put it on the chassis dyno, or whatever they're doing, they're at the mercy of what the guy gives 'em. A guy walks around when the race is over and kicks both front fenders in a foot, knocks the spoiler up in the air another two or three degrees, or whatever might happen before it gets into the wind tunnel. Or then they put it on the chassis dyno and the engine blows up. Wow! Wonder how that happened?" In the world according to D.W., there was too much of this "jacking around" in the name of parity. "Racing was not meant to be managed. When you have the desire to have a Pontiac, a Chevrolet, and a Ford come across the finish line side by side every week, that's not realistic. They should leave 'em alone like they always did. Some guys are just having a hard time accepting the fact that some other guys might just drive a little harder than they do." And, because it "costs us ten thousand dollars every time they [NASCAR] make a little change," some protection should be given the smaller operations in their struggles against what he called the A Teams, the big ones like Hendrick and Childress and Roush. "On January the first they ought to say, 'Here's the rules and this is the way they'll be for one year.'"

And another thing: "If some of these guys weigh a hundred and fifty pounds and I weigh two hundred and my brother weighs two-thirty, and we've all got seven hundred horsepower and a car that weighs three thousand and four hundred pounds, who's got the most horsepower now? The car with the lightest driver. I think you should weigh the cars with the drivers in 'em. When we go to Japan, I might find me a good little driver, and"—playing for a laugh here—"while I'm at it I'll get me a crew chief called Win One Soon." And another thing (no names, but Earnhardt came to mind): "Reckless driving. I'm tired of hearing 'just racin'.' It's 'just *wreckin*'.' NASCAR has allowed certain big-name drivers to create an image that young drivers think is the way to go. If you're going to stop people from speeding in the pits, you've got to stop the big guy first. If you're going to stop people from being reckless on the racetrack, you've got to stop the big guy first. The punishment never fits the crime. They'll go get some guy like Jimmy Spencer and put him in the penalty box every week. Let another guy do something twice as bad and they'll turn their head. You could make a highlight film out of that every week." And another, with a long stretch of racing on dangerous big tracks coming up: "We should have a designated driver for our car for a period of time when the driver is injured. This crap of having to crawl in and out of race cars when you can't even walk, just to get points, is ridiculous. If a doctor says a driver shouldn't drive, says, 'This man needs to be out of the car for three or four weeks,' you should be able to have a relief driver and it should be the same one. We've got guys getting banged up every week now. You've got to get back out there and go again, make a few more laps for points and money, and that's not right. It's dangerous."

Lord, lord, here was a man with an opinion about everything. Indy versus NASCAR: "I like Indy cars. When I was younger and starting in this business [in his home state of Kentucky], I didn't seem to have a niche here. It looked like I was more suited for Indy-car racing. They were open-minded then, more willing to listen to young upstarts up there than they were down here. I was happy until they said they were going to take twenty-five spots and give them to designated people. If it's reserved for 'twenty-five of my closest friends,' that's wrong. . . . We don't drive Lolas and Cosworths and Menards to work, we drive Fords and Chevrolets. We've got ourselves a pretty neat deal here. We've got twenty-five drivers and fifty corporations promoting NASCAR races in a big kind of way, spending big bucks to make their cars and their drivers and our sport look good. Our sport is being marketed a lot better than any other sport." On the new technology: "Until they get a computer to sit in that race car and carry it into the first turn at Talladega at a hundred and ninety or two hundred miles an hour and go through the bumps and everything else that's on that racetrack, it's all irrelevant. A car that sits in the wind tunnel, it ain't going anywhere, it's sitting still. The racetrack is the best dyno we've got." Because of the new tracks being built, how many additional races would the drivers accept? "We don't *want* weekends off. The people who want weekends off ain't the people who have anything to do with it. Most of the guys will tell you they'd just as soon race seven days a week. If there's an off-weekend in November, and Texas says they're going to have a race and it's going to pay a million dollars, all of us would go, whether NASCAR sanctions it or not. If they don't give us a race, we'll *make* a race. I was going to do that in Nashville ten years ago on an off-weekend. If you pay enough money, everybody will be there." On hiring new people when things aren't going well: "A new crew chief walks into the building and says, 'I can't believe you're running that. Nobody runs that. Boy, you're screwed up. Here, let me fix it.' The first thing you know, all the cars you have, it's whack-whack-whack, cut-cut-cut. The guy says, 'Now we're getting somewhere, how do you like that?' 'Well, I don't know, it doesn't feel like that car I had before.' 'Oh, you'll get used to it.' Then you go along with that guy, and the first thing you know he's out the door and here comes another guy. 'Man, nobody runs that stuff, we've got to have this.' Whack-whack-whack, cut-cut-cut. *Provisional.* 'Oh, no, we're right back where we started.' It's frustrating. You've got to have continuity."

That was all very well and good, but what everybody wanted to hear was Waltrip's assessment of his own career, now in its twilight. The soliloquy he offered, with all its bittersweet resonances, was a classic musing from an old soldier not quite ready to die. "The thing that bugs me is that I haven't won any races in the last four years," he said. "But I still love the sport and I still love being in it. Every time you write a story, and it don't even make the front page of the sports section, it bugs you. Sometimes you write something you get letters to the editor about, other times nobody cares, but you still keep writing. You still go get your paycheck. You probably still bitch about where you've got to work, you probably don't like the parking place you've got, but you've still got to do the same things over and over. You do it because, a), what else would you or could you do? and, b), because you love what you do. I need to be on the front page, too, but I'm not. That's the bottom line. Everybody's got to win, but they can't. Somebody's got to be twenty-eighth; but he's had a great career and he loves being out there, likes competing, likes racing, likes the media, likes the fans, likes to travel. I mean, every time I go play golf I don't hit a hole in one, but I go buy a new set of clubs and try to get better. If I find out when I buy those new clubs that they aren't as good as my old ones, then I look for a course that complements my slice or my hook; and, believe me, I've got 'em both."

It was his way of saying he was looking for a way to ease out of driving full-time, but still keep his hand in the game that he once dominated as Earnhardt did now. "I can take my knowledge, my expertise, whatever little bit of clout I have, and what I've done, and I can still be a factor in this sport," he said. "I don't want to just have breakfast and have a big time with you guys. Yeah, I'm thinking about replacing the driver [himself], but the crop ain't too good. Why do I want to put somebody in my race car? I might not run too good, but most of the time I bring it back in one piece. I can work on 'em, I can chop-chop-chop and cut-cut-cut. I've got to go through that developing stage with a [new] driver and I've got to consider who that's going to be. . . . [But] I'm going to run Bristol until they quit running Bristol, and I'll always run Martinsville, so I guess I'll only semi-retire. I can't have all these toys sitting around and totally quit. I would like to have the option with my sponsor of running any race I wanted to, maybe Daytona or wherever, when I wanted to. That's how I'd like to stay on the payroll. If you're only fifty years old when you decide to stop, you've got to figure you could still be competitive or at least be out here and be a part of the show. That's the biggest difference between then and now. I used to be the show. Now, I'm just a part of the show."

The brunch with Waltrip had taken place on the Thursday before the running of the Coca-Cola 600, on the second day of Winston Cup qualifying (D.W. would go out and qualify poorly again, running more than three miles per hour slower than the pole winner, Gordon, to put him at the twenty-eighth starting position), at a time when many were still buzzing about the raucous success of the previous weekend. The grandstands had been jammed on that Friday past for a full day of all sorts of racing: a ubiquitous Legends race (Humpy, it seemed, couldn't open the gates without holding one), qualifying for the ARCA neophytes and for the Winston Cuppers hoping to run in the weekend's wildly popular Winston Select; plus round three of the IROC four-race series. Although the IROC race turned out to be pretty much a snoozer, with Mark Martin leading all the way after four of the identical Pontiac Firebirds were destroyed in his wake on the ninth lap, the fans even at CMS didn't seem to mind; they, like everybody except the Pontiac people, couldn't care less about the whole idea of IROC in the first place. But racing was racing, and, besides, they knew the good stuff was yet to come on Saturday: the glitzy, hellish spectacular known as the Winston Select.

The Select was another of Humpy Wheeler's babies, a spirited shoot-out divided into three segments of thirty, thirty, and then ten laps. Variations of such an all-star race had been held for many years, but it had taken its current form in '92 when the lights were added to CMS. The idea was to take twenty of Winston Cup's hottest drivers—the fifteen winners of the most recent Cup races, plus the top five finishers in the fifty-lap Winston Select Open, held immediately prior to the Select itself—and throw them together in what amounted to a series of three wild and woolly sprint races. Even the mode for qualifying was different; for the Select, times were based on three laps sandwiched around a two-tire pit stop. It was a nonpoints race that would have nothing to do with the season championship, but the overall winner would get $200,000, the third-largest purse of any race on the circuit, and a whopping $350,000 if he won all three of the sprints. There were some who disapproved, most notably Darrell Waltrip: "It's not a race. It's not what we normally do. It's an event developed for the fans. The thing is, the fans get their money's worth, and we end up paying the price for it most of the time." That last referred to the mangled race cars sure to result from such a series of mad dashes, with so many dollars at stake; which was, naturally, why the fans loved it. The Winston Select had become one of the hottest tickets on the circuit.

Anyone who felt favorably disposed toward Jesus, America, the Republican party, country music, tobacco, and stock car racing would have thought he had stumbled into heaven when he hunkered down into a seat at Charlotte Motor Speedway on Saturday. Humpy Wheeler had them all covered. From the moment in the late afternoon when a Winston blimp was released from its mooring in the infield until late in the evening when a final cluster of fireworks filled the sky, one would have thought it was VE Day all over again. A racing helmet was presented to the honorary starter of the Winston Select, the state commissioner of agriculture, giving him the opportunity to take a shot at the White House. Ned Jarrett gave an invocation. Joe Gibbs, the former coach of the NFL's Washington Redskins (now owner of Bobby Labonte's Winston Cup car), started the ARCA race. When that was over, in little more than an hour, the time came for the Winston Select Open. As the thirty-six drivers stood beside their cars along pit road, out came the delectable country singer Suzy Bogguss with the National Anthem, while some high school ROTC boys raised the flag and jet fighters screamed overhead. The racing was becoming almost incidental; the Winston Select Open was won by Smokin' Joe's Camel himself, Jimmy Spencer, who got a check for $28,000 and a spot in the Select (as did Lake Speed, Hut Stricklin, Jeff Burton, and Michael Waltrip) for less than an hour's driving. And then . . . but wait; the night was young.

Somewhere in there, an entourage led by Richard Petty in his plumed cowboy hat had hustled out to the Charlotte airport to greet ex-Senator Bob Dole, the Republican challenger to President Bill Clinton, and in due time the man who would do something about this anti-tobacco foolishness was introduced to the packed house. Like most politicians stumping in the provinces, he wore a blue shirt opened at the throat to show he was just another working stiff. The fans reverently applauded when Dole was presented a racing helmet and then said a few words about America and smoking and racing and other God-given rights before getting into a Camaro convertible for a parade lap around the track. Soon, he was out of the car and shaking hands with the twenty drivers who would run in the Winston Select. On and on it went, with nobody sitting anymore in their grandstand seats—just proud to be Americans!—and the proceedings tumbled ahead toward the real business at hand. Another country singer, Jesse McGuire, warbled "America the Beautiful" as fireworks lit the darkening skies; and finally, with the drivers buckled in and their wondrous rolling billboards gleaming under the lights, Dole intoned the magical words: "Gentlemen . . . start your engines!" And all hell broke loose.

The extravaganza was being broadcast, live, on TNN cable, and it offered a splendid appetizer to those around the country who might be planning to watch the Memorial Day showdown, on television, between Indy- and NASCAR-style racing in order to make their own judgments. Nobody put on a show better than Humpy Wheeler, the P. T. Barnum of racing, and his speedway at night looked like a diamond necklace sparkling against black velvet in a showroom window. The crowd was estimated at 140,000, amazing for a nonpoints race, and when the cars burst away for the first segment they were on their feet like bettors at a greyhound track (*Heeere's . . . RUS-teee!*), knowing that such a short race can be won or lost by the slightest slip. There was much desperate charging into the corners, side by side, tires squealing, metal clanging, sparks flying from brakes, Dale Jarrett blowing past Gordon halfway through the race and holding on to take the checkered flag. They barely had time to let the engines cool and reverse the field before they were off again, the second thirty-minute dash being won by Earnhardt when he overtook Terry Labonte with five laps to go, in the tri-oval right there in front of the main grandstand. But the real surprise came in the final segment, a ten-lap sprint that could be compared to a hundred-meter dash, when D.W.'s younger brother, Michael, zipped past Earnhardt and Terry Labonte on only the second lap, while they were preoccupied with swapping metal on the second turn, and stayed in front to take the win and the total payout of $211,200 that went with it. Talk about parity in Winston Cup racing: Michael Waltrip had not won a Winston Cup race in ten years on the circuit (309 starts), and on this night he had barely slipped into the field, having gotten the last available spot by finishing fifth in the Winston Select Open. He had no sooner gotten out of his car in Victory Lane than his brother, D.W., who had finished a miserable eighteenth overall, rushed up and bear-hugged him and said, "I love you, man!" By the rockets' red glare, as bombs burst in air, Bubba 'n' them went home with joy in their hearts. Let the Yankees chew on *that* one.

And so, on the following weekend, the big day finally arrived. Not since 1969, when Joe Namath led the upstart "outlaw" American Football League out of the swamps in a head-on confrontation with the established NFL that forced a merger of the two leagues, had there been such an opportunity for a shift in the balance of power in American sports. Unlike the brash Namath, who had correctly predicted victory for his New York Jets over the Baltimore Colts, in a championship game that would become known as the Super Bowl, the NASCAR people seemed content to let the relative quality of the shows and the ensuing television ratings speak for themselves. But they were aglow already, given the scintillating success of their own Race Week in Charlotte and, at the same time, the reports emanating from the Indy-car camps at Indianapolis and Michigan. The tickets for Indianapolis Motor Speedway's 285,000 permanent seats had sold out long ago, before the split between IRL and CART, but apparently many of them would go unused; scalpers were trying to unload them at face value, and motel rooms were available in and around Indianapolis. At

Brooklyn, Michigan, 250 miles to the north, there were banners all over the place—"The real cars . . . the real stars . . . the real race. The U.S. 500. The Real 500"—but the crowd was expected to be 110,000, less than one third of what the Indy 500 was accustomed to drawing, and the taunting from the veteran open-wheel drivers was becoming a bit unseemly ("The magic is gone," said one Gary Bettenhausen). Let 'em talk, was the thinking in Charlotte, where scalpers were getting rich by auctioning off tickets for a race that had been sold out for nearly a year.

Except for the presence of a handful of drivers with names like Davy Jones and Tony Stewart and Scott Sharp, the starting lineup for the Indy 500 sounded like the cast of a film at Cannes. Arie Luyendyk was one of the few open-wheel stars who had chosen not to bolt IRL and join in the boycott, leaving the fans at Indianapolis to scratch their heads and choose between an international crowd of rookie drivers named Vélez and Matsuda and Salazar and Gregoire. Compared to the familiar stock American cars of Winston Cup, these Reynards and Lolas looked like lunar vehicles that would fall apart if a fellow so much as kicked the tires. But off they went, at noon, and with all of those rookies in the field it went pretty much as everyone had feared. The attrition began early, when one car's transmission was discovered shot on the pace lap, and before they had gone 100 laps ten others had gone to the garage with a multitude of injuries ranging from fire to gearbox problems. The Brickyard had never been known for side-by-side racing, with its flat banking and narrow corners, and the whole day might have been a good time to take a nap in front of the television set if not for a hellacious crash on the final lap that wiped out three cars and allowed a fellow by the name of Buddy Lazier to win. Only three cars were in the lead lap, and just nine of the thirty-three were still running at the end. All in all, it had been pretty dull stuff.

Behind the wheel of the pace car at Michigan was Paul Newman, the actor and, in his younger days, an open-wheel race car driver, and he might have muttered the most famous line from *Cool Hand Luke*—"What we have here is a failure to communicate"—when he looked into the rearview mirror and saw the disaster behind him before the green flag had even dropped to start the U.S. 500. All week long the veteran drivers of CART had been ridiculing the Indy 500, with all its rookies, but just as they came out of the fourth turn on the final pace lap at Michigan all hell broke loose: the two leading cars touched, wheels and struts began to fly, and eleven of the twenty-seven cars were destroyed or badly maimed before the race had begun. Everything stopped, and it took sixty-one minutes for the teams to prepare their backup cars so they could try to get this thing right the second time. It would have been hilarious—"the worst first impression in the history of motor sports," one writer put it—except for the sheer horror of the crash and the sobering thought that, hey, this was the day CART was supposed to assert itself. Although there would be eleven more caution periods, and just eleven of the cars would be running at the end, it turned out to be a day of few surprises. The race was won in a backup car driven by pole winner Jimmy Vasser, the instigator of the mess on the pace lap, who cruised home alone over the last ten laps. Said a disgusted Michael Andretti, of the famous open-wheel racing family, who had gone out early in the race: "I'm sure the folks in Charlotte are loving this. Just loving it."

Humpy Wheeler didn't order the rain that struck Charlotte Motor Speedway in the late afternoon, delaying the Coca-Cola 600 by more than an hour, but it was a fortuitous stroke for NASCAR; it nudged the start of the race closer to prime-time Sunday night, giving the television viewers out there across the land a chance to grab something to eat and shake off the memory of the sour Indy-car performances before settling down to see what the good old boys had to offer. The lads from Charlotte didn't disappoint. (Could Humpy do Patriotic, or what? The call to start the engines came from an astronaut, no less, a North Carolina boy speaking from the spaceship *Endeavour* as it orbited 150 miles above the earth.) It wasn't the greatest race of the Winston Cup season by any means, Dale Jarrett coasting out front for the last 121 laps to beat Earnhardt by the rather large margin of twelve seconds, but the race had, well, *personality*. There were a half-dozen crashes that took out five cars, the only serious one coming when Benson and Craven tangled, leaving both drivers groggy and their cars reduced to skeletons; there was the always breathtaking sight of Earnhardt (this time driving a red-white-and-blue Chevy freshly minted to honor the upcoming Olympics in Atlanta), coming on strong after starting far back in the twentieth position; there was the unusually high number of green-flag pit stops, the most critical kind of all; there was the news that Jarrett, now having won two of the designated races necessary to take the Winston Million, could cash the $1 million check by winning the Southern 500 on Labor Day at Darlington; and there were the shenanigans of Kyle Petty's car owner, the volatile Cuban Felix Sabates, after Kyle had been penalized five laps for "rough driving" and Felix filled the airwaves with such invective, directed at a NASCAR pit official, that he drew two more laps' penalty.

It wasn't quite like rushing down to Sardi's to knock down a few and wait for the early reviews of a play in the *New York Times* early edition, but there was more than a little anxiety as everyone awaited the television ratings. This was about ego and bragging rights, to be sure, but also at stake could be millions of dollars in future advertising. If the figures showed that Winston Cup racing had hung in there in the showdown with Indy-car racing, especially against the entrenched Indy 500, it would likely give much pause to the corporations around the country who wanted to get in on this automobile racing stuff. NASCAR had won on one field, the sports pages, where it was almost universally being claimed the "winner," but it wanted more. And when the results came in, later the following week, there it was in cold black figures. The Indy 500 had attracted 6.5 million homes to ABC, a decent figure, but the worst in the race's history. The U.S. 500 in Michigan, on ESPN, was a pitiful 1.9 million. The Coca-Cola 600 at Charlotte? In spite of being on cable, and coming at the close of a long day of televised racing, it had made its way into 3.1 million homes. *Mama!* And all across the great sprawling Southern outback, wherever Moon Pies are sold, the good old boys were smiling.

12

SATURDAY NIGHT AT DIXIE SPEEDWAY

On the last Saturday of June, while the Winston Cup boys were enjoying a rare off-week before plunging into a fierce stretch of fourteen races without a break, it would be business as usual for Rodney Dickson. All during the week he and and the three men under his employ at Greater Design, a landscaping maintenance operation, had hauled their clattering equipment around the sprawling new subdivisions of Fayetteville—a fast-growing town some thirty miles south of downtown Atlanta—mowing lawns and trimming hedges and tidying flower beds in the stultifying Georgia heat, and now, finally, it was time to go racing. An energetic twenty-seven-year-old with bright brown eyes and a thick black beard on a chunky five-eleven, 200-pound frame, Rodney found himself suddenly leading the points standings in the Late Model Division at Dixie Speed-way, a classic three-eighths-mile dirt oval located in Woodstock, another middle-class town thirty miles on the *other* side of the city. If he were to win both the pole and the Late Model feature on this night at Dixie he would take home a total of $2,050 and move a step closer to the $5,000 bonus given to the track's overall points champion. Those figures paled in comparison with the phenomenal Winston Cup paydays, of course, but no matter. "Good thing I'm not in it for the money," he said. "Whatever I win goes back into the car, and it's a losing battle."

Rodney lived with his wife and nineteen-month-old daughter two doors down a country road from the roomy brick house where he grew up, and by noon he and his father, Jerry, a mechanic for the U.S. Postal Service in downtown Atlanta, were hovering over the car in what amounted to their racing shop—a cluttered cinder-block garage under the trees in Jerry's backyard big enough to hold six cars—as they surveyed the damage. Rodney had won the Late Model feature at Dixie on the previous Saturday night but had wrecked the next night at the dirt track in Rome, Georgia, and he was worried that the chassis had been knocked out of alignment. Every night during the week, after finishing his day's work, he had gone over to the garage to work on the car with his father, who served as his mechanic and crew chief, and their assessment now was that it was about as ready as they could make it. Since they had no dynamometer, no wind tunnel, no track to test on, they were left to guesswork. If the alignment was terribly off, Rodney would simply have to drive accordingly.

Unlike the machines on the Winston Cup circuit, with their thin illusions of appearing to be production Fords or Chevys or Pontiacs, these dirt-track cars were pure lightweight racing machines of thin-rolled aluminum draped over an orange steel roll-bar cage. They weighed 2,130 pounds, against Winston Cup's 3,400, and their V-8 one-carburetor engines produced about 500 horsepower (against 700) to create speeds of up to 110 miles per hour on straightaways. Rodney figured he had about $28,000 invested in this one (and another $20,000 or so in the enclosed car-hauler parked beside the garage in the ninety-degree heat), and that he had driven it in more than fifty races over the past two years at Dixie and Rome and the half-dozen other tracks within a three-hour drive of Atlanta that he frequented. It was painted bright yellow with a white bottom this year, adorned with the number 18 and logos for his various local sponsors (plus the legend "Thanks to Sonia Kayla," a bow to his long-suffering wife and daughter, who saw little of him during the six-month racing season);

outfitted with the same wide slick racing tires and rear spoiler and bucket seat and removable steering wheel of the Winston cars, but not much else. For starters, there was no windshield; rather, an angled sheet of aluminum soldered above the dashboard to deflect the mud and dust and bugs encountered on hot Southern nights at a dirt track ("The first thing you do when you get home is hose yourself down").

This was how the other half lived; automobile racing at the grassroots level. Although Rodney Dickson of Fayetteville, Georgia, was faring better than most of his peers in terms of equipment and sponsorship and driving ability, he was representative of the thousands of young men who would be rolling away later in the day to the 600 or more dirt tracks spread over the American landscape, primarily in the South and Midwest, to have at it on raucous little dirt bullrings carved out of the countryside. Soon there would be sightings on the highways of doughty race cars in tow, sporting hand-painted letters announcing their sponsor ("Joe's Garage") and some whimsical monicker like "The Other Woman," jouncing along behind pickup trucks crammed with the drivers' brothers and cousins and buddies who constituted their crew, all of them headed off into vigorous weekly combat in the mud and the blood and the beer. You could ask Rodney Dickson why he kept doing this week after week and year after year— spending all of that time and money, taking real chances on getting hurt when there was a family to support, having little hope that it would lead to much more than a scant mention in the Atlanta newspapers—and he would shrug and look you in the eye and say, quietly and firmly, "Because I love it." That seemed to be a sufficient explanation. About the danger of flying around those treacherous ill-lighted dirt tracks alongside wild-eyed rookies with more desire than good sense, he was stoical: "It's there, but except for getting my bell rung a couple of times I've never been hurt." That would change two weeks later at Dixie when he would go fender-to-fender with his father-in-law, Billy Clanton, and wind up with a badly wrenched wrist after a spinout.

His background was no different from that of most drivers who had gone on to Winston Cup: small-town, blue-collar, visceral, son of a man who worked on vehicles for his livelihood. Jerry, his father, "got interested in racing about the time Rodney was born, helping a friend who was into sprints, open-wheel, but I never had the money to go into racing 'em myself." Rodney began going along with his father to the races as a tyke, and by his early teens he was racing dune buggies and learning all about race cars by helping older friends who had managed to convert their street cars and run them on the local dirt-track circuit. The only other sport that had interested him was wrestling, but that ended with high school graduation. He scraped together enough money to refit his own car, a Vega, and when he entered it in the Cadet class for American compacts at Dixie Speedway, at the age of eighteen, he finished fourth. And he was hooked. They couldn't keep him away from Dixie, even when he married and began his own business and, much later, became a father. "He was a hard charger from day one," said Mike Swims, co-owner of Dixie Speedway with his father, Mickey. "There's a saying in racing, 'Go fast, go left, or go home,' and Rodney understood that right off. He's our Dale Earnhardt out here. I don't know if he gives any thought to going Winston Cup one day. His immediate goal in life is to outrun Stan Massey," a much older veteran in the dirt-track wars, owner of a wrecker service in the town of Mableton, the king of Dixie when he showed up.

At this do-it-yourself level, it paid to have well-connected friends. Rodney and his father did most of the work on the car during the week, and on weekends at the track they were joined by a reedy older man named Larry Watkins, who worked beside Jerry in the motor pool at the post office; Rodney's older brother Richard, a mechanic for Delta at the Atlanta airport; and any number of old high school pals who shared his love of racing. The sponsorship deals were laughable when compared to Winston Cup, but you took what you could get. Rodney's principal sponsor this year was Peacock Construction, a local firm, which loaned him a company truck to pull the car-hauler and bought him a new set of racing tires every two weeks or so (at $412 a set). Peacock's reward was to see its logo on the hood of the car, a facsimile of the multicolored NBC peacock, and to hear relentless bleatings over track public address systems about "Rodney Dickson in the Number 18 Peacock Construction car." Garner Concrete Sawing and Coring was paying for all fuel; Active Auto Parts would sell him parts at wholesale, which Rodney said could mean a saving of nearly $3,000 a year; and the owner of RSD Enterprises, in the nearby burg of Rex, let Rodney use his racing shop whenever he had some serious work to be done. And that was it. Everything else came out of his track winnings and, sooner or later, his own pocket. "I had my best year in '95," he said with a rueful shake of the head. "Won fourteen thousand dollars. Went two thousand in the hole."

This was his tenth year of running a circuit of dirt tracks ringing Atlanta—at Dixie and Rome and Cordele and Hartwell in Georgia, Phenix City in Alabama, Greer in South Carolina, Cleveland in Tennessee—and sometimes it was possible to enter three races on a weekend. He had won "thirty-five or forty" in his time, almost always finishing in the top three or four, and he was happy to report that he ran "pretty good" at Senoia, a few miles south from Fayetteville, the only asphalt track he had experienced ("The difference is you can't slide on asphalt, and that's what dirt is all about"). Did that give him ideas about pursuing a Winston Cup career? "At my age I'm open to anything," he said. "Sure, I know the odds. You've got to move up one level at a time, first to asphalt and then to ARCA and then to Grand National. And, hey, there's only one rookie out of forty-something drivers in Winston Cup this year, right? Nah, I'm happy where I am right now. Mike [Swims] is right about me and Stan Massey. When he shows up, he's the man to beat. But I figure he puts his britches on one leg at a time."

The two rusty old water trucks had been at it since the sun broke over Dixie Speedway that morning: trundling down to the banks of the twenty-five-acre lake beyond a stand of trees encircling the property, siphoning water until their cylinders were full, bumping back up to the parched track, emptying their loads, going back for more. They dumped 100,000 gallons on the track every race day, and when it had become as slick as moss the water trucks were joined by a bulky ten-wheeled dump truck and even the early-arriving drivers in their race cars; all of them slipping and sliding until the mud had been packed into a glistening clay. "We tore up the asphalt and went back to dirt in '77," said Mickey Swims, a drag racer in his time who now co-owned Dixie and its sister track in Rome, about thirty miles northwest near the Alabama line. "We found that everybody likes dirt better. It might be ten times the trouble for us, but asphalt is three times as expensive for the driver because of tire and engine wear. The fans love dirt, watching those roostertails fly when the cars start sliding into the corners." He solemnly reported that there had been only one racing death in Dixie's twenty-eight years, that coming in the early eighties when a rookie named Sammy Burks had his neck broken when he slammed down against the pit wall.

There were three dozen race dates every year at Dixie (plus eight more at Rome, on Sunday nights), the total purses now having exceeded $1 million in one season for the first time, and before the schedule played out there would be some sort of racing for everybody. If it's got wheels, a Southerner will get around to racing it: Late Models, Super Late Models, Monster Trucks, Outlaw Pony Stocks, Modifieds, Sportsmen, Demolition Derby, Daredevil Motorcycle Jumps. (Once, at Atlanta Motor Speedway before a Winston Cup race, the drivers' sons furiously pedaled away in the Big Wheels 590, that being the length of the course in feet and the number on the dial of the sponsoring country music station.) The biggest event of every year at Dixie was the Hav-A-Tampa Shootout on the last weekend of September, the culmination of a series characterized by Mike Swims as "sort of the Winston Cup of dirt-track racing," with a prize of $30,000 for the winner of that championship finale. For three years running, in the mid-eighties, when Winston Cup drivers still could afford to mess around like that, the Swimses paid Bill Elliott and Dale Earnhardt $10,000 each to show up and race at Dixie ("Ten thousand fans, ten bucks a head, *sure* we could afford it," said Mike). There was seating for 8,000—a few hundred of those for the drinkers, exiled to undesirable rickety wooden bleachers on the turns—and the average attendance held at 4,000 with hardly any promotion outside of word of mouth and posters nailed to telephone poles. Not until Tuesday did the Atlanta papers get around to publishing the weekend's local racing results, in a roundup on the back sports pages at that.

"It's a family operation all the way around," Mike was saying. It was five o'clock and the gates had just opened for the first fans to trudge in, some lugging seat cushions and coolers and sacks from KFC or McDonald's, most swapping first-name greetings with Swims. "There's Mickey and me. My mother runs the concessions and keeps the books, my sister handles T-shirts and souvenirs, and my wife does the computer stuff and stats. The drivers and the fans are family, too, sort of, since they come from around Woodstock and know each other in that small-town way." Soon he would be heading across the track to begin checking in the 150-odd drivers of every stripe who would be paying $15 apiece for an infield pass that would serve as their entry fee. "My dad warned me to do anything except go into race promotions, so of course that's what I chose to do. I tell you, I've never seen the same race twice out here, and when they drop the green flag the hair on my neck stands up and tingles. Bill Elliott and Jody Ridley are the only two we've had who started here and went on to Winston Cup. We've got an attorney, one of those kinds you see advertising his business on television, who comes here and races sometimes in Pony Stocks, in a four-cylinder Pinto. But the ones you've really got to admire are the guys who go to a job all day and work on their car every night and then come out here and drive their guts out on Saturday night so they can win maybe sixty dollars. They'll be here pretty soon. They're what Dixie is all about."

Just as there were people who had walked away from country music the day it went corporate and moved out of old Ryman Auditorium in downtown Nashville, and those who had turned to minor-league baseball in disgust after the unseemly major-league money squabbles that had brought on work stoppages in the mid-nineties, there were many longtime auto racing fans who would take a night at Dixie Speedway anytime over the gaudy, expensive, and time-consuming spectacle of a Winston Cup race. Like minor-league baseball, stock car racing at the grass roots was cheaper and closer and, in its own way, more *fun* for spectators. "I don't know if fans are down on Winston Cup now that it's gotten so big," Swims said. "I do hear some of 'em say they're getting put out about the inaccessibility of the drivers, the money they make, the ticket prices, the traffic jams, and all of that. It's gotten so big it might scare some of 'em off. A lot of our folks say they'll never go back to AMS [Atlanta Motor Speedway] until they do something about the traffic. But, you know, the television has gotten so good for Winston Cup these days, with the cameras inside the cars and all, they can come here on Saturday night without any hassle, bring the whole family and enjoy our show without spending a lot of money, and sit back and watch the big boys on Sunday on television. There's room for both of us, Dixie and Winston Cup."

The sun was hovering like an orange ball over the speedway as the three heavy trucks began circling the track, gradually tamping the slick surface into clay. There would be the usual full schedule on this night—three heats of Bomber divisions (a euphemism for true stock cars, "street stocks," driven by enthusiastic good old boys), a Sportsman race, Rodney Dickson's Late Model feature, a series of mad one-lap sprints by fans in the very cars they had driven to the track, all of it capped by a maniacal Demolition Derby—and the concrete grandstand was filling up in a hurry. Dixie Speedway sat in a natural bowl, less than a mile from an interstate highway spur connecting Atlanta to the north Georgia mountains. Surrounded by rolling pastures that served as a parking lot, the track was illuminated by lights on telephone poles ringing the grandstand and on two glistening new steel spires whose powerful beams were aimed at the backstretch. There was a twenty-foot-high catch fence around the outside edge of the track itself on the grandstand side, a gravel infield with cinder-block buildings holding concessions stands and rest rooms, and an array of two dozen billboards on the backstretch advertising such local services as banks, wreckers, gas stations, tire outlets, and a radio station. While the public address system piped country music, barely audible over the rumbling of the trucks, a woman sat calmly in the grandstand and nursed her baby.

By now, Mike Swims had set up for business in a one-room shack beyond the backstretch so he could record the entries in the Bomber division races. Thirty-two years old, with a full head of thick black hair, he sat on a swivel chair beneath a whirring window air conditioner, wearing a polo shirt and blue jeans and sneakers and wraparound sunglasses. The Sportsman and Late Model starting positions would be determined in qualifying heats, but the entrants in Bomber and SuperTrucks and Demolition Derby would have to draw for positions. The Bombers were the kids,

the rookies, the guys next door who simply had a hankering to race—
"what Dixie is all about"—and the three divisions were determined by
their experience. They would park their battered heaps outside in the dust
and step into the shock of the air-conditioning, outfitted in the cutoffs and
T-shirts and gimme caps and sneakers that were their racing uniforms, to
sign in and draw a numbered chip from a red plastic dispenser shaken by
Swims. There would be about sixty of them, and Mike knew the names
and hometowns and car makes of nearly every one of them as he scribbled
the information on sheets held by a clipboard: "Jake, how's it going over at
Chatsworth? . . . Still driving that ol' number 8 Pontiac, Bobby? . . . You
mean four guys, four cars, four divisions? . . . Your daddy get over that
heart attack? . . ."

He paused when one of them, a scrawny older fellow, said he would be
entering the Bomber Two class tonight. "Wait a minute, you've won four
in a row in Bomber Two if I'm right," said Swims. "Naw, five," he was told.
"You win tonight, you're gonna have to move up a class, ol' buddy," and
with that the fellow swelled up and grinned as though he had been pro-
moted from Grand National to Winston Cup.

"Lookie here, Mike, I got a little situation," said another, a pear-shaped
kid in a T-shirt and unlaced hightop basketball sneakers.

"Let's hear it," Swims said.

"It ain't me, understand, it's my sponsor."

"I'm listening."

"See, when we get out there and run around the track, helping y'all
pack it down, mud gets all over the car and you can't read my sponsor's
name no more."

"You could hose it down before the race."

"Naw, there just ain't enough time. I was wondering if maybe I could
just bring an old junker over here for that part and then park it somewhere
during the week. Run my regular car in the race. I'd leave you the key so
you could move it if you had to, ain't no skin off my nose."

Swims said, "It's a good idea, but if everybody else did it I'd have a
hundred cars out here all week."

"Like I said, I got to keep my sponsor happy."

"Tell you what, I'll bring it up with Mickey and let you know next
week."

■ ■ ■

Rodney and his father had spent the afternoon putting the final touches on the race car—tightening bolts and belts, mounting new tires, filling it up with gas and oil and water, hosing off the layer of caked mud from the previous weekend—and they were muscling it up the ramp into the car-hauler by the time the rest of the crew arrived. Larry Watkins and Richard Dickson would be joined this night by a teenager with his arm in a cast, Barry Peacock, son of the sponsor, and an old high school friend of Rodney's named Chris Peacock (no relation). They secured the car in the hauler with a winch, tossed in an extra set of tires and a floor fan and a coolerful of soft drinks and snacks, and then bumped out of the backyard and onto pavement for the sixty-mile drive along Atlanta's interstates to Dixie Speedway. Rodney's wife and daughter and mother would follow shortly, when his mother got off work at the dry cleaner's.

By the time they arrived in the infield, at six o'clock, the place had the feel of a noisy convention; which it was, in a way. A dozen of the Bombers were still out on the track, groaning around behind the big trucks in low gear, helping to pack the surface into hard clay, while the infield rumbled with the thunderous cacophony of more than a hundred machines of every color, size, condition, and ilk: shiny new SuperTrucks, long-snouted twenty-year-old Pontiacs and Oldsmobiles not seen much on the roads anymore, feisty little Pintos and Camaros wearing their dents and bruises proudly, crumpled Demolition Derby junkers marked for death. The lights came on and the cars gleamed under their pale glare, revealing the numbers and sponsors and mottos—"With God Your [*sic*] Always a Winner" and "Bearly [*sic*] Legal" and "Need for Speed"—and around each car whirled a ragtag bunch of grease-stained boys and men, family and friends, in earnest last-minute preparations. "Reckon them tahrs'll make it? . . . Where's that five-eighths wrench at? . . . That sumbitch cuts in on me again, he'll hear from me this time . . . Earl, the motherfucker's gon' be too loose, I tell you . . ." In the middle of it all was a supply truck, a virtual rolling auto parts store, whose back doors had been swung open to display a cornucopia of emergency supplies ranging from fan belts and batteries to rolls of Bounty paper towels and spray bottles of Windex. There would be no ominous inspection station crawling with grim uniformed NASCAR technical inspectors, not here at Dixie Speedway, just one man wandering from car to car to warn against outside mirrors or oversized engines or a piece of dangling metal that ought to be taped down for safety's sake.

"They don't watch 'em too close here," Jerry was saying, stroking a close-cropped white Hemingwayesque beard. They had parked the rig against a fence near the pit road and unloaded the car, in line with a half-dozen of the other better-heeled outfits, while Rodney went to the truck to wriggle into his racing outfit. "A man's a damned fool to spend all that time and money, and then have the race taken away from him for cheating. Fellow there"—he nodded to the red 47 car in the gravel next to Rodney's—"he came here from a different track, and after he'd won a couple of races they told him he'd have to change all kinds of stuff. Height, skirts, mirror. He wasn't cheating, he just didn't know." Jerry fished a clean blue rag out of his hip pocket, thinking to touch up the Peacock logo on the hood, and scanned the infield to see which of his son's big rivals were there tonight. He saw the 81 car of Granger Howell, a handsome thirty-four-year-old who owned a muffler shop in nearby Cartersville, a consistent winner at Dixie for at least a decade. He saw Phil Coltrane, owner of a speed shop in Canton, Rodney's closest competitor in the points race at Dixie. And then he saw the main man, Stan Massey, and a glimmer of envy flashed in his eyes. "Look at that. We're strictly family, but Stan's got himself some experienced mechanics, a regular racing team. He's been racing almost as long as Rodney's been alive. Well. He's here, and so are we." When Rodney emerged in his driver's suit, a pair of worn black Simpson shoes and a loose-fitting nylon jumpsuit striped in black, white, and purple, Jerry nodded toward Stan Massey's group. Rodney smiled grimly and put on his game face.

There would be twenty-two entries in the Late Model feature, the headline event of the evening, and as soon as the trucks and junkers finished packing the clay Rodney and Coltrane and Howell and Massey and the others were allowed a few minutes of "hot laps," like Winston Cup's Happy Hour, to check out their machines. Rodney put on his full-face helmet and crawled into his car and rumbled out of the infield to take a half-dozen laps around the track, swerving from side to side in order to heat the tires and to test the chassis alignment, floorboarding it on the straightaways, pumping the brakes in the turns, running high and running low in search of his groove. When he rolled back into the infield and parked behind the hauler only five minutes later, he was slowly shaking his head. There was much work to be done between now and qualifying, scheduled for immediately after the first race of the night, and the way that one went it looked like they might have all night to fine-tune the car. It was the first Bomber race, a fifteen-lapper involving twenty of the rawest rookies and the least dependable junkers, and a scramble that might have taken five minutes raged on for more than half an hour. They would barely complete one lap before there would be a spinout, the caution flag would go out, a tow truck would drag away the wreckage; another green flag, another crash, another yellow, more carnage. The crowd was on its feet, laughing and pointing and cheering the bravado, loving every minute of what felt more like the running of the bulls at Pamplona than an automobile race.

Larry and Jerry had spent their time during the Bomber duel tightening lug nuts, lowering the gear setting, revving the engine so as to check the cooling system and the rpm's, topping the fuel tank from a red plastic gas can they had brought along, doing whatever Rodney recommended ("If the driver doesn't know what's wrong, who does?" said Jerry). When the winner of that first race had limped around the track, pumping his fist out of the window on a joyous victory lap, and the last Bomber had been dragged to the infield, it was time for Late Model qualifying. Each driver would have one lap to build up speed and two laps to establish a time. The four men constituting Rodney's crew grabbed white plastic bucket chairs and scrambled up a ladder to the top of the trailer while Rodney took his place in line on pit road, staring directly at the legend on the trunk of the car ahead—"Jesus: Believe or Burn"—and checked out the radio headset connecting him with his father, who stood on the trailer to get a view of the track. "Let me know the times, okay, the *fast* times," said Rodney. "Gotcha," Jerry told him.

The Late Models roared away from pit road, each in its turn, throwing up roostertails of clay chunks as they got up to speed, then thundering down the backstretch on their solo runs. First out had been Howell, a crowd favorite, who once had entertained thoughts of going NASCAR but now found himself in his mid-thirties with a wife and two kids. "What'd Granger do?" Rodney said over the headset to his father. "Sixteen-thirty-four on the first lap and . . . hold on, here he comes . . . sixteen-twenty-six on the second," Jerry reported. "Where's he running?" "Low to halfway up." And so it went. Phil Coltrane, of the dashing name, turned the track in a poor sixteen and seventy-two-hundredths seconds, "running low and doesn't look good at all." Rodney seldom qualified well, probably because he thrived on car-to-car competition, and this night would be no exception. His car was loose, sliding all over the track, partly due to the damaged chassis suspension, and he qualified twelfth in the twenty-two-car field with a time of sixteen-forty-three, which translated to 82.174 miles per hour. Stan Massey? On the pole, in a breeze.

When he rolled back into the infield and parked the car, nobody was smiling. His mother and his wife and daughter had arrived at some point during the qualifying. Sonia, a pigtailed blonde wearing hiking boots and tight denim shorts and a T-shirt, sidled up to Rodney, shifted Kayla to the other hip, kissed her husband on the cheek, and innocently said, "What's wrong, honey?" Rodney blurted, "The sonofabitch won't run, that's what's wrong." Since her father and three brothers still raced on Georgia's dirt tracks, she was no dummy about racing; it was Rodney's language in front of their daughter. When she flinched and nodded toward Kayla, cute as a Kewpie doll, he stroked his little girl's blonde hair. "Sorry," he said. "I don't know. We'll work it out." As the races continued—more Bomber races, then SuperTrucks, then Sportsmen—he spent the next couple of hours wandering about the infield: worrying, thinking, checking to see how the track surface was changing as the night droned on, now and then consulting with his father and Larry Watkins. In the end, all they did to the car was adjust the spoiler to gain some down force. "The track's gotten drier and looser, and this ought to make it stick a little better," Rodney said.

Finally, at 10:45, it was time for the thirty-lap Late Model feature race. There were no pit stops at Dixie, due to the brevity of the races, nor any ceremonial call of "Gentlemen, start your engines." Rather, once the twenty-two cars had lined up in the order of qualifying, there was a wave from a flagman standing at the pit-road entrance to the track on the first turn, indicating it was time to crank 'em up. There came the same deafening roar of a squadron of engines being revved simultaneously, not unlike that tingling instant one experiences at Daytona and Bristol and all of the other stops on the Winston Cup circuit, and, with the fans on their feet to celebrate the moment, the flagman began waving the cars onto the track. Bucking and weaving, jockeying for position, champing at the bit, eager to get on with it, being admonished by the main flagman in a crow's nest at the start-finish line to form eleven orderly rows, two-by-two, the drivers shifted into high gear after the second warmup lap. When they came around again, flying out of the fourth turn at about seventy miles an hour, they spied the mad waving of the green flag and gunned it. *They're off!*

Racing on a small dirt oval was an entirely different matter from cruising the huge paved superspeedways like Talladega and Daytona. There was some drafting involved, when the cars went nose-to-tail at more than a hundred miles per hour on the straightaways, and over the course of a long season the spoils usually went to the more powerful engines. But here aerodynamics and raw horsepower often would take a back seat to the sheer *arrogance* of a driver, his compulsion to let the others know, *Outta my way, asshole, here I come.* Dirt-track racing was a three-round flurry of punches, not a fifteen-round war of attrition, and it was up close and personal. This was where almost all of the Winston Cup drivers had begun, and over the course of the '96 season more than one of them, during post-race interviews in Victory Lane, would describe his winning move as "a little thing I learned on dirt one night at Hickory when I was just startin' out." Jerry Dickson said, "Yeah, but it's still like Winston Cup. It takes three things: the car, the setup, the driver. No, better make that four. Takes luck, too." It was a mad dash of only thirty laps, not quite fifteen miles, a race that would take less than ten minutes were there no caution flags, and it could be won or lost on the corners, depending on how well a driver controlled his slides in and out of the turns.

There would be cautions galore on this night, a total of four, each of them resulting when two cars tried to muscle into a turn where there was room for only one, and Rodney managed to stay free of the early wrecks.

"Go, go . . . clear, clear," he heard on his radio from Chris Peacock, his spotter during the race, who was standing on the roof of the trailer. "How many behind me now?" Rodney radioed after a series of moves on the corners had enabled him to begin picking off other cars, one at a time. "Twelve," said Peacock. "*Twelve? That all? Damn.*" Stan Massey had avoided all of the trouble on the track the simple way, by staying out front well ahead of the pack, and his lead was growing on every lap. "Git 'im, honey, git 'im," Sonia was shouting, jumping up and down on the roof of the hauler, still holding Kayla on her hip, causing the hauler to rock. Rodney was on the back straightaway now, diving low and trying to take Granger Howell on turn three. "Git 'im, honey, git 'im, honey, git 'im!" And he did. Howell spun out and had to be towed from the track, and when the green flag came out again Rodney came up on the tails of two cars, both carrying the number 66, threatening to run over their backs like a rude tailgater on the interstate. *Git 'im, honey, git 'im.*

He picked off one of the 66 cars, to move into sixth place, but time was running out. The other 66, either unmindful or caring less that he wasn't allowed to be outfitted with a rearview mirror at Dixie, began driving with the mirror. In the best tradition of Dale Earnhardt and the other superstars who had been teethed on dirt tracks, aware that the 66 car was keeping his eyes on him and him alone, Rodney tried feinting right and feinting left, but to no avail. The fellow was blocking him out, quite adroitly, countering each move. Rodney tried frightening him, literally bumping him, hoping his adversary would lose his cool for the instant it would take to get inside for the fatal tap on his left rear flank that would spin him out of the way. If it had worked, with the four leaders spread out the way they were, he might have been able to make a sprint to the finish line with Stan Massey. But, alas, time ran out. Stan Massey had won again.

Only when it was over and they were loading the car into the hauler did they notice that it had all taken place under the eerie glow of a perfectly full moon, as orange as the afternoon sun due to the cloud of dust lingering over the speedway. Out on the track, like teenage hot-rodders racing side by side on a country road—*Rebel Without a Cause!*—fans who had simply come out of the stands and fired up their street cars were now fishtailing around the course, two at a time, in one-lap scrambles. From the gravel parking lot on the hill beyond the third turn, a line of crumpled junkers began lumbering down the hill to the track for the grand finale of the evening, the Demolition Derby. A thick coat of red dust blanketed everything.

"The guy pulled the same stuff on me last week," Rodney was saying as he trudged toward the cinder-block building doubling as a concessions stand and a pay window. "You think he doesn't know you can't drive here with a mirror? I'd go after him, but the problem is he's a good guy, a friend of mine." Ah, well. Another night, another race. On the July Fourth weekend, while the Winston Cuppers were running the traditional Firecracker 400 at Daytona, Rodney would be chasing Stan Massey again at Dixie Speedway in a pair of 200-lappers on Friday and Saturday nights, the latter paying $7,000 to win, then going on to Rome Speedway on Sunday night for the Firecracker 50. He stood in line for his winnings, $250 in cash, while his father and his brother and his two friends tied things down and locked the doors on the hauler, and they rolled away from the track at midnight. They stopped at a Waffle House near the interstate for a greasy breakfast and much animated discussion about the race, swapping friendly insults with fans who recognized Rodney. They got home around two in the morning.

13

LONG HOT SUMMER

Thirty-one races spread over nine months, with only seven weekends off for mending injuries to the drivers and the cars, had the makings of a forced march, an excruciating odyssey, something that only the fittest could survive. The season was roughly divided into three phases—spring, summer, fall—and the most punishing of them all was the eleven-race summer season, with its long and expensive road trips to the northern and eastern points, and races at all four of the different types of tracks, and only two off-dates between the Memorial Day and Labor Day weekends. Like the month of August in major-league baseball's 162-game season, this was nut-cutting time, when the men were separated from the boys; or, more accurately, when the better drivers and the richer teams simply wore down the others. Tempers flared into so's-your-old-man shoving matches in the pits, anxious sponsors grew antsy, rattled owners began delivering ultimatums, frustrated mechanics and engine builders stepped up their efforts at "creative engineering," drivers and crew chiefs jumped ship or got fired, equipment shortages began to tell, and long-held grudges were settled on the track.

Felix Sabates, the quick-triggered Cuban owner of Kyle Petty's car, never one to shun the spotlight even in ordinary times, jumped into the summer madness ahead of everybody else. It was shaping up as another rotten year for the son of The King, who was running eighteenth in the points standings after eleven races, but Sabates was still focusing on the crash at Charlotte that had drawn a five-lap penalty for Kyle and two more when Felix leapt over the retaining wall and rained profanities on the NASCAR inspectors. "Kyle was one lap down, [Ted] Musgrave two," he was explaining a couple of days after the Coke 600. "Common courtesy says Musgrave lets Kyle pass, but when Kyle went up to pass, Musgrave went down. Hell, even his spotter told us on the radio, 'My fault.' If anything, Kyle's not aggressive enough. He's not a dirty driver. I went crazy when they said, 'Bring him in, rough driving.' This is the twentieth century, not the Medieval Ages. I was mad, cursing, raising hell on the radio, and I guess everybody heard me. Rough driving? How about Mr. Excitement? We didn't hit [Musgrave] any harder than [Earnhardt] hit [Hamilton] at Rockingham. I gave Gary Nelson my credentials and said, 'Gary, I won't be back for a while.' That's all I got to say."

He did have more to say, as it turned out. True to his word, Sabates didn't show up on the first weekend of June at Dover Downs International Speedway, about an hour south of Philadelphia, hard by Delaware Bay, but he was there in spirit. Kyle's car was painted Earnhardt black and bore the legend TODO ES JUSTO EN AMOR Y CARRERAS—"All's fair in love and racing"—and Kyle could only shrug: "This was Felix's deal, his idea. He says black cars [Earnhardt] don't get penalized." It didn't matter whether Sabates was there or not, for Jeff Gordon won both the pole and the race, the first time such had happened in twenty-one years on Dover's rough concrete "Monster Mile," to move up from fourth to third in the points race. The Kid led 307 of the 500 laps of a race that eleven drivers failed to finish due to engine failures and crashes. Earnhardt held on to the points lead in spite of finishing third behind Gordon and Terry Labonte, but he bade farewell to Delaware with his usual growl: "It was just one of those long days at Dover, running on sidewalks," bitching to the end about the concrete surface.

■ ■ ■

If everybody was going to keep taking these potshots at Jimmy Spencer, as John Boy and Billy had done at North Wilkesboro ("Gentlemen, *and Jimmy Spencer,* start your engines") and Sabates after the Charlotte race, it seemed fair enough to let the man speak for himself. At six-one and 220 pounds, the least athletic driver on the circuit—doughy, sweaty, wheezing, baseball cap sitting cockeyed on a damp mop of straw hair, with the countenance of a jolly hayseed who had been up to some mischief—he was, in a word, endearing. He had been called onto the carpet late in the '95 season by RJR's T. Wayne Robertson for a lecture about safe driving habits, but for the most part the sponsor of the Smokin' Joe's Camel Ford still gaily bandied the Mr. Excitement monicker he had attracted in his rambunctious earlier years on the circuit. He had been keeping his nose clean lately, and he was candid enough now to admit to the errors of his youth: "I've done some dumb things in the past, but I've gotten to where I'll tell a guy I'm sorry if I've done him wrong. I used to think, when there'd been a wreck, 'Well, he'll understand,' but it turns out they don't. So now, I told Michael Waltrip I was sorry when I took him out at Richmond, and he told me he was sorry when he took me out at Bristol."

Spencer was one of the handful of drivers who had been reared not in the bosom of Southern stock car racing but on the dirt tracks and short paved ovals of the Northeast; in his case, along the stretches of the Susquehanna River in eastern Pennsylvania. His father had been a short-track terror, and his brother, Paul, still raced asphalt modifieds back home. He claimed to have learned to drive, in fact, when he and Paul raced junkers around a track they had carved out beside a junkyard, driving them until they were destroyed. "My dad said I could be a lawyer if I wanted to, but, hell, I couldn't have been a lawyer; I would've been in contempt of court all the time." So he chose racing and his legend as a hell-raiser grew when he got on the public address system after his first win and said he had "whipped [the local favorite's] butt" and was roundly booed. He got the nickname the night his front brakes went out early but he still managed to bull his way to a second-place finish; and it truly blossomed one day at Talladega when he rolled the car six times, landed on his tires, and kept on going. Now he was thirty-nine, in his sixth year of racing full-time in Winston Cup, winner in only two of his 185 races, but calming down a bit and, as a result, finally on his way to better things. For sure, the folks at RJR liked the way he handled his end of the sponsorship deal. "I used to drive for McDonald's and did a lot of stuff with kids, you know, so they'd go to McDonald's for their hamburgers, but it's different with RJR. I'm not allowed to go around to children, to schools and all that, and say, 'I want you to smoke Camels cigarettes.' Hey, up in Dover there was this kid about sixteen who'd snuck into the pits and he had a pack of Camels in his pocket. He was kinda proud of himself. So I grabbed him and said, 'Listen, bud, you're too young to smoke,' and I took 'em off him. I wish the damned government would get off our backs."

The occasion was the week off between the Dover race, where his sixth-place finish was the best of the year, and the upcoming race in the Poconos not far from his hometown of Berwick, Pennsylvania. Was he a lovable rogue, or what? "I don't know about that; I'm just giving a hundred percent for my team, trying to do my job. But, hey, a lot of people just don't know John Boy and Billy. You oughta hear 'em make fun of themselves on the radio. They just wanted to have some fun. First they asked Earnhardt if they could do it ["Gentlemen, and Dale Earnhardt . . ."] with him and he said, 'I don't want to mess with that stuff, I just want to drive,' and then they asked me and I said fine, it sounded like fun, good for business." How about Sabates's comments? "You know how car owners go off on a tangent now and then, but Felix was totally out of line. They say RJR with its Camels car gets favors, but that's not true. If anything, they spend extra time on me in the inspection line because of that. If NASCAR thought I was unnecessarily rough, they'd penalize me. Felix oughta make amends. He's making it harder on Kyle when he says stuff like that."

Spencer's car owner, a veteran crew chief by the name of Travis Carter, had spoken of the long apprenticeship necessary to make a top driver. "You've got to have a lot of physical strength, desire, enormous willpower, and control," he said. "It's an ongoing process and it takes time. Jimmy Spencer needed polishing. He's learned to control his emotions and be patient." The fans and the media who liked to tune in to Spencer's frequency on the radio scanners, whether during practice or in a race, might have found that to be news or wishful thinking—"Christ a-mitey, where'd *that* sonofabitch come from?" he yelped one day when another driver tried to cut him off at the pass—but Mr. Excitement, for himself, saw an older and wiser man. "At Dover," he said, "we knew we had a sixth-place car and we took that. That's what I've been learning. If you've got a tenth-place car, live with it. When the car's running good, you can't go wrong. If you try to push it, you'll crash and all you've got is a wrecked car and a bunch of guys mad at you because they've got to fix it and you haven't done anything for your sponsor." Maybe he was learning, after all, for in each of the three races following Dover he would finish in the top ten and move up to sixteenth in the overall points standings. It got to where his detractors were sort of missing the former Mr. Excitement.

Although there were no figures to show how many in the army of faithful Winston Cup camp followers took advantage of the cultural possibilities inherent in traveling to foreign lands, as it were, like dropping in on the Amish while in Pennsylvania to see how in the world anybody ever got along without a car, the opportunities were certainly there during the summer schedule. This was vacation time, and one would think that Bubba 'n' them might load up the RV and tie in their race watching with a little exploration—check out the resort areas of the Poconos in Pennsylvania, run up to Detroit to see the automobile plants in Motor City, maybe pop in on Harvard Square on the way to New Hampshire, or stroll through the wineries of upstate New York while en route to the road course at Watkins Glen—but no, *au contraire.* The Southernization of America had been underway for a long time now, at least since 1968 when George Wallace won thirteen percent of the national vote during his first run for the presidency ("Y'all know what the 'New South' is, don't you? South *Boston*"), and that was precisely what happened whenever the Southerners invaded the North and East. During the week leading up to the races, Indianans and Pennsylvanians and New Yorkers and Michiganders and the Yankees of New Hampshire acquiesced in the face of the invasion of the Sun Belters; became Bubbas for a week, kicking tires on the show cars, standing in line to marvel at *Bee-yul* Elliott's amazing drawl during an autographing at a McDonald's, finding themselves dangerously close to saying "y'all." The Southerners, in the meantime, hardly noticed any of this. They drove straight through to the track in, say, the Irish Hills seventy miles from Detroit, parked their rigs, set up camp, hoisted their Confederate flags, put their Hank Williams, Jr., CDs in their boom boxes, broke into their cases of beer, and settled back in their lawn chairs. *See one track, you've seen 'em all.* It might as well have been Rockingham or Darlington.

In the middle of June, the tour made the first of its two stops of the summer at Pocono Raceway, in the lush forests of the Pocono Mountains in northeastern Pennsylvania. The track was a bitch to drive, a relatively flat two-and-a-half-mile tri-oval with sharp turns that required much shifting of gears, and a lot of the big-name drivers didn't get anywhere at all; there were thirteen DNFs in the starting field of forty-one, and both Jarrett and Irvan were out of the race by the thirty-seventh lap. This being the UAW-GM Teamwork 500, it would have been poetic if Earnhardt had won in his workingman's like-a-rock Chevy, but that was not to be on this day. A valve broke in his engine, forcing him behind the wall little more than halfway through the race, marking only the third time in twelve races that he hadn't finished in the top five, and he had cause to be a little antsy. Gordon won his third straight pole and his second straight race, and now the two were separated in the standings by only sixty-four points. "This really hurts," said Earnhardt. "The kid's team doesn't seem to miss a beat." Indeed, everybody was beginning to see Gordon in their rearview mirrors as the season neared the halfway point; his pole-winning speed had broken the track record by five miles per hour, the pit stops were the stuff of highlight films, and all in all the mighty Hendrick Motorsports factory was on a roll. The only driver who seemed to threaten the anticipated Earnhardt-Gordon duel for the championship was Terry Labonte, Gordon's teammate at Hendrick, whose Corn Flakes Chevy was finishing in the top five of nearly every race and now stood second in the standings.

They loaded their machines and equipment onto the car-haulers and trudged the 600 miles back home to Charlotte, to spend a hectic week tending their crumpled cars and bruised psyches, and then headed out again, this time on the 800-mile trip to Michigan. ("This summer schedule is probably harder on the truck drivers than anybody else," said one of the veteran crew chiefs, Musgrave's Howard Comstock, noting that the drivers and principal crew members got to travel by air.) Michigan International Speedway, where the open-wheel CART race had been run on Memorial Day weekend, was another big flat track with around 100,000 grandstand seats and room for the usual horde of 20,000-plus in the infield, and everyone was aware that this was the site of the most recent near-fatal Winston Cup track accident; the place where Ernie Irvan had nearly lost his life during a routine morning practice run in '94. As though to show that everything was going to be all right, Irvan put his daughter in a stroller and pushed her around the pits, proclaiming with a shrug, "I'm not spooked about coming back, because I don't remember the wreck." The drivers were kept busier away from the track there than at any other stop on the circuit, it seemed, running back and forth to the sprawling Detroit metropolitan area for personal appearances during a week-long centennial celebration of the American automobile. But all of the forty teams making the trek qualified for the race, which turned out to be a tame affair, attended by a full house in perfect seventy-four-degree weather. There were only two brief caution periods, to clear debris from the track, and with so much green-flag racing it came down to gas mileage. Rusty Wallace, a short-track specialist not always a factor on the big tracks, had learned his lessons well in recent outings—at Michigan in '95 he had been leading with five laps to go but ran out of gas and finished third, and in the spring race at Darlington, his tank bone dry, he had coasted across the finish line to manage a fourth—and this time he "kept one eye on the track and the other on the fuel pressure gauge," running the final fifty-two laps (104 miles) on one full tank of gas to win the race. Gordon had the stuff to win, but he had to settle for sixth place when the Rainbow Warriors sent him out after a pit stop with a lug nut missing; a NASCAR inspector ordered him back to the pits, to have one put on, and sent him to the rear of the field. Since Earnhardt chugged in at ninth place, there was little change in the standings.

There was a reminder that these sponsors meant business; that they didn't plunk down cash to buy decal space on the cars just to add a dash of color to the televised proceedings. The list of "special awards" attending each of the thirty-one races ran to more than a dozen—from the $1,000 Goody's Headache Powders consolation prize to the $5,000 RCA Pit Strategy bonus—but a team wasn't eligible if it didn't carry that sponsor's decal. The most important of all these special contingencies was the Busch Pole Award, offered by the "Official Beer of NASCAR," not so much because of the $5,000 that went to the pole winner of each race but because it meant automatic qualification for the next February's Busch Clash at Daytona. But the smile on Bobby Hamilton's face didn't last very long when he climbed out of his Pontiac after winning the pole on Friday because never, in his long career, had Richard Petty, his car owner, consorted with the evil breweries. "My mother would probably shoot me if she saw a beer sticker on my car," said The King, who should have been celebrating his first pole as an owner. "Kyle has one on his [Coors Light, in fact, was his son's primary sponsor], but she ain't had a whole lot of control over Kyle." Hamilton's Pontiac was the only car in Winston Cup without a Busch decal, and neither Petty nor Busch was budging. There would be no Busch Clash for Hamilton in '97, even though he would win a second pole later in the season.

Kyle Petty. If there was a single enigmatic figure left in Winston Cup racing, in this modern era of the button-down driver obediently marching to the orders of corporate executives and facile public relations advisers, it was the son of The King. Kyle had won the very first stock car race he entered, an ARCA 200-miler during Speedweeks of 1979, when he was only eighteen years old, and from that very first day he was in the spotlight. "You know how to win," his father famously remarked that day, "and now it's time you learned how to drive." Following Richard's advice that he not waste time matriculating on dirt or at small tracks, he plunged right into Winston Cup, first under the banner of Petty Enterprises at Level Cross and later with the Wood Brothers, and in 1986 he became the first third-generation driver (behind his grandfather Lee and his father) to win a Winston Cup race. He was young, he had the bloodlines, and he seemed to be on his way just when a new generation of drivers, led by Earnhardt, was coming to the stage. With his ponytail and earrings and persona as a peripatetic guitar-playing Harley-riding Wild Child, Kyle Petty was a fresh breath of air who would be attractive to the young fans and to the nontraditional outsiders that RJR hoped to bring to the tracks and to the television audience.

Unlike his father ("Richard Petty, The King," he obediently reminded readers at every opportunity in his weekly newspaper column in the *Atlanta Journal-Constitution*, which often barely touched on racing), Kyle had a life beyond the track. He performed his duties for his sponsors over the years, to be sure, like the time he gleefully poured drinks at a bar in Manhattan in behalf of Coors Light, but there was much more to him. The modest frame home he shared with his wife and three small children, on a large spread out in the countryside near where he was born, overflowed with rare first editions that he actually *read* before putting on the shelves. He wrote and performed children's songs and folk ballads, capably accompanying himself on the guitar. He was inquisitive and politically liberal, in contrast to his rigidly conservative father, and loved to sit around and chat with people of differing views and lifestyles. (In fact, when the promising young driver Tim Richmond died of AIDS, contracted from one of the groupies along the way, Kyle bought multiple copies of Randy Shilts's *And the Band Played On*, about the AIDS epidemic in San Francisco, and passed them out in the Winston Cup garages. The drivers, once notorious for frolicking with the many camp followers on the NASCAR circuit, began keeping their britches zipped after that.) There was a warming little story about him and a poor ten-year-old kid named Rodney, who lived in a shanty near Team Sabco and spent his afternoons hanging around the shop. Kyle had somebody buy him a new bike to replace the piece of junk he was riding, and when Rodney reported that none of his classmates believed it was a gift from his friend Kyle Petty, Kyle took measures; clearing it with the teacher, he walked into Rodney's class one day, unannounced, and sat down beside the kid until the bell rang. Kyle had no enemies that anyone knew of.

But greatness never came for him on the racetrack. He had not a single Winston Cup victory to show in the 140 races he had driven for his father, only two in 115 for the Wood Brothers, so when he teamed up with Felix Sabates, in 1989, it seemed to most that his fortunes would change. They seemed a natural pair, two gregarious souls who genuinely enjoyed each other's company, and in the beginning the relationship paid off; Kyle winning eight poles and five races over their first five years together. But then Kyle won only one race in sixty-one starts, over the '94 and '95 seasons, and this '96 season had become hell for the fourth-longest driver/ owner relationship in Winston Cup. He ranked eighth in miles completed, showing fortitude, but there was little else to brag about. After fourteen races, Kyle was yet to finish on the lead lap; he had no top ten finishes, only seven top twenties, and he stood twentieth in the points standings and was going nowhere. "Aw, hell, we missed the setup again," was Sabates's terse answer, week after week, when Kyle continued to qualify poorly and finish even worse.

When the teams arrived in Daytona for the Pepsi 400 on the July Fourth weekend, formerly the famous Firecracker 400, where King Richard had won his last race as a driver, no one was really surprised, then, to hear that Felix and Kyle had agreed to end their relationship. They spoke warmly of regarding the other "like a father" and "like a son," but one win in three seasons wasn't cutting it. Speculation flared immediately that Kyle would return to the family fold at Petty Enterprises in Level Cross, after riding out the season with Sabco, but that hadn't worked before and he wasn't so sure it would this time: "The first thing I did was call Bobby [Hamilton] and his wife" to tell them the famous Petty blue number 43 STP Pontiac was "his as long as he wants it and Richard wants him," and that he wasn't interested in being the number two man at his father's shop. "Maybe we'll set up PE-II or something," he said, indicating that he didn't think a father-and-son arrangement was a probability. As for Felix, he admitted to having been watching the young Indy-car driver Robby Gordon for more than two years, and later in the summer he would sign a three-year deal for Gordon to get behind the wheel of the Coors Light number 42 beginning with the '97 season. "I saw an Indy-car race where he blew his engine, and when he got out and kicked the car I said, 'That's my man,' " Sabates said. "Robby said he also wants to run the Indy 500 next year, that it's always been his dream to win that one, so, hey, we'll work it out. I'll have a plane at Indy. He can change uniforms on the plane while we fly him to Charlotte for the Coke 600, and we'll get him to the track in a chopper. I'm gonna like this kid."

That was only the beginning of the silly season, as it turned out. As they reached the midpoint on the schedule, firings and rumors of firings were rife. Steve Grissom (twenty-ninth in the standings) and Mike Wallace (thirty-ninth) lost their rides for the season, replaced by Greg Sacks and Dick Trickle, respectively. Several other drivers were tenuously clinging to their jobs after poor showings in the first half, most notably Morgan Shepherd and Robert Pressley, while it was announced that John Andretti and Jeremy Mayfield would simply switch cars and sponsors at some point later in the season. Poor Ken Schrader, even though he stood seventh in points, was told that he was the odd man out behind Gordon and Terry Labonte at Hendrick Motorsports and would be replaced by Ricky Craven in '97. Richard Childress, tired of seeing Earnhardt getting hung out alone in the draft, began preening Mike Skinner as a second driver on what would become a two-car RCR team in '97 ("You can't pass on the superspeedways without help, and those guys [like the Hendrick and Roush teammates] aren't going to work with anybody but their own").

The one man who seemed immune to all of this panic, a desire on the part of owners and sponsors to change drivers if only for the sake of change, was the indefatigable Dave Marcis. His best day had been in the Daytona 500, when he finished fifteenth, and he hadn't had a top twenty since; indeed, with three DNQs and three DNFs, he was thirty-eighth in the points standings. But even his sponsors at Prodigy understood that Marcis was judged differently, that the very sight of the dogged old grandfather out there on the track, plugging along in his purple number 71 car, was a sort of repayment in itself. In fact, when a busted oil pump threatened to keep him from qualifying for that weekend's race at Daytona, which would give him a record for active drivers of 800 starts, Earnhardt loaned him his own qualifying engine and Marcis went out and qualified. It was repayment for all the times the loyal and dependable Marcis had run tests so Earnhardt could make his GM-Goodwrench appearances or simply go fishing. "You don't see things like that in football, baseball, or other sports," said Marcis. On the morning of the Daytona race, Bill France, Jr., presented him a trophy adorned with a new pair of black wingtip shoes. "If I know Dave," said France, "he'll be wearing 'em next week."

That return race at Daytona, delayed for two hours and then shortened from 160 laps to 117 by storms sweeping across Florida ahead of Hurricane

Bertha, was won by Sterling Marlin—his eighth victory in the last seventeen races at Daytona and Talladega, the restrictor-plate tracks—but not without some adventures. The son of the redoubtable old driver Coo Coo Marlin had been sailing ahead of the pack for thirty laps in his powerful Kodak Chevy when suddenly his ignition shut off; unable to find the backup ignition switch, he fired the engine the old-fashioned way by shifting into third gear and letting out the clutch. Then, advised over the radio that a $10,000 bonus was his if he could take the lead on the eightieth lap, the scheduled halfway point in the race, he caught a draft and passed six cars in half a lap to take the lead and the money. And finally, when a three-car accident on lap 101 sent most of the others to the pits for a splash of gas under caution, he followed the terse advice of his crew chief, Tony Glover ("Stay out, it's gonna rain"), and won under a caution when the rains finally came. Terry Labonte was a close second, Earnhardt fourth, and now The Intimidator led Labonte by only five points as the tour headed back to the East again. What did the resident sage, ol' D.W., think about that? "Earnhardt wants [the championship] badder than he lets on. He's obsessed by it. An eighth would make him the greatest driver of all time, at least in *his* mind. Gordon, now, he's just twenty-four, energetic, maybe too much aware of Earnhardt. Me, I'm picking Texas Terry."

And so it came to pass, on the following weekend at New Hampshire International Speedway, that Labonte, the soft-spoken Texan of French-Canadian heritage, took the points lead for the first time in the season. There was something otherworldly about racing in the dank evergreen forests of New Hampshire, on the edge of the forbidding White Mountains, where the woods were so thick and canopied that headlights had to be turned on as the car-haulers negotiated the country back roads leading to the track. Due to the hard New England winters, the surface of the track was buckled and cracked, and it got worse when more than 16,000 car laps were run on Friday—by the Winston Cup, modified, and Busch North Grand National cars competing that weekend. Then on Saturday, all activities were washed out by a brush from Hurricane Bertha. "The track might look good on television," said Waltrip, "but you've got to keep taking shovels and scooping up the stuff [chunks of asphalt and rubber] that's out there." Ricky Craven hadn't been faring well at all since surviving his frightful airborne crash at Talladega, but he excited the locals (he was from Maine and had lived in nearby Concord, New Hampshire, during his BGN North apprenticeship) by taking the pole before the rains came. It took forever to run the Jiffy Lube 300 on Sunday, due to numerous pauses to clear the track of more debris, but for the fans it was worth the wait; Ernie Irvan took his first victory since his near-fatal crash in '94, and when he crossed the start-finish line he screeched into a Bootlegger Turn and circled the track clockwise in what the boys called a "Polish Victory Lap" in memory of the deceased Alan Kulwicki and Davey Allison, both of whom had been stars of the Yates racing team. But as others were celebrating Irvan's return (except for his wife and young daughter, ironically, who normally made all of the races), Labonte was quietly backing into the points lead by finishing sixth while Earnhardt ran out of gas on the last lap to finish twelfth and Gordon came up thirty-fourth when he developed ignition problems late in the race. It may have been a rough weekend on a battered track, but everybody was sobered when they read of events elsewhere around the racing world: a driver and a course worker were killed in a CART race at Toronto, five spectators died when a car got loose and sailed into the crowd on Bastille Day in France, and a biker and a track official were killed in Belgium.

Although Rusty Wallace would win the next Sunday's Miller 500 in his Miller-sponsored Ford at Pocono, his fourth victory of the year, all conjectures about who might win the points championship and the $1.5 million bonus that went with it now very much included the name of Terry Labonte, aka Texas Terry, the Iron Man, and the Ice Man. He had had his ups and downs over the years, winning the '84 championship as a twenty-seven-year-old (when it paid only $150,000) but then parking his car and walking away in disgust during the middle of a race in '91, but he had been thriving for three years now as the number two man, behind Gordon, at Hendrick Motorsports. He was proving to everyone in Winston Cup, once again, that consistency pays; he had won only one race, against Gordon's five and Earnhardt's two, but he had threatened to win nearly every start except four (Daytona, Rockingham, Martinsville, and Pocono), which turned sour. "Everybody was watching Earnhardt and Gordon [in the points race] and I guess I sort of snuck in there," he was saying over a pay phone in a hotel lobby in Grand Rapids, Michigan, where he was doing some business for Kellogg's Corn Flakes and Bayer Aspirin on the Tuesday following the Pocono race. The din of conventioneers in the background was such that he had to fairly shout to be heard over the phone. "It's the first time I've been in the lead since '85, but the run for the championship is still the same. Consistency. I mean, sure, you're aware of your closest competitor because he's the one you've got to beat. I mean, you don't want to come down to a situation where the guy you're racing against gets four new tires and gas, and you don't do anything. But you don't change your game plan. You try to get ahead and stay ahead for as long as you can, and if you do it every week you'll win the championship."

And now, in the dead of the summer, big bad Talladega awaited their return. Nobody needed any reminding of the violent airborne disasters in the spring race, least of all Ricky Craven and Bill Elliott, whose chances at anything approaching a successful season had been squashed on that day. Craven had been running fourth in the points standings before his frightening flight, and now he was fourteenth and fading fast. Elliott had gotten back into his car a month ahead of schedule, at Daytona in July, but after missing five races due to his smashed left femur he found himself thirty-fifth in the standings ("We've been behind the eight ball ever since"). And now, on the last weekend of July, there was another factor for the drivers to contend with: the insufferable Alabama heat. The temperatures inside a modern stock car routinely reached 130 degrees, which wasn't that much of a problem in the coolish early and late portions of the season, but with a heat index of 100 predicted for the weekend at Talladega it was something to dread. Chad Little, one of the Busch Grand National drivers scheduled to compete in Saturday's preliminary race, was trying something old and something new to beat the heat. "Air-conditioning can spoil a driver," he said, then telling of how he had been driving around in his street car with the windows rolled up and the heater running full blast, an old trick Buddy Baker had used some thirty years earlier, to prepare himself for the steamy Labor Day Mountain Dew Southern 500 at Darlington. The new was a

NASA-designed cooling helmet, sixteen pounds and shaped like a pump-kin, that kept the temperature thirty-four degrees cooler than that in the cockpit. "I turn it off during cautions to save the battery," he explained, "and when I turn it back on it feels like I'm sticking my face in a refrigera-tor." Many of the drivers or their emissaries crowded around Little's garage stall just to have a look, like show-and-tell time at school, for there had been a futile ongoing search for some way to beat the heat and they were ready to try anything.

But then, with the coming of the ubiquitous "late afternoon and eve-ning showers" of summertime in the Deep South, the weather cooled considerably; the primary beneficiary of the sudden drop in temperatures being young Jeremy Mayfield, whose turn to qualify came just as a cloud cover cooled the track by fifteen degrees and greatly enabled him to win the pole. The problem now wasn't the heat but, rather, the possibility of a rainout, something no one wanted. NASCAR would do anything to get this race in, for coming up was the rich Brickyard 400 at Indianapolis, a Saturday race that would require the teams to depart from Charlotte a day earlier than usual. So while everybody kept one eye on the skies and the forecasts of fickle thunderstorms, they could ponder other matters. The Winston leader bonus had rolled over and now a driver who vaulted into the points lead by winning this race would collect a check for $160,000; and both Gordon and Earnhardt were close enough to Labonte to cash in if either won and Labonte fared poorly. Between contemplating such a windfall and working out the kinks during practice sessions, they found time to give a standing ovation to Joe Gibbs, the owner of Bobby Labonte's car, for having just been installed in the National Football League's Hall of Fame for his tenure as coach of the Washington Redskins (so noted on the hood of Labonte's car for this race only), and to consider the terrorist bomb that had interrupted the Olympics 100 miles away in Atlanta. Now, it seemed, some of the drivers were prepared to talk about the death threats that they had kept quiet about over the years. "It's scary that race fans can get so opinionated and volatile," said Rusty Wallace, who revealed that his wife seldom came to races anymore because of the fans' profani-ties. He talked about the 1987 season, when Earnhardt was assigned FBI agents for a month after some aggressive driving on his part brought death threats; and about the time two years later when he was sent home from Charlotte Motor Speedway with two security guards in tow, courtesy of Humpy Wheeler, after a run-in on the track with Darrell Waltrip had enraged the masses. Obviously, having the most devoted fans this side of international soccer and professional wrestling worked both ways.

Gordon had qualified on the outside pole, Earnhardt fourth, and with Terry Labonte starting far back at twenty-ninth, each of them could smell the fat Winston bonus as they checked in for the race on Sunday morning. Another rowdy Talladega crowd was assembling, along with a full team from CBS-TV, but it had rained in torrents throughout the night, turning the grassy stretch between pit road and the frontstretch into a lake and putting the race in doubt. It was NASCAR's call to make, not CBS or any of the racing teams, and since there seemed to be no viable makeup date, Bill France, Jr., showed no inclination toward calling it off, even when the network gave up at half past three in the afternoon and switched over to coverage of a Professional Golfers' Association Seniors tournament. Finally, at four o'clock, the green flag was waved and the race began. From the very beginning, it was restrictor-plate racing at its worst, with the lead constantly changing hands as the drivers slipped in and out of the draft. All along, there was the constant threat of darkness that would shorten the race's intended 200 laps, but onward they roared on the treacherous high banks, through green-flag pit stops and near misses and the ever-present danger of another horrendous airborne flight into the darkening Alabama sky, miraculously avoiding serious accidents until, on lap 117, there came the moment that would forever define the 1996 Winston Cup season.

Earnhardt got creamed. His black Chevy had been in the lead on seven different occasions, and he was struggling to maintain the lead when the Fords of Sterling Marlin and Ernie Irvan bumped, going into the first turn at nearly 200 miles per hour, and when Marlin was slung into Earnhardt's right rear it sent The Intimidator spinning hard into the retaining wall. The fans were on their feet now and time stood still as Earnhardt's car caromed off the wall, flipped on its side, and, thus exposed, was smacked in the roof by three oncoming cars. Demolished race cars were strewn all over that end of the track, a total of twelve of them knocked out for the day, and with the red flag out all attention turned to the scurrying of men as they pried Earnhardt from his machine. A huge roar went up from the crowd of more than 100,000 when he emerged, wincing and gently holding his left shoulder, in severe pain as he groggily shuffled to the ambulance that had been driven to the scene. (So as not to worry his fans, he had insisted that they not make a big deal out of cutting the roof to extract him from the car, and that he be allowed to walk to the ambulance.) He was airlifted out of the infield to a hospital in Birmingham—surely, by now, surgeons over there had learned to be on full standby alert during race weekends at Talladega—and soon word came back to the track. Earnhardt had a fractured sternum and left collarbone, and it would be a miracle if he could drive anytime soon. To miss a single race would cost him that eighth championship now, and coming up were two of the most demanding races on the schedule: the rich Brickyard 400 at Indianapolis, with its flat track and high speeds; and the road race at Watkins Glen, with all of the frenzied hands-on driving required on a meandering road course.

Once the wreckage was cleared and it was announced that darkness would shorten the race to 129 laps, Jeff Gordon got an unexpected push in the draft from a rival Ford driver, of all things, Jeff Burton, to burst past Dale Jarrett in a thrilling five-lap sprint following the final caution to win by fourteen hundredths of a second. He had been "lucky" to avoid the big wreck, he said, just "saw a hole and got through it before the spinning cars could get to me." It was a huge payday for The Kid, more than $272,000 when the Winston bonus and others were totaled up, and now, for the first time this year, he had the points lead. There was the usual finger pointing in the aftermath of the accident, of course, Irvan and Marlin blaming each other before adding, interestingly, with no remorse, that they hadn't done anything that Earnhardt didn't do all of the time ("When somebody goes to pass *him*," said Irvan, "he just runs right into 'em"). The Intimidator could be excused this time for leaving the building prematurely, being laid up in a hospital and legitimately unavailable for comment, so now the stock car fans out there in TV land could focus their ire on CBS. They would have to wait until the following Sunday to see the wreck that, in all likelihood, had done Earnhardt in, that being the day CBS promised a truncated two-hour taped version of the race; but in the meantime they gave the network and its affiliates unrelenting hell for showing them golf, for God's sake, instead of racing. The CBS station in Johnson City, Tennessee, near the Bristol track, reported receiving 1,000 angry phone calls on Sunday and Monday; and the week was young.

Now, like never before, all eyes were on Earnhardt as the Cuppers geared up for the final leg of the summer schedule. He had refused the surgery that would have derailed his season, deciding to ride out the pain, and by Tuesday he was back home at the Richard Childress Racing shop in Welcome, where the crumpled remains of the Talladega car were already on display at the RCR museum ("I'm kinda bruised up, sore, and in some pain, but the car looks a lot worse than I do"). He was being outfitted with special harnesses, was practicing getting in and out of the car, and Childress "saw something in his eyes that said if his body will let him, we'll have to pry him out of that car." NASCAR rules allowed that the driver who started a race was the driver of record, so the general plan was for Earnhardt to start and go as long as he could until he was relieved by Mike Skinner, the thirty-nine-year-old Californian who had already been contracted to drive a second car for RCR in '97. Childress had tried to hire Al Unser, Jr., the Indy-car driver, who had practically been raised racing at the Brickyard, but Unser's team, itself crippled by injuries, needed him to test cars at Sebring, Florida. So it would be up to Skinner, who was leading NASCAR's new truck series but had completed only 700 Winston Cup laps during this season (his best turn being a twelfth at Rockingham), to carry the RCR banner at the Brickyard. The points race was as close as it could get, with Earnhardt trailing the leader, Gordon, by only twenty-three points, and second-place Labonte by fourteen. All Skinner had to do was bring the black number 3 home intact and in a decent position so Earnhardt could pick up some points. "I'm just going to take my time and try to stay out of trouble," said Skinner. "If I could finish in the top fifteen, it would be great. My job is to go out and get some points for 'em and try not to wreck the car or make any stupid rookie mistakes."

Nobody needed any reminder of the fallout from the crash at Talladega, although one was supplied—no sooner had the teams set up their stalls on Wednesday, than Irvan and Marlin got into a shouting match in the garage area over who had been at fault (". . . sunglasses were thrown," read one impish report). The center of attention, of course, was the RCR/ Earnhardt camp. Earnhardt, obviously in great pain, went onto the track for only nine practice laps while Skinner spent what seemed like hours out there, introducing himself to the car and the track. And then, when it came time to qualify on Thursday, the first of two minor miracles of the weekend occurred. Gordon had already gone out and won the pole with a record-setting run when Earnhardt buckled himself into the car, fired the ignition, gave his crew a lame thumbs-up sign, and dug out. The sharp, relatively flat corners of the Brickyard made steering difficult for any man on any day (the healthy Hamilton, Rudd, and Craven, in fact, would fail to qualify that day), and the track had been made more treacherous with a new layer of asphalt ("I always cringe when I hear somebody's repaving," said Mark Martin). But the Man in Black took his warmup lap without result, brought the car up to full power, and when it was over he had qualified, remarkably, for the twelfth starting position. And then, on Saturday, with the largest crowd of any Winston Cup season on hand to watch the chase for the biggest purse on the circuit, Earnhardt took it to the first caution, on only the sixth lap, and reluctantly turned it over to Skinner ("This is my life, right here," Earnhardt said, his voice cracking, when an ABC-TV reporter stuck a microphone in his face). He was back in his RV with his wife, resting and watching the proceedings on television, as Mike Skinner did exactly what he said he would do; he stayed out of trouble and brought the car home in fifteenth place, without a scratch ("I didn't get nervous about driving; I was nervous about tearing it up"). The better news for Earnhardt was that Gordon had crashed on lap twenty-three and Labonte finished third (the winner was Jarrett, whose $564,035 payoff doubled his father's entire career winnings). Earnhardt had actually moved up to second in the standings, due to Gordon's misfortune, and was still only sixty-one points behind the leader, Labonte.

The real test of Earnhardt's mettle, however, would come on the following weekend, at the Bud at the Glen race in upstate New York. It was one thing to floorboard the car and go into a continuous left turn for three hours or so, but quite another to negotiate eleven esses over a twisting 2.45-mile road course like the one at Watkins Glen. Mark Martin, for one, always enjoyed it, and reckoned the reason he had won the last three at The Glen was because "driving with my dad on all those curvy, hilly back roads back home in Arkansas was like driving on a road course." There were the esses, followed by a 160-miles-per-hour backstretch, and then a tricky inner loop akin to a slalom run; all of it requiring a furious pumping of all three pedals (accelerator, brakes, clutch), vigorous shifting of gears, and violent steering. It would seem to be an impossible task for a driver in Earnhardt's current condition, barely able to lift his elbow away from his waist, but he would by-God try. Before the wreck at Talladega, he had experienced few significant injuries during his career—he missed four races during his rookie year, 1979, when he broke both collarbones at Pocono, and when he broke his kneecap at the same track in '82 he refused to sit out—and he was trying to shrug this one off, like Superman. "I'm not trying to be an iron man, I'm just trying to do my job," he growled before slipping into the car on Friday for qualifying. And what did he do? He not only won the pole; hell, he set a course record doing it. Admitting he was "really pumped up" for qualifying, he sounded like Bear Bryant when the incredulous media gathered around him afterward: "To rassle the car like I rassled it on that lap, and to put that effort in there, I'm pretty proud of it. It hurts, but it's a good hurt."

For this race, Childress had hired an experienced road-course driver, Busch Grand National points leader David Green, to relieve Earnhardt at the first opportunity, just as Skinner had done at Indy. They had even gone so far as to install Green's narrower seat in the car to replace the wide truck-type seat Earnhardt had always preferred, the thinking being that Earnhardt wouldn't be in it for very long. But Ironhead's startling perfor-mance in winning the pole had changed everything. The fans were into this drama, too: a whole batch of T-shirts reading "It Hurts So Good" had been produced overnight at the little Earnhardt factory in North Caro-lina, rushed in by plane and put on sale at his souvenir stand along the promenade, and they were sold out long before noon Sunday. There were naysayers in the media and among the fans—most of the opposition coming from those who saw this as just some more egomaniacal grand-standing from a macho dude out to prove something, at the risk of endan-gering the rest of the season—but, like Earnhardt himself, they would see how it went. Not lost on anyone was the news that two other regulars who had gotten banged up lately, Elliott and Petty ("Even my hair hurts," Kyle joked, telling of how somebody had stepped on his pigtail as medics were pulling him from his car after a wreck at Indy), had opted for relief drivers in this one.

Sunday had turned out to be another splendid day for racing, and the fans spread out on grassy banks all along the meandering course, picnic-style, to await the start of the ninety-lap (221-mile) race under blue skies and scudding clouds. Those with scanners were tuned to Earnhardt's frequency so they could hear what amounted to a play within a play. Down on pit row, in the number 3 stall, Earnhardt fired his engine and looked straight ahead with all of the grimness of a kamikaze pilot. On the other side of the low concrete wall, David Green stood beside the chair on stilts, like a tennis judge's perch, whence Richard Childress would direct the operation beneath a big colorful umbrella, the designated relief driver wearing his fireproof driving suit and holding his helmet by its strap. When the pace car eased along pit road, Earnhardt followed it and led the thirty-eight other cars onto the track. The way Childress had it orchestrated in his mind, there would be some early trouble that would bring out a caution so Earnhardt could hustle into the pits and turn the car over to Green.

They got the early yellow they had hoped for when Musgrave spun out on the fifth lap, and now Green was donning his helmet and standing on the top step of the tall chair so he could consult with Childress. This was the moment they had anticipated . . . But wait. Earnhardt had already won five bonus points for leading a lap and he was still in the lead by a comfortable margin. "It's your call, Dale," Childress radioed, and got nothing but silence. Earnhardt wasn't going to tempt himself by coming into the pits, not even for a splash of gas under caution, so he stayed on the track while Musgrave's car was arighted. He powered away, again, when the green flag resumed racing, and that more or less signaled the crossing of the point of no return. He had built his lead to two full seconds after thirty laps, when everybody hauled into the pits for four tires and fuel, and now Green was taking off his helmet and Childress wasn't even discussing a driver switch. It was too late to change now, anyway; not only would the switch take too long, NASCAR rules would force the number 3 car to the rear of the field. So Earnhardt was in and out of the pit in a sensational 19.2 seconds, and he would lead a total of fifty-four laps during the afternoon, as late as the sixty-fourth lap of ninety, before he finally began to flag. When it was over, he still had managed to come in sixth. Labonte had finished second, Gordon fourth, but Earnhardt had maintained his hold on second in the points standing.

The winner was Geoff Bodine, a local favorite who had grown up down the road at Chemung, New York, but there wasn't much interest in his post-race comments; especially when they turned into a maudlin recitation of his personal woes, from his wife's leaving him to his squabbles with his brother Brett. The story was Earnhardt, and it was a stirring one that had the media and fans comparing his courage with such memorable moments as the Dodgers' Kirk Gibson limping off the bench to hit a game-winning homer in the '88 World Series, and, more recently, gymnast Kerri Strug's nailing of a team gold medal at the Atlanta Olympics on a twisted ankle. Let the arguments that he may have delayed his recovery and thus risked his chances to win his record eighth Winston Cup championship be damned. This had been a stirring moment for the ages, a tale of raw grit and courage, and the man was entitled to savor it, no matter what lay ahead. He had even managed to win over some members of the press who had never been big fans in the past. "For sure," wrote the columnist George Webster of *Performance Racing News*, "right now he is almost single-handedly saving Winston Cup racing from the terrible blight of the slick, plastic blahs."

They had a hard time getting him to the phone on Tuesday morning for the weekly media teleconference, for only his second appearance there all year ("Dale's tied up with several business opportunities," said RJR's Chris Powell, saying that Earnhardt was "out of his driving suit and into his business suit today"), but in due time the man of the hour checked in. "I've got a dull ache in my shoulder and a burning in my chest, and I'm sore from [Green's] small seat because it was pushing on my rib cage in the corners," he said, "but I've got to admit it gave me better support. It never got unbearable. Coming out of the esses, I was shifting with my right hand and steering with my left. It was get out or continue, on that first caution, but the car was running so well that I decided to stay with it. The desire to drive that race car was greater than the pain. I faltered at the end, just got tired and started wearing down. But, hey, at this point last year we were three hundred points down and we almost made it back, so we're going for it. The concern is endurance, not pain." Then he promptly went out to his farm that afternoon and got pissed off at his bulldozer and gave it a shot with a sledgehammer, jarring his collarbone and sternum again, setting his recovery back to where it had been before Indianapolis. And finally, when he showed up for the following weekend's race at Michigan, somebody presented him with a Superman outfit, tights and all. "At least he had the good sense not to wear it in the race," wrote Webster, a skeptical Canadian who still wasn't entirely sure of what to make of the man.

14

THE SOUTHERN BY-GOD 500

Eight of the eleven summer races had been held on foreign soil, to hear the Southerners talk, and now they were bringing it home for the final stretch. Except for the fall return to Dover, Delaware, and the arduous trek out to the rocky barrens of Phoenix, Arizona, for the next-to-last race of the year, the remainder of the season would be played out on their home turf in the Deep South. And there was no better place to embark on the beginning of the end than on Labor Day weekend with the forty-seventh staging of the Southern 500 at quirky old Darlington Raceway, in the scrub-pine Sandhills area of northeastern South Carolina, hard by the banks of the mighty Pee Dee River; for Darlington was, in nearly every respect, the most traditional of all the stops on the Winston Cup circuit. It was called, variously, the Lady in Black and the "Track Too Tough to Tame," the latter referring not only to the rigors of the track itself but also to the rowdy infield crowd it attracted.

It was there at Darlington, in fact, where the early perceptions of stock car racing as a lawless activity of the South's white lower classes, "white trash," first took hold and flourished; a stubborn notion that NASCAR, nearly half a century later, was still busily trying to airbrush if not totally deny. (There had been an outburst in the garage area of Daytona at the beginning of the season when a press agent for one of the drivers jumped a writer new to the scene: "All I read outside of the trade press is that it's a bunch of Southern illiterates who drool tobacco, run moonshine, marry their cousins, and screw everything in sight." *Well*, the writer thought, *we'll always have Darlington.*) It was here, in the shank of a Labor Day afternoon in the early sixties, that a writer named Bill Robinson, of the *Atlanta Journal*, sat inside the chicken coop of a press box perching perilously on the first turn, where more than one errant race car had come for a visit, just passing through, and pecked out a line on his portable typewriter that was still being quoted with misty eyes by the old-timers still on the NASCAR beat; a lyrical passage about how the most thrilling spectacle in the world of sport just might be the sight of three battered race cars, "side by side on the backstretch, running flat out, bellies to the ground, chasing the sun. . . ."

When Darlington was scooped out of the sand in 1950, it became NASCAR's first fast high-banked superspeedway: a paved 1.4-mile pear-shaped oval that traced its odd configuration to the refusal of a neighboring farmer, Sherman Ramsey, to drain his minnow pond in order to make way for the normal line the architects had drafted for the track's first and second turns; thus forcing the builders to work around it. "We were like a bunch of New York City cab drivers," said Tim Flock, the youngest of the Flock boys from Atlanta and one of seventy-five starters in that inaugural Southern 500, which saw only twenty-five of them running at the end. "With that many cars, you could start lapping folks on about the second lap." Even at qualifying speeds of only eighty miles per hour, the drivers were ill-prepared to handle a track like that, with its uneven layout and rippled asphalt surface and relatively high banks of more than twenty degrees, and from that very first race there arose the term "Darlington Stripes." "Yep," many a driver would grin, assessing the white streak on the right-hand side of his machine as it was being towed away, "went to Darlington and earned my stripes."

Just as Sherman Ramsey's obstinance had helped create a unique race-track, another factor beyond the builders' control also brought distinction, if that is the word, to Darlington. The track was so far out in the boondocks that there were few motel rooms for miles around in those pre-interstate days, prompting the promoters to issue an invitation for fans to come early and camp in the infield for the weekend, at $5 per vehicle. And so the ragged hordes poured in, all manner of good old boys, a volatile conglomeration of sandhill peckerwoods and sawmill hands and tobacco farmers and shade-tree mechanics (and prostitutes to serve them from covered trucks and customized hearses). The promoters had expected a crowd of 5,000, but 25,000 showed up. The infield at Darlington became a lawless village unto itself, a rowdy world of arrant yahoos who drank, smoked, fought, fornicated, and even killed. Hundreds would be arrested during a weekend, many of them simply locked up in a makeshift jail right there on the first turn until they sobered up, and there was a large tent with a red cross on it, something right out of *M*A*S*H*, for the wounded. They still talked about the flood of 1975, when seven inches of rain fell in less than an hour, swamping the two tunnels and turning the infield into an untidy lake awash with tents and portable toilets and everything else that would float.

Both Bubba and the South had cleaned up their acts somewhat since the fifties—but not that much—and so here at the approach of the millennium, Darlington still wore the rough edge that set it apart from all of the other venues on the circuit. Here there were no air-conditioned condominiums for the fat cats, nor oak-paneled boardrooms for the sponsors. The track was still a bitch to drive, even more so when you consider that qualifying speeds were nearly 100 miles per hour faster these days than in 1950, and the infield was still the place to be; albeit a little more nearly refined, and a lot more expensive. Now there were hot showers and rest rooms inside cinder-block buildings in the infield, which had been paved and grassed and lined off to bring some illusion of order, and on race weekends it was filled with hundreds of RVs that cost more than twice the price of any race car on hand and were charged as much as $500 for parking and hookups. Changing the race day from Labor Day to Sunday hadn't cut down on anybody's drinking time, so it was still what it had always been: a wild party, all-white and pugnacious, in a sea of portable barbecue grills and tents and boom boxes playing country music and junky pickup trucks bearing jerry-built viewing platforms that held Confederate flags ripping in the breeze. This was Bubba's Last Stand, where he could drink and smoke and wench and eat pork and use the word "nigger" if he damned well wanted to, without any shushing from the politically correct, and he was there to celebrate all of that. Forget, hell.

As the fans and the teams and the media converged on the old track, there was a tension in the air not felt since the giddiness of the season's unfolding back in February at Daytona. The phone lines had been crackling throughout the stock car kingdom, from NASCAR's headquarters at Daytona to R.J. Reynolds's big house in Winston-Salem, ever since President Clinton's long-anticipated formal signing of a bill a week earlier that could pave the way for the outlawing of tobacco-company sponsorship of sporting events. (The timing must have seemed downright morbid to RJR's T. Wayne Robertson, whose father finally died of lung cancer the day after the announcement.) Clinton had brought the hammer down, dropped the first shoe, just as the '96 presidential campaigns were getting underway, and now RJR and NASCAR were mounting their counteroffensive. The first piece of paper to be tacked up on the bulletin board of the infield media center at Darlington was a statement from RJR, announcing its intentions to sue if it came to that. The timing was ironic, if not strategically planned by the White House, for this Labor Day weekend of the Mountain Dew Southern 500 happened to mark only the fourth time that RJR found itself in the position of making its grandest gesture of all: paying out the Winston Million, the size of the check that would go to Dale Jarrett should he win on Sunday.

To take the $1 million, a driver had to win three of four selected races during the season: the Daytona 500 (the most prestigious), the spring race at Talladega (the fastest), the 600-miler on Memorial Day weekend at Charlotte (the longest), and the Southern 500 (the oldest). It had been accomplished only once, when Bill Elliott became known as "Million Dollar Bill" in '85, and only two other times had drivers had a shot at it when the moment of truth came down to Darlington: Darrell Waltrip in '89, and the now-deceased Davey Allison in '92. Jarrett, of course, had won the Daytona and Charlotte races this year, and would have already nailed the Million had he not finished second to Sterling Marlin, by only two car lengths, in the spring race at Talladega (the day of the airborne crashes that had taken out Elliott and young Ricky Craven). The son of the old champion-driver-turned-broadcaster Ned Jarrett, raised not fifty miles from Darlington at Camden, was having a superb season. He was third in the points race, tops in earnings with more than $1.8 million, and to win this race would put him in a special orbit. Except for a poor performance on the road course at Watkins Glen, he had finished fourth or better in the last seven races, and in preparation for this big one he and Robert Yates had dropped nearly $75,000 for three days of testing "my favorite car" on the Darlington track. If he could stay focused through the crush of the media, he said, he ought to be all right. "With a chance to win a million dollars, there *should* be a lot going on."

And so, during the weekly media teleconference on the Tuesday before Darlington, it was all Jarrett and the Million and, as an extension of that, the despised president's threat to end RJR's twenty-six-year stewardship of Winston Cup racing. The latter issue came up early on, an invitation for Jarrett to respond with the practiced company line that would be parroted, like a drumbeat, in the long tug-of-war sure to follow for many months. "This is the United States of America," he said, measured and not a little defiant, an echo of T. Wayne Robertson's soliloquy of the spring. "We all have our choices to make, whether it's smoking or whatever. I've never seen the tobacco companies target the youth of the country. All they're interested in is getting people to use *their* products. We have more serious problems with the youth of America than whether they're going to smoke cigarettes, anyway. We ought to be worrying about drugs and firearms, not this, and we'll fight right along with R.J. Reynolds on this. Sure, they [NASCAR] could find other sponsors to step in. But it just wouldn't be right if it wasn't Winston Cup."

That said, Jarrett and his inquisitors turned to the race for the Million. Nervous? "I'm more nervous about Todd than anything," he said, referring to his crew chief, Todd Parrott, who wouldn't be there in the pits; he had slipped and torn up his knee while chasing down a tire in the pits at Bristol the previous Sunday, had surgery, and now was on crutches. The car? "Like I said, it's my favorite, the same one we won with in the Coca-Cola 600 at Charlotte and at Michigan in August, the same one we had at Darlington in the spring when we scraped the wall and then ran out of gas and finished fifteenth. After we tested it here last week, we touched up the paint and wrapped it." He still intended to run another car in Saturday's 200-mile Busch Grand National race (driving a Ford sponsored by Band-Aid, he had run in thirteen of twenty-one BGN races and collected $121,000): "The main reason is, we'll be trying to learn about tire wear and track conditions. Running those races is a big advantage, I think. Whenever we've run on Saturday, we've always had a better Sunday." Reaching, one of the writers asked if his teammate, Ernie Irvan, would get out of the way with, say, five laps to go, so he could win one for the Yates team. "We've joked about that, but I can guarantee you that Yates isn't about to get on the radio and ask Ernie to step aside so I can win the Million. Ernie's got Texaco, Havoline, and Ford to look out for, not Dale Jarrett. He wants to win as badly as I do." Well, come on now, surely the pressure is building. "You have pressure every week. There are nine races left for the points championship, and this is just one of 'em. Now it might be different if we were personally putting up our own million dollars and we'd lose it if we didn't win the race. That would be pressure. But this is gravy, a bonus, and it's great for the sport. I will admit, though, that like any athlete I tend to get up for the big ones."

His father, Ned, came on the line. He had won the Southern 500 in 1965, taking $22,600, "and that was a lot of money back then. This is exciting. The furthermost thing in my mind back then was that someday you could win a million dollars. And it's my son with that opportunity." Ned would be in the booth Sunday for ESPN, and someone wanted to know if he would be asked again to "take your boy home" if it came to that. "We've heard from a few people saying they don't like that, and I think we've done enough of it. When Dale was winning at Michigan and it came down to the wire, I saw 'em talking to the truck about having me do it again and I shook my head no in no uncertain terms. But, yeah, I've talked to ESPN about it and agreed to do it. I hope people will understand it if I do it one more time." They were obviously very close, and Ned wanted to say something else about a son who, lately, had begun to out-Jesus even Jeff Gordon in his public pronouncements: "Fans are always coming up to me and saying how proud I must be of Dale's driving. Well, I'm more proud of the kind of father he is to his kids, what kind of husband he is to his wife, what kind of son he is to his parents. He opened the church on Sunday morning of the Michigan race with a prayer for the people killed in the jet airplane crash [Flight 800, over Long Island] and I was beaming. I was more proud of him then than when he went out and won the race that afternoon."

Praying for the dead was the last thing on the minds of Bobby Lee Turbeville and Bryan ("You can call me Hoss") Hause and their ragged gaggle of pals as a full orange moon rose over Ramsey's Pond, just outside the west tunnel of Darlington Raceway, on Friday night. Hause, a thirty-two-year-old carpet layer from Lexington, South Carolina, about an hour's drive from the track, had wheeled his battered '73 long-bed Chevy pickup into place at noon Thursday, claiming the "pole position" in a line of cars and trucks and campers that stretched into the woods for at least half a mile. Bobby Lee, a twenty-five-year-old butcher from Dillon, the town that serves a monstrous souvenirs-and-fireworks emporium on the state line known as "South of the Border," had followed soon after and parked his truck fifth in line, or, as he put it, "third row on the pole." They had been coming to the Southern 500 for a long time—Bobby Lee's first stock car race, in fact, happened to be the one when Bill Elliott won the first Winston Million—and they had their act down pat. They always spent Thursday and Friday nights camped right there in the gravel, in the company of maybe a thousand other fans strung out around the pond and through the woods, so that when the gates opened at six o'clock Saturday morning they would be assured of claiming their usual ground at the end of pit road with a worm's-eye view of the first turn. Given that a room for two at the Days Inn ten miles away in Florence had been bumped up to $80 a night, and restaurant meals weren't free, this was the way to go. Camping in the infield for Saturday and Sunday cost $50 per vehicle plus $70 per person. "Correct me if I'm wrong," Hause was saying, "but

I-don't-think-sooo. That's a hundred and ninety dollars for me and my wife here. I don't know what the fuck they're charging for the grandstand, maybe eighty bucks apiece, and we'd wind up sitting between a couple of fat shits rootin' for that damned Earnhardt. Eats? Hey, I'll wait till I get back home to eat *goor-may.*" In the meantime, they were subsisting on red meat and beans and beer. Lots of beer.

" . . . *Rrrrraawwwwwwoooooww!*"

"Fuckin'-A. Damn right!"

"Here comes Rusty. *Rrrrraawwwwwwoooooww!* Sounds like a damned catsaw. *Rrrrraawwwwwwoooooww!* Catsaw'll go through anything: nails, knots, brick walls, you name it. That's Rusty when they get that Ford right. *Rrrrraawwwwwwoooooww!* Out o' th' way, assholes."

"Well, Hoss," somebody said, "he ain't doing so hot."

"Well, hell, what's he gonna do when a couple of idiots not even on the lead lap cut right in front of him? Shit, you saw Wilkesboro. Bodine and Andretti, lookin' at the scenery, out for a little Sunday drive, sumbitches never saw him comin'. Sounded like somebody mashing a beer can. *Crunch.* 'Sorry 'bout your car, Rusty.' Correct me if I'm wrong . . . *but I-don't-think-sooo.*"

Bryan Hause had the floor, as usual, the floor in this case being the tailgate of his truck. He was a fit man, bronze and slightly shaggy, and his uniform for the weekend consisted of a pair of blue gym shorts and thong sandals. He had made six Winston Cup races so far this season, starting with Speedweeks, and he planned to make four more. Except for the Daytona trip, he had been accompanied by his wife of twelve years, Brenda, and they always left their three young children with a friend who didn't much care about racing. Brenda was tall and leggy, in denim cutoffs and a halter top and sandals, and smiled brightly through her husband's shenanigans and ravings. His likes and dislikes were many, fervently held: he despised the city of Atlanta (whence they had moved to Lexington because he perceived it as a haven for "folks on welfare"), IROC races ("How can you root for a True Value Hardware Pontiac with 'Gordon' painted on the door?"), and Earnhardt ("You call hoping to finish fifth in one piece 'intimidating'?"). He loved Miller Lite ("I was drinking it before they invented cans"), Rusty Wallace and Bill Elliott ("That big old McDonald's T-bird looks like a red dick comin' at you"), and this, camping with friends at Darlington. But a Ford man with a Chevy? "Well, it's a piece of shit like everything else GM builds. Notice I got a decal on the window, a little boy peeing on the Chevy emblem. What can I say? I got a good deal on it." The bed of the truck was piled thick with carpet remnants taken from jobs, a good enough place for privacy and sleep once he and Brenda draped a tarp over it, and it was topped with a sturdy five-foot-high platform mounted on four-by-four legs and floored with black and white linoleum squares forming a checkered-flag design. Already unfurled and flying high, like the sails of a schooner on the high seas, were three flags clipped to an aerial: Confederate, Ford, and Rusty Wallace. His buddy, Bobby Lee Turbeville, wore the regalia of Mark Martin, but that was all right by Hoss; Martin drove a Ford, too.

"Hell," Hause was saying, "Ford is *America*. Henry Ford, father of our country, cross your heart. Picture it. Our great-granddaddys out there drivin' them T-Models, right off the line, first cars ever made. Then came our granddaddys, driving them Ford tractors on the farm. Then our daddys got their first cars—Fords, what else?—and we got the Mustangs, every red-blooded American boy's dream, and what's good enough for all of them is good enough for Rusty Wallace, and so on and so—"

"Ker-*blooomm!*"

"What th'—"

"Hot damn, got the Yankees on the run now!"

The first explosion of the evening came at 9:30, from down in the woods and the pastures surrounding Ramsey's Pond, where hundreds of cars and trucks and campers were dug in under the trees like General Robert E. Lee's troops in bivouac. Whatever caused it, a cannon or one of those giant cherry bombs available at South of the Border, it ceased the chirruping of the cicadas and brought a wave of whoops and Rebel yells reverberating through the trees. And now, not two minutes later, here came a pair of nifty little white golf carts laden with red fire-extinguishing equipment, being driven by earnest young men wearing the white uniforms of the raceway's security staff. They slithered to a halt beside Hause's little band, whose bleary eyes were now lit by the ashen flickers of a Coleman lantern, and one of the young men said, importantly, "Where'd that come from?"

"What?" said Hause.

"Sounded like a cannon or something."

"Oh, they're probably having a firefight down in the woods."

"The woods? That where it was?"

"I wouldn't go down there if I was y'all."

"Well, we've got to look into it."

"You got flashlights? Weapons?"

"Hunh?"

"Be careful, buddy. They don't take prisoners."

The young security guard gave Hause and the others a long look of disgust, like a railroad guard who had stumbled upon a hobo camp, before motioning for the other to follow him. As they passed the long jumble of cars and trucks and disappeared into the darkness on their humming electrified golf carts, Hause and Turbeville and the others howled and cracked open another round of beers and began to talk about getting some sleep. The moon rose higher, and the cicadas and other creatures of the night resumed their serenade. Six o'clock would come damned early.

On the outside listening in, as it were, they had missed the practices and the first round of qualifying that had taken place all day Friday. The Winston Cup car-haulers had rolled into the infield at daybreak after their eighty-mile trek from the shops around Charlotte, and the cars were on the track by eleven o'clock, with a crowd of maybe 8,000 basking in a blistering sun that promised to get even hotter during the weekend. It was still the Dale Jarrett show. "When I hear Robert Yates saying he's given Dale the best car he ever built," mused Jeff Gordon, "that means he's got a guided missile out there." Jarrett pretty much agreed with the assessment: "I think I do have a better car than everybody else, a better car and a better engine." Nobody was surprised, then, when Jarrett recorded the fastest times during the midday practice sessions and then went out in the afternoon and aced the track with a Darlington record qualifying speed of 170.934 miles per hour that won him the pole for Sunday. "There's no telling what Jeff Gordon or anyone else could run in this car," he said. "But it's mine, and he's not getting it."

The record time aside, nobody was venturing that the track "too tough to tame" had finally been brought to heel. When the first round of qualifying was over, the whitewashed retaining walls were streaked with ugly black scars left by drivers who had lost control—"Here," said Earnhardt, "you can *see* your mistakes"—and the most ghastly of all was where little Ward Burton, only ten minutes into the qualifying round, had lost it coming out of the fourth turn. The car was tight and his line was too high, and when he slammed into the wall he was thrown back down across the track into the pit wall. There, in a car fully loaded with twenty-two gallons of gasoline (a foolish NASCAR rule designed to equalize car weights during qualifying), the fuel cell cracked and a sheet of gas *whoosh*ed into a ball of orange flames like napalm skidding across the Vietnamese landscape. It had happened directly in front of about 4,000 fans seated in the shade of the tin-roofed grandstand on the fourth turn, and they were treated to the sight of Ricky Rudd, who had been standing beside his car at the rear of the line of qualifiers, leaping over the low retaining wall in his bright orange Tide suit, to help the frantic Burton escape his car. "It wasn't too *hahd* a hit," Burton said moments later, in his laconic rural Virginia drawl, then echoing the greatest fear expressed by fighter pilots from the Second World War: "I didn't want to *buhn*. I'll go one day, but I don't want to *buhn*."

It seemed that the only safe haven for Jarrett was on the track, in his car, because every time he climbed out of the cockpit he was being hustled off to the press box for another session with the horde of media, which was nearly twice as large as it had been for the March race. Quite understandably, the RJR/Winston Cup/NASCAR people were squeezing every possible line of type and second of airtime out of this grab for the Winston Million, and they were fortunate to have a willing partner in Jarrett. So, at the end of the first day's qualifying, he took the elevator up to the press level of the modest Winston Tower overlooking the first turn and submitted to another chat. He was good, very good, even self-effacing at times, although there were signs that he and the writers were becoming weary of the talk and ready to get on with the race. There were more paeans to his father: "There weren't a lot of guys who were very polished [in his] time, but Dad took the time to make sure he was able to handle each and every situation." There was a tidbit about pit-to-car communications: "Some things we can discuss on the radio and some we can't, because we've certainly found out that with success comes people getting in on your radio line, and we don't want to give any of our secrets away." Yes, he intended to sweeten his team members' paycheck if he won the Million; no, he didn't expect to have trouble sleeping Saturday night ("I'll be chasing my kids around the motor home until they go down around nine or nine-thirty; and, anyway, the day I stop getting nervous before a race is the day I'll get out of this business"). "Briefs, in the race car, anyway," was his answer to the question "Boxers or briefs?"—the sure indicator that enough was enough.

But in the course of these little fireside chats, Jarrett had revealed, to the delight of Motorheads everywhere, some insights into exactly what made Darlington such a difficult track and how a driver dealt with it. Basically, it came down to the fact that the track had been built for a slower generation of cars. "You have to be patient here, even with a good race car. It gets to feeling good but then it only takes a split second to miss the line—we're only talking about six or eight inches—and you're into the wall." The turns, he said, were totally different, and that's what made it so difficult. "Turns one and two have a narrow groove and when you get in there the car wants to slide up the racetrack. You come very, very close to the wall, especially as the race goes on. Getting off turn two is extremely tight and you feel like you're going to hit the wall exiting there every lap. Turns three and four are probably the most difficult turns we have any-where. You're on such a high line to run fast through there that you just have to give yourself room. Three and four were pretty slick [when he qualified] and we saw some cars have some trouble up there, so I probably lost half a tenth up there by barely squeezing out of the throttle. Ward [Burton] had a great lap going, but his crash certainly got everybody's attention. You've got to race the track here, not the other cars."

Saturday morning found Bryan Hause and Bobby Lee Turbeville long gone from their two-night encampment at the head of the line of revelers, having fired up their trucks at the first glint of daylight and a wave from a security guard, triumphantly rumbling through the tunnel to stake their claims in the infield, like settlers dashing westward in tattered prairie schooners during the Oklahoma land rush. Now, around ten o'clock, in a pasture the size of a football field, some 2,000 parents and children sat back in webbed aluminum folding lawn chairs or else sprawled out on the lush green grass, cheering and singing along with a Christian rock band. "Danny Nicholson and Heart of Love," read black letters on a white oilskin banner tied to the same fence where, only the night before, Bryan and Bobby Lee and the gang had staggered over to pee when the authorities weren't looking. Backed up to the fence were two flatbed trailers, serving as the stage for the five-piece band and their electrified equipment.

" '. . . and open the door and let it shine on your life' . . . One more time, all together now . . ."

" '. . . let it shine, let it shine . . .' "

"Aw-*riiighhttt!* 'Let It Shine.' Thank you good folks very much." Danny Nicholson had 'em in his hands now. No odors of stale beer drifted through this crowd, nor traces of cigarette smoke, and certainly there were no earnest discussions of drivers trying to knock each other's asses over the retaining walls. The racing T-shirts and caps here proclaimed Jeff Gordon and Dale Jarrett, not Dale Earnhardt and the other perceived bad boys, and mostly they wore Christian stuff—crucifixes, their church softball team's T-shirts, scarves with biblical scripture printed on them—while some held umbrellas with Republicanisms dealing with family values.

"Totally cool! Come on, let's hear it!"

". . . total . . . cool . . ."

"Repeat after me. Totally cool!"

"Totally cool!"

"That's it. That's right. Some folks say it isn't easy, but we know better. It's totally cool to be a Christian. Let's sing it now. 'Totally Cool . . .' "

Well, there had been a couple of problems during the night, but that was behind them now. One of Bryan's buddies had dragged in past midnight in a cloud of marijuana smoke, but that worked out all right because a cop came around and simply took the bag from him without a word. Then, around three or four o'clock, nobody remembered exactly when because of the beer and the wee hour, this old boy from West Virginia got up and stretched and decided he'd had about enough of this and figured he'd just as soon drive on to Myrtle Beach. Bryan had helped the fellow wiggle out of his parking spot and had Brenda mark it off with a cooler and some lawn chairs while he went down the line and kicked Bobby Lee's Ford Ranger to wake him up and advise him that he was now sitting on the outside pole.

"Just bombed out on us, that's all. Spent two nights drinking and eating and arguing with us, and then he split. Probably sitting on the beach right now. Stop me if I'm wrong about this, *I-don't-think-sooo*, but some folks don't take their racing serious." This was Hoss Hause, spiritual leader of his new kingdom down there on the grass near the first turn, holding court from beneath an umbrella as he reclined in a lawn chair on top of his platform. Brenda had treated herself to a long hot shower as soon as they had claimed their spot and gotten organized. Then she and Bryan had taken a long stroll around the infield, for him to shake off the effects of the beer from the night before; and now, with the bright noon sun overhead, they sat together beneath the umbrella and surveyed the scene. Their number had swollen to twenty now, including Hause's brother John, from Atlanta, and—surprise of surprises—a handsome young black man from Columbia named Russell Watson, who had been joining them at Darlington for three years now. "You wouldn't have seen this at a Winston Cup track five years ago," Hause said. Russell Watson was also a carpet layer, same as Hause, and was a friend of one of the others in their company. "All of Russell's friends are white. Hell, he even goes fishing with Roland Martin, the guy with the fishing show on television." But Russell didn't spend the night with them in the infield anymore. "He tried it a couple of years ago, but it got pretty drunk out that night and when some other ol' boys started in with the 'nigger' stuff he decided he'd better get the hell out." This was in line with what Tom Stinson, one of the *Winston Cup Scene* columnists, had learned earlier in the year when, upon the emergence of the brilliant young black golfer Tiger Woods, he had pondered in print whether it was time for NASCAR to join the lily-white PGA in erasing the color line; Stinson could hardly believe the pile of bilious racist letters he received, most of them starting with "nigger" and going downhill after that. Relatively speaking, Bryan Hause and Bobby Lee Turbeville and their tatterdemalions looked like social workers.

Some late arrivals in their corner of the infield were still frantically hammering away, assembling their platforms on the spot, while others were tossing horseshoes. ("We tried it for a while," said Hause, "but we were so hungover I had to drop it from twenty-one points to ten, and finally I had to declare a time limit. 'First one that hits the stake wins.' ") Pennants for favored drivers rippled in the light breeze, and all about there was the aroma of steaks and hamburgers and hot dogs sizzling on portable grills. Out on the track, the second day of qualifying for the Mountain Dew Southern 500 was drawing to a close. Soon, at one o'clock, the green flag would drop for the Grand National race.

"Hey, Hoss," said Bobby Lee, waggling a cap holding slips of paper and $5 bills, "you gon' get in on the pool?"

"Hell, no, I'm not."

"You ain't gon' take a chance on Rusty?"

"I wouldn't take a chance on *anybody* at this track. Especially when he qualified twenty-eighth. *I-don't-think-soooo.*"

Bobby Lee, putting on his game face a full twenty-four hours before the start of the 500, tugged on his Mark Martin cap and reminisced about that very first stock car race he had seen, when Bill Elliott won the first Winston Million in '85. "My daddy's uncle, that's my great-uncle, was a real racing fan and he came up from Jacksonville just for the Southern 500. He was a big Bill Elliott fan, too. We were sitting over there in the stands, and when Elliott won the race my uncle went crazy. He was dancing around, hugging people he didn't even know, shouting, carrying on something fierce. He reached into his cooler and got out a couple of beers and pushed one in my face and said, 'Here, boy, have a beer.' Hell, there I was, eleven or twelve years old, and I didn't know what to do. My daddy just leaned over and said, 'No, no, I don't believe so.' It was a hell of a day, I tell you, a hell of a day. I haven't missed a race at Darlington since."

The sun rose like a ball of fire on Sunday, the big day, and the 60,000 or so fans gathered in the sizzling aluminum grandstands and roiling in the infield grass were asked to sit through prerace ceremonies that threatened to last until Halloween. They bellowed their special appreciations for Dale Earnhardt and Dale Jarrett during the driver introductions, of course, but expressed little interest in expending their energy on the likes of Ted Musgrave and Chad Little and Loy Allen, and then they had to sit back and endure a parade of politicians, Pepsi executives (for this was, after all, Pepsi's Mountain Dew Southern 500), Miss Winston and the Unocal Race Stoppers, and a stretch limo–ful of account executives bearing presentations like the Plasti-Kote Winning Finish Award. Up to the microphone came U.S. Senator Strom Thurmond, the indefatigable racist demagogue, nearly as old as the century itself, in a blue shirt and a straw hat, to reenact his cutting of the ribbon to open the track when he was a middle-aged governor in 1950. Up came the current governor, David Beasley, to take a free shot at President Clinton: "We need to get Washington and Clinton [no "president," just "Clinton"] out of stock car racing." Up came the star of the show, Dale Jarrett, with a kid slung on his hip and more loving words for his masters on earth: "I won't go into the political issues here, but R.J. Reynolds made our sport what it is today." They saluted these throwdowns of the gauntlet, but they were clearly exhausted by the time Old Glory was raised and the Gatlin Brothers crooned the National Anthem.

It took less time than all of that for Jarrett's bubble to pop. He had taken over the lead on the twenty-sixth lap and was looking good, his powerful Yates engine roaring with the authority of a Panzer plowing across France in overdrive, until what Richard Petty liked to call "one o' them racin' deals" came up and bit him. The least-known driver in the field that day was one Ed Berrier, the thirty-four-year-old owner of an auto shop in Winston-Salem, who had driven his pickup truck down to Darlington and somehow managed to qualify thirty-third in a jerry-built Thunderbird that was co-owned by his father and sponsored by a pickle grower. It was only his second start in a Winston Cup race and he had gone on about having been "just happy we made The Show." His car had begun leaking oil from the outset, so imperceptibly at first that he was never black-flagged by the NASCAR spotters, and that would make him the bad guy on this day. Jarrett was still leading the pack when he took his normal line on the third turn, ducking down low in order to negotiate the least forgiving corners of the entire track, but at the very bottom he hit Berrier's oil slick and lost control; sliding up and hitting the wall, leaving a Darlington Stripe at the top of the fourth corner, bringing about a caution, essentially losing his shot at the Winston Million right there. In the ensuing minutes he fell hopelessly behind, rushing in for *nine* pit stops as his crew frantically tried to repair the severely damaged infrastructure—broken shock, bent control arm, damaged ball joint, screwed-up floorboard and A-frame and right-side panels—and he would have to settle for fourteenth place and, thanks to NASCAR's mystical bonus payoff system, a grand total of $128,165 to go along with the mere pittance of $4,385 for his eighth-place finish in Saturday's BGN race.

There would be a total of twenty-nine lead changes throughout the day, with fourteen different drivers taking the lead at one point or another (seven would go behind the wall, due to crashes or engine breakdowns), but in due time it began to appear that Jeff Gordon and his well-heeled cohorts at Hendrick Motorsports would prevail once more. This stuff was getting old. Only five times during the twenty-two races had Gordon finished out of the top ten, winning six of them, and he was inexorably closing in on Terry Labonte's lead in the points race. Perhaps it wasn't so surprising that in the drivers' introductions before this race, for the very first time this season, he had been met with a chorus of boos; it could have been that Darlington attracted more Earnhardt fans than did the other tracks, but it seemed just as likely that Winston Cup fans in general were looking for someone other than the usual suspects to root for. Hey, if Ed Berrier—Ed *Who?*—could mess up Jarrett's day, maybe somebody could do something about Gordon. Besides, as the fans who had scanners knew, it was getting hot and surly out there on the track:

- Earnhardt to David Smith, his crew chief, as he kept slipping behind and losing himself among the Dave Marcises and Derrike Copes: "David, something's wrong with this car. It ain't drove like this all week."
- Pit to Terry Labonte: "You know what [Darlington] is all about, buddy. Remember, you came back and beat David Pearson here one time." Labonte to pit: "Yeah, but there's not three guys here who know who David Pearson was."
- "Whooooaa! Son of a *bitch!* Look at that idiot! What th' hell's he thinkin'?"

- "Rubber and sand's so bad out here, it looks like Saturday night at a dirt track when I leave the pits."
- "Watch it, watch it, there's three of 'em comin' up on the outside" [like aerial combat].
- "Clear, clear, go, go . . . Well, *shit.*"
- "Okay, bud, don't worry. Remember, this is Darlington."

Victories in the first twenty-two races of the season had gone to only eight different drivers, so it came as an answer to the fans' yearnings for somebody new to root for when, as the day wore on, here came a journeyman by the name of Hut Stricklin, who still needed an introduction after a decade of Winston Cup racing. Affable, bulky, moon-faced, thirty-five years old, Stricklin hailed from the peaches-and-cattle country around Calera, Alabama, halfway between Birmingham and Montgomery, and had known only fleeting moments of joy since the days he had been a teenaged hotshot on the tracks of rural Alabama. He had dabbled at Winston Cup with three races in '86, and in his first full season, 1989, had been runner-up to Trickle for Rookie of the Year. He had hooked up briefly with Bobby Allison, an uncle by marriage, finishing sixteenth in points for the Alabama Gang in '91; but mostly he had wandered about from season to season, shop to shop, looking for a ride, sometimes getting one as a relief driver. His best run this year had been an eleventh-place finish in the spring race at Bristol, his biggest payday $66,560 for an eighteenth-place finish in the Brickyard 400, and his career totals in Winston Cup were little to write home about after 214 starts: no wins, eight top fives, twenty-six top tens.

But now and then a miracle happened or, at least, appeared to be a distinct possibility. From time to time, every other year at best, everything would come together for a driver whose lot in the scheme of things was to try to stay out of trouble long enough to win some lap money and maybe gain a little respect. Nobody could figure it out, least of all the boys in the rival shops, especially the ones who had more time and resources and expertise and history on their side. It just happened, is all they could say. A perennial also-ran would show up and on that one glorious day everything would somehow be right: the setup, the driver's frame of mind, pure luck in avoiding traffic, even the weather. The old bromide "The race may not always go to the swiftest, but that's the way to bet" would be set aside for that one brief shining moment when the swayback nag would thunder past Man o' War, when the journeyman pitcher would throw a no-hitter, when the third-string jitterbug halfback would return a punt for the winning touchdown. 'Twas a puzzlement.

Nobody, except perhaps the boys at the Stavola Brothers shop outside of Charlotte, had any inkling that this might be one of those magical days for Hut Stricklin. On Saturday, in the BGN 200-miler, driving a Ford sponsored by Smokey Mountain Chew, Stricklin had crashed on turn one, two thirds through the race, and finished thirty-sixth. But that was another car, another race; for, down in the garage area, he and his crew chief, Philippe Lopez, had a car they thought might work in Sunday's big one. The odds were greatly stacked against them, of course. "We've got a new team, only twenty-two of us, and we've been making do with old equipment," said Stricklin. "So we can't build our own cars, and there's a six- to eight-week waiting period when you're buying from outside sources." Lopez (Mexican father, French mother) revealed that the team had started from scratch in December and hadn't been able to catch up in its building program until around July, and fretted that the Thunderbird they had prepared for the Mountain Dew Southern 500 was "okay for a four-hundred-mile race but not for five hundred." Still, they had taken the car to Richmond for three days of tests in the early part of the week and when they hauled it into the garage at Darlington on Friday at daybreak they felt a slight tingle. Stricklin qualified the car tenth that afternoon, allowing the team to set up its pit operation on the preferred frontstretch rather than on the back side, and then they wrapped it and prayed.

Gordon had been in the top ten all day and had led at the halfway point to pick up that bonus money and points, and it had begun to appear that he would weather the attrition taking place as the heat rose and the tempers grew short and the track became more treacherous from the buildup of sand and rubber scraps. Although hardly anybody noticed at first, Hut Stricklin, too, had been steadily moving forward in the field. It was after the halfway point that the number 8 Circuit City Ford began making itself known—twice before, Stricklin had taken the lead for stretches of about fifty laps—and when he zoomed past Gordon on lap 305 of 367 it became a two-car race to the checkered flag, with only Mark

Martin staying with them on the lead lap. *Flat out, bellies to the ground, chasing the sun. . . .* Stricklin was keeping his eyes on two things, both of them problematical: the clever Gordon in his rearview mirror, and the rising temperature gauge on his dashboard. They had installed an inferior shaker screen in front of the radiator, and the buildup of crap was clinging to it. With Gordon right on his tail, probing low and probing high, the crowd sensing an upset, the two of them thundered on through the lapped traffic. Stricklin was trying to stay cool, remembering a particular race from all the way back in 1978, when he was running Limited Sportsman cars in Alabama, and "got excited and started counting my chickens before they hatched" and blew it. Now, as he would later explain, "I'd been fighting overheating all day, watching the temp gauge, thinking 'there's no way this thing's going to live,' praying every single lap that I'd just finish. I was so hungry for a win, you wouldn't believe it. I didn't want second place, but maybe I was destined for it."

Stricklin's car had also tightened up, forcing him to muscle it to stay low when flying out of the corners, and that was what Gordon had been focusing on. The Kid nearly took him with twenty laps remaining when Stricklin "had a confrontation with another car" on the hazardous fourth turn and temporarily lost the handling. It seemed a matter of time now when the dream would end for Calera's finest, and it happened with sixteen laps to go when Gordon ducked down to the apron and waved goodbye. Gordon had done it again, to the consternation of fans who, like the New York Yankee haters of the fifties and the NASCAR fans of the same era who had turned against old Carl Kiekhaefer for winning too often, were lusting for new faces. They weren't interested in hanging around to watch the same old scene of Jeff Gordon and his Rainbow Warriors whooping it up down in Victory Lane, the delectable Brooke Gordon messing up her lipstick with a kiss for her husband, and they had long forgotten Dale Jarrett's run for the Winston Million. "In the meantime," the columnist Steve Hummer of the *Atlanta Constitution* was typing out in the press box as they gathered up their coolers and scanners and umbrellas, "if Jarrett wants his million from the big cigarette maker, he'll just have to stand in line and sue for it like everyone else."

15

DOWN TO THE WIRE

Stirring though it might have been, Earnhardt's determination to drive through his injuries, come hell or high water, was ill-advised. He had certainly made his point when he refused a relief driver at Watkins Glen and drove to a sixth-place finish, one of the gutsiest performances in recent memory, but it became clear as the season began to grind toward its conclusion that grit would carry him just so far. Of his noms de guerre, Ironhead fit him better now than The Intimidator. He brushed it off as "too little, too late" when Irvan finally apologized for causing the wreck at Talladega, which replays proved to be the case ("It's not my place to tell him how to live his life, but he made a mistake and it took him two weeks to call or come by"), but it had become a moot point, anyway. Even before the wreck, he had begun to lose the substantial lead in the points race that he had built early in the summer, and his twelfth-place finish in the Mountain Dew Southern 500, two laps down, was a harbinger of what was to come. As heartening as it was to see the intrepid old warrior grimacing and sliding into his car to do battle, week after week, something was missing. And that something was, very simply, endurance. He wasn't there at the end, anymore, an ominous black shadow filling the leader's rearview mirror, threatening to run up his tailpipe if he didn't move over, and he wasn't getting any younger. His next birthday, in April, would be his forty-sixth.

By the time Gordon had moved up to second in points with his fifth-place finish in the August race at Michigan, breathing down Terry La-bonte's neck, the race for the championship had come down to those two. No one else would ever lead again, and it looked more and more like the championship once more would be decided in the final race, at Atlanta Motor Speedway in early November. The message was writ loud and clear, for all of the one-car operators to see: the future belonged to the rich multi-team operations. It was sweet to think that a lone-wolf owner-driver like, say, Ricky Rudd, could hang in there against the conglomerates like Hendrick Motorsports—his thirty-man shop against Hendrick's 160 or so —but it wasn't realistic, even though Rudd had been hanging around sixth in the points all year long. At the halfway point in the season, around the time of Earnhardt's crash at Talladega, the top twelve places belonged to the eight drivers representing multi-team operations. Except for Earnhardt and the short-track master Rusty Wallace, who had won four races before Labor Day, the one-car outfits rarely visited Victory Lane and weren't expected to now that wear and tear were becoming major factors. The same laws applied here as in college football, where a three-deep Nebraska was always going to wear out a thin Kansas in the fourth quarter.

It was all about numbers. NASCAR allowed each *car* seven testing sessions per year on Winston Cup tracks (everybody got around that one by running a few additional tests at non-Winston tracks here and there, like the Birmingham Fairgrounds), which meant, of course, that a three-car shop such as Hendrick could triple the number of computerized test results it had to draw from back at its one shop. Entering two cars in a race doubled an owner's chances, of course, and, as Irvan noted, "having twenty shop people for one car doesn't necessarily mean it takes forty for two cars." It "helps to be a multimillionaire," said Travis Carter, the owner of Jimmy Spencer's Camel car, but obviously it was more cost-effective for one shop to field more than one car.

There were some problems in running a multiple-car operation, how-ever, and the people involved with those teams were the first to bring them up. "Race cars are like snowflakes, no two of them being alike," said Howard Comstock, crew chief for Ted Musgrave of Roush Racing. "All three of our cars are built at the same shop, but what's good for Ted isn't necessarily good for Jeff [Burton] or Mark [Martin]. We take the information from testing and tailor it to each chassis and each driver's style." The independent owner-drivers were the loudest to shriek about NASCAR's incessant changing of the rules whenever it appeared one car make had an edge over the others. "Every time we have to cut the body off to meet the new rules, it costs us a bunch of money," said Rudd, "and Hendrick, with all of those employees they've got over there, can respond quicker to all of these changes. I don't think Yates can do that, and I *sure* can't." Said Geoff Bodine, parroting Darrell Waltrip: "I just wish they would lay down the rules in January and stay with 'em." There was some sympathy for that, and for changing the rules about testing, from a surpris-ing source, Robert Yates of the Irvan-Jarrett shop: "There are just so many days in a year, and I'm for reducing tests. I say try to do it in the three days you're there before a race. You spend money and you tire everybody out, and when you get back to the track [for the race] it's changed since you tested there. There's a lot of wasted motion."

Some of the owners and drivers and crew chiefs seemed to have the same conflicted feelings about all of this as they did about the demise of the traditional old tracks like North Wilkesboro. "To tell you the truth," said Yates, "having forty cars with forty owners, all of them racing to the start-finish line with an equal chance to win, that's what the sponsors and the spectators and NASCAR want." The basic stock car racing fan, fan-cying himself as the last rugged individualist, looked upon these big-budget conglomerates such as Hendrick Motorsports with the same disdain he held for big government and huge faceless corporations like U.S. Steel and General Motors. But both the fans and the principals knew the future when they saw it, and the future was 163,000-seat Texas Motor Speedway and Hendrick Motorsports, not little 40,000-seat North Wilkes-boro and Junior Johnson's shops out back in his barn. The first indication that the move toward multi-car teams was on in earnest had come when Richard Childress announced he was adding a second car, driven by Mike

Skinner, to team with Earnhardt so RCR could pool resources and data. Soon after, in the late fall, Felix Sabates would reveal his more grandiose plans: not only had he hired young Robby Gordon from Indy-car racing to replace Kyle Petty as his top driver, he was adding Joe Nemechek and Wally Dallenbach to form a three-car operation at Team Sabco for '97. "Building a multi-car team is a three-year project," he said, announcing that he also was dumping Pontiacs and going to Chevrolets while he was at it. "But I can promise you that in five years the only cars in the top twenty will be from multi-car teams."

All anybody had to do was look out there on the track to see what all the fuss was about. With his own personal fortune from automobile dealerships, plus solid sponsorships for his three entries (DuPont for Gordon, Kellogg's for Labonte, Budweiser for Ken Schrader) and the purse money that kept rolling in from having all three in the top ten, Rick Hendrick had the wherewithal to do just about anything he chose to do: expand his shop, hire the best engine builders and mechanics available, buy the best toys, run every sort of test known to man. It wasn't enough that Gordon and Labonte were fighting it out for the points championship; the weak link at Hendrick was the veteran Schrader, and even though he had been in the top ten throughout the summer it had already been announced that he would be replaced by the more promising young Ricky Craven in '97. The smattering of boos that had met Gordon during the driver introductions at Darlington, the thanks he got from the fans for his success, was an omen of what would happen to the Hendrick drivers for the rest of the season as their juggernaut rolled on past the competition. "If you can't beat 'em, you might as well join 'em," said Richard Childress, throwing up his hands, ready for this season to be over with so he could get going with his new two-car deal.

Still dogged by the hurricanes flitting about in the late summer and early autumn, they were forced to qualify on the afternoon of the Saturday night race at Richmond, giving them scant time to switch to their race setups and engines. This was where Gordon had turned his season around earlier in the year, winning the Pontiac Excitement 400 after the embarrassing DNFs at Daytona and Rockingham, and although he didn't repeat —Irvan nipped him by one tenth of a second in front of a crowd that hit 90,000 capacity in spite of rain and power outages and threats of more mischief from Hurricane Fran—he closed Labonte's lead to four points when Terry came in fifth. Next up was the return trip to Dover, but first Gordon and his crew chief, Ray Evernham, had another record to set: the first formal appearance on an Ivy League campus by the NASCAR crowd. They had been invited to lecture to a class of freshman engineering students at Princeton, in New Jersey, up in the neighborhood of Dover, and they showed up with a number 24 DuPont Chevy show car to illustrate their points. This was great for Evernham, who had made a routine of wearing an Albert Einstein T-shirt in the garage on Saturdays and now could replenish his supply with a run by the great man's house, now a shrine, near the campus. In their exit interviews, as it were, both revealed their remorse in not going beyond high school. "I partied too much, I drank too much, and I didn't think there was life after modifieds," said Evernham.

The only constant at Dover the following Sunday was that Gordon won again, his eighth victory of the season, to crawl ahead of Labonte in the standings. It was getting worse by the week for Earnhardt, who dragged in at twentieth, for now his own crew was admitting that his physical discomfort was affecting his concentration and some other teams were accusing him of unnecessarily rough driving in his desperation to salvage the season. A total of ten cars went out prematurely, due to crashes, and tempers were short throughout a race that took nearly five hours to complete: Spencer tried to punch Dallenbach through his window mesh after a wreck, Irvan's crew chief ambushed Derrike Cope and began shouting as the driver left the infield infirmary following a run-in with Irvan, and Kyle Petty had to be restrained from jumping Michael Waltrip right there on pit road after a fender-banging on the last lap; all of this extracurricular activity bringing a total of $17,000 in fines from NASCAR. For years, drivers had been complaining that the 500-milers at Dover were too long ("You can run for two and a half hours and it's devastating to look up on the board and see it's just halfway over," said Jeff Burton, who hadn't had to worry about that on this day, since he went out in a crash on the third lap), and, as it turned out, the most significant positive result of the long day was that Dover officials finally agreed to shorten their races by 100 miles.

The end was so near now that they could smell it. While the powerhouse multi-car teams were racing among themselves at the front, the lesser ones were running out of equipment and patience. Every day, it seemed, there was another defection in the lower ranks; not only by drivers but by crew chiefs and engine builders and fabricators and the lowliest gofers, all of them looking for a better deal during this, the silly season. All of those grand plans that had been laid out with great fanfare during the media shop tour back in January—Pontiac's promise to be a factor, Darrell Waltrip's grim vow that he wasn't ready to be counted out as a competitive driver, Felix Sabates's expressions of a never-ending love for Kyle—had either noisily imploded or conveniently been forgotten. John Andretti and Jeremy Mayfield had, indeed, simply swapped cars now rather than wait until '97; Mike Wallace would take over the Spam car the next season in place of Lake Speed, who would drive for a team to be sponsored by the University of Nebraska, of all entities (surely, the car would become known as Big Red); the drivers Robert Pressley and Steve Grissom had been fired at one place and quickly hired at another; the Hooters restaurant chain announced it was bailing out of Winston Cup sponsorship, while Hot Wheels said it was getting in (with Kyle Petty as its driver); and here came another Indy driver to join Robby Gordon on the Winston Cup circuit, this one a chap named Tony Stewart.

There would be the cross-country trek to Phoenix for the penultimate race of the season, but all of the others would be held down home. There were six to go and counting, and for many teams and drivers it was all over but the shouting when they hit the slow little track at Martinsville in late September. With the fight for the points championship and the $1.5 million bonus that went with it down to Gordon vs. Terry Labonte (second place this year would fetch a not-inconsiderable half a million), a passel of others were scrambling to "make the stage," meaning be seated at the main tables down front at the Waldorf-Astoria during the season-ending banquet, reserved for the top ten in the points standing, and the rest were already concentrating on saving face and looking ahead to the '97 season.

Among those sitting on the bubble as far as the top ten was concerned was Bobby Hamilton, the flaxen-haired country boy who drove the famous blue STP number 43 for Richard Petty. The shot he had taken from Earnhardt at Rockingham in the second race of the season, costing him an almost certain victory with only ten laps to go, had made it an uphill climb for him all year long; if not for that, he might be comfortably ensconced in the top ten. But he had endured, in spite of running out of gas on the next-to-last lap in the spring at Darlington and going out in an accident on the sixth lap of the second race at Pocono and losing his timing chain early on at The Glen, and now he was primed for a serious run for a spot at the top ten. He and Petty made an interesting pair, Hamilton seeming to be the agreeably pliant son to The King that Kyle had never been, and even when he checked into Martinsville and remained ineligible for the '97 Busch Clash in spite of winning his second pole of the year—Petty still refused to put a beer decal of any sort on the car—he took his medicine quietly. He went ahead and finished third in the race (the winner was Gordon, with Labonte four car lengths behind in second place) to jump to eleventh in the standings, only ninety-six points behind Sterling Marlin. "It ain't bad when you lead so many laps [332 of 500], sit on the pole, and have Pontiac's best showing of the year," he said.

Gordon, Gordon, Gordon. The Kid won his third straight, the next weekend at North Wilkesboro, making that ten victories on the year and stretching his lead over Labonte to 111 points. (Earnhardt came in a distant second, his best finish since the Coca-Cola 600 at Charlotte on Memorial Day, but he was lagging 351 points behind Gordon and, with only four races to go, was more or less out of it.) Since it was the last Winston Cup race ever to be run at North Wilkes, ESPN and even the *New York Times* had come down to mark the occasion. "It's kinda like when a cranky aunt dies," a former Winston Cup spokesman told Joseph Siano of the *Times*. "You hate to see her go, but what the heck." Junior Johnson, again, didn't bother to show up, but his ex-wife, Flossie, whipped up another of her gargantuan breakfasts for a few of her longtime favorites like Bill Elliott and D.W. In his weekly column, dictated to the Atlanta paper, Elliott gave the usual company line on the situation ("The truth is, this sport has outgrown the track") and told a story about North Wilkesboro, a track that had no tunnel for access to the infield: "This fella was gonna help us on race day, but he got there late. The guard at the crossover gate told him he'd get him across the track on the first caution. Well, the first caution didn't come out until lap 385 [of 500]. The fella got to the pits in time to celebrate our victory."

When they moved on to Charlotte Motor Speedway for the UAW-GM Quality 500, Humpy Wheeler was ready for them. It was never enough for NASCAR's resident P. T. Barnum simply to open the gates and let the boys race on a weekend at CMS. The man who had given the world mock helicopter "invasions" and funky little "Legends" cars and the call to "start your engines" from an orbiting astronaut knew he had a captive audience of maybe 100 media people lolling around—bored, tired, willing to take any scrap of information under advisement at this late point in the season—and he wasn't about to pass up the opportunity. In the five days leading up to Sunday's Winston Cup race, Humpy orchestrated a total of eighteen news conferences, car unveilings, and other "special activities." Never mind that most of the news conferences dealt with plans for '97 that had already been published, that nobody much gave a damn what the new Spam paint scheme would look like, that the ultimate stretch was to stir the media's interest in a new motor oil being marketed jointly by NASCAR and Unocal. Humpy was still drumming away when race day finally arrived on Sunday, a mite shamelessly this time, when he put a six-year-old boy on a float and paraded him around the track; the boy having become something of a cause célèbre in those parts for having been suspended on the grounds of sexual harassment after kissing a little girl at school. One mindless act had begat another. They did manage to get the race off on time, and when it was over NASCAR had its tightest points race at this juncture of the season since 1979. While Gordon was having all sorts of problems and finishing thirty-first, Labonte handily won and pulled within a point, with Dale Jarrett suddenly a factor, only ninety-two points back.

After a free weekend, their first after fourteen straight races, it was back to old Rockingham, The Rock, where Bill Elliott remembered making his Winston Cup debut exactly twenty years earlier. "I've been coming here so long," he said, "that the new motels I stayed in then now look like they should be condemned." Labonte took over the points lead by finishing third while Gordon loped in at twelfth, but the real story was the win by Ricky Rudd. It marked the fourteenth straight year that he had won at least one race, quite an accomplishment for someone who had never reached stardom, and this one hadn't come easily for an independent owner-driver who had started the year by suing Sabates for allegedly stealing his three main men in the shop. Nobody could remember a day when a driver had won a race with such poor work in the pits. Rudd was certainly dialed in for the 400-mile run, but every time he pitted something went wrong—lug nuts fell off, tire changers dropped tires, guys bumped into each other like circus clowns—and after he had gone in at second and come out tenth one time too many Rudd put out an SOS for volunteers from teams whose car was out of the race, his call being answered by Bobby Allison's crew. "Good thing I do my best driving when I'm mad at somebody," he said. He had seen enough, and he chose to run the final seventy-four laps on old tires rather than pit like his closest challenger, Jarrett ("We couldn't gamble at that point on some foul-up in the pits again"), and the tires held up. Rudd was one of those who seemed to cherish being on his own, rather than part of a multi-car operation; but still, he admitted, life as an independent was getting tougher every year: "You're gonna have off-days like we did in the pits, and the truth is we've been so busy with other things that we hadn't been able to practice pit stops. When we're at the top of our game we're like a great college football team. But when Gordon and his people are at the top of their game they're a good *pro* team."

There would be 105,000 paying customers at Phoenix International Raceway the following Sunday, for the next-to-last race of the season, enough to make the arduous 2,000-mile trek to the desert worthwhile from a box office standpoint. But this sure wasn't home. The track was stuck out there in the desert, some fifteen miles from Phoenix, and for one thing there were the rattlesnakes that had to be chased from the banks on the corners that had evolved as a favored place for viewing the races. Another was the constant looming possibility of sudden dust storms; and, sure enough, no sooner had the car-haulers arrived to set up in the garage area than here they came. The Winston Cup season was so long that every year they got a taste of just about everything nature had to show them—the brisk winds of Daytona in February, the snows of March in the Blue Ridge, the spring rains, the insufferable heat of the Deep South at midsummer, the perfect days of spring and fall in the North and East—so why not sandstorms? They got so bad that qualifying was canceled on Friday, but not before a practice round earlier in the day that saw Terry Labonte spin out of control and hit the wall head-on and come out of it with a broken bone in his left hand. This was nothing compared to the injuries Elliott and Earnhardt had suffered ("I shoot a gun right-handed," Labonte said, of the hunting trip he planned as soon as the season ended), but with the points race so close between him and Gordon, when the least slip could be costly, it was worth close attention. They wrapped it in a splint and wired the hand to an electrical stimulus, and he borrowed a smaller steering wheel from Joe Gibbs, his brother Bobby's car owner, and he went out and finished third to Gordon's fifth to stretch his points lead to forty-seven as they headed into the final race, at Atlanta, two weeks hence. The biggest celebration of the day, though, took place down in the Richard Petty pits after Bobby Hamilton roared home with the first victory for a Petty Enterprises car in thirteen years. "With two laps to go," said Hamilton, "I noticed the electricity in the stands. No telling how it would've been if we'd won it in North Carolina." The trip to Victory Lane came at a most welcome time for The King, who hadn't had much good news lately.

Ever since the day he first crawled behind the steering wheel of a race car, back in 1958 at the age of twenty-one, Richard Petty had been one of the most beloved people in the world of automobile racing. He represented everything held dear by the blue-collar American South, the crucible of stock car racing: small-town roots, religious, conservative, patriotic, son of a race car driver, the amiable down-home sort who stayed humble and accessible to his fans and the media in spite of his overwhelming success. Although he had persisted in driving well past his prime, not winning a single race over the next eight years following that glorious 200th victory, at Daytona in 1984 with President Ronald Reagan in attendance, he remained very much a part of the Winston Cup scene as a living idol (The King) and the twangy television spokesman for Goody's Headache Powders

("Now *that* was a Goody's headache," he would intone as a violent crash involving his famous number 43 "Petty blue" race car flashed on the screen), and, now, as a car owner whose shop was right there on the same scrap of land where he had spent his life.

His decision to run for the office of secretary of state in North Carolina was embraced, at first, by Republican party officials both in the state and in the nation; the more Republicans in office, the better, and their hope was that other candidates might ride the coattails of The King during the elections. Petty, for himself, was promoting the facts that he had served as a county commissioner for sixteen years and that, as the head of Petty Enterprises, he knew a thing or two about running a big business. The office he sought, secretary of state, involved securities regulation, the registering of lobbyists, and the chartering of new businesses. His Democratic opponent was a fifty-year-old woman named Elaine Marshall, a lawyer from the obscure little town of Lillington. A mere *woman* against The King? Forget about it.

The press loved it, of course, some newspapers dispatching reporters on the campaign trail with Petty, itching to use the headline "Petty Politics," and Petty had a big lead when the politicking began. But it didn't take long for the politicos to begin blanching. Going out on the hustings only two days a week, between Winston Cup races and commercial appearances for his Winston Cup sponsors, Petty was gaily presenting himself to the voters more as a sports legend than a candidate for political office. He would stump in eighty of the state's 100 counties before it was over, but those appearances were more like an extended Richard Petty Appreciation Day than a serious opportunity to deal with the issues. He seemed to be enjoying every minute of it as hundreds of fans flocked to his advertised political events where Petty, sporting his signature boots and plumed cowboy hat, talked racing and signed autographs for crowds that often were dominated by nonvoting adolescents and teenagers. Whenever pressed about the nuts and bolts of the job he sought, Petty allowed as how he didn't know a whole lot about it right now but he planned to pick people who did to make the decisions and, as for himself, he intended to personally put in, shoot, two whole days each week at the state capital in Raleigh. Meanwhile, as the earnest lady lawyer from Lillington, on Buies Creek, went around the state discussing the issues, Petty's lead began to weaken.

Then came the tailgating incident. Petty was headed home from Charlotte Motor Speedway on a Wednesday afternoon in early September, between the Richmond and Dover races, when he roared up behind a Mazda traveling a mite too slowly, for his tastes, on I-85. The King first blinked the headlights of his Dodge pickup, signaling that he wanted to pass, and when that failed he began to ride the man's bumper. They were both doing seventy miles per hour, slightly over the speed limit. Perturbed, the Mazda driver tapped his brakes, and that was when Petty made contact with his bumper. The man got on his car phone and called the highway patrol, and not until the troopers had hauled Petty over, forty-five miles down the road, did anyone know who was driving the Dodge pickup. *Great shades of Darlington! Another one o' them racin' deals!* Petty paid $25 for the scratch on the Mazda's bumper, plus $65 in court costs, but it cost him much more than that. "Now if it had been a NASCAR showdown, he'd o' been over in the ditch somewhere," he cracked in a television interview, trying to kiss off the incident with all of the good-natured intentions of a post-race commentary. It was probably a setup, anyway, he said, arranged by Democratic party operatives in Raleigh to besmirch his name and make sure he got beat.

The newspaper pundits were amused ("You can take Richard Petty off the racetrack, but you can't take the racetrack out of Richard Petty," said the *Atlanta Constitution*), but the voters weren't. When they went to the polls on the Tuesday before the last race of the '96 Winston Cup season, North Carolina's voters saw to it that Petty took a drubbing. He got only forty-five percent of the vote as Elaine Marshall became the first woman ever elected to a seat on the Council of State and continued the Democratic party's century-old domination on the council. That wasn't racin', it was politics. "People aren't stupid," said a political analyst in the state. "They figured out he wasn't running a serious campaign." If Petty felt any remorse over his defeat, he never showed it when he checked in at Atlanta Motor Speedway on Thursday to prepare for the final race of the season. The only kind of setup that concerned him now was the one he would install for Ol' Blue, Bobby Hamilton's Petty Enterprises number 43 STP Pontiac.

16

END OF THE ROAD

There would be no tomorrow. Neither the racing teams nor the sponsors nor RJR had reasons to hold anything back when the last race of the season loomed up on the second week of November. The one piece of urgency was, of course, the battle for the points championship that would be determined by the running of Sunday's NAPA 500 at Atlanta Motor Speedway. But this was the last chance for the public relations types to do their thing, as well, so by Monday of that week the sprawling Atlanta metropolitan area was teeming with every available show car, parked at malls and fast-food joints, auto parts stores, and new-car dealerships within a fifty-mile radius from downtown; searchlights and giant helium balloons filling the sky to mark the spot, the Bubbarazzi falling all over themselves for this one last chance to mingle with their heroes before the hollow days of winter set in. On Wednesday, the Georgia Dome was converted into a Motorhead's paradise—Ford Fan Appreciation Day—with a dozen Ford drivers, from Rusty Wallace to Hut Stricklin, there to sign autographs and answer questions. On Monday, the day after the race, the annual Breakfast of Champions would be held in the infield at AMS, with such eminences as Gordon and Labonte eating their Spam-'n'-Eggs off of paper plates just like the thousands of fans likely to have lingered overnight in the infield. And on the same day, an hour up the road in Dawsonville, more than 3,000 members of the Bill Elliott Fan Club were expected for the perennial Most Popular Driver's own tenth annual fan appreciation day, to tour the shops and watch a pit stop demonstration and ride in a Winston Cup simulator.

Not since Dale Jarrett's failed attempt to cash in on the Winston Million at Darlington on Labor Day had RJR been presented with such a chance to call attention to itself, with the $1.5 million championship payoff on the line, so its Sports Marketing Enterprises publicists were missing no opportunities to showcase the last-race showdown at AMS. The race teams wouldn't be allowed to enter the track until daybreak Friday to off-load the cars and set up shop in the garages (although the handful who hadn't used up all seven of their authorized tests had arrived a day or two earlier), but RJR summoned the three drivers who had a chance at the championship, Labonte and Gordon and Jarrett, for a press conference just past noon on Thursday in order to get some more ink and airtime. About two dozen of the beat reporters showed up at a high-rise hotel hard by the interstate in Marietta, north of downtown Atlanta, and were joined by a covey of Atlanta radio and television reporters.

Jarrett had been forced to rush back home when his brother-in-law was seriously injured in a head-on collision with a pickup that killed the other driver, leaving Gordon and Labonte alone to meet the press. When the buffet lunch was finished and Gordon had arrived, running late from another luncheon at another hotel, the two were led to a table on a dais, with the ubiquitous red-and-white Winston Cup banners as a backdrop. As it is with movie stars, who always appear larger than life on the screen, one was reminded, once more, of how *small* most of the drivers are when confronted away from the track. Labonte was listed at five-ten and 165 pounds (though he seemed to be shorter than that), Gordon at five-seven and 150, and they had the appearance of well-dressed jockeys; neatly coiffed little guys, bright-eyed and healthy and full of quiet confidence, personable and well spoken in their own ways (as opposed to Earnhardt, whose demeanor on such occasions was that of someone who had been pulled away from more important matters, like fishing). Each wore pressed slacks and a crisp short-sleeved shirt bearing his sponsor's logo stitched above the breast pocket, as though somewhere in the Winston Cup kingdom there was a wardrobe room with duds marked "press conference" hanging on a rack.

The simple mathematics showed that Labonte would take the championship if he finished eighth or better on Sunday, no matter what Gordon and Jarrett did, and, since he had done just that in twenty-three of the thirty races this season, only fools were betting against him. (Only a fool would bet on *any* Winston Cup race, in fact, there being so many variable factors involved.) Gordon could take it if he led the most laps and won the race, provided that Labonte led not a single lap and finished no better than ninth; Jarrett could become the champion by winning the race and leading the most laps while the others were finishing far back in the pack. So it appeared to be in the bag for Labonte, busted hand or not, even though he knew as well as anyone in the room what can happen when forty-two cars get out on a track, all eyes on the prize, in a mad scramble through high-speed traffic for more than three hours. It was unfortunate that Jarrett wasn't there to replay how he lost the Winston Million when he hit somebody else's oil slick at Darlington. Labonte was on the verge of winning the season's points championship by virtue of consistency, having only two victories against Gordon's ten, but everybody was very much aware that on six occasions some sort of disaster had struck and he had failed to finish in the top twenty. The season had been a huge success—he had already won nearly $1.9 million in purses and bonuses, Gordon $2.4— but to win the championship meant not only an additional $1.5 million (he had gotten only $150,000 from RJR when he won in 1984) but all sorts of additional exposure and financial windfalls, not the least being able to realize the dream of every red-blooded American boy: seeing his likeness on a box of cereal.

Jarrett's chances being so dim, it was all but guaranteed that Rick Hendrick was about to become the first car owner since Carl Kiekhaefer, in the mid-fifties, to win back-to-back championships. Earlier in the week, he had brought together all three of his teams for a sort of season-ending pep rally at the huge Hendrick Motorsports complex on Papa Joe Hendrick Boulevard in Harrisburg, outside Charlotte, a meeting that Gordon hailed as "a class act on Rick Hendrick's part." All was happiness and light, apparently, something that couldn't be said of all the multi-car operations. "I think it's still going to take some time for other teams to catch up with what Hendrick has to offer," said Gordon, the more effusive of the two. "It's all about communicating. If the teams don't communicate and if they're battling with each other, it tears the place apart, and that's something we don't have. I remember after the season was over last year and we had our Christmas party, those guys [Labonte's team] would say, 'Congratulations, you guys won this year and we want to win it next year.' Now [if Labonte wins] it's going to make us step up our program for next year. So it makes the whole organization better and even more competitive." Both drivers downplayed the advantages that might be gained by pooling technical data gathered by three teams rather than only one. "If we're running like crap, we can walk up there [to the Gordon team] and they're going to help us, and vice versa," Labonte admitted. But, as Gordon said, often the information is worthless because what works for one driver doesn't necessarily work for another: "[In recent tests] Ricky Craven was running very well in the 25 car. I got in his car and I couldn't drive it the way he had it, couldn't run the speeds he was running. But I could come over and run the speeds in *my* car."

Labonte's left hand was still bandaged, but he said it was no big deal; he would use a splint and a smaller steering wheel again, and he would get a shot before the race to soften the pain, but steering at Atlanta was easier than at many of the other tracks. Would he play it safe Sunday? "As close as the points are, you can't go out there and ride around. We're going to have to race, run as hard as we can because something can always come up." As for Gordon, concerned that he hadn't run well lately at AMS, he and his team had brought two cars to Atlanta for tests right after returning from Phoenix: "We're putting a lot of pressure on ourselves because we've got to, the way Terry's been running. We've either got to win or finish up there in the top three or four. And, believe me, I know from experience that there's a whole lot of difference between finishing first and finishing second." And, no, he had no quarrels with a points system that found him, with ten victories, trailing a man with only two: "You still race to win because winning pays the most points, but those finishes are very important and can really hurt you a lot if you don't finish. Those five DNFs is the one thing we know is preventing us from being in the lead right now."

The gathering trailed off after some banter between the two: a long-suffering veteran who had won his first and only championship when The Kid was only thirteen years old. "Most of the guys are in their late thirties or early forties, with the exception of Jeff, who'll be retired by the time he's thirty-five," said Labonte, smiling at his joke. "Hey," said Gordon, "I didn't even know what Winston Cup was at that age. I knew what the Daytona 500 and the Indianapolis 500 were. I was racing go-karts and getting ready to make the move to sprint cars. I was always racing on Sundays, so I didn't get a chance to watch Winston Cup."

There had been tornado warnings throughout north Georgia on Thursday night, and Friday broke wet and cold at the track as the car-haulers rolled through the tunnel after their six-hour rumble down the interstate from Charlotte. The Busch Grand National drivers had already ended their season, even had their banquet at the Fontainebleau Hotel in Miami Beach (the champion, thirty-five-year-old Randy LaJoie of Norwalk, Connecticut, had earned more than $500,000 on the year, nothing in the million-dollar range but still more than Dave Marcis would take home from his doleful Winston Cup efforts), so the Winston Cup finale was the big draw for the weekend; although there would be a thirty-three-lap Shelby Pro Series race for lightweight racing machines and a full 500-miler for the ARCA drivers.

The big news, as far as the fans were concerned, was that Bruton Smith had heard their wails about the impossible traffic situation at AMS, and now they were met by a system of brand-new paved roads that had been carved out of the red earth since the March race, bringing a semblance of order to the flow of traffic, and Smith was promising that they wouldn't recognize the place in '97. He had already added a second tunnel leading into the infield, and over the winter he would be reconfiguring the track by moving the start-finish line to what had been the backstretch, putting in 37,000 new grandstand seats, building forty-four more luxury suites above what would become the new frontstretch, and adding a little Legends track and new garage areas and refurbished shower and rest room facilities to the infield. This was small stuff, of course, for a man audacious enough to build a 163,000-seat racetrack on the Texas prairie at the same time he was plotting to plop a dome on the Bristol track to make it the world's first indoor racing facility.

So crowded was the schedule of "PR opportunities" that a detailed listing was posted in the infield media center. At 9:30, the folks who make Lovable bras trotted out Tammy Jo Kirk, a thirty-four-year-old who had been racing motorbikes and stock cars since she was nine, to announce that she would be driving the pink Ford pickup, now parked outside and available for photo opportunities, in the '97 NASCAR Craftsman Truck series (free for the taking were bumper stickers reading "Burn Rubber, Not Bras"). At 9:50, here came BellSouth to announce it was jumping into the Winston Cup business as primary sponsor of Team Sabco's number 42 car, which had formerly graced Kyle Petty's Pontiac but now would go on a Chevy driven by Joe Nemechek. At exactly 10:05, photographers were invited outside to jostle with the clamorous Bubbarazzi for shots of Childress Racing's number 31 Chevy, the one Mike Skinner would be driving as the second man at RCR behind Earnhardt. The crammed little pressroom (it, too, was going to be expanded) swirled with flacks, flashing smiles and press kits, as lunch was served. Still to come, in the afternoon, were announcements about the upcoming Suzuka Thunder Special 100 exhibition race in Japan two weeks hence, some sort of a summer racing camp at AMS for twelve- to seventeen-year-olds, and a raft of new sponsorships lined up for the coming year. If the Winston Cup sponsorship was in trouble, you couldn't tell it by R.J. Reynolds's T. Wayne Robertson, who stood outside in the brisk air, his chipmunk cheeks aglow as he told of his son Toby's winning the points championship at the Hickory track, in the red Pontiac with "Tobacco Pays My Bills" on its hood.

Meanwhile, in the garages, the mood matched the weather. It had been a long haul for everybody, and, except for the three who had a shot at the championship and those like Bobby Hamilton (with a tenuous hold on tenth place) who still might make the stage of the Waldorf-Astoria with a stirring run on Sunday, most of the drivers were reflective, happy to be saying farewell to the '96 season. "There were a bunch of races we should have won, and that's what irks you," said Rick Mast, one of the veteran independents, who had finished in the top ten of only four races for Hooters, and had just been picked to replace Morgan Shepherd in the number 75 Remington Arms car for '97. "Something would happen, and we just wouldn't win." Bill Elliott's season had been a downer from that instant he went airborne at Talladega in the spring, his injuries keeping him out of seven races, and he had about run out of words: "This is like my home track, and it's been real good to me. Hopefully, on Sunday, it'll remember who I am." Nemechek was running thirty-fourth in the points in a year where "everything that can go wrong went wrong," and, although he could take comfort in looking ahead to being the second man in Felix Sabates's new three-team operation, "it sure would be nice to end this year with something good." Another who had struggled but had a new deal for '97 was young Jeremy Mayfield, who had only two top tens as Cale Yarborough's driver before moving over to the Kmart/Little Caesars car in September, and at least he had a sense of humor left: "There isn't a four-leaf clover within a solid mile of our shop because we've gone out and found every one of them. We hit an import-export store and took every Buddha they had, and we encourage people to rub the bellies during breaks. I sure wouldn't want to be a rabbit anywhere near our place." Johnny Benson, the '96 Rookie of the Year by default, had learned a thing or two: "We didn't have a lot of drafting partners at the superspeedways, but that's to be expected. I would pull out of line and everyone else would go by like I was standing still. They looked like they were having fun, though, so I'm kinda looking forward to doing that to some rookie next year."

In the first round of qualifying, held on Friday afternoon, Gordon and Labonte and Jarrett did what they had to do, qualifying for second, third, and fifth, respectively, but the big story was Terry's younger brother. Bobby Labonte hadn't won a race thus far in the season, but he was putting on a strong finish for his popular owner, Joe Gibbs. He had won the pole for three of the past six races and now, suddenly ranking twelfth in the points standings with this one last race to go, he seemed to have a legitimate chance to overtake Ernie Irvan and make the stage at the Waldorf-Astoria. The next to last to make his qualifying run late that afternoon, when the track had cooled, he posted the fastest time of the day and the fastest in AMS history to win the pole. This was considered fortunate for Terry, who might receive some favors from his little brother if the need arose, but Bobby had other ideas: "Everybody's got something to race for Sunday. We're gonna race our car, and they're gonna race their car. Maybe they'll give *me* a break."

The track was even faster on Saturday's second round of qualifying, when Ricky Craven recorded the seventh-fastest time (although he would start at twenty-sixth, according to rules that lock in the first day's top twenty-five qualifiers), but there were some long faces in the garage when no fewer than five full-time Winston Cup drivers failed to make the cut. Among those was Kyle Petty, who had no remaining owner's provisionals to draw from, and in the late afternoon there was the somewhat poignant vision of the son of The King loading up his cars for the last time as a member of Team Sabco so he could beat the traffic home to North Carolina and ponder the future. He had secured Hot Wheels as a sponsor and would set up a shop of his own in Concord, to be called pe^2, loosely aligned with his father's Petty Enterprises in Level Cross, but he appeared to have a mountain to climb after two miserable years. "Kyle just didn't have his heart in qualifying," said Jon Sands, the Sabco media representative, clearly saddened that it had come to this. "But it's been like that ever since he and Felix split."

There was no way Bobby Lee Turbeville and Bryan Hause were going to miss out on this chance to spend a weekend in "Hotlanta," even if it meant camping in the cold on the second turn at Atlanta Motor Speedway. Bryan and his wife, Brenda, had dropped off their kids with friends from their days of living in Stone Mountain, east of downtown, and on Friday they had met up with Bobby Lee at their traditional campsite in the infield. Only four others of their gang had made it, their black friend Russell Watson being among the no-shows, but that didn't lessen their spirits. With the '97 Daytona 500 three months away, this was their last chance to howl before the off-season, the dreaded "void," arrived. They had brought the usual provisions and refreshments.

They knew how to improvise, even in the big city. There hadn't been much for them to root for on Friday afternoon, during the first round of qualifying, when Bobby Lee's beloved Bill Elliott posted the thirteenth-best time of the day and Hoss's Rusty Wallace failed to qualify at all, and it was cold and grubby down there. This was a far cry from Labor Day in Darlington, when Hoss had spent the entire weekend clad in shorts and sandals. With a push from Brenda, her hair already a tangle of smoke and grease, six of them had piled into one of the pickups around dark of that first day and gone to a motel out on the highway, where Hoss negotiated a deal to rent a single room, at $30 for an hour and a half, so they could take turns in the shower. On Saturday, Hoss had his day ruined when Rusty managed a thirtieth-place starting position during second-day qualifying; but he salvaged something, at least, when he led the gang to a nearby sports bar with a giant screen, where they plunked down $20 a head to watch Atlanta's Evander Holyfield thrash Mike Tyson to take back the world's heavyweight boxing championship.

Theirs was a great location for watching the races, in the shadow of the pricy high-rise condominiums called Tara Place, and it would be even better next year when the track was reconfigured and they would find themselves in the fourth turn with a good angle on the start-finish line and the entrance to pit road. During Saturday's ARCA race they had seen several messy wrecks right in front of them, where the less-experienced drivers had lost control. One of them, a kid from near Junior Johnson's turf in North Carolina, had to have his left hand amputated. "Well," said Hoss, upon hearing this piece of news, "that'll show you this ain't all fun and games. Just a little ride on Saturday afternoon? *I-don't-think-sooooo . . .*"

With Veterans Day coming up on Monday, the Sunday race afforded one more opportunity for an orgy of patriotism on a bright cold day perfect for racing. An Air Force Reserves band moved into place near a portable stage on the frontstretch before noon, after an hour or so of serenading by a couple of country music groups, and thus began another bow to America. The NASCAR All-American Veterans Day Salute brought to the stage a horde of drivers and owners and officials, military veterans all, each being handed a little American flag as he was introduced. Here came country singer Kenny Chesney to sing "America the Beautiful" while a giant American flag, thirty-by-fifty-feet, was unfurled. Out there on the roads leading into the track, tempers were flaring and horns were honking in the swirling dust, the show pressing on without the late arrivals. On and on it went, through the driver introductions and the presentation of a dozen awards like the Plasti-Kote Winning Finish and the UAW-GM Teamwork of Excellence and such, of more importance to the sponsors than the winners, everybody having a tiny flag shoved into their hands as they trudged across the stage. "Georgia on My Mind" was sung, and the National Anthem, and the colors were presented and taps was bugled and four F-16 jets came flying by, and finally here was Bruton Smith himself with, for the last time in '96, the call to start the engines.

Jeff Gordon to his crew chief, Ray Evernham, over the radio as the drivers rumbled along behind the pace car: "It's a great day. God's on our side. I can feel it." Earnhardt, on his radio, from far back in seventeenth position: "We've got dirt and stuff all over turn three out here." His crew chief, David Smith: "They're going to take a couple of extra pace laps so maybe the cars'll blow it off." The fans, an estimated 140,000 of them overall, were on their feet, eavesdropping on their scanners, watching through their binoculars, waiting for the play to unfold. The ground began to move, the air to shimmer, as the forty-two cars picked up speed and got in line on the distant backstretch. This was it, the last dance until Daytona in February, and there was a particular intensity as they flew out of the fourth turn behind the old driver Elmo Langley, in the Pontiac pace car (his last time around, as it would turn out, for he would die of a heart attack two weeks later, halfway around the world, while in Japan for the exhibition race). Suddenly, Elmo dipped for safety onto pit road, his job done forever, the flagman high in his aerie began to madly wave the green flag, and, finally, the cars were off and running for the end of the road.

The race had hardly gotten underway when it looked, for a moment, as though the Lord didn't want anything to do with Gordon. On the ninth lap, startled when his car began shuddering violently, The Kid hit the brakes and got no response. "The brakes are gone, the brakes are gone!" he shouted to his crew, tossing in a "damn" for the first time in anyone's memory. The brakes finally caught and he hauled into the pits, where it was found that the problem was a loose left wheel. Gordon was fortunate to lose only two laps while the best pit crew in Winston Cup racing, Evernham's Rainbow Warriors, jacked up the car and replaced the wheel. Meanwhile, Bobby Labonte had roared off the pole to lead the first six laps but then was passed by his brother for a couple of laps, earning Terry five bonus points that now meant he could clinch the championship with only a tenth-place finish, and by the time Gordon was back on the track the race had already begun to take shape. In all, the lead would change hands twenty-seven times among twelve drivers and seventeen of them would finish on the lead lap—a high number on all counts—with only four crashes occurring, which was just enough to keep everybody sober and on their toes.

To his credit, Terry Labonte had chosen not to be a "stroker" on this day, a pejorative for one content to stay out of trouble, but rather to go for his championship the hard way. His brother would sum it up afterward: "He wasn't going to ride around and win [the championship] by the skin of his teeth. It looked like he was going to win [the race] there for a while." Indeed, Terry led for a twenty-five-lap stretch at about the one-third point in the 328-lap race, and for the next hour or so he plowed ahead, staying in the top five or ten, while his brother and Gordon and a host of pretenders battled back and forth for the lead. This was, after all, exactly how he had run all year to lead the points race in spite of winning only two races. It was more evidence of Hendrick Motorsports' domination of Winston Cup racing; build a strong car, put a durable and smart driver in it, give him an excellent pit crew, and you're going to win over the long haul. If anybody was concerned when Terry slipped back to twelfth place late in the race, it wasn't the Ice Man. His busted hand was aching as the painkiller wore off, but it didn't appear to be affecting his driving, and with forty laps to go, just as his little brother was grabbing the lead for the last time, he began to pick off the cars ahead of him one at a time until finally, on lap 300, he established himself in fifth place and finished there to nail down the 1996 Winston Cup championship and all the goodies that went with it.

From the whoops crackling over the airwaves, it sounded as though a fighter squadron had completed a successful mission. It had come down to

Bobby Labonte taking his first victory of the year, crossing the finish line about three car lengths ahead of Jarrett, those two closely followed by Gordon and Earnhardt, but the man of the moment was the quiet Texan in the bright red-and-yellow Corn Flakes Chevy.

"Congratulations, man, good job," Labonte was hearing from his crew chief, Gary DeHart.

Somebody else chipped in with, "Awesome, champ."

His teammate, Gordon, got on the line: "Congratulations, guys, you did it."

DeHart, again: "Okay, champ, forget about Bobby. Stay out and take your *own* cool-down lap, and then follow the convertible to pit road."

"Convertible?" said Labonte.

"They didn't tell you about the convertible?"

"I don't know nothin' 'bout nothin'."

"Well, there's gonna be one out there, so follow him in."

It was a great day for the Labonte boys, anyway, as Bobby rolled his car into Victory Lane for the obligatory session for the photographs that would lead the Monday sports pages—high-fiving his crew, spreading his arms in the V-for-victory pose, plopping cap after cap on his sweaty head out of duty to his many sponsors (the "hat dance," they called it), hugging his wife and his car owner—while Terry, the new champion, cruised around the track on his own victory lap. Soon the brothers were touring the track together on another victory lap, and then they were talking to MRN on a live hookup that could be heard throughout the speedway over loudspeakers. The Ice Man's voice cracked with emotion, at some point, and he had to pause to pull himself together. He had been dismissed as a has-been only four years earlier, but now he had been raised from the dead in his third year with Hendrick Motorsports. Nobody in the history of Winston Cup had gone so long between championships. "When I won the championship twelve years ago, I thought, 'Hey, this is pretty neat, I'll probably do it again next year,'" he said. "I didn't think next year was ever going to get here."

"Earnhardt has left the building," one of the MRN announcers said during a commercial break, and that was figuratively true for the other drivers on this last day of the season. Being stuck in the midst of all this rampant celebration with no place to hide was like losing the final game of the World Series on the road, having defeat rubbed into your nose, and all they could do was sneak off to the RV for a shower while the crew loaded up the cars and equipment for the last run back home. Except to congratulate Labonte and opine that his effort on this day represented "the hardest I've ever drove here," The Intimidator had been no more eager to explain his finishing fourth in the points race than he had wanted to talk about losing another Daytona 500 back in February, so he was out of there, on his way to Montana for some hunting. There had been no changes in the top ten, although Bobby Labonte nearly overtook Ernie Irvan, who barely clung to tenth in the points despite going out of the race after a violent collision with the wall seventy-three laps from the end. There were more losers than winners when the final point standings were tallied, in fact, and there were some big names in the group who failed to finish in the top twenty; most notably, Petty at twenty-seventh, Darrell Waltrip at twenty-ninth, Elliott at thirtieth, and the beloved Dave Marcis at thirty-eighth, dead last of what were considered the full-time Winston Cup drivers. It was no surprise that only Waltrip wanted to talk about it: "We've got a good car for sale, if you want to run by a Western Auto store [his sponsor] and get it."

Not until two hours after the race had ended did the Labonte brothers finally begin trudging under escort to the press box, high atop the main grandstand, for the usual post-race mass interview with the sportswriters. Terry was already being reminded of how it would go as the reigning champion, having had a hell of a time breaking away from sponsors and fans and photographers just to work in a shower and a change into street clothes. ("When I was following him in '91," said Richard Huff of the *New York Daily News*, who had written *Behind the Wall*, a narrative of Labonte's '91 season, when times were bad, "he had all the time in the world. This weekend, the best I could do was get through the crowd to shake hands.") The writers had been fed quotes from all the other drivers and owners and crew chiefs, and, while they awaited the stars of the day, they clattered away on their laptops. Gordon had pronounced everything as "great" and "awesome" and "wonderful," was "real happy and real proud," in fact: "You better watch out. It might be one-two-three next year for Hendrick Motorsports." Bobby Hamilton, who had been 105 points out of tenth place with two races to go, had made the stage at the Waldorf-Astoria: "Nobody's going to write *me* a speech for the banquet in New York. I'm gonna do it off the cuff." Wally Dallenbach, who had sent Loy Allen to the hospital when they collided late in the race: "I went over there to make sure his eyes were open and everything, and that was the case." Gary DeHart, Terry Labonte's crew chief: "The guys will take a day off, and then be back at the shop Tuesday, working on the Daytona cars." Michael Waltrip, on the upcoming exhibition race in Japan, two weeks hence, where four of the entries would be Japanese drivers new to the game: "If it was Talladega, I'd be nervous about that, but if they aren't very good we won't see 'em much when the race starts."

The Labontes were a good act. Back in the spring, right there in the empty grandstands at Atlanta Motor Speedway, they had taped one of the better television commercials of the season, for Chevrolet; the two of them arguing about who was the best driver, the best singer, the best dancer ("Yeah, but who's the best-looking . . . ?"), the best whatever, in the tradition of competitive siblings. The family's roots were in Maine, but their father had fled the winters up there by joining the U.S. Navy and finally settling in Corpus Christi, on the Gulf Coast of Texas. After proving everything they could prove on the small tracks in that part of the country, both boys moved to North Carolina in the late seventies to go Winston Cup. (The father, Bob, now looked after their Busch Grand National interests out of a shop behind his house.) Their parents had been there at AMS for this final race, and about the only improvement on the day for them would have been to see Bobby pick up the forty-two points he needed to beat out Ernie Irvan for tenth place in the final points. Even so, Bobby, the younger brother by seven years, had become one of the eleven drivers to earn more than $1 million in purses during the '96 season. They had far outshined the four other brother teams, the best of those being the Wallaces, with Rusty finishing seventh in the points, Kenny twenty-eighth, and Mike forty-first.

Sitting beside each other on the long front-row table of the press box, their backs to the darkening track far below, where a fireworks display was entertaining thousands of weary fans who would be stuck in gridlock for another two hours, they bantered with the reporters looking down on them from rising tiers of tables. They talked racing stuff, for the most part, Bobby saying that he had been "on a mission" that day, needing to "lead the most laps and win the race and have some other guys have tough luck," Terry saying that it had seemed like "the longest race I ever ran," and that "at the end, we rode it out." In the giddiness of the moment, Terry dropped his guard and confessed to some small-scale collusion with his brother before the race. "I told him, I said, 'Now look. If you're leading a lap and let me lead the race, I'll let you get back around me.' He said okay. I needed those five points for leading a lap, and after that I just found a spot and rode it out." What are brothers for, anyway? "Bobby and I are maybe a little different than some of the other brothers in racing," said Terry, not having to mention to this crowd the long feud between Geoff and Brett Bodine. "I mean, we actually like each other and get along good. It was pretty special today, it really was."

"Yeah," said Bobby, "taking a victory lap together was about the coolest thing we ever did."

"Second coolest," said Terry.

"What?"

"The time we shot Dad's pickup was the coolest."

"Oh, man, I'd forgotten about that."

Like little boys giggling over some adolescent romp, they told of the day when their father's battered old pickup simply gave up, and of their decision to do the humane thing and put it out of its misery by filling it full of bullets. How times had changed. Little more than half a century earlier, this would have been the two devilish whiskey-running cousins from Dawsonville, Lloyd Seay and Roy Hall, having run one-two in a Sunday race at dusty old Lakewood Speedway in Atlanta, now sitting around a stove at the Pure Oil station and recounting tales of outsmarting the sheriffs hiding in ambush along the old highway leading from the stills of Dawson County to Atlanta. But maybe times hadn't changed at all. For at the heart of the matter, then as well as now, it was all about dashing young men and their racing machines.

EPILOGUE: DINNER IN MANHATTAN

Talk about raining on a parade. As the hour of the annual Winston Cup awards banquet in Manhattan approached, on the first Friday night of December, the NASCAR family had every reason to gloat. All of the numbers were up—attendance, television audience, purses, sales of collectibles, sponsors' outlays—and the folks at R.J. Reynolds thought they could forget, if only for a moment, the government's threat to come down against tobacco advertising. There were those who felt that the natural place for the banquet would be, say, at the gaudy Opryland Hotel in Nashville, but they had been holding it in New York because of the validation it afforded (not that any of the good old boys felt that New York City was anything more than a nice place to visit). Some 2,000 of the principals and their ladies were expected at the Waldorf-Astoria, where ESPN would do a live broadcast of the proceedings from the Grand Ballroom. Sponsors had booked hospitality suites, RJR had written checks for nearly $7 million, and, parked out front of the hotel, on the streets of Manhattan, were Terry

Labonte's gaudy Corn Flakes race car and a bright red Winston Cup show car. Down home in North Carolina, country mechanics were renting their first tuxedos and outfitting their women in spangled gowns and double-checking the time their chartered flights were to leave for the Big Apple. But then, like a thunderclap, the news broke on Wednesday of that week: Rick Hendrick of Hendrick Motorsports, the paradigm of the modern racing organization, had been indicted by the federal government for alleged hanky-panky in his automobile dealerships.

Rick Hendrick had come a long way since his childhood on the family tobacco farm in Virginia. He was keeping the farm's trucks and tractors going when he was ten years old, messing with stock cars at fourteen, and he had helped pay his way through college by working on automobiles. His father had taught him about hard work, he often said, and his mother, a banker, had "taught me the ninety-day note." In the mid-seventies, at the age of twenty-five, he borrowed $50,000 to start his first automobile dealership, in South Carolina, and in the ensuing years he had become one of the biggest car dealers in the United States, his Hendrick Management Corporation controlling sixty-six auto and truck dealerships, employing 4,500 people, and producing annual revenues of more than $2 billion.

Specifically, a grand jury in Asheville, North Carolina, was charging him with thirteen counts of money laundering and one each for conspiracy and mail fraud. The Feds were saying that he had bribed executives of American Honda to ensure that he had a steady flow of their popular little imports for Hendrick Automotive Group, a subsidiary that had become the largest Saturn and Honda dealer in the country. The trail had traced back to a trial in New Hampshire, in March of '95, when a Honda executive testified that Hendrick had helped him purchase two homes as a way of buying influence. If the charges stuck, Hendrick would spend the rest of his life in prison and pay up to $7 million in fines.

It was in the hands of the lawyers now, with Hendrick and his people saying he would be exonerated once the facts were presented in court, but before they clammed up the NASCAR and Winston people complained out loud about the curious timing. They still remembered how the Feds had taken the first step toward effectively taking RJR out of racing on the eve of Dale Jarrett's shot at the Winston Million, on Labor Day weekend at Darlington, so they could be forgiven their paranoia. "Some might wonder if the timing of the indictment was made to promote an unrelated agenda," Bill France said, jut-jawed, at a terse press conference the day before the banquet. "If one drop of rain falls on Terry and his team's parade, it will be one drop too many. It's inexcusable." Hendrick had "graciously consented to an interview," one of the ESPN announcers said, in the cozy manner of Winston Cup reportage, and he was given his chance to proclaim his innocence on a taped lead-in to that night's broadcast.

So the show went on. Like any awards banquet, it was an orgy of self-congratulations, a parade of notables and the top ten drivers to the stage as highlights of the '96 season flashed across the big screen serving as a backdrop. Here was Earnhardt, wearing a black shirt under his tux, asking T. Wayne Robertson if they could just "round that off at four hundred thousand" when he was presented a fourth-place check for $397,000. Here was Bobby Hamilton, speaking extemporaneously, as promised, as he fondled a check for $163,000. "Richard [Petty] and me might fight over this." Here was Jimmy Spencer, waddling up to the stage as winner of the Sears DieHard Racer Award, for completing more laps than anyone in the field. Here came Dale Jarrett, reversing the field by thanking God and his family first, his sponsors and crew second. And, finally, toward the end of the two-hour show, the time came to crown the new champion. The script had been written to read, "Terry Labonte epitomizes the modern race car driver," but it came out wrong. "Terry Lobotomy . . ." the emcee began. A good laugh was had by all, even Labonte, who was so overcome by the moment that he forgot, in the course of thanking everybody in his universe, exactly how long he had been married to his faithful racing widow. When they hauled out a poster-sized facsimile of a check made out to him for $1,942,500, he could only blink and say, "That's a lot of money."

Gober Sosebee, the Dawson County boy who had gone on to win three Daytona races in stock car racing's earliest days, didn't make it to his eighty-second birthday. On the day following the final race of the '96 season in Atlanta, as thousands of Bill Elliott fans swarmed into Dawsonville, Gober died. He had been clearing his land with a front-end loader when he lost control and the machine fell on him. The official cause of death was a heart attack triggered by the accident—his wife, Vaudell, was at his side when he breathed his last breath—but there was a sort of sweet irony that he had died on the job. "All of those boys knew what hard work was, Lloyd [Seay] and Roy [Hall] and Gober," said Raymond Parks, the former bootleg whiskey baron who had been the first multiple-team stock car owner even before NASCAR was formed. Parks drove up from Atlanta in his restored black '39 Ford coupe ("I was doing seventy, passing people") for the burial at a cemetery just blocks from the one where, fifty-five years earlier, he had installed Lloyd Seay's fanciful tombstone. He was joined by Gordon Pirkle, owner of the Dawsonville Pool Room, who had just announced formal plans for a $6 million Georgia Automotive Racing Hall of Fame and Museum in Dawsonville. The first car to go under the roof of the 50,000-square-foot building would likely be the number 50 Cherokee Garage Ford coupe that Gober had driven to victory at Daytona in the forties.

Young Rodney Dickson wound up winning the 1996 Late Model points championship at Dixie Speedway, and the $5,000 check that went with it, and suddenly his horizons began to expand. That bonus had swelled his earnings to nearly $25,000 on the year, and, as usual, he poured it back into racing. First, he sold his old yellow-and-white number 18 car to another driver on the Georgia dirt-track circuit; then he and his father drove a rental truck to a factory in Indiana, to take delivery on two new racing chassis right off the production line; and, finally, he finished building a garage of his own, right beside his house in Fayetteville, being careful to keep peace with his wife, Sonia, worried that he might tacky up the neighborhood, by dressing it with the same roofing and siding as the house so that passers-by "can hardly tell it's a garage." Although he wasn't about to give up his day job, his landscaping business, he had been emboldened enough to begin thinking more seriously about making the move into the big American cars on the asphalt ARCA circuit. For the time being, though, he planned to race more often and at tracks well beyond little

Dixie Speedway so he could "get my name around a little more at some other places." Dixie would still be his home track in '97, he said; and, besides, there was some unfinished business there: "I still haven't beaten Stan Massey."

So while another piece of the past died with Gober Sosebee, and perhaps a taste of the future arrived with Rodney Dickson, the Winston Cup people had enough on their hands wrestling with the present as another Daytona 500 bore down on them. Even as the annual awards banquet in New York came and passed, there was more shuffling in the ranks. Earnhardt sold the plant that had been generating so much income in collectibles, perhaps an admission that he had been spreading himself too thin as some had argued, and then he offered a salary of $300,000 to lure Larry McReynolds, one of the best crew chiefs in the business, away from Ernie Irvan's shop at Robert Yates Racing. The Cola Wars spread to Winston Cup; when Jeff Gordon found that Coca-Cola intended to continue using him only in regional NASCAR-related commercials, he followed such luminaries as Shaquille O'Neal, Deion Sanders, and Ray Charles to the Pepsi stable in hopes of becoming a national icon ("We wanted to keep him," said a Coke spokesman, "but not enough to make him a Shaquille O'Neal"). The televised Winston Cup races had always been a staple in the Atlanta Braves' clubhouse during Sunday games, and now four Braves, including first baseman Fred McGriff (a black man!), were pooling a few million dollars and hastily assembling an entry for the '97 Winston Cup season; shops in Statesville, North Carolina, car and driver and crew and sponsor and everything else to be announced; all they knew was, they wanted in on this stuff.

Except to count the driver's weight in the total package during prerace inspections, to eliminate the edge that had always gone to the lightweights like Gordon and Andretti and Ward Burton, NASCAR had made no noticeable rules changes in advance of the '97 season. Everyone remained stymied on what to do about the dangers of restrictor-plate racing at Daytona and Talladega, but they couldn't agree on a plan. The same went for testing, which was prohibitively expensive for the low-budget operations and of questionable value to the multi-car shops. In the heat of any season, there had always been squawking about one make or another being "give the candy store," as Earnhardt had snipped after losing by a nose to Jarrett's Ford in the Daytona 500, but that seemed to have settled into a rare calm; Chevy had won six of the first races in '96, but Ford had come roaring back after some concessions to win eleven of the next seventeen (a Pontiac, Bobby Hamilton's, didn't win until the next-to-last date), so it was decided not to fix something that wasn't broken.

The only real issues left hanging on the eve of a new Winston Cup season, in fact, were more or less out of NASCAR's hands. To be sure, RJR's not inconsiderable lobbyists were working overtime to divert the White House away from its anti-tobacco stance; and, just as certainly, Rick Hendrick had employed something more than an ambulance-chaser to take on the federal government in *his* moment of angst. (In fact, Hendrick had bigger troubles. Between the last race and his indictment he was found to have leukemia, a bone-marrow cancer, likely to sideline him during the '97 season as he underwent treatment.) But even if both RJR and Hendrick were to lose, they could be replaced in a blink. The sport had become bigger than one tobacco maker and one millionaire car owner by now. Indeed, things were running so smoothly that some within the family were having to create something to worry about. And that led them directly to Bruton Smith, the rotund little racetrack baron whose Charlotte-based Speedway Motorsports, Inc. had become bigger than the France family's International Speedway Corporation.

While everybody else was off on vacation between the season-ending race in Atlanta and the banquet in New York, Smith was blandly announcing that he had bought Sears Point Raceway at Sonoma, in the California wine country north of San Francisco. Suddenly it dawned on the folks at NASCAR headquarters in Daytona Beach that, hey, this one man now owned five tracks where one fourth of the thirty-two races on the '97 Winston Cup schedule would be held. And he had the audacity to squawk that Bill France still owed him a second date at his new Texas Motor Speedway, in the Fort Worth–Dallas area ("France promised me one, but I had to buy that one [by purchasing North Wilkesboro and closing it down], so he still owes me"). Was Smith playing semantics with the

France family, or was he threatening to start his own major-league stock car circuit, thereby creating division in the kingdom à la Indy-car racing? There were big tracks at Miami and Las Vegas that had no Winston Cup dates at all, four with only one (Texas, Phoenix, Indianapolis, and the new California Speedway east of Los Angeles), and still others either in Bruton Smith's dreams (Long Island?) or on the drawing board at places like Kansas City. Ol' Buck Baker's plea to "give everybody a drank o' likker and drop the green flag" seemed more plaintive than ever now. The good old boys were long gone.